The Collected Works of Gerard Manley Hopkins
Volume VII

THE DUBLIN NOTEBOOK

The Collected Works of Gerard Manley Hopkins

GENERAL EDITORS
Lesley Higgins and Michael F. Suarez, S.J.

Volumes I and II
Correspondence
R. K. R. Thornton and Catherine Phillips

Volume III
Diaries, Journals, and Notebooks
Lesley Higgins

Volume IV
Oxford Essays and Notes
Lesley Higgins

Volume V
Sermons and Spiritual Writings
Jude Nixon and Noel Barber, S.J.

Volume VI
Sketches, Notes, and Studies
R. K. R. Thornton

Volume VII
The Dublin Notebook
Lesley Higgins and Michael F. Suarez, S.J.

Volume VIII
The Poems
Catherine Phillips

Gerard Manley Hopkins

THE DUBLIN NOTEBOOK

Edited by
LESLEY HIGGINS
and
MICHAEL F. SUAREZ, S.J.

OXFORD
UNIVERSITY PRESS

OXFORD
UNIVERSITY PRESS

Great Clarendon Street, Oxford OX2 6DP,
United Kingdom

Oxford University Press is a department of the University of Oxford.
It furthers the University's objective of excellence in research, scholarship,
and education by publishing worldwide. Oxford is a registered trade mark of
Oxford University Press in the UK and in certain other countries.

First Edition published 2014

Impression: 1

Published in the United States of America by Oxford University Press
198 Madison Avenue, New York, NY 10016, United States of America

British Library Cataloguing in Publication Data
Data available

Library of Congress Control Number: 2014933918

ISBN 978–0–19–953402–9

Printed and bound by
CPI Group (UK) Ltd, Croydon CR0 4YY

Hopkins's room, 86 St Stephen's Green (now Newman House, University College Dublin).
Photo by Michael Flecky, S.J.

I am in Ireland now; now Í am at a thírd
Remove.

   —Hopkins, 'To seem the stranger'

ACKNOWLEDGEMENTS

Funding for this project has been provided by the Social Sciences and Humanities Research Council of Canada, the Faculty of Liberal Arts and Professional Studies, York University (Toronto, Canada); Fordham University; Campion Hall, Oxford; and the University of Virginia.

Brian Dunkle, S.J. was an exemplary Consulting Editor for the classical materials: thorough, intellectually resourceful, and obliging. Ross Arthur provided invaluable assistance as forensic classicist and Pindar explicator. Bonnie Blackburn was our exceptional copy-editor: equally adept with Latin, music, and literature. Any errors that persist are those of the editors.

Many people have been generous with their time and knowledge. In Ireland: Archives, Ollscoil na hÉireann (National University of Ireland): John Foley and staff; Clongowes Wood College: Bruce Bradley, S.J., Rector; Margaret Doyle, Archivist; Irish Jesuit Archives, Dublin: Fergus O'Donoghue, S.J., Archivist, and Damien Burke; Special Collections, James Joyce Library, University College Dublin: Eugene Roche; Archives, University College Dublin: Seamus Helferty, Principal Archivist; Royal Irish Academy: Petra Schnabel, Deputy Librarian, and Amy Hughes, Assistant Librarian. In England: the Staff of Imaging Services, Bodleian Libraries, University of Oxford; University of Oxford: Simon Bailey, Archivist, and Alice Millea, Assistant Keeper of the Archives; Royal Academy Library: Andrew Potter. In the United States: Stephanie Edwards Plowman, Special Collections Librarian, Gonzaga University, Spokane, Washington. The research notes of the late Anthony Bischoff, S.J. were invaluable, and have been cited throughout the volume. We are fortunate to have been able to make extensive use of the *Correspondence of Gerard Manley Hopkins* (2013), skilfully edited by R. K. R. Thornton and Catherine Phillips, which comprises Volumes 1 and 2 of the *Collected Works*.

We would also like to thank Jacqueline Baker; Noel Barber, S.J.; Leofranc Holford-Strevens; Andrew McNeillie; Phyllis Weliver; the Campion Hall Jesuit Community; the British, Irish, and New York Provinces of the Society of Jesus; and our colleagues on the *Collected Works* project: Kelsey Thornton, Catherine Phillips and Jude Nixon. We are particularly indebted to the friendship and gracious hospitality of Marie-Christine and Bruno Leps.

Research assistants from the Graduate Programme in English, York University, have included: Bruce Douville, Eadaoin O'Boyle, Taryn Ortolan, Tanya Pikula, Bianca Rodrigues, Jonathan Vandor, and Cathy Wazczuk. Mia Spiro was vital to the archival work, and endlessly resourceful. Amanda Paxton deserves special credit for her exemplary assistance. We have also benefitted from the assistance of Megan Burke at Fordham University and Michael Pickard at the University of Virginia.

The photographs featured in this volume have been made available by a very generous individual and two benevolent institutions; their copyrights are reasserted here. The frontispiece and Figures 4, 5, and 6 are photographs by Michael Flecky, S.J. that originated in *Hopkins in Ireland: Pictures and Words* (Omaha: Creighton University Press, 2008). The two group photos taken at Clongowes Wood College, Co. Kildare, Ireland, are courtesy of the Rector of Clongowes and the Irish Jesuit Archives, Dublin. The digital images of Campion Hall MS GI.a, 'The Dublin Notebook', are courtesy of Campion Hall, Oxford and the Trustees for Roman Catholic Purposes. The photograph of Hopkins first appeared in *Donahoe's Magazine* in 1902 (photographer and origin unknown).

CONTENTS

LIST OF ILLUSTRATIONS

LIST OF ABBREVIATIONS

Bod	Bodleian Library, University of Oxford
BRC	Bischoff Research Collection, Foley Library, Gonzaga University (Spokane, Washington)
CH	Campion Hall, Oxford
CW	*Collected Works of Gerard Manley Hopkins*, 8 vols.
CWC	Clongowes Wood College, Ireland
DN	*Dublin Notebook*
EPM	*Early Poetic Manuscripts and Note-books of Gerard Manley Hopkins in Facsimile*, ed. Norman H. MacKenzie
G.I.a	GMH manuscript known as 'The Dublin Notebook'; one of two large notebooks from his years in Ireland
G.II	GMH notebook featuring revised outlines for teaching 'Roman Literature and Antiquities'
GMH	Gerard Manley Hopkins
HQ	*The Hopkins Quarterly: A Journal of Critical, Scholarly and Appreciative Responses to the Lives and Works of Gerard M. Hopkins, S.J., and his Circle: Robert Bridges, R. W. Dixon, and Coventry Patmore*
IJA	Irish Jesuit Archives (Dublin, Ireland)
LPM	*Later Poetic Manuscripts of Gerard Manley Hopkins*, ed. Norman H. MacKenzie
ODNB	*Oxford Dictionary of National Biography*, <www.oxforddnb.com>
PW	*Poetical Works of Gerard Manley Hopkins*, ed. Norman H. MacKenzie
RUI	Royal University of Ireland
RUIC	*Royal University of Ireland. The Calendar*, published annually
UC	University College (Dublin, Ireland)

CHRONOLOGY

1883

Robert Louis Stevenson, *Treasure Island*; Mark Twain, *Life on the Mississippi*; Friedrich Nietzsche, *Also sprach Zarathustra*.

13 January	Seventeen members of the Irish 'Invincibles' responsible for the 'Phoenix Park murders' of Lord Frederick Cavendish and Thomas Burke on 6 May 1882 are arrested; five executions take place 14 May to 9 June.
May	GMH is teaching at Stonyhurst; composing 'Mary Mother of Divine Grace Compared to the Air we Breathe' ('The Blessed Virgin').
July	Robert Bridges, *Prometheus the Firegiver*.
26 July	GMH describes himself to Bridges as 'Fortune's football', uncertain as to his next teaching or pastoral assignment.
28 July	GMH's 39th birthday.
29 July	Meets Coventry Patmore.
1 August	Told he will continue to teach at Stonyhurst; but on 10 August goes to Church of Holy Name, Manchester, to assist for a week. Correspondence with Patmore begins.
16 August	Begins summer visit with family in Hampstead and takes part in a trip to Holland.
26–27 August	Eruption of Krakatoa, the volcano (and volcanic island) in the Sunda Strait, Indonesia.
3 September	Begins annual eight-day retreat at Beaumont (near Windsor).
12 September	Returns to Stonyhurst.
4 October	The Orient Express rail service begins between Paris and Varna, Bulgaria (with additional ferry and train service to Istanbul).
6 October	Three members of Clan na Gael, an American-based Irish nationalist organization, carry out bomb attacks on two London underground stations; several citizens injured.
23 October	The bishops of Ireland having agreed, earlier in the month, that the Society of Jesus should be put in charge of University College (UC; formerly the Catholic University established by John Henry Newman), the Jesuits sign an agreement to take over the buildings on St Stephen's Green (84, 85, and upper 86), and retain the existing faculty and staff. Fr William Delany, S.J. will be the president.
2 November	In Dublin, classes commence at UC.

12 November	GMH writes to *Nature* magazine regarding the after-effects of Krakatoa; the letter is published on 15 November. Subsequent letters are written on 21 December 1883 (published 3 Jan. 1884) and 19 October 1884 (published 30 Oct. 1884).
18 November	Canadian and American railroads introduce five standardized continental time zones.
29 November	Edward Purbrick, S.J., Provincial of the English Province of the Society of Jesus, writes to Delany to agree that GMH could be appointed to new academic positions at UC and the Royal University of Ireland (RUI).
Early December	Delany visits GMH at Stonyhurst to explain the Dublin appointments.

1884

4 January	Fabian Society founded in London.
5 January	Debut of Gilbert and Sullivan's *Princess Ida; or, Castle Adamant*.
30 January	After heated debate, GMH is elected to a fellowship at the RUI. He is also Fellow in Classics and Professor of Greek and Latin at UC.
1 February	First volume of the *Oxford English Dictionary* published (–1928).
18 February	Moves to 85–6 St Stephen's Green, Dublin; writes to Newman on 20 February to announce his new appointment and new address.
22 February	Meditation on St Peter's Confession.
24 February	Berlin conference on Africa.
27 February	Ash Wednesday. Lent begins. Prose meditations in *DN* focus on Christ crowned with thorns; the Lance and Nails; the Transfiguration; the Five Wounds; and the sorrows of the Virgin Mary.
3 March	As reported in the *Freeman's Journal and Daily Commercial Advertiser*, a Dublin newspaper, GMH is elected to the Gaelic Union council. A modified version of Henrik Ibsen's *A Doll's House* is performed under the title *Breaking a Butterfly* at the Prince's Theatre, London.
12 March	Siege of Khartoum, Sudan begins.
2 April	GMH presents the Gaelic Union with a letter 'relative to the teaching of Irish in the National schools'.[1]
13 April	Easter Sunday. Visits Clongowes Wood College for several days.
22 April	Earthquake in Colchester, England.

[1] *Freeman's Journal and Daily Commercial Advertiser* (Wednesday, 2 April 1884), 5.

12 June	Feast of Corpus Christi.
28 June– 2 August	London conference on Egypt.
5 July	Begins extensive travels in west Ireland, including cliffs of Moher in Co. Clare, Connemara, Galway, and Killarney.
22 July	Begins annual eight-day retreat at Clongowes Wood College.
28 July	GMH's 40th birthday.
31 July	Feast of St Ignatius Loyola.
2 September	RUI students take the first examination set by GMH: the paper in Latin translation, grammar, and composition for the First University Examination in Arts. GMH also sets two parts of the Greek exam for the Second University Examination (honours), administered 23 September, and is an examiner for the BA in Greek Composition.
September– October	Grades examination papers.
1 October	Matriculation examinations begin. An international conference in Washington, DC decides that the Greenwich meridian will be the 'prime' global meridian of longitude. Resumes composition for 'St Winefred's Well' (a 'tragedy' or verse drama he began in autumn 1879): 'Caradoc's Soliloquy' for Act II.
22 October	RUI is the nation's first institution of higher education to grant a BA degree to women.
November	Working on 'Sibyl's Leaves' (informs Bridges 26 Nov. 1886 that the poem is finished).
22 November	Meditation notes for St Cecilia.
December	Redistribution Bill (Third Reform Bill), 1 December, extends suffrage in Britain, including Ireland, to all males, age 21 and above. The Representation of the People Bill, enacted 6 December, which enables tenants to vote as well as landowners, increases the Irish electorate from 126,000 to 738,000.
10 December	GMH attends performance of Antonín Dvořák's *Stabat Mater* at Trinity College.
25 December	Spends Christmas with Lord Emly[2] (who had supported GMH's appointment in Dublin).

---

[2] William Monsell, 1st Baron Emly (1812–94; *ODNB*).

1885

2 January	Visits Clongowes, until 16 January.
13 January	RUI Scholarship examinations begin.[3]
26 January	Fall of Khartoum; death of General Charles Gordon.
February	Walter Pater, *Marius the Epicurean*.
5 February	King Leopold II of the Belgians declares Congo Free State to be his personal possession; the State is officially established on 2 May.
11 February	Death of Edward Cardinal McCabe, Archbishop of Dublin.
18 February	Ash Wednesday. Lenten meditation subjects include St Gregory; the woman taken in adultery; the feeding of the 5,000; St Patrick; St Joseph.
20 February	James McNeill Whistler delivers 'Ten O'Clock Lecture' in London.
March	Émile Zola, *Germinal*.
1 March	GMH and Fr Mallac attend a political meeting in Dublin's Phoenix Park; nationalists are protesting the expulsion from parliament of Bill O'Brien, an Irish MP.
14 March	London premiere of Gilbert and Sullivan's *The Mikado; or, The Town of Titipu*.
5 April	Easter Sunday.
7 April	GMH attends post-Easter celebrations (students' athletic competitions, special dinners) at Clongowes.
8 April	Edward, Prince of Wales (he will become King Edward VII, 1901–10) and his wife Alexandra, Princess of Wales, visit Dublin; some members of the Dublin Corporation refuse to greet them.
10 April	Death of GMH's friend Martin Geldart (a possible suicide, off the Newhaven-Dieppe ferry).
May	GMH writes 'Strike, churl', 'No worst', and '[Ashboughs]'. In a letter to Bridges, late May, GMH refers to two poems—'if ever anything was written in blood one of these was'—assumed to be among the 'sonnets of desolation' ('I wake and feel', 'No worst', 'To seem the stranger', 'Carrion Comfort', 'My own heart', 'Patience'). Christina Rossetti, *Time Flies*.
1 May	Irish Loyal and Patriotic Union established.
4 June	Feast of Corpus Christi.
9–10 June	RUI First University Examinations in Latin and Greek.

---

[3] See fos. 2ʳ and 3ʳ for GMH's list of texts and requirements. Notes made while grading the Scholarship exams begin on fo. 22ʳ.

9 June	Gladstone resigns; the public holds him responsible for Gordon's death at Khartoum.
23 June	Dr William Joseph Walsh is appointed archbishop of Dublin; consecrated in Rome on 2 August.
30 June	RUI Matriculation Examination begins.
6 July	Louis Pasteur successfully tests vaccine against rabies.
Late July	GMH sails to England, where he stays three weeks; visits with family, William Addis, and Patmore. Stays at family's holiday house in the South Downs; travels include Midhurst, Hastings, and Rye.
28 July	GMH's 41st birthday.
31 July	Feast of St Ignatius Loyola.
2 August	Preaches at Sydenham (a sermon also delivered in London, 1878; Oxford, 1879; Clitheroe, 1883).
	Returns to Dublin by 20 August.
21 August	Begins his annual eight-day retreat at Clongowes.
1 September	In a letter to Bridges, describes four sonnets that have come 'like inspiration unbidden and against my will'.
15–19 September	RUI First University Examinations in Latin and Greek.
21–30 September	RUI Second University Examinations in Latin and Greek; BA and MA Examinations.
29–30 September	RUI Matriculation Examination.
22 September	The new archbishop, Dr William Walsh, visits UC.
30 September	H. Rider Haggard, *King Solomon's Mines*.
November	Burma is annexed to British India; officially 'presented' to Queen Victoria on 1 January 1886.
	Tennyson, *Tiresias, and Other Poems*
14–28 November	War between Serbia and Bulgaria; Serbia is defeated at Battle of Slivnitsa, 17–19 November.
24 November–9 December	British general election: the Liberals under Gladstone, 333 seats; Conservatives under Salisbury, 251; Irish Party, with Parnell, 86. Salisbury becomes prime minister. On 17 December, Gladstone's support of Home Rule is made public.
December	Bridges, *Eros and Psyche*.
Christmas	GMH spends holidays with MacCabe family in Donnybrook, south of Dublin.

1886

January	Robert Louis Stevenson, *The Strange Case of Dr Jekyll and Mr Hyde*.
10 January	RUI Scholarship examinations.
25 January	Ulster Unionist Party is established to oppose movement for Irish Home Rule.
28 January	Salisbury's government resigns.
29 January	Karl Benz patents the first successful gasoline-driven automobile.
February	Marie Corelli, *A Romance of Two Worlds*.
1 February	Gladstone forms his third Liberal government.
11 February	In a letter to Alexander William Mowbray Baillie, GMH describes academic project 'on Homer's Art'.
20 February	Triple Alliance of Austria, Germany, and Italy confirmed.
March	Gold is discovered in the Main Reef of the Transvaal hills, South Africa by George Walker.
10 March	Ash Wednesday.
8 April	First Home Rule Bill for Irish independence, supported by Parnell and Gladstone, is introduced in British parliament; defeated 7 June.[4]
20 April	Travels to England, where he visits with family, Baillie, the Paravicinis (in Oxford), and Bridges (6 May).
25 April	Easter Sunday.
9 May	Returns to Dublin. Corresponds with Sir Robert Stewart regarding his musical compositions; Stewart finds that 'nearly everything in your music [is] wrong'.
10 May	Thomas Hardy, *The Mayor of Casterbridge*.
15 May	Emily Dickinson dies.
29 May	Attends Dublin Musical Society Concert; programme includes Beethoven's *Mass in C*, J. S. Bach's *Motet* for double choir, Arthur Sullivan's *The Lost Chord*, Mendelsohn's 'Morning Prayer' and 'Hear My Prayer', and the 'Hallelujah' chorus from Beethoven's *Mount of Olives*.
Late May	Additional letters are exchanged with Stewart, who deems GMH's musical compositions 'wanting in coherent plan'.
8–12 June	RUI examinations: First University (honours).
21–23 June	RUI examinations: Matriculation; First University (pass).

---

[4] For the Hansard text of Gladstone's speech introducing the Bill, see <http://hansard.millbank-systems.com/commons/1886/apr/08/motion-for-leave-first-night>.

June 23	France banishes Bonaparte and Orléans families.
30 June–10 July	RUI examinations: Second University (pass and honours).
July	John Ruskin publishes vol. 1 of *Praeterita: Outlines of Scenes and Thoughts perhaps Worthy of Memory in my Past Life* (vol. 2, 1887; vol. 3, 1888–9).
1–17 July	British general election; Salisbury becomes the Conservative prime minister on 25 July.
12–17 July	RUI examinations: BA (pass and honours); MA.
28 July	GMH's 42nd birthday.
31 July	Franz Liszt dies.
	Feast of St Ignatius Loyola.
August	Drafting a study of 'Light and the Ether'.
September	Holiday in North Wales with Robert Curtis; returns to Dublin 4 October.
21 September	Tenants' Relief Bill endorsed by Parnell's Irish Party is defeated in the House of Commons.
	Twentieth anniversary of GMH's reception into Roman Catholic Church.
October	W. B. Yeats, *Mosada*.
5 October	RUI examinations: Matriculation; First University. GMH then takes a brief holiday in North Wales.
7 October	William Barnes, English poet and philologist, dies.
12 October	RUI Scholarship Examinations.
13 October	Informs Bridges that he has been translating Shakespeare's songs and Bridges's 'In all things beautiful' into Latin.
November	Visits John B. Yeats's studio at 7 St Stephen's Green; meets Katharine Tynan and W. B. Yeats.
12 December	Austria, Italy, and Britain sign a treaty on the Near East.
Christmas	GMH visits with Mary Cassidy in Monasterevan, Co. Kildare; begins to write 'On the Portrait'.

1887

1 January	H. Rider Haggard, *She: A History of Adventure*.
3 January	GMH returns to Dublin.
February	*Irish Monthly* publishes GMH's Latin translation of Shakespeare's 'Come unto these yellow sands'.
17 February	Meeting with Katharine Tynan.
17–18 February	In a letter to Bridges, GMH marks 'three hard wearying wasting wasted years' in Ireland.
23 February	Ash Wednesday.

7 March	The London *Times* begins a series on 'Parnellism and Crime', in which Irish Home Rule leaders are accused of various outrages during the Land 'War' and described as being 'essentially a foreign conspiracy'. In the final article, 18 April, letters purported to be in Parnell's hand are quoted; they express support for the Phoenix Park murders in Dublin (6 May 1882). A special parliamentary commission is eventually established to investigate.
15 March	Thomas Hardy, *The Woodlanders*.
26 March	GMH visits Monasterevan.
10 April	Easter Sunday; visiting with Bernard O'Flaherty in Co. Wexford.
27 April	Attends farewell recital of Romola Tynte at Dublin's Antient Concert Rooms.
June	Pater, *Imaginary Portraits*.
14–18 June	RUI examinations: Matriculation; First University (pass and honours).
21 June	Queen Victoria's Golden Jubilee (50 years as monarch). On 27 June, a garden party at the Royal Hospital, Dublin is attended by Victoria's sons, Prince Albert and Prince George. Although the Jesuit community is told not to go, to avoid political disagreements, GMH's friend and colleague Martial Klein, S.J. not only attends but speaks controversially. He is subsequently recalled to London. Klein leaves the Society of Jesus in November.
23 June–2 July	RUI examinations: First University (pass and honours); Second University (pass and honours).
4–17 July	RUI examinations: BA (pass and honours).
28 July	GMH's 43rd birthday.
31 July	Feast of St Ignatius Loyola.
August	Holiday in England, including visits with Baillie and Bridges; goes to Inversnaid; attends Manchester Exhibition. Returns to Dublin on 27 August.
September	His 'broken holidays' continue in Dromore, Co. Down; drafts 'Harry Ploughman' and 'Tom's Garland', and works on musical compositions. On 15 September, he begins his annual retreat at Loyola House, Dromore. On 26 September, he attends the Dromore novices' 'evening recreation'.
27 September	RUI examinations: Matriculation; First University (pass and honours).
4–5 October	RUI examinations: MA.
6 October	GMH consults an oculist.
11 October	Sends Bridges a copy of 'Harry Ploughman'.
November	*Irish Monthly* publishes GMH's Latin translation of Shakespeare's 'Full fathom five'.

12 November	Emile Berliner is issued a patent for his gramophone.
13 November	'Bloody Sunday': more than 10,000 demonstrators (including Annie Besant, Robert Cunninghame-Graham, and George Bernard Shaw) converge in Trafalgar Square, London urging independence for Ireland; they clash with more than 2,000 police and 400 troops. Hundreds are injured, including women and children; there are at least three deaths. Further demonstration, with casualties, on November 20.
Christmastide	Visits Mary Cassidy in Monasterevan; departs 3 January.

In 1887, writes 'Harry Ploughman' and 'Tom's Garland', and works on '[Ashboughs]'.

1888

28 January	Military agreement between Germany and Italy.
February	George Moore, *Confessions of a Young Man*.
15 February	Ash Wednesday.
24 February	Mary Arnold Ward [Mrs Humphry Ward], *Robert Elsmere*.
27 March	Robert Carbery, S.J. is chosen as superior of the Jesuit community at St Stephen's Green and the new president of UC.
1 April	Easter Sunday.
12 April	Everard Hopkins weds Amy Sichel. Subsequently, GMH begins 'Epithalamion' in their honour.
15 April	Matthew Arnold dies.
May	Oscar Wilde, *The Happy Prince, and Other Tales*.
31 May	Feast of Corpus Christi.
June	Annie Besant organizes three-week strike by London's 'match girls' (women working at the Bryant and May match company manufacturing products with yellow phosphorous).
15 June	Frederick III of Germany dies; Wilhelm II becomes emperor.
29 June	The first known classical music recording: Handel's *Israel in Egypt* is recorded using a wax cylinder at the Crystal Palace.
26 June	RUI examinations begin: Matriculation; First and Second University (pass and honours); BA.
4 July	RUI Matriculation examination.
July	Arthur Conan Doyle, *A Study in Scarlet* (the first Sherlock Holmes adventure; originally published in *Beeton's Christmas Annual*, 1887).
26 July	GMH writes out a fair copy of 'Heraclitean Fire'; sends it to Bridges on 7 September.
28 July	GMH's 44th birthday.

31 July	Feast of St Ignatius Loyola.
August	Two-week holiday in Scotland with Robert Curtis, S.J., including a visit to the Glasgow Exhibition, and hiking in the mountains near Fort William (including Glencoe and Ben Nevis); then, Whitby, Yorkshire to visit his brothers Arthur and Everard. Works on 'Heraclitean Fire'.
August	First victims associated with Jack the Ripper are found murdered in London's East End.
4 August	George Eastman registers the Kodak trademark and patents a camera that uses film on a roll.
13 August	Special commission on 'Parnellism and Crime' established.
6 September	GMH's 20th anniversary of entering the Society of Jesus.
mid-September	RUI examinations: First and Second University (pass and honours); BA.
22 September	Manley Hopkins's *Cardinal Numbers* is reviewed in the *Saturday Review*, but GMH's contribution regarding 'the mental visibility of numbers' is treated dismissively.
28 September	Early draft of 'In Honour of St Alphonsus Rodriguez' has this date.
14 October	Louis Le Prince films the first motion picture, *Roundhay Garden Scene*, in Roundhay, West Yorkshire, England.
30 October	By signing the Rudd Concession, King Lobengula grants Cecil Rhodes mining rights in Matabaland, Africa.
2 October	RUI Examinations: Matriculation; First University.
9 October	RUI Scholarship Examinations; also, MA and D.Litt.
November	Matthew Arnold, *Essays in Criticism* (2nd series).
Christmastide	Spends the holiday with Mary Cassidy in Monasterevan.

1889

January	William Butler Yeats, *The Wanderings of Oisin, and Other Poems*.
1–6 January	On retreat at St Stanislaus College, Tullabeg.
21 February	At the 'Parnellism'/*Times* Commission, Irish journalist Richard Pigott, who initially sold the incriminating letters and documents, begins his testimony. On 23 February, he reveals under cross-examination that the papers were forgeries. Subsequently Pigott flees England to avoid arrest, and commits suicide in Madrid, Spain.
1 March	GMH informs his mother, 'I continue to be a Home Ruler: I say it must be, and let it be'.
6 March	Ash Wednesday.
17 March	Drafts '(Thou art indeed just)'.
31 March	Eiffel Tower is inaugurated in Paris (opens to the public 6 May).

3 April	Revises and dates the text of 'The shepherd's brow'.
April	Sees Francis de Paravicini, who is visiting Dublin; Frances de Paravinci will summarize the reunion in a letter to Kate Hopkins after GMH's death.
21 April	Easter Sunday.
22 April	Drafts 'To R. B.', and sends it to Bridges a week later.
Early May	Significant illness; on May 6 informs parents he has 'a sort of typhoid'; his parents are summoned, 5 June.
7 June	First British production of Henrik Ibsen, *A Doll's House*, at Novelty Theatre, London.
8 June	GMH dies of 'typhoid fever' and 'peritonitis'.[5]
11 June	Funeral mass at St Francis Xavier's Church; GMH is buried in the Jesuit plot, Prospect Cemetery, Glasnevin, Dublin.

[5] GMH's death certificate, dated 18 June 1889, states, for 'Certified Cause of Death and Duration of Illness', 'Typhoid Fever | 41 days | Peritonitis 4 days' (BRC 11: 5).

INTRODUCTION

'I am in Ireland now.' Two days after his arrival in Dublin on 18 February 1884, Gerard Manley Hopkins sat down to write his annual birthday letter to John Henry Newman,[1] explaining that he had just taken up residence at St Stephen's Green to begin work as Professor of Classics at University College (UC) and Fellow of the Royal University of Ireland (RUI). Soon thereafter, Hopkins, always one to organize himself by writing, searched among his effects and found a large, empty notebook that he had purchased some twenty years before when he was an undergraduate at Oxford.[2] On the first two leaves, he neatly copied out the list of required texts for the various examinations that would come to dominate his working life both as a teacher of UC students and as an RUI examiner, 'helping to save and damn the studious youth of Ireland'.[3]

On the 21st of February, he put the *Notebook* to a different use, the first of many seemingly random entries: planning the course of his meditation on the gospel (St Peter's confession of faith) to be read and prayed over the following morning. After these notes on a text set by the Roman Catholic Church for liturgical and individual prayer, there immediately follow further instructions for a Scholarship exam and its set texts that would not be administered for another eleven months. A few leaves later, Hopkins wrote out from memory William Collins's 'Ode to Evening', the inspiration for a musical composition then in progress. Next, one finds a draft of 'Caradoc's Soliloquy', for his verse tragedy *St Winefred's Well*. Subsequent leaves include teaching notes on 'Roman Lit. and Antiquities'; pages in which he tallied exam marks and commented on students' performances; intermittent musical jottings; lists of correspondents to whom he owed letters; attendance records; drafts of a short biography for publication; various practical memoranda; a commentary on Cicero; and preliminary versions of 'Sibyl's Leaves'.

A unique document among the extant Hopkins manuscripts, the *Dublin Notebook* occupies a distinctive place in the *Collected Works*. According to the surviving evidence, Hopkins routinely kept multiple journals and notebooks to order, administer, catalogue, and memorialize the professional, personal, and spiritual aspects of his life. Diary-like entries were made in small journals (see *CW* iii); academic work was accomplished in specially assigned notebooks (*CW* iv, vi); sermons and religious writings had their places as well (*CW* v). Copies of poems were carefully preserved (by Robert Bridges) in separate scrapbooks (*CW* viii). Drawings were committed to sketchbooks (*CW* vi). Moving to Dublin in the winter of 1884, however, Hopkins suddenly found himself 'at a

---

[1] See Biographical Register.

[2] The signature 'Gerard M. Hopkins' appears on the inside front cover; written in pencil, it is an example of GMH's handwriting in the 1860s. Typically he would put his name in a notebook when it was purchased, not when he began to use it. See also G.II (*CW* vi).

[3] GMH to Dixon, 30 June–3 July 1886.

third / Remove'. Displaced from his own Jesuit province, his family, his much-beloved country, and from the company of politically and religiously like-minded friends (many of them also middle-class converts to Roman Catholicism), he suffered under 'dark heaven's baffling ban', discovering himself 'a lonely began' who would 'hoard unheard'.[4] As the *Dublin Notebook* gives witness, compositional protocols he had formerly lived by no longer obtained. Whether one should read this textual commotion as a sign of his profound alienation or not remains a matter open to debate. What one can be certain of, however, is that the *Dublin Notebook*, in the cumulative effect of its fragmentary parts, embodies Hopkins's experience of extreme dislocation.

The contents of the *Notebook* are dispersed throughout the *Collected Works*: classical notes, for example, appear in vol. vi; poetic texts, in vol. viii. Only in facsimile, however, does the iconic force of the manuscript become apparent. By presenting the *Notebook* as it was left by Hopkins, we hope to provide the reader with a deeper understanding of the author's textual selves and working practices in Dublin.[5] It is only by reading the complex and highly various contents of the document in their originary context that one can apprehend their meanings and the processes that created them. The *Notebook* indicates, for example, how the apocalyptic 'Sibyl's Leaves' comes to Hopkins in the midst of the 'killing' work of marking seemingly endless examination scripts. For most of his major poems, the only extant manuscripts are 'fair copies', often subsequently corrected; in the case of 'Sibyl's Leaves', however, the *Dublin Notebook* provides three rough working drafts from the early stages of its composition. We can see 'Evening, dealing the dark down, time's drone, sullen hulk-of-all, hearse-of-all night' gradually evolve into 'Evening strains to be time's-well, world's-pit, womb-of-all, home-of-all, hearse-of-all night', and then fragment into:

$$
\text{Evening strains to be time's} \left\{ \begin{array}{l} \text{harbour} \\ \text{hush, world's haven} \\ \text{dock, world's den} \end{array} \right.
$$
doom-of-all, womb-of-all, hearse-of-all[.][6]

At this juncture, the poem goes into arrest: Hopkins did not produce a finished text until November 1886,[7] by which time all six of the so-called 'terrible sonnets' had been committed to paper.[8] Thus, the *Dublin Notebook* teaches us how to read 'Sibyl's Leaves'

---

[4] 'To seem the stranger'.

[5] Of course, no reproduction is the same thing as the manuscript. Furthermore, as Henry Woudhuysen states, 'facsimiles are themselves editions, involving a whole range of editorial and critical choices, and the dream of an unmediated text is no more than a dream'. Woudhuysen, '"Work of permanent utility": Editors and Texts, Authorities and Originals', in Lukas Erne and Margaret Jane Kidnie (eds.), *Textual Performances: The Modern Reproduction of Shakespeare's Drama* (Cambridge: Cambridge University Press, 2004), 46. See also G. Thomas Tanselle, 'Reproductions and Scholarship', *Studies in Bibliography*, 42 (1989), 25–54.

[6] See fo. 15[r] and note and fo. 20[v].   [7] See letter to Bridges, 11 Dec. 1886.

[8] There is no established canon of GMH's 'terrible sonnets', also sometimes called the 'sonnets of desolation' or simply the 'dark sonnets', but these six poems, most of them written in the summer of 1885,

as framing some of Hopkins's most harrowing works. The 'dragonish' drama of 'self ín self steepèd . . . / Disremembering, dismembering all' would not be completed until the tumultuous sonnets had found their expression. In addition, the *Notebook* enables us to view 'Sibyl's Leaves' (fos. 15ʳ, 20ᵛ, and detached fragment) contextually: both as it responds to Collins's 'Ode to Evening' (fo. 8ʳ⁻ᵛ) and as it informs 'Caradoc's Soliloquy' (fos. 9ᵛ, 21ʳ).

Close scrutiny of the *Notebook* not only encourages the discernment of 'under-thoughts' in correlations and resonances such as these, it also allows us to dispel a number of myths surrounding Hopkins's Dublin years. He teaches his University College students responsibly, preparing them for the RUI examinations that they will be facing.[9] His own class preparations are extensive and reflect a concerted effort to accommodate the material to students of moderate abilities. Pages flooded with check-marks are not a sign of debilitating compulsion—scaling the worth of examination answers into quarter points, as is often alleged—but merely reflect the mandated RUI grading system, in which a total of 1,200 possible marks per examination paper was assigned to Latin and Greek. Hopkins computes exam grades competently; the anomalous figures are candidates' identification numbers.[10] In sum, for all his limitations, he did his job thoroughly; the manuscript shows just how sedulously he worked to fulfil the duties assigned to him. This is not to suggest, however, that Hopkins was not beset by 'fits of sadness' and 'continual anxiety'—his letters attest to 'that coffin of weakness and dejection in which [he] live[d]'.[11] The spiritual writings in the *Notebook* similarly reveal his agitated state, 'For indeed it seems a spirit of fear I live by' (fos. 21ᵛ, 22ʳ). Yet, the quotidian materials that punctuate the manuscript manifest something of Hopkins's attempts to function usefully despite 'joyless days, dejection'[12] and to carry on in the midst of manifold difficulties. Thus, as a biographical record, the *Dublin Notebook* adds depth and complexity to Hopkins's self-reporting to his correspondents.

are often considered to be among their number: 'To seem the stranger', 'I wake and feel', 'No worst', 'My own heart', 'Carrion Comfort', and 'Patience'. The order in which these were composed cannot be definitively determined, and the last of them may have been written as late as the spring of 1886. It is likely that GMH made revisions to some of them in Sept. 1887. 'Spelt from Sibyl's Leaves'—apparently begun in Oct. 1884 and most likely completed in Dec. 1886—although not ordinarily understood as belonging to this group, certainly exhibits strong resonances with these poems variously written during its long and intermittent composition. ('Thou are indeed just', a later production of Mar. 1889, is also occasionally counted among these works.)

[9] *Pace* reports provided by Robert Bernard Martin, *Gerard Manley Hopkins: A Very Private Life* (New York: G. P. Putnam's Sons, 1991), 375–6; Norman White, *Hopkins, A Literary Biography*, 385–6; Paul Mariani, *Gerard Manley Hopkins: A Life* (New York: Viking, 2008), 333.

[10] On the eleventh line of fo. 10ʳ, for example, one reads '8 = 48 − 10 = 38 290'. This is a kind of shorthand for the following calculation: for candidate 290, losing eight marks yields a score of 48; losing another ten marks gives a total 38 for this question.

[11] Letter to Bridges, 17–29 May 1885; to Dixon, 7–9 Aug. 1886; to Bridges, 1–2 Apr. 1885.

[12] 'Heraclitean Fire'.

Because the *Notebook* was meant exclusively for Hopkins's private use, its meanings
are not always immediately apparent, nor are its markings always legible. Accordingly, in
order to help the reader gain a full measure of access to this heterogeneous document,
this edition provides introductory commentary, full diplomatic transcription facing
each leaf of photographic facsimile, and extensive annotations. Appendices provide
ancillary matter that otherwise would be difficult to obtain, such as documents relating
to his appointment, one of the RUI examinations he set, and the published text of the
biography of Richard Watson Dixon he laboured over in the *Dublin Notebook*.[13]

Hopkins began to use the *Notebook* in February 1884 and continued to make entries,
albeit intermittently, until late autumn (probably December) 1885. During these
twenty-two months, he worked his way through it sequentially, but occasionally
returned to earlier leaves to add fresh material. Hence, the close reader of the *Notebook*
must continually bear in mind that its spatial order does not invariably correspond to a
strict temporal sequence. On fo. 9ʳ, for example, three different iterations of text,
distinguishable by ink and pen nib, as well as corrections made subsequently, indicate
that Hopkins inscribed the page on four discernible occasions. On fo. 11ʳ, changes in ink
and nib reveal different stints of burdensome examination work. Although it is not
always possible to assign precise dates to particular entries, we have been guided by a
number of reference points, both internal and external, in making chronological
determinations: religious feast days, references to contemporary events, RUI
examination dates, links with extant correspondence, Hopkins's UC teaching schedule,
and the occurrence of the intercalary 29 February 1884.

The *Dublin Notebook* was often a starting point, a work space in which new texts, both
academic and poetic, were first generated. Further drafts or fair copies of what he
had begun in the *Notebook* were made elsewhere, some of which do not survive. We
know, for example, that the teaching summaries for 'Roman literature and antiquities'
(fos. 22ᵛ ff.) were augmented and substantially revised in the notebook now catalogued
as Campion Hall G.II, the other unused workbook from the 1860s that Hopkins brought
with him to Dublin (see *CW* vi). Yet, only a few of his numerous studies for the
'Dorian-Measure' project have been located.[14] Thus, the *Dublin Notebook* was many
things, but perhaps most interestingly it was a kind of nursery for new ideas, new under-
takings—a place in which Hopkins could experiment and engage privately with material
he would later make public, whether as teacher, examiner, or poet.

The *Dublin Notebook*, spanning the months that yielded 'To seem the stranger' and
the 'terrible sonnets', chronicles his personal unravelling even as it documents his
nascent and hard-won pedagogical competence. Occasional memoranda in the *Notebook*
('Athenaeums at the Royal Irish Academy' (fo. 17ʳ)) remind us that daily life for

---

[13] See Biographical Register.

[14] *DN*, 17ᵛ, 18ʳ⁻ᵛ. In addition to the comments made in letters to Bridges (see '"[T]ime's eunuch"' and
'"Sound effects were intended"', in the Introduction, below), GMH identified the Greek translations of
'Tell me where is Fancy bred' and 'Orpheus with his lute made trees' as exercises in the 'Dorian Measure'.
See *LPM* 294–6.

Hopkins meant adjusting to and interacting with a new physical and social environment. As we discuss below, neither Dublin nor the Irish situation was congenial to his thoroughly English sensibilities. In addition to the city's material and cultural impoverishment, the political unrest—and sometimes violent agitation—concerning Home Rule and land reform were especially disturbing to him. 'Politically, the times are most troubled', he lamented to John Henry Newman in 1888; 'There is a great strain of feeling. I live, I may say, in an air most painful to breathe and this comes home to me more, not less, with time.'[15] Fascinated by Irish English, and compassionate towards the Dublin poor, he found himself caught between two camps—a disturbing duality perhaps best exemplified in his title as Fellow of the *Royal* University of Ireland.

AN 'HONOUR AND AN OPENING' AND A 'DISCOURAGEMENT': THE DUBLIN APPOINTMENTS

So fraught were the circumstances and repercussions of Hopkins's double appointment to UC and the RUI that they generated enough emotion for one of the melodramas so popular with Victorian audiences.[16] Aside from the egos and aspirations involved, the complex machinations on multiple fronts reveal very different approaches to improving university-level education for Catholics in colonial Ireland, and the role of an international society such as the Jesuits in Irish affairs. Yet, only if one temporarily disentangles the seemingly inextricable UC and RUI connections (and animosities) can Hopkins's position as 'Fortune's football'[17] be fully understood.

As happened so often in Hopkins's life, there was a Newman connection to the crisis. In 1845, three Queen's Colleges (in Cork, Galway, and Belfast) were established by royal charter to constitute the Queen's University of Ireland, but a papal 'rescript' of 1847 condemned them as being 'detrimental to [the Roman Catholic] religion'. A renewed impetus for a Catholic-based institution resulted in the 1851 establishment of the Catholic University, in Dublin, with Newman as the first rector. Classes began in November 1854, but the Catholic University soon faltered for several reasons, most notably because it did not have a royal charter and, hence, could not grant degrees. Newman departed in 1858. When, in the late 1870s, the Society of Jesus was invited to assume control of the Catholic University (renamed University College, and officially a Jesuit institution as of 23 October 1883), its first president, William Delany, S.J.,[18] was

---

[15] GMH to Newman, 20 Feb. 1888.

[16] When GMH announced his 'new departure or a new arrival and at all events a new abode' to Bridges in Mar. 1884, he declared himself 'unworthy of and unfit for the post . . . It is an honour and an opening and has many bright sides, but at present it has also some dark ones' (7 Mar. 1884). GMH's 'new year's' letter to Bridges in Jan. 1887 quickly became a short disquisition on 'discouragement': 'Our institute provides us means of discouragement, and on me at all events they have had all the effect that could be expected or wished and rather more' (2 Jan. 1887).

[17] Letter to Bridges, 26 July 1883.   [18] See Biographical Register.

wholly committed to its success.[19] To his mind, that meant bringing in faculty from various Jesuit provinces; only they could hope to rival the scholars at Dublin's Trinity College.[20] Edward Purbrick, S.J., Provincial Superior of the English Province, was both unable and unwilling to oblige him: 'our good men . . . the cream of the Province', were 'absolutely not to be spared', he informed Delany in November 1882—and Hopkins most definitely would not be an asset ('Fr Hopkins is very clever & a good scholar. But I should do you no kindness in sending you a man so eccentric').[21] Although temporarily stymied, Delany continued to plan and lobby.

At the same time that UC was being (re)organized, efforts to provide degrees for Catholic-educated university students were coming to fruition. Again, however, there were compromises and complications, all with imperial, nationalistic, and sectarian undertones. The University Education (Ireland) Act of 1879 enabled the formation of a new degree-granting body, the Royal University of Ireland—but it would exist as an examining entity only, serving University College, the three Queen's colleges, and other schools.[22] The requisite academic Fellowships, each worth £400 per annum, would be divided among the Roman Catholic institutions and Trinity College (and thus among Catholics and Protestants). Delany hoped to secure all fourteen of the 'Catholic' RUI fellowships for his community, not merely for the prestige, but because the salaries would

[19] UC would serve 'a rising Catholic middle-class for whom education was primarily a passport to careers and respectability'. Jill Muller, *Gerard Manley Hopkins and Victorian Catholicism* (New York and London: Routledge, 2003), 102. Muller, who depends greatly on White's biography, concludes that compared with Newman's 'surprisingly tolerant view of the Irish cause', GMH was 'incapable of any such open-mindedness' (ibid. 104); GMH's eventual, albeit reluctant support for Home Rule and his acute sense of divided loyalties are not considered.

[20] In the 1884–5 academic year, the members of UC were as follows: President, Revd William Delany; Vice-President and Dean of Residence, Revd John J. Hughes; Catechetical Lecturer and Librarian, Revd Denis Murphy; Professors: *Mental and Moral Philosophy*, Revd Thomas Finlay (FRUI) and Revd James Mallac; *Greek and Latin Language*, Revd G. M. Hopkins (FRUI) and James Stewart (FRUI); *Greek and Latin Literature*, Robert Ornsby (FRUI); *Classical Tutors*, W. J. M. Starkie, M. T. Quinn, and R. Campbell; *Mathematics and Mathematical Physics*, John Casey (FRS, FRUI), Morgan Crofton (FRS, FRUI), Revd Robert Curtis (FRUI); *Mathematical Tutors*, E. Hughes Dowling and Joseph Casey; *Experimental Physics*, Revd Gerald Molloy (FRUI); *Physics Tutor*, Joseph McGrath; *English*, Revd John Egan (FRUI) and Thomas Arnold (FRUI); *English Tutor*, Daniel Croly; *Modern Languages*, Mons. L'Abbé Polin (FRUI) and Revd J. J. O'Carroll; *Irish Language, History, and Archaelogy*, Revd J. J. O'Carroll; *Biology and Zoology*, George Sigerson, MD (FRUI) and Revd L. Martial Klein (FRUI); *Biology Tutors*, J. S. McArdle and Joseph O'Carroll; *Chemistry*, John Campbell (FRUI); *Tutor in Law*, M. McD. Bodkim.

[21] Purbrick to Delany, 10 Nov. 1882; IJA J456 / 51 (2). Letters pertinent to GMH's Irish appointment are reproduced in Appendix A. Delany had previously consulted George Porter, an English assistant to the Jesuits' Superior General in Rome, who replied 5 Nov. 1882: 'I think F. Purbrick might be induced to let you have Hopkins or Walford: I do not think he would part with Rickaby or Lucas. Walford is a first class teacher: Hopkins is clever, well trained, teaches well but has never succeeded well: his mind runs into eccentric ways.' The original letter is in the Delany Papers, IJA; see also BRC 36:16.

[22] The charter for the RUI was granted 27 Apr. 1880. Twenty-eight years later, the Irish Universities Act of 1908 established two new institutions, the National University of Ireland and the Queen's University of Belfast; the RUI was dissolved 31 Oct. 1909.

fund UC operations.[23] In November 1883, when Catholic-designated RUI Fellowships in Natural Science and Classics became vacant, he secured Robert Curtis, S.J. for the science position and resumed efforts to prevail upon Purbrick for a creditable classicist. This time, Purbrick replied that he had 'no objection' to losing Hopkins, then teaching at Stonyhurst (preparing students in their penultimate or final year to succeed in the matriculation—entrance—examinations for the University of London):

As far as I am concerned I have no objection to your writing Fr Gerard Hopkins to stand as a Candidate for a Fellowship. He is the only man possible. You know him. I have the highest opinion of his scholarship & abilities—I fancy also that University work would be more in his line than anything else.

Sometimes what we in community deem oddities are the very qualities which outside are appreciated as original & valuable.[24]

Purbrick also suggested that Delany approach Hopkins in person, which Delany did in early December 1883.[25]

---

[23] Thomas J. Morrissey, *Towards a National University: William Delany, S.J. (1835–1924): An Era of Initiative in Irish Education* (Dublin: Wolfhound Press, 1983), 79. How significant was each Fellowship salary, in terms of operating expenses? The annual rent for 84, 85 (excluding the great hall), and the upper two storeys of 86 St Stephen's Green was £200, plus £30 in rates and taxes. Ibid. 75, 77.

[24] 29 Nov. 1883; IJA J11 / 456 (3). Testimonials for Hopkins were provided by a former tutor, Benjamin Jowett (1817–93; *ODNB*), then Master of Balliol College, Oxford, and Richard L. Nettleship (1846–92; *ODNB*), a former Balliol student (Greats, 1869), who became a Fellow of the college in 1869 and subsequently a Tutor in Philosophy. (For details of their academic relations with GMH, see *CW* iv.) See also Martin, *Gerard Manley Hopkins*, 362–4.

[25] Three GMH biographers differ significantly regarding the date of Delany's visit and its immediate aftermath; there is no definitive GMH-authored document to clarify matters. Working from Delany's papers, Martin suggests that the rector saw GMH in early Dec. 1883 and met him again in Feb. 1884, when GMH arrived in Dublin. White surmises that Delany 'probably saw Hopkins on 4 December. Hopkins probably travelled back with Delany for a brief introduction, visiting Clongowes Wood College . . . as well as Dublin' (*Hopkins*, 361). Mariani's highly speculative account has Fr Delany 'cross[ing] over from Dublin to Stonyhurst' after Christmas 1883, with 'a return visit for Hopkins soon afterwards' (*Gerard Manley Hopkins*, 312–13). Misinterpreted photographic evidence is responsible for some of the confusion. GMH appears in two group photographs taken at Clongowes (CWC), but both were dated incorrectly. When published in T. Corcoran, S.J.'s *The Clongowes Record, 1814–1932*, the picture featuring GMH with a biretta, seated next to Fr Kelly, S.J., then rector of CWC, was dated '1883' (although the picture itself is catalogued and marked '1884 (?)'). Kelly was rector of CWC from 1881 to 1885. The photograph, capturing a day when posing outdoors near a fully grown lawn would have been amenable, could not have been taken during the winter. The second photograph, in which a bareheaded GMH is turned to the left, towards another rector, Fr John Conmee, S.J., was also tentatively dated '1884 (?)', but Conmee was appointed 22 July 1885; the inauguration celebrations were held at CWC on 24 Sept. 1885. Evidence from GMH's letters (see *CW* ii) and the log book kept by the Minister of CWC, Fr Verdon, S.J. indicates that GMH visited Clongowes in Apr. 1884; early Jan. 1885; Easter 1885; and late Aug. 1885 (for his annual retreat). In the GMH/Kelly photograph, GMH is wearing the gown of an English Jesuit (sleeveless, with a button at the neck and the waist); the 19th-c. Irish Jesuit gown, also sleeveless, featured an 'invisible' row of buttons. (Information generously provided by Fr Fergus O'Donoghue, S.J., Archivist, IJA.) GMH's letters to the editor of *Nature* magazine in late Dec. 1883, and to Coventry Patmore on 3 Jan. 1884 (both from Stonyhurst; see *CW* ii), also indicate that he would not have had time to visit Dublin before moving there.

Delany assumed that the election of Hopkins to the Fellowship by the RUI Senate standing committee was a *fait accompli*, not least because he had been assured of such an outcome by the senior senator, Edward Cardinal McCabe.[26] Yet McCabe was soon persuaded to another point of view by Irish Catholic educators who did not trust converts, much less Englishmen, and were eager to recognize and promote national academic accomplishments.[27] Hence, the 'Irish row' over his appointment to which Hopkins alludes in a letter to Bridges (7 Mar. 1884). Opposition to Hopkins was orchestrated by the Revd Dr William Walsh, then president of St Patrick's College, Maynooth.[28] His preferred candidate for the Classics Fellowship was Fr Joseph Reffé, headmaster of Blackrock College. By many accounts Reffé was an 'inspiring teacher', but because he was educated entirely in seminaries he did not have a civil degree.[29] Delany, adroit and persuasive, lobbied other senators vehemently. As he later summarized for Thomas O'Hagan, Lord Chancellor of Ireland (see Appendix A), the final vote at the committee meeting 30 January 1884 was 23 for Hopkins, and 3 for Reffé. McCabe, feeling betrayed, threatened to resign from the Senate, but was eventually persuaded not to do so.[30]

Walsh, still smarting from defeat ten months later, decided to make the controversy public—in two countries, thereby embarrassing Jesuits of the English Province at home.

[26] Edward McCabe (1816–85; *ODNB*), educated at St Patrick's College, Maynooth, was ordained in 1839, named archbishop of Dublin in 1879, and made cardinal in 1882. University education for Catholics was a particular concern (see his contribution to the London *Times*, 1 Apr. 1879). Yet, '[i]n his politics McCabe was opposed to the campaign for home rule and land reform led by Charles Stewart Parnell and Michael Davitt. Though aware of the plight of tenant farmers and appalled by wholesale evictions, he had sympathy for the economic difficulties facing landlords. He regularly condemned agrarian outrages and in October 1881 issued a pastoral letter denouncing in fierce terms the Land League's 'no rent' manifesto. McCabe zealously sought to keep priests from engaging in political agitation. All of this left him isolated among his fellow prelates and increasingly alienated from the generality of Irish nationalist opinion.' W. A. J. Archbold, 'McCabe, Edward (1816–1885)', rev. David C. Sheehy, *ODNB*.

[27] Delany wrote to Walsh on 23 Jan. 1884 to summarize his meeting, the previous day, with the Cardinal and Robert Curtis. 'His eminence was very affable and pleasant' initially, but when GMH's name and appointment were mentioned, McCabe observed that 'he disliked having Englishmen and thought this place had too much of Englishmen in its past history' (Delany Papers, IJA; BRC 41a:8).

[28] William Joseph Walsh (1841–1921; *ODNB*). When Cardinal McCabe died in Feb. 1885 (see GMH's note, fo. 25ʳ), Walsh was named his successor. 'During the commission set up in 1888 to inquire into charges made by *The Times* against Charles Stewart Parnell [Walsh] provided crucial assistance to Parnell in exposing Richard Pigott as a forger. When the Parnell divorce crisis broke in 1890, he resisted pressure from both nationalist politicians and ecclesiastics, such as Cardinal H. E. Manning and Archbishop T. W. Croke of Cashel, to come out against Parnell. It was only when secret negotiations between Parnell and himself, conducted through an intermediary, failed to produce a compromise that he led the clerical attack on Parnell's leadership.' D. A. Kerr and David C. Sheehy, 'Walsh, William Joseph (1841–1921)', rev. *ODNB*.

[29] Norman MacKenzie, 'Hopkins, Yeats and Dublin in the Eighties', in Joseph Romsley (ed.), *Myth and Reality in Irish Literature* (Waterloo, Ont.: Wilfred Laurier University Press, 1977), 82. See also Martin, *Gerard Manley Hopkins*, 363–4.

[30] Walsh resigned from the Senate 'in May [1884] when his advocacy of Fr. Reffé's appointment, this time as Fellow in Modern Languages, failed even to raise a seconder'. MacKenzie, 'Hopkins, Yeats and Dublin in the Eighties', 82.

Letters were sent to the Belfast *Morning News*, 'the London *Tablet* and the Dublin *Freeman's Journal*. No candidates' names were mentioned, but . . . [it was not] necessary to advertise identities. Day after day the hard-hitting accusations and rejoinders continued.'[31] Thus Hopkins was, throughout his Dublin life, associated with a fractious, politically charged debate and a scandal that typified what one bishop, Laurence Gillooly, referred to as 'the evils with which we are threatened'.[32] The enmities in play were not merely Catholic versus Protestant or even Irish versus English; they were also 'Castle Catholic' versus nationalist Catholic, convert versus 'cradle Catholic', and 'religious' priests (members of religious orders such as the Jesuits) versus 'secular' (or diocesan) priests. Sadly, it was not an exaggeration to inform his mother, in late November 1884, 'We have enemies here—indeed what is Ireland but an open or secret war of fierce enmities of every sort? —and our College is really struggling for existence with difficulties within and without' (26 Nov. 1884). Four years later, Hopkins's sense of abjection was no less acute: during his January 1889 retreat at Tullabeg, recalling that the 'resolution of the Senate of the R.U. came to me, inconvenient and painful' only intensified his disconsolate self-scrutiny.[33]

'I LIVE IN DUBLIN'

Hopkins had already lived in London, Liverpool, Sheffield, and Leeds—could Dublin, another late nineteenth-century 'great town', really have been that much of a terrible surprise? In 1881, writing from Glasgow, Hopkins bemoaned to Bridges, 'you cannot tell what a slavery of mind or heart it is to live my life in a great town'.[34] His 'dream' environment, as he recounted in 1888, was 'a farm in the Western counties, glowworms, new milk . . . but in fact I live in Dublin':

---

[31] MacKenzie, 'Hopkins, Yeats and Dublin in the Eighties', 83. See the *Tablet*, Nov. and Dec. 1884; *Freeman's Journal*, 29 Nov., 1, 3–6, 8 Dec. See also Morrissey, *Towards a National University*, 89–97. GMH informed Bridges that the editors at the *Tablet* 'do not like Jesuits, but I have always maintained the *Tablet* is a very good[,] well conducted gentlemanly paper, unequal in ability, but some of its articles are very good and able' (14 Dec. 1885).

[32] In Feb. 1884, for example, Laurence Gillooly, CM, Bishop of Elphin and a member of the RUI Senate, informed the Jesuit provincial, Thomas Brown, S.J., that his 'unfortunate' support for GMH helped to 'rende[r] the Conflict inevitable—the results are already unfortunate and it is not easy to foresee the other evils that will follow. I take the liberty of writing to you now, to tell you how much I deplore the step you have taken and the Conflict in which it engages you and to express a hope that you will, for the sake of your great undertaking at St. Stephen's Green as well as for wider & weightier interests, remedy the mistake you have made by withdrawing the Revd. Fr. Hopkins, as you are of course still perfectly free to do' (IJA J11/1, fo. 2ʳ).

[33] Bodleian MS Eng, Misc, a.8, fo. 25ᵛ; see Appendix I, below; and *CW* v.

[34] GMH to Bridges, 16 Sept. 1881. Cf. his sister's observation, 'He was made miserable by . . . the ugliness of it all'. Kate Hopkins to Bridges, 7 Jan. 1920; quoted in Martin, *Gerard Manley Hopkins*, 432 n. 14.

What I most dislike in towns and in London in particular is the misery of the poor, the dirt, squalor, and the illshapen degraded physical (putting aside moral) type of so many of the people, with the deeply dejecting, unbearable thought that by degrees almost all our population will become a town population and a puny unhealthy and cowardly one.[35]

Although these comments anticipate twentieth-century urban studies by Georg Simmel and Osward Spengler in interesting ways, Hopkins's dire words offer few specific facts or even fictions about Ireland's capital. 'I had fancied it quite different', he informed Bridges in March 1884, '[b]ut Dublin itself is a joyless place.'[36] Neither the eighteenth-century architecture ('a few fine buildings'), nor the beauties of Phoenix Park ('fine, but inconveniently far off'[37]) offered sufficient consolation for the newcomer.

Although Hopkins's response to Dublin as lived and built environment was thus both over- and pre-determined, he was not exaggerating its fundamental municipal problems. The socio-economic (and *always* political) reasons for this predicament have been amply documented. Dublin in the 1880s was 'a declining, second-rate, ex-capital' with a decreasing population and seemingly insurmountable public health problems.[38] Although it retained its status as the legal, medical, banking, and transportation centre of Ireland,[39] it was losing international significance as a shipping hub[40] and garnering too much attention as a fractious, poverty-blighted garrison city in the British

[35] To Baillie, 1 May 1888.

[36] To Bridges, 7 Mar. 1884. R. K. R. Thornton addresses the questions 'where is Dublin in the Dublin poems' and is 'Dublin in the letters' in 'Dublin and Hopkins in the 1880s', *Hopkins Quarterly*, 14/1–4 (Apr. 1987– Jan. 1988), 105–11 at 107–8.

[37] GMH certainly enjoyed his sojourns there—enough to compose poems in his mind: 'Alphonsus Rodriquez' ('made out of doors in the Phoenix Park with my mind's eye on the first presentment of the thought', 19–20 Oct. 1888); and possibly 'Heraclitean Fire' (see the letter to Dixon, 29–30 July 1888). Yet, the Park was also strongly associated with political rallies, even sectarian violence and death. (See the discussion of the 1882 'Phoenix Park murders' in 'Extreme Political Troubles', below.)

Phoenix Park, situated 3 km north-west of Dublin's city centre, is Europe's largest enclosed urban park, covering more than 1,800 acres. (Originally a royal hunting preserve, it has a resident herd of Fallow Deer.) It was opened to the people of Dublin in 1745 by Lord Chesterfield; in 1830, as an additional attraction, what became one of the oldest zoos in the world was established there. Subsequently, it was also the site of the barracks for the British military garrison assigned to Dublin. Douglas Bennet, *The Encyclopaedia of Dublin* (Dublin: Gill and Macmillan, 2005), 191.

[38] Mary Daly, 'Dublin in the 1880s', *Hopkins Quarterly*, 14/1–4 (Apr. 1987–Jan. 1988), 96. According to the 1881 census, the city's population was 249,602; in 1891, 245,001 (ibid. 3). The percentage of Roman Catholics increased: from 80.44 per cent in 1881 to 82.21 per cent a decade later (Mary Daly, *Dublin, the Deposed Capital: A Social and Economic History 1860–1914* (Cork: Cork University Press, 1984), 122). Birth and marriage rates in Dublin were above national levels, but so too was the annual mortality rate—in 1879, it reached an unprecedented high of 35.7 persons per 1,000. Margaret Preston, *Charitable Words: Women, Philanthropy, and the Language of Charity in Nineteenth-Century Dublin* (Westport: Praeger Publishers, 2004), 26.

[39] Daly, *Dublin*, 4–5.

[40] See Preston, *Charitable Words*, 14. When protective trade duties were abolished in 1824, all of the Irish markets were opened up to foreign competition. Andrew MacLaren, *Dublin: The Shaping of a Capital* (London: Belhaven Press, 1993), 42.

empire. Although the city centre remained the focus for local business, shopping, and entertainment,[41] members of the Protestant (but also Catholic) middle class were decamping to suburbs such as Rathmines.[42]

For 'the Unemployed' and the underemployed, however, Dublin was a home fraught with hazard. Conditions were indeed 'perilous' ('Tom's Garland'): in 1884, the Royal Commission on the Housing of the Working Classes in Ireland reported that some 30,000 Dubliners subsisted in 2,300 tenement houses 'which were deemed unfit for human habitation'.[43] Pollution, overcrowding, poor nutrition exacerbated by high food prices,[44] and inadequate plumbing and drainage systems undoubtedly made the poverty-stricken even more susceptible to frequent outbreaks of infectious diseases such as typhoid, scarlet fever, measles, cholera, tuberculosis, and bronchitis.[45] The poor's physical proximity to Dublin's dairy yards and slaughterhouses meant that both their food and sewage were vectors for these and other often deadly disorders.[46] Although Hopkins certainly found the poverty and squalor of Dublin repugnant, the poor themselves elicited his compassion.

The Liberties and Bull Alley, two of the most noxious areas of Dublin,[47] were quite close to middle-class St Stephen's Green, 'the biggest square in Europe'[48] surrounded by once-elegant private establishments that were now typically rented out for professional offices, colleges, clubs, and studios. Daily, Hopkins would not only walk by a Unitarian Church, the Methodist Centenary Church, and Wesley College, but also a temperance hotel, the St Stephen's Green Club, the St Stephen's Green Bazaar, and the St Stephen's Green Turkish, Electric, Russian, and Medicated Baths.[49]

Culturally, Dublin could be very inviting. In Merrion Square, the National Gallery had opened in 1864. Twenty years later, the National, Historical, and Portrait Gallery opened. The one facet of Dublin's 1880s arts scene that Hopkins consistently enjoyed was the vibrant musical community, which seemed to defy both political divisions and economic deprivations. International artists the calibre of Italo Campanini, Joe Masas,

---

[41] Joseph Brady and Anngret Simms suggest that Daly's portrait of Dublin is too dire; despite the economic recession, the city was gradually improving its water supply and other key elements of its infrastructure, as well as improving roadways and rail communications. 'Dublin in the Nineteenth Century: An Introduction', in Joseph Brady and Anngret Simms (eds.), *Dublin through Space and Time* (Dublin: Four Courts Press, 2001), 161.

[42] Daly, 'Dublin in the 1880s', 99.   [43] MacLaren, *Dublin*, 45.

[44] Preston, *Charitable Words*, 26.   [45] Daly, 'Dublin in the 1880s', 98.

[46] Preston, *Charitable Words*, 23.

[47] The Liberties, 'a few minutes walk' west from St Stephen's Green, 'in the direction of St Patrick's Cathedral', were associated with tenements and prostitution in the 1880s, but the area included some of the oldest sites in Dublin. Daly, 'Dublin in the 1880s', 96. Daly cites a late-1860s Midlands Railway Guide to the city that warns visitors about the ' "eruption of some strange" ' and ' "squalid" ' conditions in the Liberties (ibid., 97).

[48] GMH to Bridges, 7 Mar. 1884. Twenty-seven acres of land south of the Liffey and east of the city centre were first marked out as 'open space' in 1664. A wall enclosed the park as of 1669; in the early 1880s, the Green was opened for general use. Bennet, *Encyclopaedia*, 237–8.

[49] Ibid. 238–40; and Daly, 'Dublin in the 1880s', 96–7.

Maria Piccolomini, and Thérèse Tietjens frequently performed, as did numerous Irish vocalists.[50] Concerts were staged at the Royal Academy of Music in Westland Row, the Antient Concert Rooms on Great Brunswick Street, and the Rotunda; more popular venues included The Royal, the Gaiety, and Dan Lowry's Musical-Hall.[51]

Dublin's contradictory realities also extended to the subject of reading. According to the 1881 census, more than 23 per cent of the adult population was illiterate.[52] There were, however, five daily morning newspapers: the *Freeman's Journal*, *Saunder's Newsletter*, the *Daily Express*, *Irish Times*, and the *Morning News*. The city's first public libraries—on Capel Street and Thomas Street—became available in 1884.[53] The National Library of Ireland on Kildare Street—until 1877, the Royal Dublin Society Library—was particularly important for the book-starved faculty and students of University College.[54]

Hopkins never praised the Dublin transportation system, but he certainly took advantage of it for his many visits to friends and associates, his 'supply' work in parishes, and his excursions farther afield. Horse-drawn omnibus services had begun in the 1840s; in 1881 three tram firms joined to form the Dublin United Tramway Company, which 'ran one hundred and eighty-six trams with over a thousand horses' on fourteen different routes throughout the city and its environs.[55] An 1886 city guide for visitors 'drew attention to routes to places as far flung as Dollymount, Rathdranbham or Blackrock'.[56] Although the railway termini were inconveniently located away from the city centre, the Great Southern and Western Railway, the Kingsbridge Line, and the Midland Great Western Railway made it possible to travel extensively within Ireland (to the cliffs of Moher, for example, or Sallins, near Clongowes Wood College[57]) and make ferry connections to England.

Hopkins's own home, the Jesuit community at 85–6 St Stephen's Green, embodied many aspects of Dublin itself. The buildings had lost whatever splendour and dignity they once possessed, were plagued with dry rot, and were too small for their current use.

[50] Peter Costello, *James Joyce: The Years of Growth 1882–1915* (London: Kyle Cathie, 1992), 48.

[51] Peter Somerville-Large, *Dublin: The Fair City* (London: Sinclair-Stevenson, 1996), 210. Musical presentations were also part of the RUI degree ceremonies, under the direction of Sir Robert Stewart or Dr Joseph Smith.

[52] Ibid. 205.

[53] Ibid. 210.

[54] After the state assumed control, it was administered by the Department of Science and Art. The Library's 'New Building', with its distinctive circular central reading room, was designed in 1883 by Sir Thomas Deane (in consultation with William Archer), but not open until 1890. Bennet, *Encyclopaedia*, 59.

[55] Somerville-Large, *Dublin*, 205.

[56] Joseph Brady and Anngret Simms, 'Dublin at the Turn of the Century', in Brady and Simms (eds.), *Dublin through Space and Time*, 221.

[57] Vivien Igoe notes that the trip from Dublin's Kingsbridge railway terminal to Sallins would have taken less than an hour. At Sallins, station carts with horses waited to convey passengers the remaining few miles through fields and woods to Calen Village, 'beyond which lay the 500-acre domain' of Clongowes. Igoe, *James Joyce's Dublin Houses* (London: Mandarin Paperbacks, 1990), 30.

There was sewage in the basement; rats were an ongoing problem. Soon after his arrival, Hopkins described the place as having 'fallen into a deep dilapidation', 'a sort of wreck or ruin . . . the costly last century [plasterwork] ornamentation . . . much in contrast with the dinginess and dismantlement all round'.[58] The buildings and the educational enterprise they came to represent were 'all unprovided to a degree that outsiders wd. scarcely believe'.[59] The neglected state of the plumbing and sanitation almost certainly precipitated his final illness; his death from typhoid fever allied him with more than a third of Dublin's population, whose final end was also caused by infectious disease.

DENIZENS

Although the *Dublin Notebook* starkly attests to professional responsibilities that, with cyclical and 'dragonish' regularity, would contribute to feelings of being 'selfstrung, sheathe- and shelterless' ('Sibyl's Leaves'), it also provides traces of the various personal connections and social opportunities that buttressed Hopkins's life. The names and epistolary tasks listed on fo. 22^r—'Angelo, Harrington, Fr. Bacon, verses for Bridges, . . . Aunt Ann, Fr. Rigby, Fr. Cummins, Milicent, verses for Fr. Bacon'— and the brief note on fo. 17^r—'Good editions of [Plautus and Terence]. Ask Mr. Tyrrell'—capture some of the networks he maintained and cultivated. Joseph Bacon, S.J., for example, whom he had known since Stonyhurst, was one of the rare Jesuits who encouraged Hopkins's poetic efforts.[60] Few of the dutiful letters sent to family members (his mother, Kate; his aunt, Ann Hopkins; his sister Milicent, an Anglican nun) survive, but throughout the Dublin era Hopkins was in regular correspondence with the four male friends whose textual intimacy he valued highly: Robert Bridges, Richard Watson Dixon, Alexander Mowbray Baillie, and Coventry Patmore.[61] The speaker in many of Hopkins's Dublin poems is 'undenizened', alien and 'lonely' in the extreme, yet he himself enjoyed, and sometimes took refuge in, several different kinds of friendships and friendly relationships. In Ireland, however, the personal and the political were always impinging upon one another (see 'Extreme Political "Troubles"', below). And all too often, Hopkins was typecast (as the 'padre'; as 'Castle Catholic' or pro-England sympathizer, and hence anti-nationalist; as 'the convert') before the shy and fastidious man was welcomed or appreciated.

Hopkins had little contact with Thomas P. Brown, S.J., the Jesuit Provincial of Ireland; it is not recorded whether Brown shared the sympathies of his predecessor, James Tuite, who had resisted Delany's plans to include English Jesuits among the faculty at UC because, ever since Newman's venture in the 1850s, Tuite was convinced

---

[58] GMH to John Henry Newman, 20 Feb. 1884.
[59] GMH to Kate Hopkins, 26 Nov. 1884.
[60] See Lesley Higgins, 'Uncommon Lives: Fr. Hopkins and Fr. Bacon', *Hopkins Quarterly*, 21/3–4 (Summer–Fall 1994), 77–96; and Biographical Register.
[61] See Biographical Register.

that 'English converts . . . "are sometimes— let us say—unsuited to this country and its thoroughly Catholic people" '.[62] The Jesuit community and UC faculty at St Stephen's Green consisted of remnants from the Newman-era Catholic University and new-comers like Hopkins, brought in to bolster the faculty and secure the RUI fellowships that would finance the Society's operations.[63] William Delany, S.J., the energetic and energizing president of University College and a determined leader, was praised by Hopkins for his 'buoyant and unshaken trust in God', for being someone who 'wholly lives for the success of the place. He is as generous, cheering, and open hearted a man as I ever lived with'.[64] Among the established (and quite cosmopolitan) group Hopkins joined: Thomas Finlay, S.J., professor of philosophy and economics;[65] Edmund Hogan, S.J., 'pioneering in Irish language and history';[66] John J. Hughes, S.J., Vice-President of UC and Dean of Residence; James Mallac, S.J., formerly a lawyer in France who now lectured in philosophy; Gerald Molloy, S.J., the Professor of Physics who 'occupied

---

[62] Quoted in Martin, *Gerard Manley Hopkins*, 377. The Society of Jesus was suppressed in Ireland in 1773, restored in 1812. Before 1830, Ireland was officially a Jesuit 'mission'; as of 1830, a 'vice-province'; and as of 1860, its own separate province. James Tuite was the Provincial from July 1880 to Apr. 1883, when Thomas Brown took the office; in Feb. 1888, Timothy Kenny. See Anon., 'Irish Jesuits since 1800', *Irish Monthly* (Jan. 1890), 1–16, 2.

[63] The non-Jesuit faculty included two classicists, Professors Robert Ornsby and James Stewart, and the Professor of English, Thomas Arnold. Both Ornsby and Stewart, initially appointed by Newman to the Catholic University, had been productive scholars, but they were physically frail by the time that GMH arrived in Dublin. Ornsby's Greek edition of the New Testament was published in 1860; he also wrote *The Life of St. Francis de Sales* (London, 1856) and *Memoirs of J. R. Hope-Scott*, 2 vols. (London, 1884). GMH commends 'old Mr. Ornsby, most modest and estimable of men' in a letter to Bridges, 28 Oct. 1886 (Ornsby had praised some of GMH's 'Greek verses'). Stewart's publications included *The Complete Latin Prosody of E. Alvarez* (Dublin, 1859); *Memoranda of Greek Grammar with a Complete System of Accentuation* (Dublin, 1859); and *A Latin Grammar for the Use of Schools and Colleges* (Dublin, 1860). Thomas Arnold (1823–1900; *ODNB*) does not mention GMH in his extant letters, but their lives variously overlapped and intersected several times. From 1862 to 1865, Arnold (son of Thomas Arnold, of Rugby, and younger brother of Matthew) was the classics master at Newman's Birmingham School (GMH had the post 1867–8); dissatisfaction with his salary, and the Oratorians' concerns about his 'liberalism', were reasons for Arnold's departure. He then moved to Oxford, where he worked as a tutor from Michaelmas term 1865 until 1876. Arnold and GMH both attended the sermons of Revd Henry Parry Liddon in Apr. 1865; Arnold and Liddon became friends (for GMH and Liddon, see Introduction to *CW* iv). Arnold was also friends with GMH's Oxford companion W. E. Addis, with whom he wrote the *Catholic Dictionary* (1884); his daughter Mary Augusta (1851–1920; *ODNB*) married Humphry Ward, the Brasenose colleague of Walter Pater, who was GMH's 'coach' or private tutor 1866–7. In Oct. 1882 Arnold returned to Dublin to resume the position as Professor of English at the Catholic University. In autumn 1885, he commissioned GMH to write the entry on Dixon for the *Manual of English Literature*, 5th edn. (see below, fo. 14ʳ, and Appendix D).

[64] GMH to Kate Hopkins, 26 Nov. 1884.

[65] Finlay, the co-founder of the Irish Cooperative Movement, helped to establish four journals: *The Irish Messenger* (1888–), *The Lyceum* (1889–94), *The New Ireland Review* (1894–1911), and *The Irish Homestead* (1895–1923). His papers are housed in the IJA. See also Declan O'Keefe, 'A Man for Others and a Beacon in the Twilight: Matthew Russell, S.J. and the *Irish Monthly*', *Studies*, 99/394 (Summer 2010), 68.

[66] Mariani, *Gerard Manley Hopkins*, 319.

more of [the] best rooms than could easily be spared';[67] and Denis Murphy, S.J., Lecturer in Religion, Modern Languages, and Physics (and Hopkins's spiritual director his first year in Dublin)[68]. The initial fellow newcomers were Robert Curtis, S.J. and Martial Klein, S.J.,[69] actual friends among the 'strangers' who deserve special mention. They were subsequently joined by Matthew Russell, S.J., whose remit as of 1886 was taking charge of UC's residential students,[70] and Joseph Darlington, S.J., Professor of English, who in later years provided a quite biased account of Hopkins's demeanour and behaviour.[71] Hopkins also had periodic contact with three other Jesuit communities: at Milltown Park, Dublin;[72] St Stanislaus's College, Tullabeg;[73] and especially Clongowes Wood College (some 32 km (20 miles) from Dublin, in Co. Kildare), then considered the 'Mother-House of the Society in Ireland'.[74] However forbiddingly the buildings, grounds, and staff were described in James Joyce's *Stephen Hero* and *A Portrait of the Artist as a Young Man*, Clongowes provided a comfortable, gracious, and rural place of congeniality and retreat for the man who now ordinarily lived in unwholesome and impoverished, altogether 'poor, all unprovided' circumstances.[75]

Robert Curtis, eight years younger than Hopkins, was by all accounts a gifted academic.[76] A graduate of Trinity College in mathematics and science, he joined the

[67] MacKenzie, *LPM*, 328. Molloy had been the rector of the old Catholic University. For GMH's sketches of a worker 'cleaning Dr. Molloy's windows', see *CW* vi.

[68] 'Fr. Denis Murphy', *Memorials of the Irish Province, S.J.*, 1 (1898–1904), 53–4; Mariani, *Gerard Manley Hopkins* 326. See fo. 6ʳ.

[69] See Biographical Register for both men.

[70] See [Lambert McKenna, S.J.], 'Father Gerard Hopkins, S.J., and his Poetry', *Irish Monthly* (1919), 441–8. The article is signed 'The Editor'. Previous commentators have misattributed it to Russell, but he died in 1912, after which McKenna assumed the editor's responsibilities. See also the Biographical Register.

[71] Darlington, also a convert and Oxford graduate, defended the Society's role in GMH's tortuous existence by casting aspersions on his colleague. 'By all accounts', Martin summarizes, 'Fr Darlington was a charitable man . . . but even so it would be natural to take his testimony as veiled envy' (*Gerard Manley Hopkins*, 374; see also Martin's Appendix).

[72] The Minister's Journals, examined by Anthony Bischoff, S.J., record a visit by Hopkins from 22 Oct. 1885 until at least 1 Nov. (when he said Mass at nearby Donnybrook); 1–6 Nov. 1887; 25 Mar. 1888 (one of several 'supply calls' GMH made to local churches requiring a priest on Sunday); 6–10 May 1888; 15 July and 24–9 July 1888; 16 and 24 Feb. 1889; and 31 Mar. 1889 (BRC 41a:8).

[73] GMH's notes from a Jan. 1889 retreat at Tullabeg (near Tullamore) are discussed above; see also Appendix I, below. In 1886–7 the boys' school at Tullabeg was amalgamated with that at CWC; by the time of GMH's arrival, Tullabeg had become the novitiate of the Irish Province of the Society of Jesus.

[74] Anon., 'Irish Jesuits', 11.

[75] GMH's letters and the 'house' diary kept by Fr John Verdon, S.J., CWC's Minister, attest to these visits (there may have been others): his annual eight-day retreat, begun 22 July 1884; early Jan. 1885; Easter 1885; Nov. 1885. On Easter Tuesday, 7 Apr. 1884, one of the fellow guests was William Walsh, then rector of St Patrick's College, Maynooth. Two days later, Walsh reported to Delany that he had paid the subscriptions for Loisette's memory training system for GMH, Fr Murphy, and Delany (see *CW* ii). Once GMH began visiting Monasterevan, he frequented CWC less often, and went on retreat at St Stanislaus's College, Tullabeg.

[76] Curtis was no stranger to sectarian politics: he was 'the first Catholic entrant' to Trinity College 'after Gladstone had abolished religious tests'. White, *Gerard Manley Hopkins*, 374.

UC faculty in 1883, and was made an RUI Fellow in Natural Science in January 1884 (by the same Senate committee so vexed by Hopkins's appointment). Epilepsy—both the disease and popular (mis)perceptions of it—was the reason he was never ordained, but it may also have been the rationale for permitting Curtis and Hopkins to associate and take holidays together. Typically, a friendship between Jesuits from different 'grades'—a Scholastic and a priest in final vows (even a 'spiritual coadjutor', as Hopkins was)—would not have been sanctioned. Yet, by November 1884, Hopkins was describing Curtis to his mother as 'my comfort beyond what I can say and a kind of godsend I never expected to have. His father Mr. Stephen Curtis Q.C. and mother live in town and I often see them and shd. more if I had time to go there.'[77] Memorably, they hiked throughout northern Wales together in July 1886. Their August 1888 holiday in western Scotland included scaling Ben Nevis, the highest peak in the British Isles, but Hopkins's report on the trip is decidedly disconsolate.[78]

To be Martial Klein's friend meant enjoying the company and scholarship of an 'amiable man',[79] but it also meant learning harsh and vivid lessons about Irish politics and one's vow of obedience. Hopkins and Klein shared their status as converts (Klein, ostensibly from Judaism; he entered the Society in 1878), as members of the English Province seconded to Dublin, and as ardent English nationalists. In December 1884, Klein was appointed Professor of Biology at UC and Fellow of Natural Science at RUI. Two and a half years later, he defied his UC superiors by attending a garden party organized to mark Queen Victoria's golden jubilee. The guest of honour was Prince Edward, not just the monarch's son but 'the commandant of all British troops in Ireland and ex-officio Privy Councillor for Ireland'.[80] More than 2,000 had been invited.[81] Initially, Delany had not objected to Klein's attendance, but when it transpired that a papal delegate in London had intervened in the invitation process, Klein was told not to participate for fear of injuring the position of Irish Jesuits and UC as a whole (by seeming too pro-British). Regardless, Klein went to the party on 29 June 1887; there are conflicting stories as to what he said, and to whom. Further complicating his overt defiance of authority and lack of prudence was Klein's sustained criticism regarding the operations of UC and the Irish Province, as well as emerging vocational doubts. His letter of resignation from the RUI, dated 20 August 1887, was accepted on 26 October

[77] Letter to Kate Hopkins, 26 Nov. 1884. As Martin summarizes, 'Curtis's father was a brilliant barrister who became Crown Prosecutor of the Counties of Kilkenny and Tipperary. . . . The family was prosperous, Conservative in politics, Anglo-Irish but Roman Catholic, and lived in a handsome house in North Great George's Street, to which Hopkins became a frequent visitor.' *Gerard Manley Hopkins*, 378.

[78] See GMH's letter to Bridges, 18–19 Aug. 1888.

[79] GMH to Newman, 20 Feb. 1888. For GMH's observations of a lecture by Klein, see the comments on Lucan: *CW* vi; and Fredric Schlatter, S.J., 'Gerard Manley Hopkins: Poetic Fragments, Comments on Lucan and Cicero, Essay on Duty', *Hopkins Quarterly*, 27/3–4 (Summer–Fall 2000), 41–2.

[80] Fredric Schlatter, S.J., 'Martial Klein, Hopkins's Dublin Colleague', *Hopkins Quarterly*, 29/3–4 (Summer–Fall 2002), 80.

[81] Documents relating to Klein are housed in Gonzaga University; see BRC 41b:11 (1–3).

1887.[82] There is a second-hand report that 'Hopkins wept' as he recounted attempts to make Klein reconsider.[83] Apparently without consulting Delany, Edward Purbrick, the English Provincial, recalled Klein in mid-October, informing his counterpart that 'Fr Klein has always been my subject and I had therefore the right of recalling him at any time'.[84] Klein left the Society a month later and was formally dismissed on 4 November (the brief, preprinted form announcing the dismissal was signed by Purbrick on 12 November 1887[85]). Three months later, when alluding to the Klein affair in his annual birthday letter to Newman, Hopkins admitted that his friend 'took a step to ours and his own injury', yet nevertheless pronounced him 'an able, learned, and amiable man'.[86]

Matthew Russell (1834–1912) was one Jesuit who negotiated Dublin's roiling sectarian waters skilfully. Perhaps he was too outgoing for Hopkins, but his good-natured demeanour and reputation as 'something of a non-partisan centre' for Catholic and Protestant culture workers would have been especially attractive.[87] 'He was a minor poet himself, and he admired the poetry of Bridges', Robert Martin reports. As editor of *The Irish Monthly* since 1873, Russell was encouraging the intellectual and creative efforts of 'the Catholic upper middle classes' and diplomatically promoting the Irish literary revival.[88] In October 1886, 'Father Matt' walked Hopkins across St Stephen's Green to the studio of John Butler Yeats, in order to meet the agnostic painter; his son, the fledgling poet William Butler Yeats; and his current sitter, the young Catholic poet

---

[82] BRC 41b:11 (3).

[83] BRC 41b:11.

[84] BRC 41b:11 (1).

[85] 'LONDON, *12 Nov. 1887*. | Rev. and dear Father, | P.C. [Pax Christi]. | Please let all in your College be duly informed | that *Fr. Martial Klein* | is no longer a member of the Society. | I remain, | Rev. and dear Father, | Yours sincerely in Christ, | *E. J. Purbrick, S.J.*' (BRC 22:24; bold italics indicate the hand-written elements.) The loss of income for a Fellow was remedied 'almost at once' by the appointment of John J. O'Carroll, S.J. (1837–89), reputed to know fourteen or more languages, including Irish; he proved to be popular with students and published in the *Gaelic Journal* (GMH to Newman, 20 Feb. 1888; Fathers of the Society of Jesus (eds.), *A Page of Irish History: Story of University College, Dublin 1883–1909* (Dublin: The Talbot Press, 1930), 100–1, 125, 127–8.

[86] GMH to Newman, 20 Feb. 1888. Klein, whose veracity was increasingly questioned, later argued that he was never baptized and therefore never validly ordained. He changed his name to de Beaumont, became a Unitarian minister, and in 1897 married Kathleen O'Hagan, the daughter of a distinguished Anglo-Irish Catholic family (Lady Alice O'Hagan was a descendant of Charles Towneley, a great benefactor of the British Museum; Lord O'Hagan became Chancellor of Ireland in 1868 (d. Feb. 1885)). GMH was often a guest at the home of Frances and John O'Hagan (Frances was Lord O'Hagan's daughter from his first marriage; John O'Hagan (1822–90; *ODNB*), a judge, was the first judicial head of the Irish Land Commission). Further evidence of the interconnecting circles in which GMH moved: Lord O'Hagan's first wife was Mary Teeling; GMH became friends with George Teeling, a nephew, who was Lord O'Hagan's private secretary.

[87] Martin, *Gerard Manley Hopkins*, 403. See also Katharine Tynan, 'Dearest of Friends', *Irish Monthly*, 45 (1912), 551–4.

[88] O'Keefe, 'A Man for Others', 62.

Katharine Tynan.[89] Tynan and Hopkins subsequently exchanged cordial letters, and there were at least two visits to her home, but Hopkins neither seized the opportunity— nor knew how—to be good friends with the young woman.

If the Russell-inspired opportunities to enlarge his social and cultural environment were not realized, Hopkins's non-examining life included member's privileges at the Royal Dublin Society; visits to the Royal Irish Academy (see *DN*, fo. 17ʳ); membership, at least for 1885, in the Hellenic Society; and attendance at various guest lectures and concerts.[90] He pursued some of his musical interests by associating with the Dublin Music Society. He also became acquainted with the RUI Fellows who served as examiners in music, Dr Joseph Smith and Sir Robert Stewart, both from Trinity College.[91] Although Hopkins's Oxford degree entitled him to use the esteemed Trinity College library, personal reticence and ever-present sectarian pressures severely limited his contact with that university's resources and people. The one major exception: Robert Yelverton Tyrrell, the classical scholar who at that time was Regius Professor of Greek. The autumn 1884 *DN* entry cited above—'ask Mr Tyrrell' for advice about good scholarly editions (fo. 17ʳ)—and the familiarity with which Hopkins refers to him in his letters by 1886 suggest a companionable as well as academic relationship.[92]

During his parish work in the late 1870s, vocational responsibilities (baptisms, weddings, funerals, charity work) necessarily had a social dimension. Only in his Dublin years, however, did Hopkins have the time and scope to establish bonds with individuals and families who provided, as he so succinctly explained to Bridges, the much-needed respite of 'kind people at a nice place' (2 Jan. 1887). The MacCabes, Miss Cassidy and Mrs Wheble, Judge O'Hagan and his family, and Lord Emly had in common their affection for Hopkins, their enjoyment of his fancifulness (or eccentricities), and their twin commitments to the Catholic church *and* the British government.[93] And yet, his enjoyment among such friends, however intense, was always short-lived; eventually he would always return to 85 and 86 St Stephen's Green.

---

[89] John Butler Yeats (1839–1922; *ODNB*) trained as a barrister but pursued his desire to paint in London, Dublin, and finally New York. He and his wife Susan Mary Pollexfen (1841–1900) had four children: William Butler (1865–1939; *ODNB*), the poet; Susan Mary (1866–1949; *ODNB*) and Elizabeth Corbet (1868–1940; *ODNB*), who together ran the Cuala Press; and Jack Butler (1871–1957; *ODNB*), the painter. For Katharine Tynan, see Biographical Register.

[90] The IJA has a transcription of entries from the UC bursar's 1884 and 1885 Day Book related to GMH. Among the items: personal expenses (the purchase and cleaning of clothes, rentals of MA gowns, shoe repair, eyeglasses), books, transportation costs, and bills for 'subscriptions' to journals and learned societies. IJA J11 / 39 (1–4).

[91] See the letter to his sister Grace, 4 Nov. 1884.

[92] Explaining to Bridges his publication hopes for some Latin lyrics, GMH observes, 'and the rest I believe I can and shall get published in the Trinity Hermathena by means of Mr. Tyrrell' (13 Oct. 1886). See note for fo. 17ʳ.

[93] In addition to the Martin and White biographies, see White, *Hopkins in Ireland* (Dublin: University College Dublin Press, 2002), 114–19; and Joseph Feeney, S.J., 'Hopkins and the MacCabe Family: Three Children who Knew Gerard Manley Hopkins', *Studies*, 90 (2001), 299–307. For Mary Cassidy, see the Biographical Register.

EXTREME POLITICAL 'TROUBLES'

The Irish think it enough to be Catholics or on the right side and that it is no matter what they say and do ~~on~~ ^to advance^ it; practically so, but what they think is that all they and their leaders do to advance the right side is and must be right. The English think, as Pope says for them, he can't be wrong whose life is in the right.[94]

So Hopkins summarized his fraught experience of Irish–English political relations on New Year's Day, 1889.[95] Yet, how did this ardent Tory patriot ('What can I do for the land that bred me') who loathed Gladstone and believed Charles Stewart Parnell capable of murderous sympathies come to the painful realization that Irish 'Home Rule' was a necessity?

Hopkins arrived in a country sorely undermined by the Great Famine forty years earlier[96] and riven with historically charged and religiously inflamed sectarian debate and unrest. Norman England had first claimed Ireland for its own militarily; the Tudor monarchs had reaffirmed legislative and local power; Oliver Cromwell had led the forces to 're-conquer' the country in 1649–50. But actual control of the population was managed most effectively over the centuries by controlling the land: colonizing Ireland and monopolizing land ownership (and by extension, rents) by granting land rights to English, Scottish, and Welsh settlers (known as the Anglo-Irish Ascendancy, most famously satirized by Jonathan Swift[97]). Opening salvoes of the 'Land War' that would be waged rhetorically and physically began in October 1879, when tenant farmers in County Mayo organized the first of many public demonstrations under the banner 'the Land of Ireland for the people of Ireland'. Politicians soon endorsed the struggle; one year later, the Irish National Land League (INLL) was founded, and Charles Stewart Parnell (1846–91; *ODNB*) elected its president (honorary secretaries included Michael Davitt, Andrew Kettle, and Thomas Brennan). Agitating on behalf of the 'three Fs'—fair rent, fixity of tenure, and the free sale of land—INLL activities

---

[94] Alexander Pope, 'Essay on Man', Epistle 3: 'For modes of faith, let graceless zealots fight; / His can't be wrong whose life is in the right: / In faith and hope the world will disagree, / But all mankind's concern is charity.'

[95] The retreat notes were misdated by GMH 'Jan. 1 1888 St. Stanislaus' College, Tullabeg'. See Appendix I and *CW* v.

[96] Severe failures of the potato crop resulted in more than a million deaths from starvation and hunger-related diseases, 1845–9, and the emigration of more than 1.5 million people. See E. Margaret Crawford, 'Great Famine', in S. J. Connolly (ed.), *The Oxford Companion to Irish History* (Oxford: Oxford University Press, 1998); James Lydon, *The Making of Ireland: From Ancient Times to the Present* (London and New York: Routledge, 1998), 302.

[97] Swift's deliberately outrageous satire, 'A Modest Proposal' (1729), suggests that Irish-Catholic 'yearling' children be sold for meat and manufacture, and that absentee landlords should profit first: 'I GRANT this Food will be somewhat dear, and therefore very *proper for landlords*, who, as they have already devoured most of the Parents, seem to have the best Title to the Children.' *The Essential Writings of Jonathan Swift*, (ed.) Claude Rawson and Ian Higgins (New York: Norton, 2010), 297.

included fund-raising in America; resisting tenants' evictions; establishing relief agencies; and advocating legislative reform. When Hopkins moved to Dublin, the Land Acts of 1880 and 1881 had been bitterly opposed as being inadequate; the national Land Commission had begun to reduce rents selectively; Parnell and some INLL party members had been imprisoned (from October 1881 to May 1882) for advocating a national tenant farmer rent strike; and 'land agitation' continued, often violently, throughout the country. On 6 May 1882, two British senior officials were stabbed to death near the vice-regal Lodge in Phoenix Park: Lord Frederick Cavendish, newly appointed Chief Secretary for Ireland (he had arrived only the day before) and Thomas Henry Burke, Permanent Undersecretary (the most senior Irish civil servant). Members of the 'Irish National Invincibles', a relatively unknown republican faction, claimed responsibility for the assassinations. Parnell was among the many Irish leaders who denounced the killings. Eventually five members of the Invincibles were apprehended, tried, convicted, and then hanged in May and June 1883. Yet, the ramifications of their actions haunted Irish politics for three decades.

Parnell's belief that 'Home Rule' for Ireland was paramount—he had joined the Home Rule League, established by Isaac Butt in 1873—helped him to win his first seat in the British parliament in 1875.[98] Five years later, he became president of the Irish Parliamentary Party (IPP), which tried to advance its cause by working with Liberal and Conservative governments in various legislative initiatives. Without question, the most important British politician persuaded to the Home Rule cause was Gladstone. Yet, in the general election of November 1885 Parnell did not support Gladstone. Lord Salisbury's Conservatives won by a slim margin, but were forced to resign 28 January 1886. On 1 February, Gladstone informed Queen Victoria of his intention to introduce 'a home-rule measure. On 4 February he made a public statement which was perceived to be a commitment to some form of autonomy for Ireland. A Liberal government, depending on the votes of Parnell's parliamentary party, and generally believed to be intending a measure of home rule, was now in office.'[99] The Government of Ireland Bill introduced on 8 April 1886 would have established an Irish legislature but reserved 'imperial issues' for the British parliament; it was defeated, by forty votes, in June.[100] Among those who lobbied against the bill: Gladstone's cabinet colleague Lord Harington, who was Lord Cavendish's elder brother (Cavendish's widow Lucy was Gladstone's niece). Four years after Hopkins's death, Gladstone introduced a second Home Rule Bill; it was eventually passed by the House of Commons in September 1893, 347 to 304, but vetoed by the Conservative-controlled House of Lords.

---

[98] F. S. Lyons suggests that 'Home Rule' was 'a question concerned less with self-government for a cloudily defined nation than with the desperate efforts of a rural population to survive in a period of falling prices, when even moderate rents seemed extortionate and when failure to pay brought eviction'. ' "Parnellism and Crime", 1887–90', *Transactions of the Royal Historical Society*, 5th ser. 24 (1974), 123.

[99] Paul Bew, 'Parnell, Charles Stewart (1846–1891)', *ODNB*, accessed 5 July 2010.

[100] See n. 3, above.

In the winter of 1885, Hopkins kept track of the Irish nationalists' bombing 'outrages' in London (see fos. 25ʳ and 26ʳ) and tried to pray for temperance when thinking and speaking about Gladstone (fo. 26ʳ). Among his regular correspondents, Hopkins freely discussed Irish politics with his friend Baillie. A postcard begun 6 April 1886 baldly concludes, 'What do you think of the Home Rule Bill?' More expansive comments were forthcoming 1 June when Hopkins, 'improved' by a recent vacation in England,[101] expressed his vexed and divided feelings:

Matthew Arnold has a fine paper in the <u>Nineteenth</u>[102] on the Home Rule bill, a temperate but strong condemnation of the G.O.M. [Gladstone, the Grand Old Man]. It might with truth be much stronger. Not but what I wish Home Rule to be: it is a blow at England and may be followed by more, but it is better that shd. be by peaceful and honourable means with at least the possibility of a successful working which otherwise may come by rebellion, bloodshed, and dishonour and be a greater and irretrievable blow—or have to be refused at a cost it is not worth. How sad and humbling it shd. have come to such a choice!

   I suppose now the bill will not pass. Gladstone will then go to the country and to pass this bill (for his Messiahship requires success to justify it) will, I daresay, offer other bribes, as abolition of the Church of England, and more 'in the dim and distant future'.[103]

Hopkins may have desired to achieve an 'other-man's-point-of-viewishness'[104] regarding Ireland, but the struggle to do so is verbally palpable.

   Had he been alive in December 1889, Hopkins would have been greatly distressed by the impropriety of Parnell's adulterous relationship with Katharine O'Shea (1845–1921; *ODNB*).[105] What is well documented, however, is Hopkins's reaction to the protracted political scandal and ferocious 'propaganda war',[106] 1887–9, generated by an anti-Parnell campaign in the pages of *The Times*. (To 'discredit Parnell and his party was not just an end in itself', Francis Lyons observes; 'it was the means towards a greater end, to discredit Gladstone and *his* party'.[107]) In March 1887, *The Times* launched a series of articles on 'Parnellism and Crime', in which Irish Home Rule leaders were accused of various criminal acts and sympathies, including 'notorious and continuous relations with avowed murderers'; furthermore, because of their American supporters, they were identified as 'essentially a foreign conspiracy'.[108] The final article, published 18 April, included an alleged letter by Parnell that virtually supported the Phoenix Park murders. Parnell wanted to sue the newspaper for libel, but was dissuaded

---

[101] GMH to Bridges, 1 June 1886; he had seen Bridges during his holiday.

[102] Arnold, 'The Nadir of Liberalism', *Nineteenth Century*, 19 (May 1886), 645–63.

[103] Gladstone used this phrase in a Nov. 1885 speech; it reappeared in H. Rider Haggard's *She*, which was serialized in *The Graphic*, Oct. 1886–Jan. 1887.

[104] GMH to Bridges, 11 Dec. 1886.

[105] The relationship between O'Shea and Parnell began in 1880; her husband, Capt. William O'Shea, filed for divorce 24 Dec. 1889 and was granted a *decree nisi* in Nov. 1890.

[106] Lyons, '"Parnellism and Crime", 1887–90', 124.

[107] Ibid., 125.   [108] *The Times*, 7 Mar. 1887.

because cross-examination would enable *The Times*'s lawyers (on its behalf, and the government's) to widen their verbal attacks on the Irish leader and assail other Home Rule and Land League advocates. Fifteen months later, the government finally agreed to establish a Special Committee of the House of Commons to investigate the charges; a panel of three judges was subsequently appointed. Between

14 and 22 February 1889, the court and the world heard from *The Times*'s representatives how they had purchased the letters from E. C. Houston, secretary of the Irish Loyal and Patriotic Union, with totally inadequate precautions to establish their authenticity; from Houston how, with similar gullibility, he had bought them from Richard Pigott.[109]

On 25 February 1889, Pigott (1828–89; *ODNB*), an Irish Roman Catholic journalist and newspaper proprietor previously suspected of financial improprieties, black-mail, and pornography, admitted under cross-examination that he had forged the incriminating evidence. Immediately after his court appearance, Pigott fled to Paris and then Madrid, where he committed suicide when apprehended by the police.

Hopkins followed the commission's proceedings avidly in the newspapers. A letter to Bridges just two days before Pigott's startling admission bristles with indignation:

And what boobies your countrymen are! They sit in court at the Commission giggling, yea guffawing, at ^the wretched^ Pigot's ~~floundering;~~ ^mess;^ making merry because a traitor to government and then a ~~trai~~ traitor to rebellion, both in a small way, has not succeeded in injuring an enemy of their own who is a traitor to government in a great way and ^on a danger on^ an imperial scale; and that after a trial which has at least shewn the greatness and the blackness of the crime ~~g~~ lawful government and the welfare of the empire have to contend with. And this I say as if Pigot were ^or employed^ the forger of those letters. For in my judgment, unless further evidence is forthcoming, I believe those letters ~~to be~~ ^are^ genuine. But no more of this misery. (23 Mar. 1889)

So much did the 'misery' of Irish affairs vex Hopkins, however, that a letter to his brother Lionel on 1 March veers away from Indo-European etymology and classical studies and crashes into current events:

My Nationalists friends are wild with triumph and joy over Pigott (one of themselves and ^sometime^ editor of their most advanced organ, the paper which under a slight change of name[110] is now United Ireland). Pigott has confessed to making, by forgery, the charge against Mr. Parnell of, after the event, faintly approving or not disapproving of a ^the^ murder ^of Lord Frederick^ ^Mr. Tom Burke^ and I want to know when his successor O'Brien is going to confess to the falsehood of his charge against Mr. Balfour of planning in general and then carrying out in

---

[109] Lyons, ' "Parnellism and Crime", 1887–90', 137.

[110] Parnell founded *United Ireland* in 1880 and named William O'Brien editor the following year; the *United Irishman* was published in Liverpool 1876–7.

particular the murder of John Mandeville.[111] The charge is far more ~~de~~ hideous. I do not ask the Irish to see this, but I should like the English dupes and dullards to see it. If you knew the world I live in! Yet I continue to be a Home Ruler: I say it must be, and let it be.

I am not convinced ^however that^ the Facsimile letter, the one about the Phoenix Park, is not genuine after all.[112]

This was one of the last substantial letters he would write before his final illness; it captures vividly the complex, sometimes competing sympathies he had developed in 'the world' in which he reluctantly lived. In politics, as in so many things, Hopkins was stringent, morally unshakeable, and unrepentantly iconoclastic.

'DEADLY WORK'

'It is killing work to examine a nation.'[113] Why did Hopkins make such an extreme statement to his friend Canon Dixon in late July 1888? The RUI was solely an examining and degree-granting institution—not only for candidates attending UC and the Queen's Colleges (Cork, Galway, Belfast), but those undergoing private study or attending more than twenty-five schools and commercial tutorial colleges ranging across the whole of Ireland.[114] Hopkins was helping to make history, in that both the female and male students of Ireland were eligible to sit the RUI examinations and be granted

[111] John Mandeville (1849–88) was a Munsterman imprisoned with William O'Brien (1852–1928; *ODNB*) on 31 Oct. 1887. He was released on 24 Dec. 1887 and died at Mitchelstown on 8 July 1888, owing, it was alleged, to ill treatment in the Tullamore jail. An inquest (fully reported in *The Times* 13–30 July 1888) was held to investigate the charge, and O'Brien gave evidence in support of the allegation. Arthur Balfour, first earl of Balfour (1848–1930; *ODNB*), then Chief Secretary for Ireland (1887–91), was British prime minister 1902–5.

[112] The judges' findings are in the *Report of the Special Commission, 1888* [C 5891], H.C. 1890, xxvii, 477–640. Pigott's testimony can be found in *Special Commission Act, 1888, reprint of the short-hand notes of the speeches, proceedings, and evidence taken before the commissioners appointed under the above act*, v, pp. 443–576 (20–2 Feb. 1889). As Lyons summarizes, '*The Times* itself cringed before Parnell and was glad enough to settle his libel suit by paying him £5,000 . . . [but] the total cost of the proceedings [was] estimated at over £200,000' and the government rejected all pleas from the newspaper for financial aid. Lyons, ' "Parnellism and Crime", 1887–90', 139.

[113] GMH to Dixon, 29–30 July 1888.

[114] The following list of institutions is based on the RUI Matriculation examination results of 1883 and 1884: Academical Institute, Londonderry; Mungret College, Limerick; Royal Academy and Institute, Belfast; Banbridge Academy; Carmelite College, Terenure; French College, Blackrock; St Colman's College, Limerick; Intermediate School, Omagh; Carlow Academy, Carlow; Wesley College, Dublin; St Kieran's College, Kilkenny; St Malachy's College, Belfast; Royal School, Armagh; National School, Dromore; Lurgan College; St Mary's College, Dundalk; St Stanislaus' College; Ladies' College School, Belfast; Holy Cross College, Clonliffe; Sacred Heart College, Limerick; Rochelle Seminary, Cork; Rye College, Peckham Rye; The Monastery, Mountrath; Portadown Academy; and Ranelagh School, Athlone. Unless otherwise indicated, information regarding the examinations has been culled from the Calendars of the RUI (a complete set is housed in the Archives of the National University, in Dublin). Each year, in addition to all the particulars pertinent to taking the examinations (fees, schedules, etc.), the comprehensive Calendar included the examination papers from the previous year.

degrees, but he was concerned about the quality of the answers, not the gender of the students.[115]

There were five possible examinations related to the BA degree: Matriculation (the entrance exam—as of 1884, held twice a year, Summer and Autumn, 'always a heavy piece of work'[116]); First University (also two sittings a year); Second University; BA pass; and BA honours. An MA examination, per field, was also available, and a Scholarship examination,[117] held in January of each year. Hopkins was a Fellow in

[115] Based on the translations they produced, he speculates as to whether two candidates are 'girls, I think', in Autumn 1884. See fo. 11^r. Throughout Ireland, women and men wrote at separate examinations centres.

[116] Walsh to GMH, 8 Sept. 1884. In Jan. 1886 there was also a supplemental Matriculation Exam, which GMH partially set; see his letter to Everard Hopkins, 23 Dec. 1885.

[117] See GMH to Bridges, 7–8 Sept. 1888: 'I have been trying to set a discursive MA. Examination Paper, in a distress of mind difficult both to understand and to explain.' Not recorded in the *DN* is the fact that GMH was awarded an honorary MA by the Royal University of Ireland. The story of GMH's MA is as follows. At Oxford and the older British universities, an MA was not an earned degree: students who had achieved a BA (hons.) could, after the twenty-first term following matriculation, apply for the award of a Master's degree, for which they might be charged an administration fee by their college. There was in theory no religious test which the student had to pass after the 1854 Oxford University Act; BA students (excluding those taking theology degrees) no longer had to subscribe to the Thirty-Nine Articles of the Church of England at matriculation or graduation; the 1871 University Tests Act removed almost all religious requirements. In the 1870s, GMH had evidently not seen the need for the largely *pro forma* upgrading of his degree. When he reached Dublin, however, there was some confusion among those referring to him, many of whom seemed to imagine that an Oxford graduate of more than fifteen years' standing would obviously be an MA. The UC *Prospectus* (1884) lists GMH as 'Rev. G. M. Hopkins, S.J., M.A. Ball. Coll. Oxford, F.R.U.I.'; the higher qualification, although representing no further academic achievement, would look more appropriate for the teacher and examiner of the Dublin universities' courses up to the MA level, and Hopkins was qualified to have it, but the assumption that he held this distinction was incorrect. On the Autumn 1884 First University Latin examination paper, dated 2 Sept., GMH is identified as 'Rev. Professor Gerard Hopkins, B.A.', as he is on the Greek 'First Paper', dated 23 Sept. On the Autumn 1884 BA—Honours examination, dated 25 Sept. 25, he is listed as 'Rev. Professor Hopkins, M.A.', but he is a BA again for the MA Second Paper in Greek, also dated 25 Sept. Throughout the 1885 examination papers, which begin in June, he is 'Hopkins, M.A.' Expenses incurred by GMH as recorded in the UC 'Day Book I 1884–5, Aug. 28th '84 to April 25 '85' include, on 12 Nov. 1884, 'M.A. gown for Fr Hopkins'—7 shillings, 6 pence. A gown was hired again on 10 Apr. 1885, for 10s. Perhaps the recurrent hiring of a gown for which he was not technically qualified spurred either GMH or his superiors to set about normalizing the position. There was in existence a formula of *ad eundem gradum* {at the same level} recognition between the universities of Oxford, Cambridge, and Dublin which allowed a graduate who was entitled to an MA at one of the institutions to proceed to the equivalent degree at either of the other universities without further examination. Permission to proceed to MA was obtained from the individual's college, and a fee was required to verify credentials. An expense item in the Day Book for 24 April 1885 reads: 'Evelyn Abbot [*sic*] bursar of Balliol fees | Preliminary to taking of M.A. degree | by Fr Hopkins'—£1 1s. 4p. (IJA J11 / 39 [1]). According to Oxford's Register of Congregation, 1879–94 (EW 2/2), that institution did not grant GMH an MA. Published university records concur: Hopkins last appears in the annual Oxford *University Calendar* for 1889, and his highest degree is listed as BA (conferred 1868). The Royal University of Ireland, however, did grant him the degree. Now housed in the Bodleian library is an ornate certificate which states: 'Royal University of Ireland | This is to Certify that the | Degree of Master of Arts honoris Causa | was conferred on Gerard M. Hopkins | Having heretofore obtained in another | University the Degree of Bachelor of Arts | at a Public Meeting of the Royal University | held in Dublin on the Twenty-seventh day of | October 1885-five. | [official seal and signed by Lord Emly] Vice-Chancellor' (Bod MS. Eng. Misc. a8, fos. 1–12, fo. 12).

Classics, which meant that for each 'examination' there would be papers in Latin and Greek literature, history, culture, grammar, and composition[118] (typically, he would be examining one language or the other). Altogether, Hopkins could count on setting parts of, and grading, between seven and ten sets of examinations per year. The overwhelmingly large numbers he reports in his letters—'557 papers on hand', a 'consignment of 331 . . . and more will come', '500 examination papers and that only one batch out of three'[119]—are corroborated by Gráinne O'Flynn, who summarizes the results provided in the *Parliamentary Papers*, Reports and Commissions, Education (Ireland): in 1884, there were approximately[120] 1,319 candidates for four sets of examinations in Classics; in 1885, 1,652 candidates for seven sets of examinations; in 1886, 1,482 candidates for seven sets of examinations; in 1887, 1,795 students, for seven sets; and in 1888, 1,774 candidates.[121] These numbers, however, tell only part of the story. The government reports do not include statistics for the Scholarship examinations— the first of which Hopkins graded in January 1885[122]—nor do they account for the doubling of papers, in Latin and Greek, for each candidate studying Classics. No wonder, then, that for Hopkins, 'the work of examination leaves leisure and strength (of mind at all events) for no other thing'.[123] Or, as he informed his mother in 1885, 'That examination work is for this time over. I never was so spent with work before.'[124]

Hopkins's RUI responsibilities were burdensome, certainly, but 'killing'? A chronic sense of dread began months before the actual work—even as he was unpacking his belongings amid the 'deep dilapidation'[125] at St Stephen's Green, and absorbing the 'welcome' from his new Jesuit community. When announcing the Fellowship to Newman in February 1884, Hopkins referred vaguely and humbly to his 'unfitness'.[126] To Bridges, a month later, he amplified the self-deprecatory language ('unworthy of and unfit for the post') and the explanation for his apprehension: 'when I first contemplated

---

[118] Greek composition was not part of the Matriculation nor the First University examination.

[119] To Dixon, 24 Nov. 1884; to Bridges, 6 Oct. 1886 ('331 accounts of the First Punic War with trimmings, have sweated me down to nearer my lees'); to Patmore, 6 Oct. 1886.

[120] They are 'approximate' because O'Flynn has tried to allow for the fact that every student, in all degree programmes and fields, was required to sit the Classics examination for the First University year. For the Second University, BA, and MA examinations, Mathematics could be substituted. Also, 'the total number of candidates is less than the total number of papers that would have to be corrected because there were at least two papers in Latin and Greek for each candidate who took Classics.' Gráinne O'Flynn, 'Hopkins's Teaching', *Hopkins Quarterly*, 14/1–4 (Apr. 1987–Jan. 1988), 177.

[121] GMH participated in the Jan. 1889 Scholarship examination but died just prior to the Summer 1889 Matriculation, 1st BA, 2nd BA, and degree examinations. As he informed his mother in May 1889, 'My sickness falling at the most pressing time of the University Work, there will be the devil to pay. Only there is no harm in saying, that gives me no trouble but an unlooked for relief.' GMH to Kate Hopkins, 5 May 1889.

[122] See *DN*, fos. 2ʳ and 3ʳ for the requirements, which GMH has copied out, and fo. 2ʳ for marks and comments regarding individual candidates. (As for all exams, the set texts routinely changed.) The Scholarship Exam was one of the least demanding, in terms of grading: 'I shall for a few days be examining the papers for the Scholarship', GMH explained to his mother, 13 Jan. 1886.

[123] GMH to Katharine Tynan, 8 July 1887. [124] GMH to Kate Hopkins, 13 Nov. 1885.

[125] GMH to Newman, 20 Feb. 1884. [126] Ibid.

the six examinations I have yearly to conduct, five of them running, and to the Matriculation there came up last year 750 candidates, I thought that Stephen's Green (the biggest square in Europe) paved with gold would not pay for it'.[127] The work came as no surprise, therefore, but nonetheless constituted a somatic and professional shock. 'I am in the very thick of examination work', he reported to Bridges on 30 September 1884, 'and in danger of permanently injuring my eyes. I shall have no time at all till past the middle of next month.' The disease motif was echoed in subsequent letters to family and friends (examining was a 'bout' or a 'plague') and the metaphorical pitch escalated: examining became 'deadly' work, akin to 'drowning'.[128]

Scrupulosity when grading papers no doubt contributed to his sense of going under, yet again one must distinguish between facts and dubious apocryphal statements.[129] The *Dublin Notebook* helps to clarify both the ordeal of marking 'many many examination papers' and the particulars involved 'in the close work of examination'.[130] Folio 7[r] features twenty-three and a half lines of checkmarks; more than 1,000 notations in all. From the spaces or pauses between groups of markings (see Codicology, Appendix K), it seems that he was keeping track of the scores on a series of questions. But the novice examiner would have had difficulty, when revisiting the page, to recall what he had discerned in the process of grading (no information about individual answers or papers is delineated). Folio 10[r], consequently, includes checkmarks, rough calculations, candidates' numbers, and quotations highlighting the students' inaccuracies or inadequacies (' "Then the Greeks goes and snatches the maiden" '). Some eleven other complete or partial folios[131] carry the same burden: identifying good work; quoting mistakes; calculating scores. The meaning or scale of the checkmarks has been misunderstood. Greek and Latin examinations were each graded out of a total of 1,200 marks. (Other 'ancient' languages such as Sanskrit or Hebrew, or 'modern' languages such as English, French, German, and Italian, were marked out of 800.) According to Tildesley's *Guide to Royal University of Ireland* examinations, 'The general pass standard [was] placed at one-third of the maximum number of marks attainable.'[132] Hopkins, in sum, was quantifying his evaluations as instructed. His acute sense of responsibility in doing so was all his own.

---

[127] GMH to Bridges, 7 Mar. 1884.

[128] See letters to Everard Hopkins, 5 Nov. 1885; to Dixon, 24 Nov. 1884. Cf. Mandell Creighton to GMH, 7 Apr. 1885, 'You say truly that the drudging of examinations is the thing which overwhelms one most.' For GMH's reports on his own health, see above.

[129] 'The story is often told with variations, of how Hopkins was so scrupulous in his marking that he would be found in the middle of the night with a wet towel wound round his forehead as he assigned grades, which he calculated precisely down to quarters and halves that he was subsequently quite unable to add up.' Martin, *Gerard Manley Hopkins*, 373.

[130] GMH to Bridges, 17–18 Feb. 1887, and to Francis Goldie, S.J., 20 Sept. 1888.

[131] *DN*, fos. 10[v], 11[r], 11[v], 12[r], 12[v], 13[r], 13[v], half of 14[r], 14[v], 16[v], one-third of 17[r].

[132] *Guide to Royal University of Ireland. Matriculation*. Tildesley's Royal University of Ireland series (Edinburgh: S. J. Tildesley & Co., 1889), 14. In GMH's undergraduate era, Oxford students relied upon Montagu Burrows's *Pass and Class, an Oxford Guide-Book through the Courses of Literae Humaniores, Mathematics, Natural Sciences, and Law and Modern History* (updated annually); see *CW* iv.

As of 1884, Hopkins's experience with university education was narrow, consisting solely of what he recalled of his own Oxford years, and helping to prepare some Stonyhurst students for University of London examinations. What could he expect from the students he would be examining? As the author of Tildesley's *Guide* discretely explained:

The Royal University of Ireland occupies an analogous position in our sister isle to that occupied by the London University in England. . . . it has been designed to perform work of a similar nature. . . . [The RUI] may be regarded as a special boon to those students whether resident in Ireland or England, who are precluded either by choice or by the necessities of their position from going into residence at any particular town or college. While the degree of the London University undoubtedly calls for a greater amount of grind and presents greater chances of failure to the average student, and is certainly of considerably greater scholastic value, yet that of the [RUI] is undoubtedly held in considerable estimation, and is a great attraction to those who are unprepared either by lack of time or want of inclination to attempt to gain the former.[133]

Less discretely: not only were the standards of the RUI lower than those of Oxford, Cambridge, and Trinity College, the students would be less thoroughly prepared than those completing degrees at the University of London. Almost certainly, then, it was not only the sheer number of exams to set and scripts to grade, but also the generally low standard of the candidates that made Hopkins's RUI examining 'a weary task indeed'.[134] The RUI 'does the work of examining well; but the work is not worth much', he confided to his mother.[135]

Hopkins's preoccupation with exam-setting responsibilities—which included 'setting, comparing, revising, and correcting proof'[136]—is evident in the manuscript fragments preserved in several archives. The earliest autograph draft of 'Epithalamion' appears on a piece of paper that also has a possible examination question on Virgil's *Georgics* (bks. 1 and 2).[137] A scrap of paper Hopkins left in the *Manuel des institutions romaines* by A. Bouché-LeClerq was meant to indicate a passage on 'p. 489' that would serve in some related capacity.[138] In Chandler's *Practical Introduction to Greek Accentuation* he inserted a directive, 'Choose for question, for 2nd Arts Honours Oral from <u>one</u> and Thucyd. VII'; Thucydides VII (C. 70, §3) was part of the Second University examination in Summer 1887.[139] Similar scraps and notes attest to the

---

[133] *Guide to Royal University of Ireland*, 5.   [134] GMH to Dixon, 18 June 1887.

[135] 5 July 1888.

[136] GMH to Baillie, 1 June 1886. Cf. GMH to Katharine Tynan, 2 June 1887: 'This being my busiest time of year or at least the most anxious, when I prepare my examination papers, I cannot now write more.'

[137] See *LPM* 320.

[138] GMH describes the *Manuel* (Paris: Librarie Hachette et Cie, 1886) as a 'first-rate book' to his brother Lionel, 1 Mar. 1889. The book used by GMH is now housed in the IJA; the piece of paper used as a bookmark is located at Gonzaga University (BRC 1:14).

[139] Bischoff found the slip of paper at p. 18, but there is no way to know if GMH had placed it there. BRC 1:14.

regular need to provide questions for the seemingly continual stream of new exams that had to be set in order to solicit from students proof of their intelligence, diligence, translation skills, and ability to memorize.[140]

Until 1887, examinations bore the name of the Fellow(s) responsible for setting and grading them, so we know precisely which papers were Hopkins's. Appendix F reproduces the first test he set for the RUI in September 1884: the First University examination, Pass, in Latin. In that same session, he was one of the examiners for the 'First Paper' for the Second University examination, honours, in Greek; the Greek authors paper focusing on Sophocles' *Ajax* and *Philoctetes*; the BA pass paper on Greek composition; the first BA honours paper in Greek (Aeschylus' *Agamemnon* and *Persae*); the MA second paper (also focusing on Aeschylus); and the MA third paper, Greek Prose Composition. The Autumn 1884 Matriculation examination took place at the beginning of October; Hopkins was responsible for the first Latin paper, dealing with Virgil's *Aeneid* (bk. 2) and Caesar's *De Bello Gallico* (bks. 1 and 2). Never before, one must remember, had he examined any university students, nor did he have any experience with the RUI system. Annual changes in the texts (or their parts) for which the candidates were responsible were discussed among the examiners and announced in the Catalogues. Appendix G (2) presents Hopkins's outline regarding 'Changes for 1886 and 1887'; these notes are particularly significant because, 'The syllabus for 1888 and the following years was considerably altered to give greater emphasis to courses in history and antiquities. . . . Hopkins was [very] involved in and contributed to the evolution of the Classics courses of the Royal University.'[141]

On the one hand, examining meant that Hopkins enlarged his circle of professional acquaintances: he met with fellow classicists from other institutions to prepare the examinations and discuss the results. (The comments about candidates one finds on various folios seem to be points for further discussion.[142]) Collegial collaboration, however, could also result in misapprehension or antipathy. At least one examination paper was drawn up by mistake (see Appendix G (1)). Bureaucratic difficulties also ensued, as a letter to his mother in November 1885 obliquely indicates: 'examination

---

[140] One fragment features GMH's translation, into Greek, of a passage from John Dryden's *Discourse concerning the Original and Progress of Satire* (1693). The MS is headed: ' "How easy is it to call rogue"—Dryden's Essay on Satire set at Royal Univ'; the cancelled final lines are: 'For Pass a passage from D'Israeli's Curiosities beginning "Da Vain, a famous chancellor" '. For the complete Greek text, see *CW* vi. The original Dryden text is: 'How easy is it to call rogue and villain, and that wittily! But how hard to make a man appear a fool, a blockhead, or a knave, without using any of those opprobious terms! To spare the grossness of the names, and do the thing yet more severely, is to draw a full face, and to make the nose and cheeks stand out, and yet not to employ any depth of shadow. This is the mystery of that noble trade, which yet no master can teach his apprentice; he may give the rules, but the scholar is never the nearer in his practice. Neither is it true, that this fineness of raillery is offensive. A witty man is tickled when he is hurt in this manner, and a fool feels it not. The occasion of an offence may possibly be given, but he cannot take it.' (*The Works of John Dryden*, iv, ed. A. B. Chambers, William Frost, and Vinton A. Dearing (Berkeley: University of California Press, 1974), 70–1.)

[141] Andrew Smith, 'Gerard Manley Hopkins as a Classicist', *Irish University Review*, 20 (1990), 302–3.

[142] See fos. 10[r], 10[v], 11[r], 11[v], 13[r], 13[v], 14[r], 14[v], 22[r], and Appendix G, items 3(a) and (b).

work is for this time over. I never was so spent with work before. And it was not work only but moral annoyance and the having to deal with officials whose behaviour was overbearing and ungentlemanly. However do not repeat this.'[143] Some time after the actual examinations, the papers were collected (and edited[144]) for inclusion in the RUI Calendar. In September 1888, D. B. Dunne, the RUI's Catholic Secretary (or registrar), had to write:

My Dear F. Hospkins [*sic*],

If you have not destroyed yet the M.A. [examination] originals, please note all the references of passages for translation, so that we need not have a hunt for them when preparing for the Calendar.

As MacKenzie speculates, 'it would appear that Hopkins on some previous occasion had delayed the editors while he searched for passages he had himself chosen'.[145] (Dunne's request has survived because Hopkins used the verso of the letter to compose lines for 'St Alphonsus Rodriquez'.)

An example of Hopkins's efforts to help prepare UC students for the RUI examinations also survives. Perhaps because he was still the 'new' man in late spring 1884 and had yet to set examinations or deliver lectures, he prepared one of the test papers for 'Collections', the sample or practice tests that served the dual purpose of monitoring students' progress and preparing them for the actual RUI examinations. As much a rehearsal as an assessment exercise, the Collections made the large academic challenge of year-end examinations incremental rather than insurmountable. The formally typeset and printed document reads:

'A.M.D.G.[146] | CATHOLIC UNIVERSITY COLLEGE. | Sessional Examination, June, 1884. | Roman History—First University Pass. | *Examiner*—Rev. G. M. Hopkins, S.J., M.A.[147] | 1. What were the principal races of ancient Italy? | 2. What and where were the Capitoline, Palatine, Aventine, and Caelian hills? | 3. What was the beginning and end of the Latin League? | 4. Give shortly the circumstances, with dates, of the battles of Sentinum, Asculum, the Aegatian Isles, the Metaurus, Pydna, Acquae Sextiae. | 5. Give short accounts of Spurius Maelius, Licinius Stolo, Xanthippus, Virathus, C. Gracchus, Cinna. | *L. D. S.*'[148]

There is also, however, a note in Hopkins's handwriting in the upper left-hand corner of the sheet: 'This paper by mistake was not set [or used] (June '84): it will do again.' We have nonetheless quoted the exam paper in its entirety both to delineate Hopkins's academic responsibilities and to emphasize, again, the close relationship between

---

[143] GMH to Kate Hopkins, 13 Nov. 1885.

[144] As a space-saving measure in the Calendar copies, for classical papers, textual passages were indicated only by references to first and last lines.

[145] MacKenzie, *LPM* 336.

[146] Jesuit texts typically begin with the motto 'A. M. D. G.', *Ad Majorem Dei Gloriam* {To the Greater Glory of God}, and conclude with 'L. D. S.', *Laus Deo Semper* {Praise God Always}.

[147] For the mystery of GMH's MA degree, see above, n. 117.   [148] BRC 1:17.

the knowledge required by the examinations and the substance of the lessons he was drafting in the *Dublin Notebook*'s second half.

Exhaustive analysis of all those examinations known to have been set by Hopkins is work for other, specialist scholars. In relation to the *Dublin Notebook*, and to Hopkins's own intellectual imagination and professional aspirations as a classicist, one paper deserves particular mention. Of the six exams presented for the September 1884 'Examination for the Degree of M.A.' (three for Latin, three for Greek), the tripartite Second Paper focused on Aeschylus (*Persae* and *Agamemnon*), Pindar (*Nemean* and *Isthmian Odes*)—both Hopkins's responsibility—and Arisotophanes (*Nubes* and *Aves* {*The Clouds* and *The Birds*}), to be examined by Professor T. Hastings Crossley (Queen's College, Belfast). The Pindar segment required the candidate to translate sixteen lines from the fourth *Nemean Ode* (as well as 'Supply by note or bracket all that is needed to bring out Pindar's meaning'); translate sixteen lines from the eleventh *Nemean Ode*; answer two contextual questions; and do the following:

3. In the first extract, supposing, what is likely, that the 4th, 5th, 6th, and 8th lines (in each stanza) are of one type and are really equal in musical time, show, by the conventional Greek marks or otherwise, how the 8th lines . . . are made to fill up the due length.

4. In the second extract, scan the line ἀγλααὶ &c. and its fellow, and the line ἰσχὺν &c., by dividing them into their bars or measures; and say what are the two names this bar or measure bears.[149]

Hopkins was asking the candidate to consider correlations of poetry, Greek prosody, and music similar to his own work, especially during the Dublin years (see below). Remarkably, these exam questions proved to be the springboard for his theory of the 'Dorian-Measure'—what Hopkins believed to be a prototypical rhythm of classical verse. Folios 17^v and 18^r (and the first four lines of 18^v) show Hopkins trying to determine the pattern of long, short, rising, and falling syllables that Pindar—notorious among classicial authors for the variety of his lyric metres—uses in *Isthmian Odes* 3 and 4 (see Appendix E). At this highly preliminary, very exciting phase of his deliberations, Hopkins employs arrows of two different lengths, and musical markings, to investigate and record the nuances of stress and silence he is discerning. To complement the metrical findings, he also begins analysing various linguistic, etymological, and figurative aspects of the odes. Once he had filled fo. 18^v, Hopkins's notes on the 'Dorian-Measure' were recorded elsewhere, in notebooks or incidental sheets now lost. From his letters to Bridges, however, we know that two years after the RUI examination, Hopkins was certain that he had made 'a great and solid discovery'[150] that would indeed 'bring out Pindar's meaning' and method.

As an undergraduate in the mid-1860s, Hopkins was subject to the rise of the examination culture in British universities advocated by the likes of Benjamin Jowett (who wanted, among other things, to harness the resources of Balliol and Oxford to

---

[149] *RUI Calendar* (1885), 199.   [150] GMH to Bridges, 2–4 Oct. 1886.

develop the imperial civil service). Hopkins's brilliant 'double first'[151] in Oxford's *literae humaniores* programme demonstrated his own intellectual gifts and self-discipline. Twenty years later, as a Fellow of the RUI, he played a particular part in the drive to standardize education and its results, encourage a competitive mindset, and provide credentials. As he lamented to Dixon, 'let those who have been thro' the like say what that means'.[152]

'HELPING TO SAVE AND DAMN THE STUDIOUS YOUTH OF IRELAND'

Hopkins's academic duties were institutionally defined: for the RUI, he was an examiner; for UC, he was a professor of classical literatures, which meant instructing small classes.[153] The new arrival assumed his examiner's responsibilities in the spring of 1884, but, because someone else had been engaged as interim Classics lecturer, Hopkins did not begin his professorial work until autumn 1884.[154] The academic terms were scheduled as follows: Michaelmas, 'beginning on the first Tuesday in October, and ending on the 20th of December'; Hilary, 'beginning on the second Tuesday in January, and ending on Tuesday in Holy Week' (prior to Easter); and Trinity, 'beginning on the Tuesday after Low Sunday [the Sunday after Easter] and ending on the 28th of June'.[155] Therefore, Michaelmas term was approximately eleven weeks long, but Hilary and Trinity were more variable because they depended on the timing of Easter (a moveable feast determined by a complex formula dependent on the lunar calendar[156]). If Easter

[151] First-class honours in the 'Moderations' exam at the end of six terms, or his second year, and the 'Greats' examination at the end of fourth year. See *CW* iv, 74–7.

[152] GMH to Dixon, 24 Nov. 1884. Cf. GMH to his mother, 5 July 1888, 'I am now working at examination-papers all day and this work began last month and will outlast this one. It is great, very great drudgery. I can not of course say it is wholly useless, but I believe that most of it is and that I bear a burden which crushes me and does little to help any good end.'

[153] 'Students entering University College to read for a degree were required to take five subjects in their first year (First Arts): Latin, Mathematics, Experimental Physics, English Language or Literature were all compulsory. The fifth subject could be taken from Greek, French, German, Italian, Spanish, Celtic, Sanskrit, Hebrew or Arabic. In the second year (Second Arts) one could proceed either to a Science BA or a purely Arts BA. For the latter you had to take Latin, Greek, English, and two other subjects (one of which had to be Logic or Mathematics). In the third year those preparing for the BA (Arts) Pass had to take Latin and Greek plus one other subject. Only those preparing for the Honours degree could eventually drop Latin and Greek.' Smith, 'Gerard Manley Hopkins as Classicist', 304–5.

[154] Martin, *Gerard Manley Hopkins*, 372. Robert Curtis, in comparison, began teaching immediately; as of 1 Oct. 1884 he had given 105 lectures. White, 'Gerard Manley Hopkins and the Irish Row', 101. See also Joseph Feeney, S.J., 'Hopkins's Closest Friend in Ireland: Robert Curtis, S.J.', *Hopkins Quarterly*, 14/1–2 (Apr. 1987–Jan. 1988), 211–38 at 236 n. 36.

[155] *University College, Dublin. Prospectus*, 6.

[156] In the Roman rite, Easter Sunday takes place the first Sunday after the full moon following the vernal equinox (20 or 21 March).

were on 12 April (a rough middle point in the range of possible dates), then Hilary Term would be about twelve weeks long and Trinity about ten. Such variations also affected the intervals between terms. There was a full month between the Michaelmas and Hilary terms, affording a Christmas vacation, but between Hilary and Trinity only a fortnight (two weeks). The length of the 'long vacation' between the end of Trinity and the start of Michaelmas was approximately thirteen weeks. Thus, the 'year' consisted of roughly thirty-three weeks of school and nineteen weeks of 'vacation', but these figures are misleading because work was to be done by students in the long vacation and Hopkins was examining during significant parts of June and July.

In the *Dublin Notebook* one finds glimpses of how the examination-oriented syllabus was organized,[157] and how Hopkins discharged administrative tasks, as well as substantial information about his approach to teaching ancient Roman texts and their contexts. Not mentioned, however, is the fact that Hopkins's teaching preparations were eventually aimed at two different groups of students: regular 'day' pupils, and 'evening' students—what today would be termed adult or continuing education students. 'Day' lectures took place in the morning, from 10.00 a.m. until 1.30 p.m.[158] According to UC records, Hopkins taught variously in the 'Latin pass' and 'honours' curriculum from late Michaelmas 1884 to April 1889.[159] The 'lectures' were not formal events addressed to large numbers of young men—'No more than lessons', as he informed his sister.[160] Typically, he taught eight to ten students (in Michaelmas 1887, there were eleven). In 1887–8, for which the most thorough data exist, Hopkins gave a total of 221 lectures or classes in the second year of the Arts program ('2nd Arts'). During a year when 120 matriculated and 99 non-matriculated UC students were attending lectures, he was teaching eight. The evening programme was a Delany innovation, the rationale for which he outlined in a memorandum to the Episcopal Committee on 29 January 1884: students with 'promise of good educational results' who were employed during the day, or had other impediments to attending a regular university programme, could complete all of the degree requirements at night, 'at the charge of six guineas for the whole course, or two guineas a term'.[161] Evening classes took place from 6.30 to 9.30 p.m., thus extending the teaching 'day' considerably. Hopkins commenced evening instruction in 1886–7, presenting classes on Latin-related subjects Monday, Wednesday, and Friday evenings, at 8.15 p.m., to two students. (A letter to his mother in January 1887 begins by explaining why he has time for correspondence: 'my evening pupil, a young Scotch Protestant, the best and brightest of all my pupils, who takes a most visible pleasure in learning and being taught and whom therefore to teach is correspondingly a pleasure,

[157] Fos. 1ʳ and 2ʳ.
[158] *Time Table & Rules for Resident Students* (BRC 36:37, fo. 1ᵛ).
[159] The records were summarized by Bischoff; see BRC 41a:8 (1884–9).
[160] GMH to Grace Hopkins, 2 Nov. 1884.
[161] Quoted in Morrissey, *Towards a National University*, 78. See also *University College, Dublin Prospectus* (Dublin: Browne and Nolan, 1884), 6–7.

does not tonight appear to be coming'.[162]) In 1887–8, he had between two and four evening students per term. None was listed for 1888–9.

Two of the cornerstones of Jesuit pedagogy are the short written quiz and the oral recitation. Folio 20ʳ, from late autumn 1884, features Hopkins's tallies from four such exercises. (Of the eight students examined, four—MacWeeney, Maher, Kennedy, Young—scored 85/100 or better.[163]) Three incomplete sets of attendance records from February 1885 are found on fos. 23ᵛ and 25ʳ. In that first Hilary term, there were approximately eight to ten students per day class.

Why do the *Notebook* entries focus on Roman rather than Hellenic materials? Hopkins's teaching assignments depended, in part, on the preferences and determinations of his senior colleagues, Robert Ornsby and James Stewart. (According to UC records, Hopkins first began teaching Greek language and literature in Michaelmas term 1888—21 'lectures' to one student). At Oxford, Hopkins had certainly studied ancient Roman authors, texts, and history, but the emphases, especially for his final or 'Greats' examinations, had been on ancient Greece. Thus the undergraduate essays and lecture notes that he had preserved, and the notes made during his sojourn as schoolmaster at the Birmingham Oratory,[164] would not have been helpful in Dublin for the Latin/Roman-intensive portions of the curriculum. Quite simply, he had a lot to learn and to relearn, and many texts to master for the first time. That may partly explain why, instead of focusing on the so-called 'Golden Age' of Latin prose and poetry (Caesar, Cicero, Virgil), Hopkins concentrates his preparations on 'Silver Age' authors and texts (Tacitus, Lucan, Martial). Also, given the paucity of books at his and his students' disposal (see above), he had to make his classroom summaries (perhaps occasionally used for dictation) as thorough as possible.[165] Only by comparing the initial, sometimes patchwork notes in the *Dublin Notebook* with the much more seamless, well-written historical commentaries in G.II (see *CW* vi) can one appreciate how much detail Hopkins, a highly judicious if not naturally gifted teacher, absorbed and refined. One may also observe—both in the *Dublin Notebook* itself and, more readily, in the G.II extended summaries, as products of the *Notebook*—how assiduously he would interweave aspects of literature, grammar, history and 'antiquities', philosophy, culture, and geography.[166] Nonetheless, critics have been divided in their assessments of Hopkins as a classicist.[167]

The *Dublin Notebook* is not entirely silent on the subject of Hopkins's effectiveness in the classroom. On the one hand, the extended note on Roman currency as it would

---

[162] GMH to Kate Hopkins, 24 Jan. 1887. His two evening students that term were James Robertson and P. P. O'Connor.

[163] For tentative identification of the students, see the notes for the respective folios.

[164] See *CW* iv.

[165] Thus GMH's lessons for small groups were truly 'lectures', in the etymological sense.

[166] GMH may also have consulted his Highgate lesson book (Campion Hall MS BII); see *CW* vi.

[167] For a favourable evaluation, see Schlatter, 'Poetic Fragments'; for a negative appraisal, see Warren Anderson, 'Hopkins's Dublin Notes on Homer', *Hopkins Quarterly*, 14/1–4 (Apr. 1987–Jan. 1988), 179–91, esp. 71. See also Smith, 'Gerard Manley Hopkins as Classicist'.

translate into then-contemporary British coinage reveals a zest for detail that would quickly exhaust most students' patience.[168] The desire to make the information relevant to his auditors is commendable, but the exactitude ('Trecenos sestertios = 600 d. = 50s. = 2[£] 10 s. or tricenos = 60 d. = 5 s.') suggests that Hopkins was deaf to the sounds of restlessness in a classroom. His pleasure in etymological complications would have been similarly tiresome[169]—especially for students accustomed 'to memorise rather than to explore'.[170] On the other hand, paraphrases of the speeches in Lucan[171] would have been very helpful, perhaps most especially to students not at the top of the class. Hopkins not only summarizes the text but explains how it functions rhetorically (another example of him trying to make pedagogical accommodations for his students). Extensive preliminary notes for lessons on 'Roman Lit. and Antiquities BC 133–43 (death of Tib. Gracchus to death of Cicero)', which occupy much of the second half of the *Notebook*, demonstrate how Hopkins would try to promote a cross-disciplinary approach. Also, after collating the RUI examinations and the notes in the *Notebook* and G.II, we can set aside the suggestion or dispel the myth that 'he was so scrupulous about the unfair examination advantages his own students had over candidates from other colleges that at the beginning of the year he undertook not to teach his class anything which would be asked in exams'.[172] Explanations of geographical details in various poems and historical works, for example, answer to the examinations' demands for a comprehensive knowledge of ancient geography. The five-line discussion of the 'Appenines' in Tacitus's *Histories*[173] would be a boon for the student who, in Summer 1885, was writing the Latin 'First University' examination (Pass): a question on Livy invites commentary on the name of the Pennine Alps. Details about coinage may not have engrossed his auditors, but 'the Financial Administration of the Republic; [and] Roman money, Roman measures' were regular examination topics.[174] Finally, for the discerning student, Hopkins modelled a number of ways in which critical acumen and finely tuned historical sensibilities may be exercised when responding to the classical world.

[168] Fos. 19ᵛ, bottom of 20ʳ.

[169] See fo. 22ᵛ.

[170] O'Flynn, 'Hopkins's Teaching', 174: 'Much of [the students'] pre-university educational experiences had been coloured by working towards examinations: much of their pedagogical encounters had been coloured by teachers striving to train them to memorise rather than to explore. Hopkins's president in the college [Delany] was publicly known for his acclamation of examinations as a pathway to the raising of standards.'

[171] Fos. 28ᵛ–29ᵛ.

[172] White, *Gerard Manley Hopkins*, 386.

[173] Fo. 20ʳ.

[174] GMH at one point was taking notes for the 'Second Univ. 1888: Pass' examination: 'Roman Hist. and Latin Lit. B. C. 78—8. | Roman Antiq[uitie]s: Organisation of the Roman people; their classes; their legislative and executive institutions in the Republican period; also the Public Lands; the Financial Administration of the Republic; Roman money, Roman measures | And in the Honours more detail | (The Books are: for Pass: | Virgil Georgics 1, 2 | Cicero Tusc. Disp. [*Tusculan Disputations*] 1, 2 | For Honours, besides: | Martial: selections from Bks. 1, 2, 3 | Juvenal Sat. 1, 3, 10, 13, 14. | Cicero de Off. 1, 2. | Tacitus Agricola, Germania)' (BRC 1:18).

'[T]IME'S EUNUCH': WRITINGS HALF-BORN,
OR UNBEGOTTEN

Wishing to 'spur . . . on' fellow writer Coventry Patmore, Hopkins adduces reasons why his friend ought to be resolute and complete his current project: 'if not done soon it will never be done, to the end of eternity. Looking back afterwards you may indeed excuse yourself and see reasons why the work should not have been done—but . . . what might have been will not exist.'[175] Yet, in his Dublin years Hopkins was himself chronically unable to finish almost every substantial project that he began; those few he did finish were nearly all rejected for publication. Hopkins's lifelong predisposition for leaving even pleasing tasks incomplete—e.g. his sketch made at Shanklin, Isle of Wight[176]—is never more in evidence and nowhere more vexing to him than in the years when his positions as Fellow of the RUI and Professor at UC thrust upon him a perceived duty to produce 'scientific works'.[177] Some of these academic undertakings were initiated with great enthusiasm and, often, unrealistic claims about their potential importance, but became anxiety-provoking and intractable to a would-be scholar amply supplied with inspiration, but routinely short of execution.[178] Other learned projects are marked as doomed from the start, as when Hopkins reports to Baillie: 'I am struggling to get together matter for a work on Homer's Art', but then immediately (and rightly) predicts, 'I suppose like everything else of mine it will come to nothing in the end'.[179] In much the same vein, he tells Bridges 'I do greatly desire to treat' the subject of English metre, a paper his friend had requested, 'but I can scarcely believe that [a publication] on that or on anything else anything of mine will ever see the light'. Hopkins goes on to reflect on his inability to engage in fruitful labour, 'if I could but get on, if I could but produce work . . . but it kills me to be time's eunuch and never to beget'.[180]

The same image recurs more than two years later when Hopkins reveals his anxieties about the professional productions required of him. He is 'now writing a quasi-philosophical paper on the Greek Negatives', but in a series of distressed questions, he despairs of its prospects: 'but when shall I finish it? or if finished will it pass the [Jesuit] censors? or if it does will the Classical Review or any magazine take it?' Overwrought, he sees difficulties at every turn; in such an agitated state, he is brought to the brink of

---

[175] GMH to Patmore, 4 Apr. 1885.

[176] See *CW* vi and GMH to his mother, 2 Mar. 1889.

[177] GMH to Bridges, 12–13 Jan. 1888.

[178] On the importance of 'execution' to artistic enterprise, see GMH to Dixon, 30 June–3 July 1886.

[179] GMH to Baillie, 11 Feb. 1886. Portions of Homer were set texts in the RUI cycle of exams, as GMH himself noted on *DN*, fos. 1ʳ and 2ʳ. Hopkins prepared extensive lecture notes on books iv–vi of the *Iliad* in Dublin between Nov. 1884 and Feb. 1886: see *CW* vi. On the fruitless Homeric project, see GMH to Bridges, 17–18 Feb. 1887 and to Baillie, 20 Feb. 1887.

[180] 1–8 Nov. 1885; see also GMH to Bridges, 11–12 Nov. 1884. The phrase 'time's eunuch' later appears in 'Thou art indeed just' (17 Mar. 1889): see *CW* viii. See also GMH to Bridges, 12–13 Jan. 1888. In his Jan. 1889 retreat notes, GMH also refers to himself as a eunuch. See *CW* v.

despair, 'All impulse fails me: I can give myself no sufficient reason for going on. Nothing comes—: I am a eunuch'.

Chief among the unbegotten progeny of the Dublin years is his work on classical poetic metre and rhythm, the so-called 'Dorian-Measure'. He announces his new undertaking to Bridges with a characteristic admixture of enthusiasm and defeatism: 'I have made a great and solid discovery . . . and hope to publish something when I have read some more. But all my world is scaffolding.'[181] Over the next several months, he variously complains, makes extravagant claims ('[it is] the true scansion of perhaps half or more than half of the Greek and Latin lyric verse'), considers the possibility of additions 'in a second edition or in a second volume', and cavils in the face of obstacles, real and imagined.[182] In January 1887, without a shred of irony, he estimates the potential value his work: 'I believe that I can now set metre and music both of them on a scientific footing which will be final like the law of gravitation.'[183] Yet, within a month he has vacillated towards despairing of the project's—and its author's—fortunes: 'I am in a position which makes it befitting and almost a duty to write anything (bearing on classical study) . . . I do try to write at it; but I see that I cannot get on. . . . I am in a prostration.' Worse still, lacking 'a working health, a working strength', Hopkins adduces that his 'trouble is not the not being able to write a book; it is the not being fit for my work and the struggling vainly to make myself fitter'.[184] Ever dutiful, the wounded Hopkins soldiers on; after some five months, the subject disappears from his surviving letters.[185]

The *Dublin Notebook* also testifies (fos. 8^r-v, 11^r, 13^r) to an undertaking driven not by duty, but for Hopkins's own aesthetic pleasure: his setting to music of the 'Ode to Evening' by William Collins, a project begun in his year at Stonyhurst immediately before coming to Dublin.[186] Its progress is demarcated in several letters coterminous with the *Notebook* and then is never mentioned again. Hopkins was demonstrably proud of—and, it seems, absurdly optimistic about—his ongoing musical accomplishment, but no copy of the completed setting has ever been known to exist.[187] Presumably, the remains of this endeavour came to occupy a place among the 'ruins and wrecks' of Hopkins's self-thwarted ambitions, his 'old notebooks and beginnings of things, ever so many, which it seems . . . might well have been done', yet another disturbing fulfilment of his own grim self-assessment: 'I see no ground for thinking I shall ever . . . succeed in doing anything that is not forced on me to do of any consequence.' Plagued by 'daily anxiety about work to be done' such as his teaching and examining, he can 'never finish all that lies outside that work'.[188]

---

[181] GMH to Bridges, 2–4 Oct. 1886; cf. GMH to Bridges, 21–2 Oct. 1886.

[182] GMH to Patmore, 7 Nov. 1886 and to Bridges, 11 Dec. 1886; see also GMH to Bridges, 28 Oct. 1886.

[183] GMH to Patmore, 20 Jan. 1887.   [184] GMH to Bridges, 17–18 Feb. 1887.

[185] See GMH to Baillie, 20 Feb. 1887; to Bridges, 1 May 1887; to Patmore, 17 May 1887; and to Bridges, 30 July–1 Aug. 1887.

[186] See GMH to Bridges, 11–12 Nov. 1884.

[187] See GMH to Bridges, 1 Jan. 1885 and, especially, 1–2 Apr. 1885.

[188] GMH to Baillie, 24 Apr.–17 May 1885.

Insofar as we are able to determine, before taking up residence at St Stephen's Green Hopkins had had two poems rejected for publication: 'The Loss of the Eurydice' and, now infamously, 'The Wreck of the Deutschland'. While in Dublin, several of his attempts to appear in print were rebuffed; others either proved nugatory or were simply false starts. Through the auspices of Matthew Russell, S.J., editor of the *Irish Monthly* and a member of his community, Hopkins published two Shakespeare songs rendered into Latin verse;[189] the remaining compositions (three each in Latin and Greek), he told Bridges, 'I believe I can and shall get published in the Trinity [College journal] Hermathena', but he never did. Russell also suggested that Hopkins write a piece introducing Bridges's poetry 'to the fewish but not despicable readers of his little periodical', a task entirely consonant with Hopkins's other promotional efforts for his friend. Yet, despite his resolve—'this I must do, as soon as it shall become possible'—no such piece ever appeared.[190] Another commissioned work for a Jesuit-run periodical, the University College's own *Lyceum*, was completed: 'I was asked and I rewrote something I had by me', he explains to Bridges. Nevertheless—and Hopkins's attempted revisions to please his editor Thomas A. Finlay, S.J. notwithstanding—the essay on 'Statistics and Free Will' was never printed.[191] Also rejected was his paper on 'Readings and Renderings of Sophocles', sent to the *Classical Review*. By Hopkins's own account, the 'passages commented on were strung together so as to illustrate a principle of lyrical construction'; even though the kind editor indicated that 'two of the passages shd. appear in the form of Notes' in a subsequent issue, none of the essay ever saw the light of day.[192]

The one extended, non-poetic project that Hopkins successfully completed and published while in Dublin was his short biography of Richard Watson Dixon, commissioned by Thomas Arnold for his *Manual of English Literature Historical and Critical* (5th edn., 1885), although Hopkins did not submit the piece until the book was 'in the press'.[193] Hopkins also submitted fifty or more Irish words and expressions that were eventually printed in Joseph Wright's *English Dialect Dictionary* (1900), though such contributions hardly required Hopkins's closely focused effort and attention.[194] Many other endeavours, such as 'a new and critical edition of St. Patrick's "Confession"', and

[189] *Irish Monthly*, 14 (1886), 628 and 15 (1887), 92. See O'Keefe, 'A Man for Others', 62–70.

[190] GMH to Bridges, 13 Oct. 1886.

[191] GMH to Bridges, 25 Sept. 1888 and 19–20 Oct. 1888.

[192] GMH to Bridges, 25–6 May 1888.

[193] GMH to Bridges, 11–12 Nov. 1884. See *DN*, fos. 14ʳ, 15ᵛ, 16ʳ, and 17ʳ, and Appendix D. GMH's short biography of Dixon is found on pp. 470–1 of Arnold's *Manual*. See also GMH to Dixon, 25 Oct. 1884 and 24–7 Nov. 1884.

[194] See *DN*, fos. 20ʳ and 30ʳ for possible instances of GMH recording such examples; see also GMH to his mother, 13 Mar. 1888, and Norman White, 'G. M. Hopkins's Contributions to the English Dialect Dictionary', *English Studies*, 68/4 (1987), 325. GMH demonstrated an interest in the Irish language as early as Apr. 1884: according to the *Freeman's Journal and Daily Commercial Advertiser*, 2 Apr. 1884, GMH's 'long and interesting communication . . . relative to the teaching of Irish in National schools' was discussed by the council of the Society for the Preservation of the Irish Language at its 'usual weekly meeting' 1 Apr.

his work on the lyrics of Aeschylus, were taken up, only to be abandoned.[195] The inevitable failure to make an end stalks even hopeful beginnings: 'I am writing (but I am almost sure I never shall have written) a sort of popular account of Light and the Ether', he tells Dixon.[196] Nevertheless, even as late as March 1889 the ever-fatigued and indefatigable Hopkins informs Bridges that he has been 'drawing up a Paper on the Argei. . . . If I can get it done I shall try to publish it.'[197]

Writing to Dixon from UC 'in the midst of [his] heaviest work of the year', Hopkins paused from the press of making examinations to reflect on human failure. Identifying with 'Christ our Lord', Hopkins observed, 'his plans were baffled, his hopes dashed, and his work was done by being broken off undone'. Still worse: 'However much he [Christ] understood all this he found it an intolerable grief to submit to it.' For Hopkins the University Fellow and Professor, all that was 'broken off undone' in Dublin was both a symptom and a cause of his great anxiety and unhappiness. The example of Christ, he found, 'is very strengthening, but except in that sense it is not consoling'.[198]

'SOUND EFFECTS WERE INTENDED': HOPKINS'S MUSICAL INVESTMENTS

He could not sing, nor play the piano. His success on the violin was less than modest.[199] He learned music theory by reading a few manuals[200] and receiving (mostly) negative criticism from leading authorities in the field.[201] When a composition of his was actually

---

[195] GMH to Bridges, 3 Aug. 1884 and 6 Nov. 1887.   [196] GMH to Dixon, 7–9 Aug. 1886.

[197] GMH to Bridges, 20–4 Mar. 1889.   [198] GMH to Dixon, 30 June–3 July 1886.

[199] Bischoff summarized an interview he conducted with Frances MacCabe Cullinam in the late 1940s: GMH 'fancied himself musical', she recalled, 'though Sir Francis MacCabe [her father] later said that, for all his talents, the one thing Hopkins wasn't was a musician. Frances, knowing the answer full well, once asked GMH whether he could sing; and he smilingly replied, "No, but I make a cheerful noise!"' (BRC 41b:12). Music was certainly part of the Hopkins household when he was growing up; his sister Grace became an accomplished pianist. Among the Hopkins family papers in Boston College are sheet music collections belonging to Grace, to his mother, and to his sister Milicent. For a discussion of the family's musical life, see Humphry House, *The Youth of Gerard Manley Hopkins, 1844–1868*, (ed.) Lesley Higgins, *Hopkins Quarterly*, 37/1–4 (2010), 63–8.

[200] See, for example, various titles in the *Novello's Music Primers* series, edited by Sir John Stainer, including Thomas Helmore, *Primer of Plainsong* (1887); Ernst Pauer, *The Art of Pianoforte Playing* (1880), and *The Elements of the Beautiful in Music* (1883); W. H. Cummings, *The Rudiments of Music* (1877). Fo. 17ʳ includes memoranda for 'Sir Robert Stewart's lectures' on music and the *Encyclopaedia Britannica* entry on music.

[201] GMH's exchanges with Sir Robert Stewart, Professor of Music at Trinity College, were playful yet stinging. 'Indeed my dear Padre I cannot follow you through your maze of words in your letter of last week', Stewart lamented 22 May 1886; 'I saw, ere we had conversed ten minutes on our first meeting, that you are one of those special pleaders who never believe yourself wrong in any respect. You always excuse yourself for anything I object to in your writing or music so I think it a pity to disturb you in your happy dreams of perfectability—nearly everything in your music was wrong—but you will not admit that to be the case.' GMH also sent music to Sir Frederick Gore Ousley and Sir John Stainer for their comments. See letter to Bridges, 11–12 Nov. 1884.

performed, he was surprised by its 'sound effects'.[202] One has to ask, then: why on earth was Hopkins so determined to compose music, a resolve that his years in Dublin only heightened?

A full rendering of what he actually composed is presented in volume vi of the *Collected Works*. The *Dublin Notebook* provides glimpses of how thinking musically infused his sensibilities, and inspired him. Certainly, he turned to music when the 'the roll, the rise, the carol' of poetic 'inspiration' was silent ('To R. B.'), and was more and more dependent on the 'comfort' and consolations of experiments in melody and harmony.[203] His commitment and aspirations, despite a lack of training, reveal much about his temperament: 'I am now ready to send my piece of music', he informed Bridges in February 1885, 'the two first verses of the Battle of the Baltic, set of course for the piano, for what else can I do? but really meant for an orchestra—if I cd. orchestrate. But this is indeed to fly before I can walk, as a severe musician told me, (but I did not care) of something else.'[204] Disregarding adverse criticism was not simply a matter of intransigence, however. Increasingly, Hopkins was linking aesthetic and academic insights, appreciating the interconnections—the 'stress'—of accent, pitch, rhythm, modulation, counterpoint, and performance, and how they 'tell, each off the other' ('Sibyl's Leaves').

Musical connections and investments are not always immediately apparent when reading the *Dublin Notebook*, but one finds elements that are alternately technical, scholarly, thematic, social—and always personal. Why did he write out William Collins's 'Ode to Evening', apparently from memory (fo. 8^{r–v})? Seeing the text in its entirety would help him to continue a 'strange and wild' Gregorian setting for the poem

---

[202] GMH to his brother Everard, 5 Nov. 1885. See GMH to Bridges, 6 Oct. 1886: 'I had [a tune based on a poem by William Barnes] played this afternoon, but as the pianist said: Your music dates from a time before the piano was. The parts are independent in form and phrasing and are lost on that instrument. Two choristers, who were at hand, sang the tune, which to its fond father sounded very flowing and a string accompaniment would have set it off, I do believe.' George O'Neill, S.J., a Scholastic at University College during GMH's tenure there, later observed, 'He did not play on any instrument . . . . He wrote from his brain, not from his ear. So, to get one of his pieces tried over the piano, procured him a peculiar pleasure—or disappointment: then he knew for the first time how his work sounded' (BRC 24:14, fo. 3). O'Neill's essay, 'A Poet I have known', was rejected by *The Month* and the *Australian Quarterly*, but he sent a copy to Bischoff in Oct. 1944. For GMH's frustration when neither piano nor pianist was available, see his letter to Bridges, 17–29 May 1885.

[203] In late June 1883 GMH informed Bridges, 'I fumble a little at music, at counterpoint, of which in course of time I shall come to know something. . . . If I could get to accompany my own airs I should, so to say, enter into a new kingdom at once, for I have plenty of tunes ready' (25–9 June 1883). These attempts at composing and epistolary laments about his lack of success repeat the pattern of his Liverpool appointment in 1879–80 (see *CW* v for a discussion of his pastoral work). 'Work and sickness have stood in the way of the music', he informed his mother 30 Apr. 1880. As McDermott summarizes, his 'correspondence with his sister Grace about music, writing airs for her to harmonize, and occasional visits to the Hallé were prominent among his few pleasures' while in Liverpool. McDermott, 'Hopkins in Liverpool', in McDermott (ed.), *Hopkins' Lancashire Sesquicentennial Essays* (Wigan: North West Catholic History Society, 1994), 22.

[204] GMH to Bridges, 8 Feb. 1885.

that he had begun while living at Stonyhurst. Although this too came to naught or was destroyed (see '[T]ime's eunuch', above), the compositional process was its own source of pleasure: 'Quickened by the heavenly beauty of that poem I groped in my soul's very viscera for the tune.'[205] The creative daring of Hopkins's musical project—which he adjudged to be both 'singular' and 'solemn'—undoubtedly had poetic reverberations as well. Defensive remarks to Bridges about the 'variety' and 'fine differences' of the composition—'if the whole world agreed to condemn it or see nothing in it I should only tell them to take a generation and come to me again'[206]—equally apply to his canon of verse.

Throughout the autumn of 1884, musical dabbling for the 'Ode to Evening' provided a respite from the tedium and trials of grading examinations, as the three-syllable snippet on fo. 11^r and the more substantial fragment on fo. 13^r indicate. Elsewhere, he temporarily focused on Shelley's 'Ode to the West Wind' (fo. 12^v). Musical markings within his own poems are very pronounced in the *Dublin Notebook* manuscripts. On fo. 9^r, for example, 'Caradoc's Soliloquy' from 'St Winefred's Well' features two different symbols for pauses or rests, each perhaps indicating a separate duration; in a subsequent version, fo. 21^r, Hopkins is experimenting with his own hybrid signs for the emphases generated by 'sprung rhythm'. Bridges, for one, had never approved of his friend's penchant for marking texts in this way. 'You were right to leave out the marks', Hopkins admitted in October 1883, while reviewing Bridges's latest poetic transcriptions; 'they were not consistent for one thing and are always offensive. Still there must be some. Either I must invent a notation applied throughout as in music or else I must mark only where the reader is likely to mistake.'[207]

As fos. 12^v and 13^r demonstrate, Hopkins's first phase of composition depended on the basic sight-singing 'Tonic sol-fa' musical notation system—figuring tunes in terms of doh, re, mi, fa, sol, etc. Based on centuries-old European practices of using syllables instead of notes on staff paper, the Tonic Sol-fa or 'Norwich Sol-fa ladder' was devised by Sarah Glover (1786–1867; *ODNB*), a music teacher in Norwich, England in the late 1820s whose unorthodox goal was to teach young children to sing skilfully without benefit of formal musical training. She explained her method fully in the *Scheme for Rendering Psalmody Congregational, comprising a Key to the Sol-fa Notation of music, and Directions for Instructing a School* (1835) and *A Manual of the Norwich Sol-fa System* (3rd edn. 1845). Renown for the system, however, was garnered by John Curwen, a Congregationalist minister (1816–80; *ODNB*), and his son John Spencer Curwen (1847–1916), who adapted Glover's method (without permission) and ardently promoted Tonic sol-fa in public lectures, performances, journals, instruction manuals, musical scores, and books (published, as much as possible, by their Curwen

[205] Ibid. Two months later, GMH described the piece as 'a new departure' (1 Jan. 1885); and in Mar. 1885, as 'a new art, the effect is so unlike anything I ever heard' (24–5 Mar. 1885).

[206] GMH to Bridges, 1–2 Apr. 1885.

[207] GMH to Bridges, 23–4 Oct. 1883.

Press). To quote Charles McGuire's excellent study, the Curwens and their adherents 'disseminated Tonic Sol-fa notation as part of a carefully crafted plan to improve people's lives with a particularly British slant: to make such individuals morally upright, turn them into practicing Christians (preferably Protestant ones), and guide them to becoming efficient workers'.[208] Hopkins's familiarity with solmization ('substituting syllables for note names—from an oral system to a printed system'[209]) is expressed in two extant letters. In autumn 1881, while writing to Dixon about four 'tunes' in various states of development, he acknowledges that the music for 'Does the South Wind[210] . . . is not quite finished and only written in sol-fa score'.[211] Comments to Bridges in a 29 April 1889 letter confirm that he 'thought', musically, in the sol-fa mode:

I now make the canon strict in each verse, but allow a change, which indeed of itself is ^is^ besides called for by the change of words, from verse to verse. Indeed the air becomes a generic form which is specified newly in each verse, with excellent effect. It is like a new art this. I allow no modulation: the result is that the tune is shifted into modes, viz. those of La, Mi, and Sol (this is the only way I can speak of them, and they have a character of their own which is neither that of modern major and minor music nor yet of the plain chant tones ^modes^, so far as I can make out).

Items in the *Dublin Notebook* also suggest that he understood how solfège scores were prepared. As examples from the Curwens' *Tonic Sol-fa Reporter* demonstrate, the compositions were divided into 'bars' or measures with extended bar lines (|), and each bar further divided with a half-line (|), much as Hopkins divides phrases in Dublin-era poems such as 'To what serves Mortal Beauty', 'The Soldier', 'Sibyl's Leaves', and 'Heraclitean Fire'. Furthermore, Tonic Sol-fa notation uses colons (:) to 'divide each measure into its primary (strong) and secondary (weak) pulses',[212] a practice which may have influenced the way in which Hopkins uses emphatically spaced colons in his poetry and prose.

---

[208] Charles McGuire, *Music and Victorian Philanthropy: The Tonic Sol-fa Movement* (Cambridge: Cambridge University Press, 2009), p. xv. McGuire's exhaustive study, which provides examples of Tonic Sol-fa sheet music, discusses the significance of musical expression, education, and propaganda for three cultural and political reform groups: the temperance movement, missionaries, and suffragettes. The Curwens 'prescribed Tonic Sol-fa as a palliative for poverty, slavery, prostitution, alcoholism, and excess of all kinds; as a means of improving children's education; and as an aid to evangelization, missionary work, and the culture of domesticity' (3). See also Phyllis Weliver, *The Musical Crowd in English Fiction, 1840–1910: Class, Culture, and Nation* (Basingstoke: Palgrave, 2006); Bernarr Rainbow, *The Land without Music* (London: Novello, 1967); and Derek Hyde, *New Found Voices: Women in Nineteenth-Century English Music*, 3rd edn. (Aldershot: Ashgate, 1998).

[209] McGuire, *Music and Victorian Philanthropy*, 8.

[210] Dixon's 'Ruffling Wind'. See *Poems by the Late Rev. Dr. Richard Watson Dixon: A Selection with a Portrait & a Memoir by Robert Bridges* (London, Smith, Elder & Co, 1909).

[211] GMH to Dixon, 29 Oct.–2 Nov. 1881.

[212] McGuire, *Music and Victorian Philanthropy*, 11.

So musically minded was Hopkins—composing; trying to organize public per-
formances of his works;[213] teaching classical odes by Pindar and Horace; attempting
to set Sappho's ode to Aphrodite to music[214]—that theoretical considerations of
performance were almost inevitably forthcoming. The creation of 'living art'[215] was his
principal concern: only by that exacting standard could verse or drama or even visual art
both achieve and express its 'true soul and self'. As he tried to elucidate for his brother
Everard in November 1885:

Every art then and every work of art has its own play or performance. The playing or per-
formance of a stageplay is the playing it on the boards, the stage: reading it, much more writing
it, is not its performance. The performance of a symphony is not the scoring it however
elaborately; it is in the concert room, by the orchestra, and then and there only. A picture is
performed, or performs, when anyone looks at it in the proper and intended light. A house
performs when it is now built and lived in. To come nearer: books play, or perform, or are played
and performed when they are read; and ordinarily by one reader, alone, to himself, with the eyes
only. Now we are getting to it, George. Poetry was originally meant for either singing or reciting,
a record was kept of it; the record could be, was, read, and that in time by one reader, alone, to
himself, with the eyes only. This reacted on the art: what was to be performed under these
conditions for these conditions ought to be and was composed and calculated. Sound-effects
were intended, wonderful combinations even . . . (5 Nov. 1885)

In December 1886, the poem of his that most vividly embodied this ideal of 'living art'
was the 'attuneable' and taxing 'Sibyl's Leaves', the composition of which is most fully
understood in terms of the *Dublin Notebook*. Thematically, not only does the poem
function as a Hopkinsian 'Dies Irae',[216] it is in many respects his 'reply' to Collins's
'Ode to Evening'. Whereas Collins's speaker is 'pensive' and 'calm', like the goddess of
Evening who inspires him, Hopkins's speaker strains to find in either 'fire-featuring
heaven' or earth's 'being' sufficient reason not to succumb to that 'womb-of-all, home-
of-all, hearse-of-all night' (fo. 15ʳ). Technically, the 'long sonnet' is, 'as living art . . .
made for performance and . . . its performance is not reading with the eye but loud,
leisurely, poetical (not rhetorical) recitation, with long rests, long dwells on the rhyme
and other marked syllables, and so on. This sonnet shd. be almost sung: it is most
carefully timed in tempo rubato.'[217]

[213] A letter to Dixon in 1886 hopefully announces that his madrigal for Shakespeare's 'Who is Sylvia' is
'to be performed at a school-concert in Dublin tomorrow . . . set as a duet and chorus', but the postscript
oozes disappointment: 'Some hindrance happened and the madrigal was not sung. If it had been I could
not have heard it, for I was helping to save and damn the studious youth of Ireland' (30 June 1886).
[214] See letter to Bridges, 28 Oct. 1886.
[215] GMH to Bridges, 11 Dec. 1886.
[216] See note to fo. 15ʳ, below.
[217] GMH to Bridges, 11 Dec. 1886. *Tempo rubato*: from the Italian, 'robbed', a temporary disregard of
strict tempo to allow an expressive quickening or slackening of pace.

For Hopkins the classicist, these 'long dwells' on the implications and possibilities of metre and cadence led him to one of his most ambitious projects, the study of Dorian metre. His outsized, never realized expectations for this work have been adumbrated above. It should be acknowledged briefly, however, that the notes on fos. 17^v, 18^r, 18^v, and 21^r demonstrate how Hopkins anticipated twentieth- and twenty-first-century scholarship by re-examining the 'infinite flexibility' and 'beautiful variety' of Pindar's rhythmical effects.[218] Taken in the context of fos. 16^v to 18^v, which show Hopkins alternately immersed in creative intellectual work, exacting exam-grading notations, and perfunctory summaries of ancient Roman history, the search for a key to the Dorian measure emerges as a counterpoint to all that frustrates or exhausts him.

'MY GO IS GONE': HOPKINS'S HEALTH IN DUBLIN

Two days after his arrival in Dublin, writing to John Henry Newman from the very building where his quondam spiritual father had earlier attempted to establish a viable Roman Catholic university for Ireland, Hopkins confessed himself inadequate to the task before him, 'feel[ing] an unfitness [that] does not . . . allow [his] spirits to rise to the level of the position and its duties', but causes him to 'begin with weakness and fear'.[219] Some two weeks later, he declared to Bridges that he was 'unfit for the post', 'not at all strong, not strong enough'.[220] Throughout his time in Ireland, Hopkins delineated the state of his physical, mental, and spiritual health in correspondence, prayer notes, and poems, revealing a harrowing state of protracted enervation and emotional difficulty.

In the approximately twenty-two months during which he was intermittently writing in the *Dublin Notebook*—a period in which 'To seem the stranger', 'Sibyl's Leaves', and most of the so-called 'terrible sonnets' were first composed, if not completed in their final form—Hopkins variously chronicled his distress, describing himself as in an 'unsatisfactory condition, weak in body and harassed in mind'.[221] Scattered throughout his letters are repeated complaints of prostration and 'nervous weakness'; he is 'in a sort of languishing state of mind and body' that he cannot fully fathom, knowing only his 'mind is harassed with the work before and upon' him.[222] He instructs himself in the *Notebook* to 'rise above' his despondency and, on Christmas Eve 1884, attempts again to stir his downcast spirits, 'bring yourself to leave out of sight your own trials rejoicing over Xt's birth'.[223] By March of 1885, he solicited the aid of St Joseph, 'patron of the

---

[218] 'Pindar and all the poets continually pass from heavier feet . . . to lighter', so that a 'beautiful variety is given . . . . With all this the rhythm came to have an infinite flexibility, of which the Greeks seem never to have tired.' GMH to Bridges, 21–2 Oct. 1886.

[219] GMH to Newman, 20 Feb. 1884. GMH had previously expressed fears that 'my go is gone' to Baillie, 11 Jan. 1883.

[220] GMH to Bridges, 7 Mar. 1884.

[221] GMH to Bridges, 24–5 Mar. 1885.

[222] GMH to Bridges, 18 July 1884; to his mother, 17 May 1885; and to Patmore, 23 June 1885.

[223] *DN*, fos. 7^v (Sept. 1884) and 21^v (Dec. 1884).

hidden life; of those . . . suffering in mind and as I do'.[224] Two months later, he confided to Baillie about 'my disease, so to call it. The melancholy I have all my life been subject to has become of late years not indeed more intense in its fits but rather more distributed, constant, and crippling.' He is in an alarming condition and can envision no way out: 'when I am at the worst, though my judgment is never affected, my state is much like madness. I see no ground for thinking I shall ever get over it'.[225] Soon thereafter, Bridges received a similar assessment: regarding his 'languishment of body and mind—which must be and will be. . . . I think that my fits of sadness, though they do not affect my judgment, resemble madness.' Perhaps most troubling of all, Hopkins's revelation is prefaced with the reservation, 'I must write something, though not so much as I have to say'.[226]

Feeling somewhat recovered in September, he had 'some buoyancy', but nevertheless characterized 'the life I lead now' as 'one of a continually jaded and harassed mind'. More seriously, he divulged to Bridges, 'I am afraid I shall be ground down to a state like this last spring's and summer's, when my spirits were so crushed that madness seemed to be making approaches'.[227] Although no further letters survive in which Hopkins refers to his own 'madness'—and it is impossible to make an exact determination as to how he precisely understood that word—his prostrating condition never disappeared for long. He is 'troubled with sleeplessness',[228] has 'a fagged mind and a continual anxiety',[229] is 'attacked with eczema',[230] believes himself suffering from 'gout or rheumatism in the eyes',[231] and deems himself as a 'wreck' and 'feeling very old'.[232] For the fastidious, perhaps even compulsive, Fellow of the RUI, 'the work of examination' was a distressing time: 'During it all is haste and pressure, before it all anxiety and worry.'[233] Even on his many holidays 'there is no end to anxiety and care, but only an interruption of it, and the effect accumulates on the whole', so that his condition progressively worsened.[234]

Unlike the reports on his situation that he gave to his trusted correspondents, Hopkins's notes from his annual retreat in early January 1889 were intended to be entirely private. With this fragmentary document, as in the lists he prepared for

---

[224] *DN*, fo. 26ʳ.
[225] GMH to Baillie, 24 Apr.–17 May 1885.
[226] GMH to Bridges, 17–29 May 1885.
[227] GMH to Bridges, 1–8 Sept. 1885.
[228] GMH to Kate Hopkins, 11 June 1886; cf. to Bridges, 18–19 Aug. 1888.
[229] GMH to Dixon, 7–9 Aug. 1886.
[230] GMH to Baillie, 7 Sept. 1887.
[231] GMH to Bridges, 7–8, 10–11, and 13–14 Sept. 1888. On GMH's eyes, see also GMH to Kate Hopkins, 24 Jan. 1887 and 6 Feb. 1887; to Dixon, 27–9 Jan. 1887 and 29–30 July 1888; and, most tellingly, to Bridges, 28 Sept. 1887 and 12–13 Jan. 1888.
[232] GMH to Bridges, 6 Nov. 1887 and 18–19 Aug. 1888.
[233] GMH to Katharine Tynan, 8 July 1887.
[234] GMH to Bridges, 10–11 Sept. 1888; see also GMH to Baillie, 7 Sept. 1887.

auricular confession in his Oxford student days,[235] the special genre of spiritual self-examination must be borne in mind when interpreting his words. Nevertheless, this last extended record of his interior condition before his final illness indicates how desperate was his state. 'I often think I am employed to do what is of little or no use', he observed with what had become a characteristic sense of futility; 'Yet it seems to me that I could lead this life well enough if I had bodily energy and cheerful spirits. However these God will not give me.' Then, delving into a deeper realm of grief, he probed the magnitude of his distress: 'I began to enter on that course of loathing and hopelessness which I have so often felt before', a state of affliction 'which made me fear madness and led me to give up the practice of meditation except, as now, in retreat, and here it is again.'[236] We do not know when Hopkins first abandoned meditative prayer in order to distance himself from the shadow of 'madness', but we may surmise—from his correspondence, the *Dublin Notebook*, and the composition dates of the 'terrible sonnets'—that he may have taken this extreme step sometime in 1885. Whatever the date, his dread of encroaching mental instability must have been considerable. Returning to that dangerous exercise of concentrated meditative practice on his 1889 retreat, he is filled with self-recrimination and brought to the brink of despair, 'I wish then for death: yet if I died now I shd. die imperfect, no master of myself, and that is the worst failure of all. O my God, look down on me.'[237] This is not 'anxiety about work to be done',[238] but something far more fearsome. Even accounting for the author's tendency towards self-dramatizing and exaggeration ('To bed, to bed: my eyes are almost bleeding'),[239] he appears to be in a world 'Where, selfwrung, selfstrung, sheathe- and shelterless, thoughts against thoughts in groans grind'.[240]

In the light of such chronic suffering, one might be inclined to dismiss the observation Hopkins made in February 1887, 'out of Ireland I shd. be no better, rather worse probably'. As we have discussed above, a number of circumstances contributed to the alienation, distress, and sense of self-diminishment that Hopkins experienced at St Stephen's Green, but it is important to recall that his enervation and anxiety began earlier: 'I fall into or continue in a heavy weary state of body and mind in which my go is gone', he writes from Stonyhurst in January 1883, adding, that he is 'so tired or so harassed' that he is able to accomplish little.[241] 'I have been in a wretched state of weakness and weariness', he tells Bridges.[242] Some seven months later, his condition is much the same, 'I have no disease, but I am always tired, always jaded', he explains, 'though work is not heavy . . . the impulse to do anything fails me or has in it no

[235] See *CW* iii.

[236] Retreat Notes, Tullabeg, Jan. 1889, fo. 24ᵛ. See Appendix I (below) and *CW* v.

[237] Retreat Notes, Tullabeg, Jan. 1889, fo. 25ʳ. See Appendix I (below) and *CW* v.

[238] GMH to Baillie, 24 Apr.–17 May 1885.

[239] GMH to Bridges, 12–13 Jan. 1888.

[240] 'Sibyl's Leaves', *CW* viii; see *DN*, fos. 15ʳ, 20ᵛ and Appendix C (below).

[241] GMH to Baillie, 14 Jan. 1883.

[242] GMH to Bridges, 4–5 Jan. 1883.

continuance'.[243] Thus, it seems fair to say that Ireland exacerbated problems and fomented difficulties already extant in Hopkins's life. Accordingly, his protestations of unfitness for his new position as Professor and Fellow may have been as much about his evolving psychological condition as his lack of recent scholarly engagement in classical studies.

'CONSIDER YOUR OWN MISERY AND TRY AS BEST YOU CAN TO RISE ABOVE IT': HOPKINS AT PRAYER IN DUBLIN

There are twenty-nine or thirty instances—possibly even thirty-one or thirty-two, depending upon how one interprets the evidence—of Hopkins using the *Dublin Notebook* to prepare for periods of prayer.[244] Thus, the notebook is one of the principal sources for understanding Hopkins at prayer and his spiritual life in Dublin.[245] According to the practice laid down by Ignatius Loyola, one should prepare for the morning's spiritual employment by thoughtfully reading a designated Scripture passage before going to bed on the night before one rises to pray. This reflective reading—typically of the gospel to be proclaimed at Mass the following morning—should then lead to the formulation of three points, or signposts, that will guide the course of the next day's meditation. The first such entry in the notebook, for example, shows Hopkins organizing to meditate on the gospel passage in which Peter confesses that Jesus is the Christ.[246] Following the traditional method that he would have learnt in the novitiate and practised for many years thereafter, Hopkins begins by imagining 'The scene of the confession', what Ignatius calls 'composition of place'. He then turns to Jesus' question, 'Whom do men say that I the son of man am?', and its implications before applying the theme to his own time, 'Consider what men now say of Christ'.[247] On the Sunday in the Octave of Epiphany, he is even more systematic: 'Christ's three man[ifestatio]ns : at Bethlehem, at the baptism, at Cana[:] (1) Consider to whom. . . . (2) Consider as what. . . . (3) By what means . . . '.[248]

As delineated in the *Spiritual Exercises*, contemplatively moving from one pre-determined way station to the next keeps one's prayer appropriately focused on the spiritual matter at hand, while enabling increasingly deeper engagement of mind and heart. This processive movement leads finally to the 'colloquy' in which the individual at prayer, now thoroughly imbued with a sense of being in the divine presence,

---

[243] GMH to Bridges, 26 July 1883.

[244] 'Consider your own misery . . . ': *DN*, fo. 7ᵛ, meditation notes for the Feast of St Michael, Sept. 1884.

[245] Other documents showing Hopkins at prayer are his retreat notes from 1883 and 1889. The commentary he prepared on the *Spiritual Exercises* during his tertianship and, to a lesser degree, his sermons should also be consulted; see *CW* v.

[246] See the accompanying annotations.   [247] *DN*, fo. 3ʳ.   [248] *DN*, fo. 21ᵛ.

communicates her or his heart's desire and listens with a disciple's ear for the promptings of God. The meditation points recorded in the *Dublin Notebook*, then, are not ends in themselves, but stepping-stones that lead upstream towards a wellspring. As Hopkins's quondam mentor, John Henry Newman, observed, '*Cor ad cor loquitor*'—heart speaks to heart. This is the great aim of Ignatian prayer, the coalescence of human and divine desire, a grace-filled meeting of the beloved with Love. In the notebook passage that Hopkins composes to pray about St Peter's confession of faith, he adds a note directing himself towards the colloquy, 'Praise our Lord in the words of this confn'.[249]

Hopkins's use of the *Dublin Notebook* for prayer—some thirty instances over the course of thirteen months from 22 February 1884 to 25 March 1885[250]—chiefly comes in four distinct spates. First, there is an initial series of notes for morning meditations soon after his arrival at St Stephen's Green. Between 22 February and 21 March, Hopkins makes six such entries. By April 1884, Hopkins is complaining in his correspondence of 'a great weakness' and at the end of the month says he is only now 'recovering from a deep fit of nervous prostration'.[251] Yet, even allowing for Hopkins's tendency towards hypochondria and epistolary self-dramatization, that professed recovery must have been either a chimera or very short-lived, for in early July Richard Watson Dixon is highly solicitous of his friend's health: 'I have been & am distressed by the news of your illness, or at least prostration of strength'.[252] Perhaps not surprisingly then, the *Dublin Notebook* shows only three examples of Hopkins preparing meditation points in the period from late March through mid-August 1884. Two of those entries are associated with Corpus Christi,[253] a feast that struck a particular chord for Hopkins.

The second cluster of prayer notes bears no date, but is almost certainly associated with the Feast of the Assumption of the Blessed Virgin Mary, on 15 August. Then, in the autumn, when Hopkins is feeling overwhelmed with work—in late October, he reports being 'now drowned in the last and worst of five examinations'[254]—we encounter only two sets of meditation points. Both of these focus on the lives of saints, Michael and Cecilia, because of their appearance in the liturgical calendar (September 29 and November 22, respectively). The third tranche of prayer activity in the notebook comes during the Christmas season; between 20 December and 10 January, he makes eight such entries, with a ninth on 19 January. The importance of the holiday and the respite that it afforded together were conducive to directed effort at formal, private prayer. The final sequence comes in March 1885, during the third and fourth weeks of

---

[249] *DN*, fo. 3ʳ.

[250] Throughout this discussion and in the annotations of GMH's text, we adhere to the dates that GMH uses in the *DN*, and, similarly, assign the undated entries the date of the appropriate liturgical memorial or feast whenever possible. It should be remembered, however, that, according to traditional practice, GMH would have actually composed his prayer points at night for the following morning's mediation; thus, for example, his entry for 'March 8 The Transfiguration' was most probably made on 7 Mar.

[251] GMH to Bridges, 16–19 Apr. 1884 and 30 Apr. 1884.

[252] 9 July 1884.   [253] *DN*, fo. 5ʳ.   [254] GMH to Dixon, 25 Oct. 1884.

Lent, when Hopkins is more regular in his prayer activity than anywhere else in the *Notebook*. In the eight days between 12 and 19 March, he records meditation points five times; then, six days later, he makes a final entry, this time for the Feast of the Annunciation on 25 March. Approximately three-fourths of the meditation notes in the *Dublin Notebook* belong to these four groups. Leisure seems to have been particularly important for Hopkins in sustaining meditative prayer. During the eight days spanning 3–10 January 1885, for example, he makes outlines for his morning prayer four times; not incidentally, he was away at Clongowes from 2 to 16 January.

Typically, Hopkins begins his preparatory prayer notes by seizing upon particular aspects of his subject; 'consider' is the most common instruction he imparts to himself; 'admire', 'remark', and 'appreciate' also convey similar habits of mind and soul. He frequently notes that he ought to make specific petitions: 'Ask for [St Patrick's] help for Ireland in all its needs and for yourself in your position'; 'Pray to be on the watch for God's providence, not determining where or when but only sure that it will come. And apply this to all your troubles and hopes, to England and Ireland, to ~~go~~ growth in virtue'; 'Wish for the strength [Divine Wisdom] gives to reach through your life'.[255] Perhaps most importantly, Hopkins directs his affect, pointing his heart towards the time of colloquy: 'you cd. practise what you did at Roehampton in the tertianship, entering into the joy of our Lord, ~~or into~~ not his joys but the joys of him'; 'Crown him king over yourself, of your heart'.[256] In addition, he makes practical recommendations and resolutions: 'Try to attach yourself more to God's will and detach yourself more from your own by prayer at beginning things'; '["]Let him that is without sin [cast the first stone"]—Pray to keep this spirit and[,] as ~~for~~ far as possible[,] rule in speaking of Mr. Gladstone for instance'.[257] A number of the later entries, though seemingly unremarkable, include material in which one may descry the spiritual lassitude, the wearied and wearying lifelessness, that intermittently afflicted Hopkins long before he came to St Stephen's Green, but which became most debilitating, frightening, and bewildering in its recurrences from the spring of 1885 onwards. The final meditation in the *Dublin Notebook*, for example, which under better circumstances might have reflected the joy of one so devoted to Mary and committed to the Incarnation, exhibits instead the aridity, or torpor, that he repeatedly complains of in his letters.[258]

The *Notebook* also records Hopkins's struggle to maintain the Ignatian practice of rigorous self-examination: 'I must ask God to strengthen my faith or I shall never keep the part[icular] ex[amen]. Must say the stations for this intention'; 'Consider the part. ex. and the prayers for it', he writes in mid-August 1884.[259] A month later, he is grappling with his own despondency and, once again, looks to the discipline and structured prayer that have been central to his spiritual formation for help: 'Consider

---

[255] *DN*, fos. 26ʳ and 21ᵛ (twice).   [256] *DN*, fos. 3ʳ and 4ʳ.   [257] *DN*, fos. 3ʳ and 26ʳ.

[258] *DN*, fo. 26ᵛ; on GMH's expressions of dissatisfaction about his health in his correspondence, see '"My go is gone": Hopkins's health in Dublin', above.

[259] *DN*, fo. 6ʳ. On the examen, see the annotations to GMH's text.

your own misery and try as best you can to rise above it, by punctuality, ~~fervour~~ and the particular examen'.[260] As he increasingly came to feel professionally harried and spiritually 'jaded', the *Notebook* attests, Hopkins appears to have been less and less able to create the interior disposition of mind and heart required for different kinds of formal private prayer.

One cannot definitively establish that the intermittent appearance of Hopkins's preparatory prayer notes reflects a correspondingly sporadic habit of carefully prepared, meditative prayer. Yet, the notes he made seem to point towards the notion that, during his first two years in Dublin, Hopkins's prayer life had primarily migrated away from formal Ignatian meditation towards other methods that he found less mentally and emotionally demanding.[261] In his retreat notes of January 1889, he observes: 'I was continuing this ~~reflexion~~ ^train of thought^ this evening when I began to enter on that course of loathing and hopelessness which I have so often felt before, which made me fear madness and led me to give up the practice of meditation except, as now, in retreat, and here it is again.'[262] The final documented occasion of formal meditation in the *Notebook* is 25 March 1885. The information we have about the composition of the 'terrible sonnets', albeit incomplete, interpreted in concert with the *Notebook* and Hopkins's correspondence, suggests that he may have abandoned contemplative prayer altogether, with the exception of his required annual retreat, sometime in the spring of 1885, a period of extreme emotional stress and distress. For Hopkins the ever-dutiful and admirably obedient Jesuit, this inability to experience the affective intimacy with God that is the defining aspiration of Ignatian meditative prayer may have been both a precipitating cause and an exacerbating effect of his feeling alienated from the One who truly was 'the very buttons of [his] being'.[263]

We do not know if Hopkins kept a daily prayer journal, although we may surmise from the *Dublin Notebook* that he most likely did not. Were he to have done so, then we might reasonably expect that the notes comprising points made for his meditations would have been kept in that notebook, instead of being juxtaposed higgledy-piggledy with lists of correspondents; petty-cash accounts; the sketch of a recycled sermon; attendance rolls; examination tallies; draft compositions of poetry, biography, and music; lecture notes, and the other quotidian, miscellaneous inventories found in the *Dublin Notebook*. Yet, because the bulk of his working papers were burnt at his death—to say nothing of Hopkins's own predilection for destroying personal papers—one can never be certain. The absence of any jottings in the *Notebook* reflecting on how his prayer sessions went, as prescribed in Ignatian meditative practice, further suggests that Hopkins, once the scrupulous recorder of his movements of heart and soul,[264] was no

---

[260] *DN*, fo. 7ᵛ, Sept. 30 [1884]; cf. GMH's 1889 retreat notes, fo. 25ʳ: 'I think it may be well to resolve to make the examen every day at 1.15' (see *CW* v, or Appendix I, below).

[261] In addition to daily Mass, GMH's prayer life would routinely have included his daily examen (quite possibly, twice a day), saying his breviary (at least twice a day), litanies, etc.

[262] See Appendix I, fo. 24ᵛ.

[263] GMH to Baillie, 22 May–18 June 1880.   [264] See *CW* iii.

longer registering his spiritual progress in 1884–5. Another sort of material evidence also strongly implies that Hopkins did not keep a spiritual diary during his Dublin years: his surviving retreat notes for January1889, occupying eight sheets, are not torn from a journal or exercise book, but instead are recorded on loose sheets of paper, the first and third sheets being printed stationery from 'LOYOLA HOUSE, | DROMORE, | CO. DOWN.'[265] It is strange to contemplate the possibility of Hopkins taking this jumbly exercise book recording fragmentary episodes from the most public and private aspects of his life into the house chapel—or into the seminar room. Yet, that is what the heterogeneous nature of the *Dublin Notebook* compels us to do.

All four sequences of prayer activity in the *Notebook* are prompted by a particular impetus, most obviously, Hopkins's arrival in Dublin, Christmastide, and Lent. But what about the undated series of meditations that appear in the summer of 1884? There is a cluster of what seem to be at least three (and as many as five or six) separate instances of meditation points in the *Notebook*, that most likely were made in mid-August.[266] The first of these is a fairly straightforward reflection and guide for prayer on the 'Principle and Foundation' of the *Spiritual Exercises*.[267] Hopkins begins with the core idea of the contemplation: that true spiritual freedom comes from judging all created things and all human experiences according to the degree to which they lead one towards the praise, reverence, and service of God, and the salvation of one's soul. Hence, even 'weakness, ill health[,] every cross is a help' for the one who knows how to use them for true spiritual good.

It is hardly unexpected that Hopkins—in the throes of intense depression and malaise, and suffering from baffling incomprehension of his condition and of God's role in his misery—should seize upon the negative aspects of the exercise ('sickness . . . poverty . . . dishonour') closest to his own situation. Remarkably, however, he then associates his own anguish with that of Jesus during his time of greatest trial, the agony in the Garden of Gethsemane, 'Calix quem Pater meus dedit mihi non bibam illud? {The chalice which my Father has given me, shall I not drink it?}' (John 18: 11).[268] On one level, Hopkins's identification with the Christ in his passion is a spur towards acceptance of his painful situation, but the readiness with which he associates his own condition with Christ's also indicates the depth of his suffering.[269] He diagnoses his condition, 'this present state of lethargy', as *acedia*, a pervasive spiritual enervation and dissatisfaction, a religious torpor or spiritual sickness akin to but not identical with depression as a mental illness. This is 'that coffin of weakness and dejection in which

---

[265] See Retreat Notes, Tullabeg, Jan. 1889, *CW* v, or Appendix I, below.

[266] GMH's use of two writing instruments—his usual medium-nib pen with black ink and, for the first time in the *DN*, a purple pencil—suggests that he spent multiple sessions preparing the meditations on fo. 6ʳ; see Appendix J: Campion Hall MSS and GI.a Codicology and Analysis of Inks and Writing Stints.

[267] See notes corresponding to fo. 6ʳ, where the full text of the exercise is given.

[268] See the corresponding note at fo. 6ʳ.

[269] Cf. GMH's undated meditation points on Psalm 16 (*DN*, fo. 5ʳ), in which he introduces the notion of 'Christ's joy in spite of his sorrows'.

I live, without even the hope of change'.[270] He is burdened with 'a fagged mind and a continual anxiety', 'grief's gasping, joyless days, dejection' from which no entreaties to God will afford him sustained relief.[271]

After this set of reflections, there follows a meditation for the Feast of the Assumption of the Blessed Virgin Mary, after which there is another set of prayer topics and observations on the 'Foundation Exercise'. As before, Hopkins begins with the opening words of the meditation, but this time he prompts himself to 'consider what Father D[enis] M[urphy] was talking about'. It seems that Murphy, the spiritual director at the time, was giving Hopkins points for his meditation, but Murphy may have been providing edifying reflections on the Principle and Foundation to the whole Jesuit community, as it was not uncommon to have a brief preached retreat in preparation for the Assumption, a liturgical feast on which many Jesuits pronounced their vows. For Hopkins, it would have been the second anniversary of his professing final vows, so meditating on the cornerstone of the *Spiritual Exercises* would have been entirely fitting. Whatever the exact circumstances, in between these two sets of points on the Principle and Foundation, Hopkins reflects upon Mary's life of fidelity and service—'her obedience, her sorrows, her prayer, her work'—and on 'her holy death', before proposing an imaginative reflection on 'the meeting between Xt and his mother' in heaven 'and how the joy of seeing Christ our Lord is from having lived for him'. He then exhorts himself, 'Pray earnestly to do this'.[272]

Perhaps not surprisingly, however, it is the dolorous Mary with whom Hopkins identifies in his state of mental extremity and wretchedness. On the previous leaf (fo. 5ʳ, leaf 6), he attempts to enumerate 'Our Lady's [Seven] Sorrows' linking particular moments from the gospel narratives with their corresponding emotional states.[273] What is sometimes known as 'the dry martyrdom' of Mary would have furnished him with ample material for reflecting on the perplexing difficulties of his own melancholy discipleship, '[t]his withered world of me, that breathes no bliss'.[274] The full degree of Hopkins's sadness and the suffering it occasioned is harrowingly captured in the notes that he made during his 1889 annual retreat:

nothing to enter but loathing of my life and a barren submission to God's will. The body cannot rest when it is in pain nor the mind be at peace as long as something bitter distills in it and it

---

[270] GMH to Bridges, 1–2 Apr. 1885.   [271] GMH to Dixon, 7–9 Aug. 1886; 'Heraclitean Fire'.

[272] *DN*, fo. 6ʳ.

[273] It may at first glance appear that GMH's inventory of the Seven Sorrows more likely corresponds to the Feast of Our Lady of Sorrows (15 Sept.), but this list is clearly linked to the points made on the subsequent leaf, not only thematically ('Consider [Mary's] obedience, her sorrows, her prayer'), but also materially, because of the unusual use of purple pencil on both leaves (see Appendix J). September would have been a highly unlikely time for such an extended meditation, because the entire month in 1884 was taken up with RUI examining, whereas August would have been far more manageable for the kind of coherent spiritual work that these several successive meditation points represent. Moreover, there is a suggestion of Mary's death and assumption into heaven in GMH's formulation, 'how the joy of seeing Christ our Lord is from having lived for him' (fo. 6ʳ).

[274] 'To R. B.', draft.

aches. This may be at any time and is at many: how then can it be pretended there is ^for those who feel this^ anything worth calling happiness in this world? There is a happiness, hope, the anticipation of happiness hereafter: it is better than happiness, but it is not happiness now.[275]

The 'sort of extremity of mind'[276] to which he was subject is not merely psychological stress because of his examining duties. Rather, it is a thoroughgoing spiritual problem because the Afflicted One to whom he turned in his own affliction gave no succour, granted no solace: 'Comforter, where, where is your comforting? / Mary, mother of us, where is your relief?'[277]

Intriguingly, the Assumption-related meditation passages in the *Notebook* are surrounded by excisions: the top portion of fo. 5 is cut away above 'Our Lady's Sorrows' and the next two leaves, 7 and 8, have been carefully removed, leaving only stubs. Leaf 9, outlining meditation points but including neither extended personal reflection nor sensitive spiritual material, is entirely intact, but there immediately follow three more leaves where nothing but stubs remain. Could it be that Hopkins had used this portion of the *Notebook* for his time of retreat and that the matter on these missing leaves was too sensitive to keep in a notebook routinely employed for the more mundane aspects of his quotidian existence? More than likely, we will never know if these missing portions of the *Dublin Notebook* contained harrowing spiritual self-examination and soul-searching of the kind found in the 1889 retreat notes, early drafts of 'To seem the stranger', or other matter. The other large excisions from the *Notebook* seem to be chiefly related to Hopkins's examination work, and these do not. Whatever may be absent, the richness of the *Dublin Notebook* as it has come down to us is considerable, bearing its 'burning witness though / Against the wild and wanton work of men'.[278]

Perhaps most especially after he found he could no longer tolerate the emotional exigencies of regular meditative prayer, Hopkins's religious life was not merely chronicled in his Dublin poems, but rather was often enacted in and through them, albeit sometimes obliquely. Whether he entreats, 'Mine, O thou lord of life, send my roots rain'; or beseeches, 'why must / Disappointment all I endeavour end?'; or arraigns, 'Wert thou my enemy, O thou my friend, / How wouldst thou worse, I wonder, than thou dost / Defeat, thwart me?'; or does all three in the same poem as in 'Thou art indeed just', it is clear that many of the Dublin sonnets aspire to make some sense of the confounding reality that the more his distress made him needful of his God, the more distant God seemed from his indigent servant. 'And my lament / Is cries countless, cries like dead letters sent / To dearest him that lives alas! away', he grieves.[279] And yet, in many of Hopkins's Dublin poems, as in his *Notebook* meditation notes, we see the stricken priest fighting hard for constancy of purpose, striving by desolate entreaty and by force of will to recover in himself and in his spiritual life the comfort that had so long eluded him.

---

[275] Retreat Notes, Tullabeg, Jan. 1889, fo. 25ʳ; see *CW* v, or Appendix I, below.
[276] GMH to his mother, Kate Hopkins, 5 May 1889.
[277] 'No worst'.   [278] 'On the Portrait'.   [279] 'I wake and feel.'

I. Gerard Manley Hopkins, *c*.1888

II. 85 and 86 St Stephen's Green, Dublin (now Newman House, University College Dublin)

III. Group photograph at Clongowes Wood College, *c*.1884, with Edward Kelly, S.J. (Rector). Back row, standing (l. to r.): Frs Lynch, Conmee, Brennan, James Murphy, John Murphy, Campbell, Wheeler, Devitt, James Colgan, Kane, Lentaigne, Cahill, Foley, Weafer, Joseph McDonnell, John McDonnell; front row, sitting (l. to r.): Frs Finlay (Rector, Belvedere), Kelly (Rector, Tullabeg), Brown (Provincial), Edward Kelly (Rector, CWC), Hopkins, William Delany (Rector, University College), Kenny (Rector, Galway), Saurin. *From the Irish Jesuit Archives (J11/34 [7]), Dublin*

IV. Group photograph at Clongowes Wood College, *c*.1885, with J. Conmee, S.J. (Rector). Back row, standing (l. to r.): Frs J. Brennan, Anderson, Tunney, Cahill, J. Kelly, Maher, Campbell, Devitt, N. A. Tomkin, Jos. McDonnell; front row (l. to r.: first two standing): Frs John Murphy, James Lynch, E. Hogan, P. Corcoran, Conmee, John Verdon, Hopkins. *From the Irish Jesuit Archives (J11/34 [6]), Dublin*

V. View from Visitor's Room, Clongowes Wood College (Co. Kildare).
Photo by Michael Flecky, S.J.

VI. Barrow River, Monasterevan (Co. Kildare). *Photo by Michael Flecky, S.J.*

VII. Cassidy House, Monasterevan (Co. Kildare). *Photo by Michael Flecky, S.J.*

EDITORIAL NOTES

MANUSCRIPT

This facsimile edition features Campion Hall MS GI.a, 'The Dublin Notebook', a large notebook (the cover of which is now detached) some 27.7 cm long and 21 cm wide. Originally, it contained forty-eight leaves. Whole and partial pages were removed at different points; notations appear variously on thirty-three rectos and versos.

Details of the manuscript's physical state are provided below ('Codicology'). For each opening, we have arranged the transcription page on the left and the manuscript image on the right so that the book (at least, to the right-handed reader) privileges Hopkins's work.

The digital images in this photo-facsimile edition were created by James Allan and his team at Imaging Services, Bodleian Libraries, Oxford. A Phase One FX was used for image capture; the colour-corrected images were resized to 600 DPI during post-production. All possible care has been taken to render the entirety of each page reproduced. The 'reader' of these scans may discern a kind of stratigraphy in each image: first, there is the substrate on which GMH wrote; in some cases, this was mounted onto a supporting leaf during conservation (see fo. 33ᵛ, for example). Each leaf of the *Notebook* was scanned while resting on a blank sheet of paper which constitutes a further layer, easily distinguishable in the images from the MS itself. Finally, there is the grey border surrounding the outer edges of each image, a so-called 'museum crop' to indicate that the reproduction has not been cropped at all. Having been privileged to spend hundreds of hours with both the original MS and the scans, we believe that—especially when accompanied by careful transcriptions—these images are adequate for most forms of study. Scholars wishing to engage in more technical or thoroughgoing analysis of the *Dublin Notebook* will, of course, wish to consult the MS itself.

PRINCIPLES OF TRANSCRIPTION

Every attempt has been made to preserve the appearance and spirit of the *Notebook*'s pages. Cancelled words and phrases are indicated with strikethrough (~~strikethrough~~) marks. The only exception to this is a cancelled dash or short line, which cannot be reproduced typographically. In those instances, we have used the symbol '÷'. For the sake of clarity, any single character or punctuation mark deleted by Hopkins is designated with a double strikethrough (ŧ). Hopkins's spelling and punctuation practices have been followed exactly. It was occasionally his habit, for example, to leave considerable space between the last character in a word and a semicolon. Although we are not certain if or how this space marks a pause on Hopkins's part, it might be meaningful. As editors, rather than predetermine the significance of the space, we have simply acknowledged it. Where the text is no longer legible, conjectured letters are indicated with italics; unreadable marks or characters are indicated with '#'. As various explanatory notes indicate, his idiosyncratic tendencies in spelling people's names and place names have been preserved. Only the seemingly interminable rows of checkmarks and mathematical calculations, indicating the grading of examination papers, have not been reproduced.

As in other volumes in the *Collected Works*, we have provided translations of non-English terms and phrases in braces { } immediately after the word or phrase. To preserve the common use of brackets [ ] for our editorial interventions or clarifications, we have translated Hopkins's very infrequent brackets into < >.

CODICOLOGY AND ANALYSIS OF INKS AND WRITING STINTS

Even the best photographic facsimile is no substitute for handling the manuscript and spending a great deal of time with it—which, thanks to the kindness of Campion Hall and the British Province of the Society of Jesus, has been our great privilege. Therefore, we are providing technical information about the manuscript that cannot be determined from the digital reproductions alone. These details are chiefly of two kinds: the structure of the manuscript itself (that is, its codicology) and evidence from variations in pen nibs used, and ink colour and density, that help determine iterations of writing and patterns of amendment. In our physical assessment of the manuscript, we distinguish between the notebook's original *leaves* of paper and the surviving *folios* as GMH used them. There were partial excisions from fos. 4 and 5. Stubs from leaves that were cut or torn out are still extant. Originally, each half of the notebook featured twenty-four leaves measuring 27.7 cm long and 21 cm wide, making 48 original leaves in all. In July 1980, at the expense of Prof. Norman MacKenzie, the notebook was de-acidified, cleaned, repaired, sewn, foliated, and covered by a conservator (Mrs Segal) at the Bodleian Library. The original covers have been preserved.

Codicology

COVERS

(Not shown.) Approximately 130 gm heavy paper (in place of board); thin, medium brown leather overlay glued down at the fold, under which the pages were stapled. Evidence of two fasteners on either side. Signed 'Gerard M. Hopkins' on the inside front cover (in an early, 1860s hand).

CONTENTS

Leaf 1 excised   The extant stub, an artefact of the conservation process carried out in July 1980, is not part of the original notebook.

Fo. 1 / Leaf 2   The edges are highly worn, perhaps from frequent referral.

Fo. 2 / Leaf 3   Compared with Leaf 2, this leaf is considerably less worn and damaged.

Fo. 3 / Leaf 4

Fo. 4 / Leaf 5   The paper is partially cut away. The missing fragment (not found) measures 12.1 cm long and 19.5 cm wide.

Fo. 5 / Leaf 6   The paper is partially cut away. The missing fragment (not found) measures 7.5 cm long and 18.8 cm wide, although the inner edge where the piece was removed has a crescent shape for the first 4 cm before becoming straight. The crescent measures approximately 0.7 cm from its deepest point to the straight edge.

Stubs of two leaves remain: Leaf 7 and Leaf 8.

Fo. 6 / Leaf 9   Complete.

Stubs of three leaves are evident: for Leaf 10, Leaf 11, Leaf 12.

Fo. 7 / Leaf 13

Stub for one leaf remains: Leaf 14.

Fo. 8 / Leaf 15   Contents: Collins's ode.

Stubs of four leaves remain: 16, 17, 18, 19. The stub for Leaf 16 shows evidence of single and double ruling on the recto; nothing is visible on the verso except a single rule mark. On Leaf 18 there is evidence, at the top of the recto, of GMH's examination grading. The stub of Leaf 17 has no markings. On the stub of Leaf 18, evidence at the top of the recto (a candidate's identification number, '772', in GMH's hand has been cancelled) indicates he was marking examinations. Some text on Leaf 18ᵛ was mostly obliterated during the cleaning and conservation work undertaken in 1980. Also, there is evidence of ruling on the verso, top, and bottom. On the stub of Leaf 19, the recto shows evidence of compartmentalization or ruling; the verso as well. Some written material was also lost during the conservation process.

Fo. 9 / Leaf 20 to Fo. 11 / Leaf 22

Stub for one leaf remains: Leaf 23. Writing on the recto and verso provides evidence of grading activities.

Fo. 12 / Leaf 24 to Fo. 14 / Leaf 26

Stubs of two leaves remain: Leaf 27 and Leaf 28. Leaf 27ʳ shows evidence of six lines of Greek text, and ruled-off sections; the verso shows the edges of ruling and cancellation marks. The stub for Leaf 28ʳ features the number 3 in the middle of a circle, as well as evidence of ruling and cancellation; the verso is blank.

Fo. 15 / Leaf 29 to Fo. 33 / Leaf 47   Complete.

[Fo. 34] / Leaf 48   Blank on recto and verso.

INK

Given that a study of the inks and pencils used in the notebook was not conducted before the MS was cleaned and conservation work undertaken, our comments about writing materials are provisional. Nonetheless, close scrutiny provides clear evidence of the serial method of composition GMH used, in several different discursive modes.

Fo. 1ʳ

GMH added 'Latin Grammar', in purple pencil, after drafting the initial list. Subsequently, he went over the words in ink. (Perhaps he did not realize at first that Latin Grammar was required.) There is no evidence of any other alterations; nothing scratched out. 'Wide' nib used.

Fo. 2ʳ

Identical to Fo. 1 in terms of ink and nib.

Fo. 3ʳ

The same, in terms of quality of ink. The date and identifying information about the religious feast day ('March 8 | The Transfiguration | The sight of our Lord's body') were initially inscribed; later, GMH went back and, with a different pen/nib (the 'fine' nib), filled in the commentary. 'Feb. 22' appears at the top of the page; then 'March 7', 'March 8', 'March 21'.

Fo. 4ʳ

Part of the page has been cut away. The handwritten intercalary date, 'Friday, February 29', indicates that GMH was writing in 1884. The next dated entry is 'March 2'.

Fo. 5ʳ

Evidence of the first extended use of the purple pencil; first use of regular lead pencil as well. Contents: spiritual meditation notes.

Fo. 6ʳ

GMH resumed using a pen with a medium nib. Someone else has added an explanation for the abbreviation, 'part. exam.' (particular examen', part of a Jesuit's 'spiritual exercises'). In purple pencil, GMH noted, 'Consider how the Blessed Virgin has praised God . . . ' Then, in ink, he went over the phrase 'Rejoice in her glory'. Subsequently, he switched back to purple pencil.

Fo. 7ʳ

GMH tallied grades in purple pencil, for the first line and a half, and then switched to ink.

Fo. 7ᵛ

Much of the same in terms of ink and nib.

Fo. 8ʳ

Some ink transfer from a preceding leaf (most probably from the verso of the leaf now represented only by the stub before fo. 8). See also 18ʳ.

Fo. 8ᵛ

Same ink and nib. A fragment of a leaf (measuring 8 cm long and 21 cm wide) found among the Bridges/Hopkins papers in the Bodleian Library, Oxford features five lines from the beginning of 'Sibyl's Leaves'. We conjecture that the page originally belonged to the first or second of the four stubs that follow Leaf 8. The fragment was originally the top part of a page. Extant markings on the lower part of the fragment suggest text from 'Caradoc's Soliloquy'.

Fo. 9ʳ

Ten lines in sepia ink; the rest appear in a blacker ink. The corrections to the first ten lines were made in black ink. Thus we have three different iterations of text, distinguishable by ink and nib. GMH corrected the third part subsequently. Altogether, the page was 'visited' or inscribed at least four times.

Fo. 10ʳ

Ink and nib appear the same.

Fo. 10ᵛ

The same.

Fo. 11ʳ

Much the same, but a different nib from 10ᵛ, indicating a different stint. When examined closely, ink and nib suggest different stints of burdensome work.

Fo. 11ᵛ

The same.

Stub

Stub of Leaf 23: the presence of numbers on the stub suggests that GMH was calculating grades, similar to 12ᵛ (adding up scores, tallying the results).

Fo. 12ʳ

Other than Hopkins's grading of examinations (a sea of checkmarks and calculations much like those already reproduced), there is but a single word: 'brinamy', in calligraphic script.

Fo. 12ᵛ

Same nib and ink.

Fo. 13ʳ

In the musical segment, there is evidence of GMH revisiting and correcting his work.

Fo. 13ᵛ

Fo. 14ʳ

The first half of page was used for grading; the second half features the first iteration of the biographical essay on Dixon. GMH revisits the Dixon draft several times.

Fo. 14ᵛ

Nib and ink for first two lines (more of the Dixon draft) are very different from the ink and nib used for grading.

Stub immediately after 14v (Leaf 27)
Extant markings indicate that this page was clearly organized in three sections, for work
of various kinds. At the top of the page, GMH was analysing a Greek text. Verso: rule
marks that continue to the edge of the page indicate he was doing very different work.

Fo. 15ʳ
Black rather than sepia ink; all one stint.

Fo. 15ᵛ
GMH wrote 'Richard Watson Dixon' and then left space to continue revising the essay.
The numerals are written in a different ink. The Dixon draft then continues.

Fo. 16ʳ
The mathematics is a later addition.

Fo. 16ᵛ
Much of the same.

Fo. 17ʳ
Three segments, three different nibs. This is the first time he used GI.a for quotidian
notations.

Fo. 17ᵛ
A substantially different nib was used.

Fo. 18ʳ
The symbol of a cross with a dot in each quadrant is similar to a remnant transfer image
on fo. 8ʳ (see above).

Fo. 18ᵛ
GMH was creating substantial teaching notes. Ink drops at bottom of folio suggest that
he was charging his pen from an inkwell during the composition of this page.

Fo. 19ʳ
No significant changes from preceding leaf.

Fo. 19ᵛ
Different nib and ink from 19ʳ.

Fo. 20ʳ
The attendance grid dominates the page; the ink is lighter in the 'St. Cecily' notes that
follow.

Fo. 20ᵛ
Uses a very thin nib for the draft of 'Sibyl's Leaves'.

Fos. 21ʳ⁻ᵛ
Two further examples of multiple uses of the page.

Fo. 22ʳ

Continues to use the page in segments; leaves room for additional commentary and new work. Ink for memoranda; ink for meditation notes; 'Scholarship Examination' is in ink, but the work that follows to tally grades is in pencil. For the bottom section, he switches back to ink.

Fo. 22ᵛ

Continues with ink. Evidence of a new pen for the 'Tacitus' work. Above that, GMH uses a different pen for the notes of 29 January.

Fo. 23ʳ

Evidence of a different pen from 22ᵛ (the Tacitus section).

Fo. 23ᵛ

Top of the page: attendance records. Comments further down indicate that GMH was rereading the work on 24ʳ and making additional notes. He was using a different nib; the script is significantly smaller.

Fo. 24ʳ

In diction and tone, there is a new formality of work in the 'Notes for Roman Lit.'. The final section, ten lines discussing the last epoch of the Republic, was written with a different ink and nib.

Fo. 24ᵛ

The whole folio is cancelled. A small drawing indicates that GMH was using a very fine nib.

Fo. 25ʳ

The name 'Byrne' is another example of GMH's calligraphy. The segment on the lower half of the page is in a different ink. The first writing stint ended with 'Absent on Sat. Feb. 27.' Another change in ink and pen at 'Quintus'.

Fo. 25ᵛ

A new, fine nib is discernible. Calligraphy with 'Lysias'. Why was the passage cancelled? Perhaps GMH did so as he completed a fuller discussion of the material in the G.II notebook.

Fo. 26ʳ

Further evidence of sectioning: the lower part of the page is reserved for separate work.

Fo. 26ᵛ

Evidence of correction, revision, and cancellation in darker ink.

Fo. 27ʳ

Evidence of correction and revision in darker ink.

Fo. 27ᵛ

The ink used to cancel memoranda is black; for the notations, it is sepia. The entire page is written in sepia.

Fo. 28ʳ
Corrections and revisions in darker ink.

Fo. 28ᵛ
Evidence of four work stints: black ink; black ink; black ink; sepia.

Fo. 29ʳ
A very interesting page, in terms of inks and pens. Sepia-coloured ink was used for approximately the first half of page. Then, GMH switched to a fine nib and a different, black ink. A sepia segment follows; additions were made in black ink, with a different nib. Extremely small additions to text. Another example of how GMH would further refine and amend the text. Again he left space, anticipating additional work, and then filled it in later. There is a break in line 7 of the second section ('Caesar to his troops'), immediately after the cancelled phrase; it is cancelled in another ink. The phrase 'a veteran out of date' begins a new phase of work.

Fo. 29ᵛ
Evidence of minor revisions in darker ink.

Fo. 30ʳ
Following his usual habits, GMH left space for additional material but added more than he had anticipated. Minor corrections in darker ink.

Fo. 30ᵛ
Halfway down, he has added notes on ancient geography.

Fo. 31ʳ
The line beginning 'Caycos' features new ink until the middle of the page, indicating that GMH went back and filled in matter where formerly he had written, '??'.

Fo. 31ᵛ
A useful page to demonstrate his process of writing and then making subsequent revisions. Eight lines from the bottom there was a switch, between the words 'immediate' and 'perception', from sepia to black ink. On the sepia part, he made corrections in black; in black part, he amended in sepia.

Fo. 32ʳ
Substantial correction and revision in darker ink.

Fo. 32ᵛ
Corrections have been made in a different ink, with a finer nib. Again, evidence of GMH revisiting his work, refining thought and phrase.

Fo. 32ᵛ
Four lines from the bottom, '§ 7. 2. Metellum', there were changes in ink and nib.

Fo. 33ʳ–33ᵛ
Minor revisions in darker ink.

CITING OTHER WORKS BY HOPKINS

All of the volumes in the *Collected Works* (*CW*) feature the same date-specific citation practices. Letters written by and to Hopkins are identified in this way, as are any sermons or spiritual commentaries. Cross-references to other *CW* volumes feature the acronym and a lower-case Roman numeral:

CW i and ii	*Correspondence*
CW iii	*Diaries, Journals, and Notebooks*
CW iv	*Oxford Essays and Notes*
CW v	*Sermons and Spiritual Writings*
CW vi	*Sketches, Notes, and Studies*
CW viii	*The Poems*

SHORT TITLES OF POEMS

All poems and poetry fragments cited in the present volume are listed below. Where a short title has been used, the expansion is given in the right-hand column.

'As kingfishers'	'As kingfishers catch fire, dragonflies draw flame'
'Caradoc's Soliloquy'	
'Carrion Comfort'	
'Epithalamion'	
'Euridyce'	'The Loss of the Euridyce'
'Harry Ploughman'	
'Heraclitean Fire'	'That Nature is a Heraclitean Fire and of the comfort of the Resurrection'
'In S. Winefridam'	
'I wake and feel'	'I wake and feel the fell of dark, not day'
'Leaden Echo'	'The Leaden Echo and the Golden Echo'
'Mortal Beauty'	'To what serves Mortal Beauty?'
'My own heart'	
'No worst'	'No worst, there is none'
'On the Portrait'	'On the Portrait of Two Beautiful Young People'
'Patience'	
'Sibyl's Leaves'	'Spelt from Sibyl's Leaves'
'The Shepherd's Brow'	
'(The Soldier)'	
'Thou are indeed just'	'Thou are indeed just, Lord, if I contend'
'Tom's Garland'	

'To R. B.'

'To seem the stranger'   'To seem the stranger lies my lot, my life'

'What shall I do'   'What shall I do for the land that bred me'

'Wreck'   'The Wreck of the Deutschland'

The Dublin Notebook

Gerard M. Hopkins°

Matric.°   Latin

Pass   —   Aeneid bk. 2
                 Caesar (de Bello Gall. bks. 1, 2
                 Grammar
                 Easy sentences into Latin
                 Outlines of Roman Hist.

Honours —   Aen. bks. 5 and 6
                 Sallust de Bello Catilinario
                 Cicero pro Milone
                 Latin Grammar

First Univ.   ~~Pas~~
Pass   —   Horace Epistles bks. 1, 2 (that is all)
                 Cicero Philippics 1, 2
                 Grammar
                 Outlines of R. Hist.
                 Short passages Eng[lish] into Latin

Honours —   Georgics bk. 1°
                 Horace Odes bks. 3, 4
                 Cicero Pro Muraena ~~et~~ and Pro Plancio
                 Latin Prose Comp.
                 Roman Hist. and Ant[iquities] of Age of Augustus

Second Univ.   —   Greek
Pass   —   Herod[otus] bk. 2
                 Odyssey bks. 6, 7
                 Gk. Prose Comp.
                 Outlines of the period of Hist. of Gk. Lit. and
           Antiquities B.C. 500–430

Honours —   Odyssey bks. 5 and 8, 9, 10, 11, 12
                 Soph[ocles] Ajax, Philoctetes
                 Thucyd[ides] bk. 5
                 Plato Phaedo
                 Gk. Prose Comp.
                 Minuter knowledge in the Period

Matric . Latin

   Pass   —   Aeneid Bk. 2
                Caesar de Bello Gall. Bks. 1, 2
                Grammar
                Easy sentences into Latin
                Outlines of Roman Hist.

   Honours —   Aen. Bks. 5 and 6
                Sallust de Bello Catilinario
                Cicero pro Milones
                Latin Grammar

First Univ.

   Pass   —   Horace Epistles Bks. 1, 2 (that is all)
                Cicero Philippics 1, 2
                Grammar
                Outlines of R. Hist.
                short passages tog. into Latin

   Honours —   Georgics Bk. 1
                Horace Odes Bks. 3, 4
                Cicero Pro Murena et as pro Plancio
                Latin Prose Comp.
                Roman Hist. and Ant. of Age of Augustus

Second Univ. — Greek

   Pass —   Herod. Bk. 2
              Odyssey Bks. 6, 7
              Gk. Prose Comp.
              Outlines of the period of Hist. of Gk. Lit. and
       Antiquities B.C. 500 – 430

   Honours — Odyssey Bks. 5 and 8, 9, 10, 11, 12
              Soph. Ajax, Philoctetes
              Thucyd. Bk. 5
              Plato Phaedo
              Gk. Prose Comp.
              minuter knowledge in the Period

B. A. — Greek (II.)

    Pass — Soph[ocles] <u>Antigone</u>, <u>Oed. Rex</u> ⎤ (1)
                Thucyd[ides] bks. 1, 2 ⎦
                Gk. Prose Comp. (2)
                Gk. Hist. and Lit. B.C. 430–322   (3)

    Honours — Aesch[ylus]° <u>Agamemnon</u>, <u>Persae</u> ⎤
                Soph[ocles] <u>Oed[ipus at] Col[onus]</u> ⎮
                Thucyd[ides] bks. 6, 7 ⎮
                Plato <u>Gorgias</u> ⎬ (1)
                Aristotle <u>Rhetoric</u> ⎮
                Demosthenes <u>de Falsa Legatione</u> ⎦
                Minuter knowledge of Period (2)
                Is there comp.?

M. A. — Greek
                Aesch[ylus] <u>Agam[emnon]</u>, <u>Persae</u> ⎤
                Aristoph[anes] <u>Nubes</u>, <u>Aves</u> ⎮
                Pindar ÷° <u>Nemean Odes</u> ⎮
                Thucyd[ides] ÷ bks. 5, 6, 7 ⎬ (1)
                Plato <u>Republic</u> bks. 1, 2, 3 ⎮
                Aristotle <u>Politics</u> bks. 1, 2 Tauchnitz° ⎦
                Greek Prose Comp[osition] (2)
                Philogy of Gk. Language (3)   (4)
                Greek Hist. and Lit. to death of Demosthenes ^

Scholarship° (Jan. '85) — Greek (II.)

                Homer <u>Iliad</u> bks. 4, 5
                Euripides <u>Bacchae</u>, <u>Ion</u>
                Soph[ocles] <u>Trachiniae</u>
                Plato <u>Republic</u> bk. 1
                Xenophon <u>Hellenica</u> bks. 3, 4
                Demosth[enes] <u>in Leptinem</u>
            III. ~~The Out~~ (a) Outlines of Hist. of Greece and Rome°

B. A. — Greek (II.)

    Pass — Soph. <u>Antigone</u>, <u>Oed. Rex</u>   } (1)
           Thucyd. bks. 1, 2
           Gk. Prose Comp. (2)
           Gk. Hist. and Lit. B.C. 430 – 322 (3)

    Honours — Aesch. <u>Agamemnon</u>, <u>Persae</u>
           Soph. <u>Oed. Col.</u>
           Thucyd. bks. 6, 7
           Plato <u>Gorgias</u>   } (1)
           Aristotle <u>Rhetoric</u>
           Demosthenes <u>de falsa Legatione</u>
           Minuter knowledge of Period (2)
           Is there comp. ?

M. A. — Greek

        Aesch. <u>Agam.</u>, <u>Persae</u>
        Aristoph. <u>Nubes</u>, <u>Aves</u>
        Pindar <u>Nemean Odes</u>
        Thucyd. bks. 5, 6, 7   } (1)
        Plato <u>Republic</u> bks. 1, 2, 3
        Aristotle <u>Politics</u> bks. 1, 2 tauchnitz
        Greek Prose Comp. (2)
        Philology of Gk. language (3)   (+)
        Greek Hist. and Lit. t death of Demosthenes

Scholarship (Jan. '85) — Greek (II.)

        Homer <u>Iliad</u> bks. 4, 5
        Euripides <u>Bacchae</u>, <u>Ion</u>
        Soph. <u>Trachiniae</u>
        Plato <u>Republic</u> bk. 1
        Xenophon <u>Hellenica</u> bks. 3, 4
        Demosth. in Septinem
    III. (a) Outlines of Hist. of Greece and Ro

Feb. 22 St. Peter's Confn.°
Comp[osition of place]. The scene of the confession; fruit
Whom do men say that I the son of man am? — Whom do <u>men</u> say
that <u>the son of man</u> is? Also there is the suggestion of son of God ?̶ .
Consider what men now say of Christ
Thou art ~~the~~ Christ the son of the living God — Praise our Lord in
the words of this confn. — There are two acknowledgments, that our
Lord was the Christ and that he was son of God. The Christ is the chosen
and anointed man, the Son of God is God

(b) ~~Jan~~ Ins[truction]° in Language and Lit. of Greece and Rome
arising chiefly out of the bks. above prescribed ɛ̸ <the
Latin bks. are <u>Aen[eid]</u> bks. 2, 5, 6 ; Horace both <u>Epistles</u>,
<u>Ars Poet[ica]</u>; Sallust <u>Bellum Cat.</u> ; Cicero <u>Pro Milone</u>, <u>de Amici-</u>
<u>tia</u> , Livy bks. 21, 22, 23)
(c) Ins[truction] in Geography arising from above bks.
(d) Comp. ; that is, translation of pieces of continuous Eng[lish]
~~pse~~ prose into Gk. and Latin

The Lance and Nails° March 7 —
Comp[osition of place] ~~the~~ / Calvary after Xt's death; grace devotion to the Passion
Seeing Christ's body nailed consider the attachment of his will to God's
will. Wish to be as bound to God's will in all things, in the attachment of
your mind and attention to prayer and the duty in hand ; the attachment
of your affections to Christ our Lord and his wounds instead of any earthly
object
March 8 The Transfiguration°
The sight of our Lord's body as a remedy for temptation
The thought of his mind and genius against vainglory and you
cd. practise what you did at Roehampton in the tertianship,° entering
into the joy of our Lord, ~~or into~~ not his joys but the joys of him
March 21 — The Five Wounds°
~~The~~ Consider our Lord's attachment to God's will at all times and this
attachment ended in the very nailing of his body to the cross. Try to attach
yourself more to God's will and detach yourself more from your own by
prayer at beginning things
The piercing of Christ's side. The sacred body and the sacred heart seemed
waiting for an opportunity of discharging themselves and testifying their
total devotion of themselves to the cause of man

Feb. 22 St. Peter's Confn.

Comp. the scene of the confession; fruit
Whom do men say that I the son of man am? — Whom do men say
that the son of man is? Also there is the suggestion of son of God //
Consider that men now say of Christ

Thou art the Christ the son of the living God — Praise our Lord in
the words of this confn. — There are two acknowledgments that our
Lord was the Christ and that he was son of God. the Christ is the chosen
and anointed man, the Son of God is God

_____

(b) ~~Ins~~ Ins. in Language and Lit. of Greece and Rome
arising chiefly out of the Chs. above prescribed ¶ [the
Latin Chs. are Aen. bks. 2,5,6 ; Horace with Epistles,
Ars Poet. ; Sallust Bellum Cat. ; Cicero pro Milone, de Amici-
tia , Livy bks. 21,22,23)

(c) Ins. in Geography arising from above bks.

(d) Comp. ; that is, translation of pieces of continuous Eng.
~~pro~~ prose into Gk. and Latin

_____

The Lance and Nails March 7 —
Comp. ~~the~~ Calvary after Xt's death ; grace devotion to the Passion
Seeing Christ's body nailed consider the attachment of his will to God's
will. Wish to be as loved to God's will in all things, in the attachment of
your mind and attention to prayer and the duty in hand; the attachment
of your affections to Christ our Lord and his wounds instead of any earthly
object

March 8 The Transfiguration
The sight of our Lord's body as a remedy for temptation
The thought of his mind and genius against vainglory and you
ed. practise that you did at Roehampton in the tertianship, entering
into the joy of our Lord, ~~as into~~ not his joys but the joys of him

March 21 — The Five Wounds
~~The~~ Consider our Lord's attachment to God's will at all times and this
attachment ended in the very nailing of his body to the cross. Try to attach
yourself more to God's will and detach yourself more from your own by
prayer at beginning things
The piercing of Christ's side the sacred body and the sacred heart seemed
waiting for an opportunity of discharging themselves and testifying their
total devotion of themselves to the cause of man

Friday Feb. 29 Christ crowned with thorns°

Christ was crowned by Gentiles King of the Jews. King of the Jews
~~mea~~ means not only king over the Jews but ~~king a~~ also born of the Jews to be king
over others, the Gentiles. These men crowned Xt in mockery, mocking
both probably at the Jews and him, at him for claiming to be a king and at
the Jews for claiming to have one. Nevertheless their act was mystical and

rights and

both the crown and the adorations were types of his true ^ royalty ~~and~~

Crown him king over yourself, of your heart

Wish to crown him king of ~~all~~ England, of English hearts and of
Ireland and all Christendom and all the world

The crown is of thorns. Consider Christ's bodily pain, then his ment-
al

Sunday March 2 — Christ tempted in the wilderness°

He was led by the spirit into the wilderness. Pray to be guided by the
Holy Ghost in everything. Consider that he was now led to be tempted and
the field and arena of the struggle was a wilderness, where the struggle wd.
be intenser but not perhaps more really perilous — to a fallen man, as Satan
might suppose him to be. Here admire our Lord in his struggle and his ser-
vants St. Antony,° St. Cuthbert,° and others

Command that these stones be made bread: The temp

Friday Feb. 29 Christ crowned with thorns   4

Christ was crowned by Gentiles King of the Jews. King of the Jews means not only king over the Jews but ~~king also~~ born of the Jews to be king over others, the Gentiles. ~~is~~ These men crowned X^t in mockery, mocking both probably at the Jews and him, at him for claiming to be a king and at the Jews for claiming to have one. Nevertheless their act being mystical and both the crown and the adorations were types of his true, *right and* royalty ~~and~~

Crown him king over yourself, of your heart

Wish to crown him king of ~~all~~ England, of English hearts and of Ireland and all christendom and all the world

The crown is of thorns. Consider Christ's bodily pain, then his mental

Sunday March 2 — Christ tempted in the wilderness

He was led by the spirit into the wilderness. Pray to be guided by the Holy Ghost in everything. Consider that he was now led to be tempted and the field and arena of the struggle was a wilderness, where the struggle would be intenser but not perhaps more really perilous — to a fallen man, as Satan might suppose him to be. Here admire our Lord in this struggle and his servants St. Antony, St. Cuthbert, and others

Command that these stones be made bread. The king

Our Lady's Sorrows° —

(1) Simeon's prophecy. (2) ~~Christ lost Jesus lost 3 days,~~ the child
~~(3)~~ (2) the flight into Egypt, (3) the loss for 3 days, (4)
the meeting on the way of the Cross, (5) the standing by
the cross, (6) the entombment, (7) ?
(1) Fear, (2) discomfort, (3) # care, (4)
(5) helpless grief, (6) bereavement

I set the Lord before me° etc — not moved. Here consider what ~~it~~
help is God's presence. Rules of modesty°
Therefore I rejoice. This joy is in hope. Christ's joy in spite of his
sorrows. Wish to enter into this
Ways of life°

Corpus Christi°
(1) Preciousness of our Lord's body, born of the B[lesse]d Virgin of David's
line, ~~crucifie~~ crucified, raised from the dead, seated in heaven; united to Xt's
soul ; united to the Word. Appreciate , . Feel your unworthiness.
(2) Its mystery: it binds the Church into one, ~~not only~~ bodily into one. It
is the pledge and means of our immortality. Revere this mystery
(3) The good it has done, sanctifying Xtians, in mass, communion, ~~at~~
viaticum. Thanksgiving
(4) It is put into my unworthy hands as a priest

June — Nobis datus°: here consider the B[lessed]d. Sacrament as
put into your hands, as ~~a comm~~ yours by your priesthood and ~~your by~~
communion. Then how well it shd. be treated. Consider occasions, mass,
visits
Nobis natus ex intacta virgine°—Here look on our Lady as the
Bestower of the B[lesse]d. Sacrament

Our Lady's Sorrows —
(1) Simeon's prophecy, (2) ~~Christ lost~~ Jesus lost 3 days
~~(3)~~ (2) the flight into Egypt, (3) the loss for 3 days, (4)
the meeting on the way of the Cross, (5) the standing by
the cross; (6) the entombment, (7) ?

(1) fear, (2) discomfort, (3) ~~her~~ care, (4)
(5) helpless grief, (6) bereavement

I set the Lord before me etc — not moved. Here consider what it
helps to ~~realize~~ God's presence. Rules of modesty
therefore rejoice. This joy is in hope. Christ's joy in spite of his
sorrows. Wish to enter into this
     ways of life

Corpus Christi
(1) Preciousness of our Lord's body, born of the Bd. Virgin of David's
line, ~~crucified~~ crucified, raised from the dead, seated in heaven; united to Xt's
soul; united to the Word. Appreciate, — Feel your unworthiness
(2) Its mystery: it binds the Church into one, not only bodily, into one. It
is the pledge and means of our immortality. Revere this mystery.
(3) The good it has done, sanctifying Xtians, in mass, communion, as
viaticum. Thanksgiving
(4) It is put into my unworthy hands as a priest.
June   — Nobis datus ; here consider the Bd. Sacrament as
put into your hands, as ~~come~~ yours by your priesthood and yourself
communion. Then how well it shd. be treated. Consider occasions, mass,
visits
     nobis natus ex intacta virgine — Here look on our Lady as the
bestower of the Bd. Sacrament

Man was created to praise° etc
Praise by the office expressly meant for this ; by ~~other~~ the mass, esp. the Gloria
And the other things on earth — take it that weakness, ill health every cross is a help. ~~The chalice~~ Calix quem Pater° meus dedit mihi non bibam illud?
Facere nos indifferentes° — with the elective will, not the affective essentially ; but the affective will will follow
I must ask God to strengthen my faith or I shall never keep the part[icular] ex[amen]. Must say the stations for this intention. Resolve also to keep it particularly even in the present state of lethargy.

————

Consider how the Bd. Virgin praised God — her obedience, her sorrows, her prayer, her work, her ~~de~~ holy death.
Rejoice in her glory. Consider the meeting between Xt and his mother and how the joy of seeing Christ our Lord is from having lived for him. Pray therefore earnestly to do this

Consider the part. ex.° and the prayers for it ; also Rules of modesty

Foundation Exercise
Man was created — Here consider what Father D. M.° was talking about
Save his soul — Consider in this life the meaning of these words. Consider peace, contentment, & good conscience
And the other things — Resolve how to get more use of them

Man was created — say ~~Xt was~~ the man Christ was created to praise etc and so to save his soul, that is / enter into ~~gl~~ his glory, and the other things ~~as a train to~~ **created** in his train
The love of the son for the Father leads   him to take a created nature and in that to offer him **ex crea** sacrifice.
The sacrifice might have been unbloody ; by the Fall it became a bloody one

Man was created to praise etc   6

Praise by the office expressly meant for this; by other the means,
esp. the Gloria

And the other things on earth — take it that weakness, ill health,
every cross is a help. ~~The chalice~~ Calix quem Pater meus dedit mi-
hi non bibam illud?

Facere nos indifferentes — with the elective will, not the affect-
ive essentially; but the affective will will follow

I must ask God to strengthen my faith or shall never keep the
pact. ex. I must say the stations for this intention. Resolve also to
keep it particularly even in the present state of lethargy

Consider how the Bd. Virgin praised God — her obedience, her sor-
row, her prayer, her work, her ~~bo~~ holy death

  • Rejoice in her glory. Consider the meeting between Xt and
his mother and how the joy of seeing Christ our Lord is from
having lived for him. Pray therefore earnestly to do this
Consider the pud. ex, and the prayer for it; also rules
of modesty

Foundation - Exercise

Man was created — Here consider what Father D. M. was talk-
ing about

Save his soul — Consider in this life the meaning of these words.
Consider peace, contentment, a good conscience

And the other things — Resolve how to get more use of them

Man was created — Say ~~Xt was~~ the man Christ was created
to praise etc and so to save his soul, that is / enter into of his glory.
And the other things as ~~entrain to exploited~~ in his train

The love of the son for the Father leads ~~~~ him to
take a created nature and in that to offer him ~~~~ sacrifice
the sacrifice might have been unbloody; by the fall it became a bloody
one

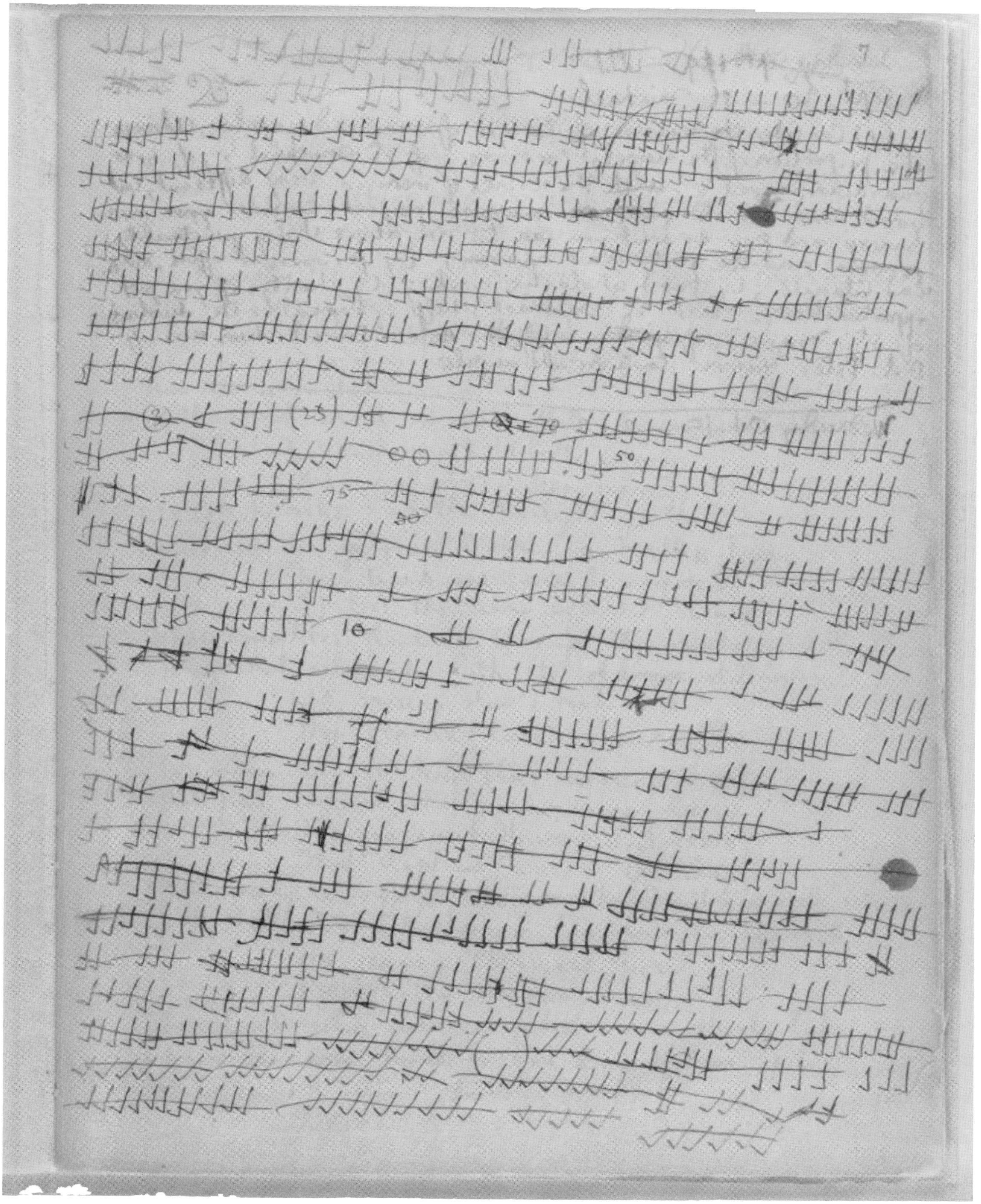

Sunday Sept. 154 — ✓✓✓
Sept. 30 — St. Michael°

(1) Consider the services ~~of~~ to God of men and angels. Admire the perfection of the angels' service, of St. Michael's, of your guardian angel's. ~~Wish~~ The service of men is very different, but good and in its ~~measure~~ measure perfect. Consider your own misery and try as best you can to rise above it, by punctuality, ~~fervour~~ and the particular examen° ; by fervour at office, mass, and litanies ; by good scholastic work; by charity if you get opportunities . Ask St. Michael's help: remember the devotion of St. Francis° of ~~God~~ ~~God~~ Assissi towards him and of Bd. Peter Favre° towards all angels

---

Wednesday Oct. 15 — 2 + 2°

Sunday Sept. 14 — JJJ

Sept. 30 — St. Michael

(1) Consider the services of, to God of men and angels, admire the perfection of the angels', service of St. Michael's, of your guardian angel's. With the service of men is very different, but good and in its ~~nearest~~ measure perfect. Consider your own misery and try as best you can to rise above it, by punctuality, fervour and the particular examen; by fervour at office, mass, and litanies; by good scholastic work; by charity of your get opportunities. Ask St. Michael's help: remember the devotion of St. Francis of ~~God~~ ~~God~~ Assisi towards him and of B.d. Peter Favre towards all angels

Wednesday Oct. 15 — 2 + 2

Ode to Evening °

If aught of oaten step or pastoral song
May serve, O pensive Eve, to soothe thine ear,
   Like thine own solemn springs,
   Thy springs and dying gales ⁊ —
O nymph reserved, while now the bright-haired sun
Sits in yon ~~tent~~ western tent whose cloudy skirts
   With brede° ethereal wove
   Oerhang his wavy bed ;
Now air is hushed, save where the weak-eyed bat
With short shrill shriek flits by on leathern wing
   Or where the beetle winds
   His small but sullen horn
As oft he rises mid the twilight path
Against the pilgrim borne in heedless hum ;
   Now teach me, maid composed,
   To breathe some softened strain,
Whose numbers stealing through thy darkening vale
May not unseemly with its ~~stilness~~ stillness suit
   As musing slow I hail
   Thy genial loved return.
For when thy folding star arising shews
His paly circlet, at his warning lamp
   The fragrant Hours and ~~e~~Elves,
   That slept in flowers the day,
And many a nymph who wreathes her brows with sedge
And sheds the ~~fr~~ freshening dew and, lovelier still,
   The pensive Pleasures sweet
   Prepare thy shadowy car.
Then lead, calm votaress, where some sheety lake
Cheers the lone heath or some time-hallowed pile
   Or upland fallows grey
   Reflect its ~~l~~ < ? > last cool gleam.

Ode to Evening

If aught of oaten stop or pastoral song
May serve, O pensive Eve, to sooth thine ear,
    Like thine own solemn springs,
      Thy springs and dying gales ;—
O nymph reserved, while now the bright-haired sun
Sits in yon western tent whose cloudy skirts
    With brede ethereal wove
      O'erhang his wavy bed ;
Now air is hushed, save where the weak-eyed bat
With short shrill shriek flits by on leathern wing
    Or where the beetle winds
      His small but sullen horn
As oft he rises mid the twilight path
Against the pilgrim borne in heedless hum ;
    Now teach me, maid composed,
      To breathe some softened strain,
Whose numbers stealing through thy darkening vale
May not unseemly with its stillness suit
    As musing slow I hail
      Thy genial loved return.
For when thy folding star arising shews
His paly circlet, at his warning lamp
    The fragrant Hours and Elves,
      That slept in flowers the day,
And many a nymph who wreathes her brows with sedge
And sheds the freshening dew and, lovelier still,
    The pensive Pleasures sweet
      Prepare thy shadowy car.
Then lead, calm votaress, where some sheety lake
Chears the lone heath or some time-hallowed pile
    Or upland fallows grey
      Reflect its [?] last cool gleam.

But when chill blustering winds or driving rain
Forbid my willing feet, be mine the hut
      That from the mountain's side
      Views wilds and swelling floods
And hamlets brown and dim-discovered spires
And hears their simple bell and marks o͡er all
      Thy ~~dw~~ dewy fingers draw
      The gradual dusky veil.
While Spring shall pour his showers, as ~~I~~ oft he wont,
And bathe thy breathing tresses, meekest Eve ;
      While Summer loves to sport
      Beneath thy lingering light ;
While sallow Autumn ~~foll~~ fills thy lap with leaves ;
Or Winter, yelling through the troublous air,
      Affrights thy shrinking train
      And rudely rends thy robes ;
So long, save found beneath the sylvan shed,
Shall Fancy, Friendship, Science, rose-lipped Health
      Thy gentlest influence own
      And hymn thy favourite name.

                        Wm. Collins

But when chill blustering winds or driving rain
Forbid my willing feet, be mine the hut
    That from the mountain's side
    Views wilds and swelling floods
And hamlets brown and dim-discovered spires
And hears their simple bell and marks o'er all
    Thy dewy fingers draw
    The gradual dusky veil.
While spring shall pour his showers, as oft he wont,
And bathe thy breathing tresses, meekest Eve;
    While summer loves to sport
    Beneath thy lingering light;
While sallow Autumn fills thy lap with leaves;
Or Winter, yelling through the troublous air,
    Affrights thy shrinking train
    And rudely rends thy robes;
So long, sure found beneath the sylvan shed,
Shall Fancy, Friendship, Science, rose-lipped Health
    Thy gentlest influence own
    And hymn thy favourite name.
               Wm. Collins

~~Whe~~
My heart,° where have we been ; what have we seen , my mind?
       blow
What ~~stroke~~ has Cradock dealt, what done? — A rebellious head
           in a body how
Struck off he has; ^ ~~and in now~~ beautiful soever
He has   bloody
~~A body~~ written ^ lessons of earnest, ~~of~~ of revenge ;
         my   my
Monuments of ~~his~~ ^ earnest, tales of ~~his~~ ^ revenge
On one who went against me , whereas I had warned her —
Warned her!~~;~~ well she knows I warned her of this work.
What work? what harm is done? Say no harm's done, none yet;
        we   Gwenvrewi
Perhaps ~~I~~ ^ struck no blow, ~~Gw Winefred~~ lives perhaps ;
⎰My mood would makebelieve : it mocked. O I might think so
⎱To makebelieve my mood was — mock. O I might think so
My heart,° ⫲ ⟊° where have we been? ; what have we seen, my
                    mind?
What blow has Cradock dealt, whát dóne — A rebellious head
Struck őff he has ; wrítten on límbs ~~as~~ lovely as may be,
⎰Lessons all in red of earnest, of revenge
⎱All in red, léssons of his earnest, his revenge

To makebelieve my mood was — mock. O I might think so
          is
But here is, here ~~a~~ ^ a workman after his day's task sweats,
I am sure   ~~it was~~ I wiped it once.
~~Strongly, as though wiped once~~ It seems, not well; for still,
Still, the scarlet swings and dances on the blade.
Steel, I can scour thee ; curtain thee ~~in thy dark sheath~~ smooth in thy sheath ; but
                              these drops,
Though wipèd once, I am sure. It seems, not well ; for still,
                 would seem,
Wiped once I am sure it was; ~~it seems,~~ ^ not well ; for still,
                not well, would seem ; for still,
Still the scarlet swings and dances on the blade.

       may
These ~~will~~ ^ never, never thrill théir blue banks again.
~~Never, never, never~~
Shall never, never, never lift their blue banks again.

⎰Thou steel, I cán scour thée, in scabbard curtain thee ; but these drops
⎱Never, never, never in their blue banks again ;
                         in thy dark
~~Stee~~ Steel, I can scour thee, curtain thee ~~in scabbard d~~ ^ scabbard ; these drops
Never etc

9

My heart, where have we been; what have we seen, my mind?
What blow has Cradock dealt, what done? — A rebellious head
Struck off he has; in a body how beautiful soever
it has written lessons of earnest, of revenge;
monuments of earnest, tales of revenge
On one who went against me, whereas I had warned her —
Warned her! well, she knows I warned her of this work.
What work? what harm is done? Say no harm is done, none yet,
Perhaps I struck no blow, she lives perhaps,
my mood could makebelieve: it mocked. O I might think so
To makebelieve my mood was — mock. O I might think so

My heart, where have we been?; what have we seen, my
                    mind?
What blow has Cradock dealt, what done? — A rebellious head
Struck off he has; written on limbs lovely as may be,
Lessons all in red of earnest, of revenge
all in red, lessons of his earnest, his revenge

To makebelieve my mood was — mock. O might think so
But here is, here is a workman after his day's task sweats,
It seems, not well; for still,
Still the scarlet swings and dances on the blade.
Steel, I can scour thee; curtain thee smooth in thy sheath, but
these drops
though wiped once, I am sure. It seems, not well; for still,
wiped once I am sure it was; not well; for still,
would seem,
Still the scarlet swings and dance not well, could seem; for still,
on the blade.

These never, never thrill their blue banks again.
Never, never, never
Shall never, never, never lift their blue banks again.

Thou steel, I can scour thee, in scabbard curtain thee; but these drops
Never, never, never in their blue banks again
steel, I can scour thee, curtain thee in thy scabbard; these drops
never etc

"Then the Greeks° goes and snatches the maiden"

"The Common Fury° of Troy and of the country ~~There~~
There were three Furies and Erinx <he means Erinys>
was one of them and the common one"

Most do not try,° the rest do wrong the scanning of two
common hexameters

"then the Greeks goes and snatches the maiden"

"The Common Fury of Troy and of the country there.
There were three Furies and Erinx [he means Erinys]
was one of them and the common one"

Most do not try, the rest do wrong the scanning of two
common hexameters/

Shew no. 1509

June 23 ~~1884~~ 1878
No. 1537 does the oratio obliqua quite right in Eng. and
monstrously wrong in Latin : ~~how~~ thus "In my own consulship
Ariovistus sought" etc of "Ariovistus in se consule° . . . appetivit."
How is this? ~~. . . . .~~

shew no. 1509

no. 1537 does the oratio obliqua quite right in Eng. and
monstrously wrong in Latin ; thus "In my own consulship
Ariovistus sought "etc" / "Ariovistus in se consule ... appellunt."
How is this?

June 23 1884 1878

spelling 1541

308 ✓✓✓✓✓ Two candidates, girls I think, being asked to give
Caesar's words <u>as spoken</u>° give an extraordinary jargon like
"The of the butcher wife of them the tails with knife off cut":
I suppose they mean it for a word for word rendering of Latin. And
this when they have translated the Latin right

177   fra-   grant   hours°
do ti re la   so re   re do

308 Two candidates, girls I think, being asked to give Caesar's words as spoken give an extraordinary jargon like "the of the Crutcher wife of them the tails with knife off cut"; I suppose they mean it for a word for word rendering of Latin and this when they have translated the Latin right

fra-   great houses
do ti re la so re re do

1676 "ecce trahebatur° passis Priameia virgo crinibus
a templo Cassandra adytisque Minervae". This he translates
"Lo, in the meantime some shepherd was being dragged from the temple
and shrines of Minerva". Then to the qu[estion] "Who is meant by 'Tro-
jaes et patriae communis Erinys'?" answers "Cassandra the vir-
gin daughter of Priam". What is the meaning of this? His Caesar
is mere jargon.

One of them quotes Anthon°

15,20,4 | 1676 "Ecce trahebatur passis Priameia virgo crinibus a templo Cassandra adytisque minervae", this he translates "Lo, in the meantime some shepherd was being dragged from the temple and shrines of minerva". Then to the qu. "Who is meant by "Tro- jae et patriae communis Erinys'?" answers "Cassandra the vir- gin daughter of Priam". What is the meaning of this? His Caesar is mere jargon

One of them quotes Anthon

2 + 4 + 3 + 1   15 + 15 + 5 + 5   176   12
6 + 6 + 6 + 7   0 + 0 + 0   208

4 + 6 + 6 + 3 =   ✗   15 + 10
252   6 + 6 + 6 + 6 + 3 + 3 + 5 + 2   0 + 20
305   10 + 10 +   236
352 212   279   353   15 + 20 20 + 10 + 10   20 + 19 + 5

4 + 6 + 6 + 6 + 8   20 + 20 + 10 + 10
6 + 2 + 4 + 6   4 + 4 + 2   4 + 4 + 5 + 5
7 + 4 + 6 + 6 + 4 = 27 352   20 + 10 + 20

10 + 10 + 5   282   6 + 2 + 6 + 6 + 11
6 + 6 + 4 + 6   20 + 15 + 5   2 + 4 + 9   15 + 20 +   185
98   273   15 + 13 + 9 (217)   45 + 9
22   32   253 293
70   15 + 20 + 10 + 10   18 + 24 =   18 + 8 + 10
83
30   305   148
273   7 + 4 + 4 + 4 + 4   5   10 + 10 +

15 + 10 + 10   Grinamy = Grin
207 199   5 + 10 + 5

6 + 4 + 6 + 2 + 3   6 + 6 + 6 + 6   15 + 10 + 10
197   216   230   153 24
10 + 18 + 10   194   187

① 93   ② 70   ② 4 + 4 + 4 + 3 = 15   ④ 15 + 20 +
⑤ + 12   5 + 0 + 0 4 + 6 + 6 + 6   15 + 20 + 5 + 10   250
5½ +   5½ + 2 + 6 + 6 + 4 + 6   0 + 0 + 0 +
⅔ line + ½ line   4 + 2 + 4 + 6 + 6   15 + 10 + 10
48   5   2 + 4 + 2 + 6   20 + 0 + 5 +   10 + 0 + 10   5

~~quitness~~ "having broken quitness" =
"rupto turbine"°

4   I   2   3, 4 ~~4,3~~ I ~~2~~2   3   4   I, –
O wild west wind,° thou   breath of Autumn's being
              <   f. p.
Do ti do do mi fa   mi do ti do   ti (ta)

7+6+6+2+18   296

15+10+10   5+15   10+10

230

2+2+2

7+7+7+5

391

"having broken quitness" =

quitness   "a rupte turbine   6+2+6+6+10   190
2+6+7+6+1

5
65
15
30
75
180

15+20+10+10   6+7+30

O wild west wind, thou breath of autumn's being
Do ti   do do mi   fa   mi   do ti do ti (ta)

6+2+7+7   5+15+5   5+3+8   200

6+6+6+6+16   15+0+5   15+5+8+10

2+7+2   2+2+6+6+9   159   6
7
18

5+5   251   15+5   6+2+4+6   40
+8

½+   15+20+5   10
183

183
10+0+   2+7+7+6+2   15+5+5   289 150

6+6+6+6+5   20+10+5 268

20+15+20   6+6+6+4+1   132
0+0+   4+7+1 ......   15+15+10   133

2+4+6+6+1   0+0+10+10q   184
7+6+6+6+2

20+0+   2+6+ 6+6   240   315   20+10+15
19+10+10   10   2+4+6+6+3   163/103

0+8   0+20+5   14+0+10+10

2+6+6+6+16   15+20+5   273
4+6   4+4+6+6   20+10+20   275

6+6+6+2+5   5+10+10
6+2+6+6   0+20+5   238   278   15+15+5
+10

What is it a lot of them mean by talking of "Tyndaris" or a
"daughter of Tyndareus" when they shd. say Helen plainly?°

For when thy fold-ing star°   a - ri - ~~sing shows~~ sing shews

                re

re   do   re mi do (do)~~mi~~ mi do ti   la   ti ~~la~~

His pa-ly circ-let, at   his warn – ing lamp

             la   la so

la so la ti ti ~~do~~ ti do re   ~~la~~ ti

The fra-

That slept in flowers the   day

  re re mi do do re ti la la

And many a nymph who wreathes her   wreathes   her

mi re do re re re mi re mi ~~re do~~ mi ti la ti la   do ti mi ti   la ti la

                         ~~ti~~

                        ~~do ti~~

     brows with sedge   ~~la so~~

    # so   la ti do   ti la mi la so la so ~~re~~

                 ~~do ti~~ mi ~~ti la ti~~   ~~la ti la~~ ~~do~~ ~~re~~ re la

And   sheds the fresh - en - ing ~~dew~~   dew and

~~Re~~   ~~mi~~ re mi do la   so

       ~~do~~

re mi re do ti

        ~~so la~~

"What is it a lot of them mean by talking of "Tyndaris" or the "Daughter of Tyndareus" when they shd. say Helen plainly?"

For when thy fold-ing star a ri ~~sing does~~ sing shows
re   do   re   mi do (do mi mi do ti   la ti

His pa-ly circ-let, at his warn-ing lamp
la so la ti ti   la ti do re   la ti

the fra-

That slept in flowers the day
re re mi do do re ti la la

And many a nymph who wreathes Her   wreathes her
mi re do re re re mi re mi re do mi ti la ti la   do ti mi ti la ti la

Crows with sedge
450   la ti do   ti la ti la so la so

And sheds the fresh-en-ing do ta mi ti la ti la ti la fa la   dew and
~~re~~ ~~mi~~ re mi do fa   so
re mi re do ti

se la

10+2+4+4+10+2   100+2+8+8+20+   2+10+6+8+10+30+10+6+6+16+4
8)500   20+8+4+4+4+4+8+8+5+10+2+8+2+10+10+10 = 308
62 ½   31

20+20+5   145   7+6+6+1 20+5
5 25   209   20+5+10   111-121

7+6+6+8   6d|6de   45+6+1   5½
6+7+2+3 = 45+6+1
2+4   103   131
2+4+6+6+7 20+20+10   257   20+5   16
4+2+4   130   2+4+6+6+5   20+5+10   15
10+0+0 206   3+10+5
7+4+6+6+7   20+0+10+10   195 176
4+4+4+4   20+10+10+10   +45   93
4+4+2+9   0+20+10+10   141   19   15+1
2+2+4+2   15+5   152   5+
10+5+8   2+4+6+4
5+   +3
          15+5   0+8   +45
4+4+4   2+4+6+6+5   20+20+10+10
                    296   4+4   225

"dehevellished
hair" = disshe-
velled°

It is odd° that no. 1458, whose paper is good and gets
316 marks out of the 400, being required to trans-
late a speech of Caesar's in or. d̶i̶ recta and then put
                              last
[it] into or. ob. does this ^ both in Eng. and Lat., quite
[rig]ht in Eng., then in Latin makes the very mistakes in
meaning which from the English you wd. say he could
[not], in fact did not make — saying e.g. my and
[ ] suis

158   $7+6+6+4+7=30$

151   $6+4+4+4+6 | 20+5$ 224

$10+/+0$ $\begin{matrix}10\\24\end{matrix}$ 13 $2+6+6$ 205

"dehevellished $\begin{matrix}25\\95\end{matrix}$ 94

hair" = dishsh- $\begin{matrix}10\\224\end{matrix}$ $15+20+10$

velled $20+20+10+10$ $3+3+5$

$6+6+6+2+9$ 261

$6+2+4+2+6$ $0+15+5, 10+20+10$ 5   278 $\begin{matrix}89\\29\end{matrix}$

$2+4$ 20

$+9+$ $18+10+10$ 81 $\begin{matrix}60\\28\\25\end{matrix}$

4 $15+20+10+10$ 219   261

$4+2+2+6+1$

15 $10+5+10$ $15+20+10$ $\begin{matrix}77\\65\end{matrix}$

$10+5$ $\{ 6+6+6+6+14$ 228 $\begin{matrix}28\\15\end{matrix}$

$10+5+10$ 223 $\begin{matrix}200\\229\end{matrix}$

$4+4+4+2+4$ $17+$ $18+$ 321   235

$14+16$ $15+20+5+10$ $4+2+6+6+8$

$+10$ $10+10+$ $8+8+8$ $4+2+1+6$

$+2+10$ $+0+$

$5+0+10$ $13+$ 280

$6+4+6+6+14$ $15+20+10$ 7   251

$20+15+0+10$ $15+10+19$ $4+4+4+4+9$ 316

$18+20+8$ $\begin{matrix}39\\100\end{matrix}$

$7+6+4+6+10$ $20+20+10+10$ $10+20+9$ $\begin{matrix}60\\31\\86\\316\end{matrix}$

It is odd that no. 1458, whose paper is good, and gets 316 marks out of the 400, being required to trans- late a speech of Caesar's in or. directa and then put into or. ob. does this both in Eng. and Lat., quite ht in Eng., then in Latin makes the very mistakes in meaning which from the English you cd. say he could not, in fact did not make — saying e.g. my and suis

‖ I gave no. 1737 31 marks on the frag-
ment of his work sent me which began at "cum Cimbris"°
of q. 5

~~The Re~~ Rd. W. Dixon° ~~born . . . . mat-
riculated at . . . College, Oxford . . . and is now~~ Rector of
Warkworth and Hon. Canon of Carlisle was born . . . . and
matriculated . . . . at . . . Coll., Oxford <no the other way>.
He is engaged on a long and learned Hist. of the Church of

In verse

England, of which ~~3~~ . . . vols. have appeared. ~~As a poet~~ he
published in . . . Christ's Company, in . . . Historic Odes, in
. . . Mano, ~~a & als~~ and in 1884 Odes and Eclogues.
ˣ ~~Mr.~~ Canon D. belongs to the same school as Mr. Wm. Morris°
and the body of writers and ~~illustrators of the~~ artists called Prae-
Raphaelites in their day, some of whom were his personal friends.

early   very

His ^ poems are ^ little known ; but the chance reading of one vol-

won

ume ~~procured~~ for him the friendship of the late D. G. Rossetti,°
a kindred mind.

~~consi~~

ˣ Christ's Company, ~~means~~ is a set of poems on St. Paul, St.
John, St. Mary Magdalen, ~~St. Thomas~~ and so on treated in single
portraits. ˣ The Historic Odes deal with Wellington,° Marlborough,°

of our

~~Flem~~ Sir John ~~Simpson~~ and other ^ national hero~~es~~. ~~These All these~~

Franklin°   ~~Mano All~~ his longest work

ˣ others have been added since   Mano ^ is a romance-epic
                                       in terza rima°: ~~the story~~

... I gave no. 1737   31 marks on the frag-
ment of his work sent me which began at "cum Cimbris"
q q. 5

... Rd V. Dixon born ..., mat
riculated at ... College, Oxford, ... and is now Rector of
Warkworth and Hon. Canon of Carlisle was born .... and
matriculated ..... at ... Coll., Oxford [no the theocracy].
He is engaged on a long and learned hist. of the Church of
England, of which ... vols. have appeared in verse he
published in ... Christ's Company, in ... historic Odes, in
... Mano, and in 1884 Odes and Eclogues.

X Canon D. belongs to the same school as Mr Wm Morris
and the body of writers and illustrators of the artists called Prae-
raphaelites in their day, some of whom were his personal friends
His poems are little known, but the chance reading of one vol-
ume won for him the friendship of the late D.G. Rossetti,
a kindred mind.

X Christ's Company is a set of poems on St Paul, St
John, St Mary Magdalen, St Thomas and so on treated in single
portraits. The historic Odes deal with Wellington, Marlborough,
Sir John Franklin and other national heroes. Mano is a romance — epic
X others have been added since   terza rima: the story

the hero is a Norman knight who died in the year 1000 A. D.: the plot,

the
which is one of ^ deepest and most affecting tragedy, turns upon
this date.

"Graiarum jubarum" "of the Greecian plum" no. 1761°
"spumeus Nereus" "the fomey Nero" ib.

To q. 4d. no. 1772 answers "The daughter of Tyndaris. (I suppose He-
len". He supposes well, but what is the meaning of talking of the daughter of Tyn-
daris? No. 1775 is much stranger about "the Tritronian woman"°

"next Ucalegon° burns (hell)"

the hero is a Norman knight who died in the year 1000 A.D: the plot, which is one of deepest and most affecting tragedy, turns upon this date.

$\int \int \int$ 4,4,4,2 | 20,15,10,10 | $\int \int \int \int$ | 20,15,5 | 247 | $5\frac{1}{2}$ $\int$ | 70,15,20,5 | $\int \int \int$

222   194   214   130

9,5 $\int$ | $\int \int$ 4,4,4 | 15,20,10,10 | $\int \int \int \int \int$ | $\int \int \int \int$ | $\int \int \int$ | $7\frac{1}{2}$

2,2,3,4   20,20,10

2,2,3,2 | 5 | $\int \int \int$ | 15,0,0 | 7,6,6,6,8 | 15,10 | $\int \int \int$ | 4,6,6,1

339

20,5 | $\int \int \int$ | 8,2,6,6,5,8 | $\int \int \int$ | 6,6,4,3,1 | 20,20,5 | $\int \int \int$ | 333

$5\frac{1}{2}$ | $\int \int$ | 4,1,5 | $\int \int \int$ | 4,6,6 | $\int \int \int$ | 4,4,4 | $\int \int \int$

"Graiarum pubarum" "of the Grecian plum" no. 1761

"spumens Nsreus" "the fomey Nero" ib.

$\int \int$ 2,4,6,6 | 20,20,5 | $\int \int \int$ | 2,9 | $\int$ | $\int \int$ | 5,20 | 10,15 | $\int \int$ | 20,15 | $\int \int$ 4,4,6,4

$\int$ | 231 | $\int \int$ | 6,6,6,2 | $\int$ | 258 | $\int \int$ | 2,4 | $\int$ | $\int \int$ | 2,4,4,2 | $\int \int$

5,1,1   222 | 20,18,10   201,194 173 193 168

$\int \int$ | 5,5,15 | $\int \int$ | 1,6,6,6 | $\int \int \int \int$

To g. 4 d. no. 1772 answers "the daughter of Tyndaris. (I suppose Helen". He supposes well, but what is the meaning of talking of the daughter of Tyndaris? no. 1775 is much stranger about "the Tritronian woman"

$\int \int \int \int$ | $\int \int$ | 1,6,6,2 | $\int \int$ | 15,1 | 222 | $\int \int \int$ | $\int \int \int$

$\int$ | 6,2,4,2,8 | $\int \int$ | 20,20 | 312 | $\int \int$ | 6,4,6,6 | 15,20,10,7 | $\int \int$ | 232 | $\int \int$

137   10,0,8 | $\int \int$ | 12,14 | 10,8,10 | 232 | $\int$ | 8,11

75 | 5,4,6,6 | $\int \int \int$ | 10,10 | 249 | 15,20,5 | 142 | 6,4,6,4 | 297

52 | $\int$ | $\int \int$ | 4,4,2,2 | $\int$ | 10,20,4 | $\int \int$

83   159

233

50 | 6,6,6,6,5 | 20,5,5 | $\int \int$ | $5\frac{1}{2}$ | $\int \int$ | 15,10 | $\int \int \int \int$ | 12 | 294

21

43 | $\int \int$ | 6,2,4,5,1 | 15,15,10,10 | $\int$ | 20, | 237 | 6,4,6,6, 18 | 5,10

18 | 10,13,20 | 271 | 2,6,6,2 | 20,20 | 192,194

137 | 20,15,1 | $\int$ | 2,4,6,6, 10 | $\int \int$ | 30 |

92

46

40

38   263

10 | $\int$ | 7,6,7,6,3 | $\int$ | 10,10 | $\int$ | 18 | 261

94

29 | $\int$ | $5\frac{1}{2}$ | 2,6,6,5 | 221

16 | 9,5 | 254 | 223 | 4,6,4,8 | 242 | 63

33

55 "next ucalegon burns (hell)" $5\frac{1}{2}$

20

5.50 | 2,4,2

Earnest,° earthless, equal, attuneable, | vaulty, voluminous, . . stupendous
s   to be   to be
Evening ⸱ strain~~ed~~ ~~into~~ dark, ^ dronedark, | womb-of-all, home-of-
-all, hearse-of- all night ;
⌠lean
The ⌊fond yellow horn ÷ light low with the west and the wild hollow
hoarlight following the height   <us,
Waste, and the earliest stars, earlstars, principal lights, overbend
Fire-featuring heaven
to
Her fond yellow hornlight wound ~~with~~ the west, | her wild hollow
hoarlight hung to the height   <bend us,
Waste and her earliest stars, earlstars, | stars principal over-
Now   ~~he~~   her
Firefeaturing heaven. ~~For~~ earth | her being unbinds; ~~the~~ dapple
                              {has unbound
                    is at an end, a-
                                      ~~lies~~ is
⌠Stray, aswarm, throughther , in throng~~s~~ ; ~~she is~~ self ~~in~~
⌊Stray and aswarm   with her or in her,
                    ~~self~~ steepèd in self ^, ~~quite~~   quite
Dismembering , disremembering all.
—————————
                                        now
Swarm, swarms, throughther , in throng ; ^ self she has ín self steeped
                    ~~of her~~
                    in her; quite (or right)
Dismembering, disremembering all.
—————————

Swarms, swarms, all througher, in throng ; self ín self steepèd
                    and flush ; ⌠quite
                              ⌊right
Dismembering, disremembering all.
—————————

Evening strains to be time's-well, world's pit, womb-of-all,
home-of-all, hearse-of-all night

15

Earnest, earthless, equal, attuneable, vaulty, voluminous, .. stupendous
Evening strainèd to the dark to be dronedark, evenb - of - all, home - of
- all, hearse - of - all night;

lean
Her fond yellow hornlight low with the west and the wild hollow
hoarlight following the height   [us,
Waste, and the earliest stars, earlstars, principal light; overbend
Fire-featuring heaven

Her fond yellow hornlight wound to the west, her wild hollow
hoarlight hung to the height   [read as,
Waste and her earliest stars, earlstars, | stars principal, over-
Fire-featuring heaven. For earth | her being now unbinds; the dapple
                                    is at an end, a-   her unbound

{ Stray, aswarm, through'ther, in throngs; the is self is in
{ stray and aswarm   self steepèd in self, quite in her,
Dismembering, disremembering all.   quite

Swarm, swarms, through'ther, in throng; now self she has in self steeped
                    of her
                    in her; quite (or right)

Dismembering, disremembering all.

_____

Swarm, swarms, all through'her, in throng; self in self steepèd
            and flush; { quite
                         { right
Dismembering, disremembering all.

_____

Evening strains to be time's-well, cold's-pit, womb-of-all,
        home-of-all, hearse-of-all night

Richard Watson Dixon   31

~~3800~~   31

100, 62, 38   50   31

50, 31, 19   <u>19</u>   <u>93</u>

450   961

<u>50</u>

950

Canon D. is engaged on a ~~hi~~ Hist. of the Church of E. on a great scale. In verse he has published—in . . . <u>Christ's Company and other Poems</u> (by the title are meant ~~St. John, Peter, St. Paul, St. John, St. Mary Magdalen, and so on : others,~~ single pieces upon St. ~~Pa~~ St. John, St. Paul, ~~St.~~ Magdalen, and so on: others have been added since) ; in . . . <u>Historic Odes</u> (on Marlborough, Wellington, Sir John Franklin etc) ; in . . . <u>Mano</u> (~~this is a romance-epic in~~ his longest work, a romance-epic in <u>terza rima</u> : Mano is a Norman knight put to death in A. D.

_{most}

1000 and the story, ~~which is one of the deepest and most affectingly tragedy ic,°~~ ~~turns upon this date) ; also in 1884 Odes and Eclogues.~~ ~~one~~ deeply and affectingly tragical, turns upon this date) ; ~~also~~ in 1884, <u>Odes and Eclogues</u>.

Canon D. belongs to the same school as Mr. Wm. Morris and the body ~~of writers and artists called in their day Praeraphaelites, that is (Medievalists), some of them his personal friends~~ (some of them his ~~personal~~ friends) of Medievalist writers and ~~the~~ artists called in their day Praeraphaelites. The chance reading of ~~one~~

_{poems}

~~of his little know almost unknown~~ early ~~pols~~ won for him the friendship of D. G. Rossetti ~~, a kindred mind.~~ . He employs sometimes the archaic style now common but with such a ~~dramatic~~ mastery and

_{most}

dramatic ~~felicity~~ as to justify a practice otherwise vicious. He has been ^

_{happiness}

influenced by Keats and ~~resembles him greatly: his images: his images br brilliant as well as cy and faithfulness of image rivals Keats' own (see the scene of the nine lovers in Love's Consolation ; the image of the heart hair fastened round the heart in Love's Consolation ; the Bride in St. John ; the figure of Joanna in Mano like a balanced tower "which seems for ever ∕~~ his imagery ~~is~~ and description is realised with a brilliancy which rivals Keats' own (see the scene of the nine lovers in <u>Love's Con-</u>

_{of}

solation, the images of the quicksilver and ^ the heart fastened round with hair ~~in the same,~~ ibidem, the Bride in <u>St. John</u>, in <u>Mano</u> the souls in purgatory and the picture of the heroine's ~~like a b~~ figure like a balanced tower "which seems for ever stepping from its place"). This richness of image is combined with a depth and earnestness of feeling which so flushes his work as to ~~affect the~~ give rise to ~~those~~ effects we look for rather from music than from verse. ~~We find a remarkable sequence of~~ To this belongs a remarkable sequence of feeling , seemingly necessary and yet unexpected, ~~by~~ acting often with

_{strokes   e.g.}

magical ~~effect~~ (see ^ in <u>Love's Consolation</u> "Ah God, thy lightnings shd have wakened me three nights before they did", in <u>Mano</u> . . "She wd have answered, underneath the boughs ") . In particular, he is a master of horror (see the dread-

Richard Watson Dixon   31

100 , 62 , 38   380   31
50 , 31 , 19   50   31
                      19   93
                      450   961
                      50
                      950

Canon D. is engaged on a hist. of the Church of E. on a great scale. In verse he has published — in ... Christ's Company and other Poems (by the title are meant St. John, Peter, St. Paul, St. John, St. Mary Magdalen and so on — others, single pieces upon St. ~~Peter~~ St. John, St. Paul, St. Magdalen, and so on: others have been added since); in ... Historic Odes (on Marlborough, Wellington, Sir John Franklin etc); in ... Mano (his longest work, a romance-epic in terza rima : mano is a Norman knight put to death in A.D 1000, and the story, which is one of the deepest and most affectingly tragic, deeply and affectingly tragical, turns upon this date); in 1884 Odes and Eclogues in 1884 Odes and Eclogues.

Canon D. belongs to the same school as Mr. Wm. Morris and the body of painters and artists called in their day Praeraphaelites, that is [medievalists], some of them his personal [friends] (some of them his personal friends) of medievalist critics and of ~~ad~~— ists called in their day Praeraphaelites, the chance reading of one of his little known [early poems] won for him the friendship of D. G. Rossetti, a kindred mind. He employs sometimes the aesthetic style now common but with such a dramatic mastery and dramatic ~~felicity~~ as to justify a practice otherwise vicious. He has been influenced by happiness Keats and resembles him greatly ~~this image~~; his ~~own (see the scene of the nine larks in Love's Consolation~~, the image of the ~~heart~~ hair fastened round the heart in Love's Consolation, the Bride in St John ; the ~~figure of ~~ in mano like a balanced tower "which ~~seems for ever~~ his imagery and description is realised with a brilliance which rivals Keats' own (see the scene of the nine larks in Love's Consolation, the images of the quicksilver and the heart fastened round with hair ~~ to move ~~ in them, the Bride in St John, in mano the souls in purgatory and the picture of the ~~towers like a~~ figure like a balanced tower " which seems for ever stepping from its place "). This richness of image is combined with a depth and earnestness of feeling which so flushes his work as to ~~give rise the~~ give rise to ~~those~~ effects we look for rather from music than from verse. We find a remarkable sequence of to this belongs a remarkable sequence of feeling, seemingly necessary and yet unexpected, ~~by~~ acting often with magical ~~its~~ effect (see in Love's Consolation "ah God, thy lightnings did have wakened me three nights before they did " in mano " she wd have answered underneath the boughs "). In particular he is a master of horror (see the dea—

               words
ful ~~live~~ about the nettles when Mano is on his way to the stake°) and of pathos, in
which ~~few writers~~ it wd. be hard to find his rival. In general we find in his poems

[mathematical calculations]

                                       inexactness
       Agst. these virtues are to be set off a certain ~~looseness~~ of form, some unpleas-
        too   what
ing rhymes, and a ^ common obscurity, ~~of expression~~ between thought and expression,
                                               clue to it
where some ~~underlying~~ deeper meaning is suggested without any decisive ~~clew~~ being left
to the reader ~~by which he can ever to reach~~ : this fault ~~is felt in~~ injures the general
effect of <u>Mano</u>.

—————

     Richard Watson Dixon, now Vicar of Warkworth and Hon. Canon
                                    but   and grandson
of Carlisle, ~~was born at Islington 1833 and educated at~~ is the son ^ of ~~a~~
well known Wesleyan divines, was born at Islington 1833 and educated at
                                           At Oxford
King Edward's School, Birmingham, and Pembroke Coll., Oxford. ~~; where~~ he
became the friend and colleague of Wm. Morris, Burne Jones°, and others of the
so-called Praeraphaelite or Mediaevalist school, to which as a poet he be-
                                    also
longs. The chance reading of one of his early volumes ^ won for him the friendship
of the late D. G. Rossetti. <He has been twice married.>
     He is engaged on a hist. of the Church of E. on a great scale <, of which 3
                                       in
vols. have appeared>. ~~A~~ In verse he has published ~~in~~ : ^ 1859 <u>Christ's Com-</u>
                    by
<u>pany and other Poems</u> (^ the title are meant single pieces on St. John, St. Paul,
                                  since
St. Mary Magdalen, and so on : others have been ^ added) ; in 1863 <u>Historic-</u>
<u>al Odes</u> (on Marlborough, Wellington, Sir John Franklin etc) ; in 1883 <u>Mano</u>
(his greatest work, a romance-epic in <u>terza rima</u> : Mano is a Norman
knight put to death A. D. 1000 and the story deeply and ~~affectively~~ingly tragical,
          upon the
turns ~~on this~~ date) ; in 1884 <u>Odes and Eclogues.</u>
     In Canon Dixon's poems we find a deep thoughtfulness and earnestness
                m   ever
and a mind ~~most keenly~~ alive to the pathos of human life, of which <u>Mano</u> is
                              likeness
~~as~~ in a single but a typical case, the faithful ~~picture~~ ; noble but never highflown,
sad without ~~straining or clamour~~ noise or straining ; everything as it most ~~comes~~
~~home to and hits~~ reaches and comes home to man's heart. He is a master of
horror (see Mano's ~~ghastly~~ words about the nettles on his way to the stake) and
of pathos; so much so that here it wd. be hard to find his rival.
            He
     ~~His muse has be~~ owes most to Keats,° and his description and imagery
is realised with a brilliancy not less than Keats' own (see the scene of the nine
lovers in <u>Love's Consolation</u> ; the images of the quicksilver and of the heart fast-
ened round with hair ibidem ; the Bride in <u>St. John</u> ; in Mano the vision of purga-
tory and the fisherman, and the ~~portrait of the~~ picture of the heroine's figure like a
balanced tower "which seems for ever stepping from its place"). This richness of
image ~~being combin~~ matched with the deep feeling which flushes his work through-
out gives rise to effects we look for rather from music than from verse. And
       is, as in music,
there ^ a ~~remarkable~~ sequence, ~~of feelin~~ seemingly necessary and yet unforeseen,
of ~~this~~ feeling, acting often with magical strokes (see e.g. in <u>Love's Consola-</u>
<u>tion</u> "Ah God, thy lightnings . . . did" ; in <u>Mano</u> "The wd . . . boughs").
     He is faulty by a certain inexactness of form ; some unpleasing rhymes ; and°

...all the nettles when Mano is on his way to the stake) and of pathos, in which ... it wd. be hard to find his rival. In general we find in his poems

$$\frac{100}{62} = 62 \quad \frac{62}{37^{?}} \quad \frac{100}{62 \times 62} = \frac{1}{x} \Big/ \frac{62^2}{100} = x \Big/ \frac{3844}{100} = x$$

$$x = 38 \qquad 38\frac{44}{100} \qquad 3844 \qquad 62$$

Apol these virtues are to be set off a certain inexactness of form, some unpleasing rhymes, and a common obscurity, of expression, between thought and expression, where some underlying deeper meaning is suggested without any decisive ... clearly left to the reader by which ... ... to reach: this fault is ... ... injures the general effect of Mano

Richard Watson Dixon, now Vicar of Warkworth and Hon Canon of Carlisle, was born at Islington 1833 and educated ... the son of a and grandson wellknown Wesleyan divine, was born at Islington 1833 and educated at King Edward's School, Birmingham, and Pembroke Coll., Oxford. ... ... he became the friend and colleague of Wm. Morris, Burne Jones, and others of the so called Praeraphaelite or Mediaevalist school, to which as a poet he belongs. The chance reading of one of his early volumes won for him also the friendship of the late D. G. Rossetti. [He has been twice married.]

He is engaged on a hist. of the Church of E. on a great scale [of which 3 vols. have appeared]. In verse he has published in: 1859 Christ's Company and other Poems ("in the title are meant single pieces on St. John, St. Paul, St. Mary Magdalen, and so on; others have been since added); in 1863 Historical Odes (on Marlborough, Wellington, Sir John Franklin etc); in 1883 Mano (his greatest work, a romance-epic in terza rima: Mano is a Norman knight put to death A.D. 1000 and the story, deeply and affectingly tragical, turns upon this date); in 1884 Odes and Eclogues.

In Canon Dixon's poems we find a deep thoughtfulness and earnestness and a mind ... alive to the pathos of human life, of which Mano is as in a single but a typical case, the faithful picture; noble but never highflown, sad without straining ..., noble or straining; everything as it most comes home to ... reaches and comes home to man's heart. He is a master of horror (see Mano's ... words about the nettles on his way to the stake) and of pathos; so much so that here it wd. be hard to find his rival.

His ... ... he owes most to Keats, and his description and imagery is realised with a brilliancy not less than Keats' own (see the scene of the nine lovers in Love's Consolation; the imagery of the quicksilver and of the heart fastened round with hair ibidem; the Bride in St John; in Mano the vision of purgatory and the fisherman, and the picture of the heroine's figure like a balanced tower "which seems for ever stepping from its place"). This richness of image ... matched with the deep feeling which flushes his work through and ... gives rise to effects we look for rather from music than from verse. And those is, as in music ... sequence, of ... seemingly necessary and yet unforeseen, of ... feeling, acting often with magical stroke (see e. g. in Love's Consolation "ah god thy lightnings ... did"; in Mano "The id ... boughs").

He is faulty by a certain inexactness of form; some unpleasing rhymes, and

"saevit tridenti" / "wages which his trident"°

3, 4, 5

20, 0/208

1, 2, 4, 9, 11, 22

10, 5, 3

10, 0

5, 15, 10

0, 0

5½

328

5½

4, 6, 6, 6

207

210

10, 15, 5

10, 0/208   10, 0, 8   137   139   201

5½   65

250   147

9   146

92
28
15
60
90
25
3/8

10, 5, 5

20, 15, 15/287

117   27   218/18   258

172

312   311

6   269   8   50, 199

12   10, 190

85   84
25   23
15   15
63   15
35

90
34
10
75
100
10

"salient trident" / "wages with his trident"

2, 6, 6, 6, +

317

5   7, 3   194

8   205   253

17   2

2, 7, 6

279

2, 2, 6, 6, 17   241   5½

153

223
80   83
17   11
35   15
58   78
10   15

328

137   128   278

35 +

10, 0

10, 15, 0   142   22   12

134

12   18

292

12   44   5½

254

2, 6, 4, 4   20, 15, 20

296

256

223   20, 0, 18

20

78
16
30   29
75   35
55   65
254   253

10

9   5½

296   236

12   128

60

20, 242

242

[*Canon Dixon cont'd*]
     We find also the very ~~g~~ rare gift of pure imagination, such as Coleridge° had
        song
(see the ~~lyrics~~ Fallen Rain and the one on the sky wooing the river). But he is
likest and owes most to Keats and ~~etc~~ his description and imagery is realised with a
truth and point not less that K's. own .

---

by an obscurity, what between thought and expression, ~~which s~~ where some deep-
er meaning behind the text is suggested, without any decisive clue to it being
left to the reader. He ~~employs~~ sometimes employs the archaic style now common,
but with such a mastery and dramatic happiness as justify a practice otherwise
vicious.

     To read° a good deal of Plautus and Terence.° Good editions of
these. Ask Mr. Tyrrell°
     Wordworth's° Early Latin
     Has Madvig° edited Livy?
     Ency. Brit.° on Music, Mythology, ~~Elect. Newle~~

     Athenaeums at Royal Irish Academy°
     Lucan's Pharsalia°
     Sir Robert Stewart's ~~art~~ lectures°
     Dr. Gunn's books°
     Irish History ~~and~~
     Gibbon°

[page begins with lines of handwritten musical/shorthand notation interspersed with numbers: 238, 51, 12, 15, 20, 10, 244, 17, 117, 27, 119, 4,6,6,8, 10,5,10, 10,13,10, 378, 134, 10,5,5, 223, 5½, 189, 200, 12, 83, 89, 10, 19, 12, 203, 198, 152, 50, 18, 70, 25, 20,0, 272, 20, 58, 233900, 22,23, 520, 5½, 20,5, 15, 260]

We find also the very rare gift of pure imagination, such as Coleridge had (see the Fallen Rain and the one on the sky crossing the river). But here latest and owes most to Keats and etc his description and imagery is realized with a truth as point noticed than his own. ... of an obscurity, what between thought and expression, where some deep or meaning behind the text is suggested, without any decisive clue to it being left to the reader. He sometimes employs the archaic style now common, but with such a mastery and dramatic happiness as justify a practice otherwise vicious.

To read a good deal of Plautus and Terence. Good editions of these. Ask Mr. Tyrrell.

Wordsworth's Early Latin

Has Madvig edited Livy?

Encyc. Brit. on Music, Mythology, ~~Stock~~ Newle

Athenaeums at Royal Irish Academy

Lucan's Pharsalia

Sir Robert Stewart's ~~and~~ lectures

Dr. Gunn's books

Irish History ~~and~~

Gibbon

↓ ↓ ↓ ↓ ↓ ↓

~~ἐκ σέθεν°~~ · ζώ | ~~ει δὲ~~ ~~πάσσον~~ μάσσων | ὄλβος ὀπι | ~~ξομένων, πλαγί~~ | ~~αις~~
~~δὲ φρένεσσιν~~

↓ ↓ ↓ ↓ ↓ ↓

ἐκ σέθεν · ζώ | ει δὲ μάσσ~~ον~~ων | ὄλβος ὀπι | ξομένων, πλαγί ‖ ~~αις~~ –

↓ ↓ ↓ ↓ ↓ ↓

ʳ ʳ αις | δὲ φρένεσσιν ‖ (= -αις ~~δε~~ δὲ φρένεσσιν

musical

By the ^ Doric scansion 2/3 of a bar are wanting, but by the verse scan-
sion the whole verse or line is ~~4 + 2 = 6~~ 4 (in Doric 3 time)
+2 (in 2 time)

ἱπποδρομί | α κρατέων ‖ · ʳ ἀνδρῶν | δ᾽ἀρετὰν ‖ ④
↑ ↑ ↑ ↑ ↑ ↑
                                                    } ⑥
σύμφυτον οὐ | κατελέγχει ‖ . ~~⑥~~ ②
↑ ↑ ↑ ↑

ἴστε μὰν Κλε | ωνύμου ‖ . ②
↑ ↑ ↑ ↑
                                    } ④
δό | ξαν παλαιὰν | ἅρμασιν · ‖ ②
   ↑ ↑ ↑ ↑

καὶ | ματρόθε Λαβ | δακίδαισιν | σύννομοι πλού | του · διέστει | χον
     ↑ ↑ ↑ ↑ ↑ ↑ ↑

τετραορι | ᾶν πόνοις ╫ ʳ ‖ ⑥
         ↑ ↑ ↑

αἰὼν δὲ κυλινδομέναις | ἀμέραις ἄλλ᾽ | ἄλλοτ᾽ ἐξάλ ‖ λαξ~~εν~~εν.
↑↑ ↑ ↑ ↑ ↑ ↑

ἅτρω | τόι γε ╫ μὰν παῖ | δες θεῶν. ʳ | ʳ ʳ ʳ ‖ ⑧
↑ ↑ ↑ ↑ ↑

123

ἐκ θεοῦ· ζώει δὲ μάσσων ὄλβος ὀπιζομένων, πλαγίαις
δὲ φρένεσσιν

ἐκ θεοῦ· ζώει δὲ μάσσων ὄλβος ὀπιζομένων πλαγί —
ρ ρ αις | δὲ φρένεσσιν || (= -αις δὲ δὲ φρένεσσιν

musical
By the Doric reantion ⅔ of a bar are wanting, but by the verse scan-
sion the whole verse or line is 4 + 2 = 6 4 (in Doric 3 time)
+ 2 (in 2 time)

ἱπποδρομίας κρατέων ρ ἀνδρῶν | δ' ἀρετὰν || ④ } ⑥
σύμφυτον οὐ | κατελέγχει. || ⊗ ②

ἴστε μὰν Κλεωνύμου || ② } ④
δόξαν παλαιὰν | ἅρμασιν. || ②

καὶ | ματρόθε Λαβδακίδαισιν | σύννομοι πλούτου διέστειχον
τετραοριᾶν πόνοις ρ || ⑥

αἰὼν δὲ κυλινδομέναις | ἁμέραις ἄλλ' ἄλλοτ' ἐξάλλαξεν.
ἄτρωτοί γε μὰν παῖδες θεῶν. ρ | ρ ρ ρ || ⑧

So also   ἄξιος εὐ | λογίαις ἀ | στῶν μεμῖχθαι ‖ may also be read, for

verse ;   ἄξιος εὐ | λογίαις ⧺ ˙ ‖ ἀ⊣ ἀ | στῶν μεμῖχθαι ‖

and the next line likewise ; that is 2 in 3 time + 2 in 2 time = 4

            down drove   ~~over~~ down,
   πλούτου διέστειχον / they made their way ~~through,~~ ^ the dangerous road
     without taking harm   all by
of wealth ~~unharmed,~~   ~~by~~ their labours in the chariot race. There is the thought
of wealth on both sides, father's and mother's, having its own dangers,
envious rivals, and so on, as if ~~an~~ in ambush on both sides ; hence

                time   them
ἄτρωτοι. Then there follows an obscure thought of ^ swaying ^ from side to
side, but no harm coming. The thought refers back to the first lines of the
ode. σύννομοι | as if their horses fed like Abraham's and Lot's° in adjoining
pastures.°
  ~~ὦ Μελισσ᾽, εὐμαχανίαν γαρ ἔφανᾶς (Μ Υ) (γ) Ισθμίοις ?~~
~~There is however~~
  ~~ἔν τ᾽ Ἀδραστείοις ἀέθλοις Σικυῶνός ὤπασεν°~~

                 ΄U U ˝
But though the above will not do it shews another thing,° that UU — U
Ú U ˝ — easily becomes Ú U ˝ U as ΄ U – – becomes ΄ U ΄ U
  θάλλοντες echoes 10. above. In this strophe the images are from
the race, — διώκειν, διέρχονται . . τέλος. Then it changes to sailing:
this is common.°
    εἴ τις ἀν – δρᾶν εὐ – τυ – χή – σαις ἢ σὺν εὐ – δό – ξοις ἀ – έ – θλοις

                    ~~la~~
  Re° do re   fa   re   do   re   la   la so la   re   re   do ~~re~~ re
                     so

  Images° in θάλλειν ⁜ ° βάσσαισιν ⧺ . . στεφάνους, νάπᾳ, θάλ-
λοντες, φοινικέοισιν ἄνθησεν ῥόδοις , φύλλ᾽ ἀοιδῶν

  πλαγίαις° φρένεσσιν, διέστειχον, κυλινδομέναις ἀμέραις etc, εὐμα-
χανίαν, διέρχονται, ἄλλοτε δ᾽ἄλλος, ποικίλων μηνῶν, γέφυραν
ποντιάδα, καμπύλον δίφρον, τέχνα καταμάρψαισα, ἔρνει Τελεσι-
άδα
   αὐτοῦ   ~~the hero's~~
 ^πᾶσαν ὀρθώσαις ἀρετὰν κατὰ ῥάβδον means laid out ~~his~~ his
    name   like his corpse
noble ~~corpse when~~ (convulsed ~~and~~ about the fatal sword) straight
   minstrel's
as his ^ wand ~~of song~~ and left it for later bards to build round
with monuments of song. Then follows image of a pyre, its beams

so also ἄξιος εὐλογίαις ἀστῶν μεμῖχθαι ‖ may also be read, for

verse ; ἄξιος εὐλογίαις ‖ ρ ‖ ἀστῶν | μεμῖχθαι ‖

and the next line likewise ; that is 2 in 3 time + 2 in 2 time = 4

Πλοῦτον διέσταχον [they made their way through, drove down, the dangerous road of wealth untraced, by their labours in the chariot race. there is the thought of wealth on both sides, father's and mother's, having its own dangers, envious rivals, and so on ; as if as in ambush on both sides ; hence ἄστρωτοι. then there follows an obscure thought of swaying from side to side, but no harm coming. The thought refers back to the first lines of the ode. σύννομοι [as if their horses fed like Abraham's and Lot's in adjoining pastures. ὦ Μέλεο, εὐμαχανία γὰρ ἔφανας [✗] [γ] Ἰσθμίοις

There is however
ἐν τ' Ἀφροδισίοις ἀέθλοις Σικυωνίας ὠπάδει
But though the above will not do it shews another thing, that ◡◡‖—
◡◡‖— easily becomes ◡◡‖◡ as ⌐◡‖— becomes —◡—◡

θάλλοντες echoes 10 above. In this strophe the images are from the race, — διώκειν, διέχονται .. τέλος. Then it changes to sailing : this is common

εἰ τις ἀπ'αρχᾶς εὖ τι χϊρ ἄεις ἢ οὐκ εὖ-δό-ξοις ἀ-ε-θλοις
Re do te fa re do te la la so la re re do re ge

Images in θάλλειν ≠ βέβαιον ✗ .. στεφάνους, νίκη, θάλλοντες, φοινικέοισιν ἄνθεσιν ῥόδοις, φϋλλ ᾿ἀιδῶν

πλαγίαις φρένεσσιν, διέσταχον, κυλινδομέναις ἁμέραις etc, εὐμαχανίαν, διέχονται, ἄλλοτε δ᾿ ἄλλος, ποικίλων μηνῶν, γέφυραι ποντιάδα καμπύλον δίφρον, τέχνα κατηγόρφανσα, ἄρχνει τελευτάσθα

ἀστῶν
πᾶσαν ὀρθώσαις ἀρετὰν κατὰ ἔξοδον means laid out (consulted like his, corrupt about the fatal sword) staight and left it for later hands to build round with monuments of song . then follows image of a pyre, its being

spreading° like those of a setting sun ~~and~~ (ἀκτὶς . . ϲ ἄσβεστος ,
ἅψαι πυρσὸν ὕμνων)
     θηρῶν shd. not be corrected : it supports the mention of two beasts
or three°

     Year 68° end . Nominal beginning of work A. D. 69
     Mutuis Cladibus prob. refers to Decebalus' victory over Domitian
and Trajan's over Decebalus
     Nero died in what ~~mn~~ month? outside ~~mom~~ Rome
     Galba came from Spain through Gaul
     War with the Albanians, Caucasian race, north of Armen-
ia, which was disputed by the Persians
     Nymphidius Sabinus° praet. praef. said he was Caligula's
natural son, tried to seize the throne on Nero's death, but was
put to death

     Galliae so Britanniae, not to speak of the Hispaniae, Moe-
siae etc and now the Russias and two ~~Sci~~ Sicilies°
     Tanquam° common of accusations
     Verginius Rufus interesting man , defeated Vindex, twice
~~or thrice~~ refused the empire under Nero, a third time after O-
tho's death , thrice consul, paneg[yric]. pronounced by Tacitus,° lived
to a great age in great honour
     Regimen etc : correct this°
     Consularis°
                              ly
     Dum° / usual^ present indic. even in or. ob., but subj. in
sense of till such ~~as~~ time as : so antequam juberentur / before
they were in the position of being ordered
     Provinces°—not governed as ours by Provincials, why : be-
cause the original meaning or idea being a charge, commission (per-
haps provincia, which is said in some MSS to be found provintia s
but ? all turns on this—= providentia) the nature of ~~the~~ offices
would vary with that of the work and Provincial wd. have only a
logical ~~gr~~ applicability : still the jurists did need such a word
and so said Praeses
     Senatorial (peaceful) and imperatorial (military), provs. not
                                   procurators
governed by proconsuls and ~~propraetors~~ respectively but ~~by varying~~
          almost
~~officers ^ indiscriminately ; the first by proconsuls, propraetors~~

spreading like those of a setting sun ~~and~~ (ἀκτῖς... ἐπ' λοββεδτοσ, ἐλαφαὶ πτερὰν ὑρανῷ)

Ὄγραν &c. not be corrected : it supports the mention of two leagues or three

Year 68 end. nominal beginning of work A.D. 69

Mutuis cladibus prob. refers to Decebalus' victory over Domitian and Trajan's over Decebalus

Nero died in what month? outside ~~was~~ Rome
Galba came from Spain through Gaul
War with the Albanians, Caucasian race, north of Armenia, which was disputed by the Persians

Nymphidius Sabinus praet. praef. said he was Caligula's natural son, tried to seize the throne on Nero's death, but was put to death

Galliae so Britanniae, not to speak of the Hispaniae, Moesiae etc and now the Russias and two ~~the~~ Sicilies

tanquam common of accusations

Verginius Rufus interesting man, defeated Vindex, twice or ~~thrice~~ refused the empire under Nero, a third time after Otho's death, thrice consul, paneg. pronounced by Tacitus, lived to a great age in great honours

Regimen etc : correct this
Consularis
Dum / usually present indic. even in or. ob., but subj. in sense of till such a time as : so antequam juberentur / before they were in the position of being ordered

Provinces — not governed as ours by Provincials, why : because the original meaning or idea being a charge, commission (perhaps provincia, which is said in some MSS to befriend provintia but? all turns on this _ = providentia) the nature of the offices would vary with that of the work and Provincial wd. have only a logical & applicability : still the jurists did need such a word and so said Praeses

senatorial (peaceful) and imperatorial (military) provs. not governed by proconsuls and ~~procurators~~ respectively : but byways ~~officers indiscriminately~~ the first by proconsuls, propraetors

the senatorial by <u>consulares</u> and <u>praetorians</u> both called <u>pro-</u>
<u>consuls</u>, the Caesarian by the emp. as <u>proconsul</u> and under him
<u>legati Caesaris</u> ranking as praetorians. The proconsuls had <u>quaes-</u>
<u>tors</u>, the legates <u>procurators</u>. Some prov. however ~~ha~~ gov[erne]d by pro-
curators (who were knights or freemen). The matter complicated

 <u>Inchoavere</u>°
 <u>Ultimum, supremum</u>°

 <u>Rubellius Plautus</u> son of R. Blandus, descended from Drusus
and nominally from Augustus, of splendid birth therefore, though
retiring and harmless, banished, then murdered by Nero
                Scribonia
 <u>Piso</u> descended from Crassus the triumvir and by his mother ^
        family
from Pompey, of splendid ~~birth~~, the Pisos (plebeian) being one
      Two of his   put to death
of the very first houses of the state. ~~His~~ ^ three brothers ~~murdered~~ by
~~different emperors~~ Claudius and Nero, the other once had the offer
of the empire
       and ordinary   ward-law"
 <u>Lege curiata</u> : this was private ^ adoption " by ~~law of word~~ ,
at the wardmate—translating <u>curia</u> by <u>ward</u>. But the ceremo-
ny here was ~~public election before the people as an army~~ clearly
something different : see cap. 18 §3. It took place nevertheless ap
~~em~~ <u>comitia</u> as appears ibid., ~~for a mere announcement need not~~
~~have been put off~~ unless the word is used loosely. There must
have been some military form of adoption, I shd. think°

 <u>Dein generum</u>° Agrippam : meaning?

 "Pessimum veri affectus venenum sua cuique utilitas" prob.
~~means~~ explained by "sine affectu peragitur" below, <u>that</u> ~~fatal~~ poison
       loyalty's truth or   turns
~~to all~~ fatal to ~~all~~ true loyalty^, which perverts it ~~makes~~ it into
a poisonous instead of a wholesome thing : the poison acts on
the flattered rather than the flatterer or just on the flatterer,
then infects (like a disease, a virus, not a poison proper) the
flattered°

the senatorial by consulars and praetorians both called pro-
consuls, the Caesarian by the emp. as proconsul and under him
legati Caesaris ranking as praetorians. The proconsuls had quaes-
tors, the legates procurators. Some prov. however he gov'd by pro-
curators (who were knights or freemen). The matter complicated

Inchoavere

Ultimum, supremum

Rubellius Plautus son of R. Blandus, descended from Drusus
and nominally from Augustus, of splendid birth therefore, though
retiring and harmless, banished, then murdered by Nero

Piso descended from Crassus the triumvir and by his mother Scribonia
from Pompey, of splendid family birth, the Pisos (plebeian) being one
of the very first houses of the state. Three of his brothers put to death by
different emperors Claudius and Nero, the other once had the offer
of the empire

Lege curiata: this was private and ordinary adoption "by ward-law",
at the wardmote — translating curia by ward. But the ceremo-
ny here was before the people as an army clearly
something different: see cap. 18 §3. It took place nevertheless as
comitia as appears did, unless the word is used loosely there must
have been some military form of adoption, I sh'd. think

Dein venerum Agrippam; meaning?

"Pessimum veri affectus venenum sua cuique utilitas" prol,
explained by "sine affectu peragitur" below, that fatal poison
fatal to loyalty's truth or true loyalty, which prevents it it as
a poisoning instead of a wholesome thing: the poison acts on
the flattered rather than the flatterer or first on the flatterer,
then infects (like a disease, a virus, not a poison proper) the
flattered

Sestertius° = semis tertius = 1 + 1 + ½ , written HS = as + as +

duodeci-
semis, written 11S or HS . It represents a combination of the ~~deci~~
mal (the as divided into 12 parts) and ~~denarius~~ decimal (denarius =

systems
10 asses) ^. It is then the ~~fourt~~ ¼ denarius and this value it kept
in spite of its name when the as was reduced from 1/10 to 1/16 of the

the   one founded
denarius (which is ~~a further~~ introduction of another , ~~the act~~ system, ^ of the
powers of 2)

1000 sestertii called sestertium, perhaps, but not certainly, a mis-
taking of sestertium = sestertiorum in mille sestertium and after-
wards used as a substantive and declined, genitive sestert~~ui~~ii etc

Nummus = sestertius. Therefore taking a sesterce or quarter
frank at 2 ~~d.~~ 1/8 d. the 100 ~~ste~~ sesterces ~~api wd.~~ apiece to the
soldiers on guard wd. be 225 d. = 18s. 9d.

Bis et vicies millies sestertium = 22,000 sestertium = 22,
000 (100,000) sesterces = 2,200,000,000 sesterces = 2,200,000
sestertia = 2,200,000 (£4 ¾) = £10,450,000, say 10 million ~~and ½~~

Sestertium = 1000 sestertii = 2 1/8 d. (1000) = £4 13s. 9d., say
£4 14s., say £4 15s. = £4 ¾

↳and a half

But take the sestertius for 2d. Then 100 sesterces = 16s. 8d. and
the sestertium or 1000 sesterces = £8 6s. 8d.

Bis et vicies millies sestertium = 22,000 sestertium = 22,000 (100,000)
sestertii or sesterces = 2,200,000,000 sesterces = 2,200,000 sestertia —
2,200,000 (£6s. 8d.) = £17,600,000 + (13,200,00 s. = ~~6,600~~
660,000 ~~£ £~~) # + (17,600,000 d. = 1,465,000 ~~d.~~ s. = 73,250 £)
= ~~30,873,250 £~~ £18,333,250

Temple of Apollo° said to be west of Palatine, nearer Tiber. Tiberius'
house on or near Palatine. Velabrum south at foot of Aventine. The
milestone was at one end of the Forum Rom.

s   agebat
Stationem etc. / was ~~the~~ on duty.° Two cohorts of the Praet. guards,
one on duty at the Palatine, the other at the camp and a ~~Ti~~ Tri-
bune with each

Cohort tenth part of legion always; varied therefore with le-
gion. But independent of legion, as with the Pretorian guards, it
is = battalion. The pretorian cohorts were 1000 strong each

Sestertius = semis tertius = $1+1+\frac{1}{2}$, written ~~IIS~~ = as + as + semis, written IIS or HS. It represents a combination of the ~~decus~~ duodeci= mal (the as divided into 12 parts) and ~~denarius~~ decimal (denarius = 10 asses) systems. It is then the ~~fourth~~ $\frac{1}{4}$ denarius and this value it kept in spite of its name when the as was reduced from $\frac{1}{10}$ to $\frac{1}{16}$ of the denarius (which is ~~a further~~ the introduction of another, the ~~as~~ ~~one fourth~~ system of the powers of 2)

1000 $\underline{sestertii}$ called $\underline{sestertium}$, perhaps, but not certainly, a mis-taking of $\underline{sestertium}$ = $\underline{sestertiorum}$ in mille sestertium and after-wards used as a substantive and declined, genitive sestertiii etc

Nummus = sestertius. Therefore taking a sesterce or quarter franc at $2\frac{1}{8}$ d., the 100 ~~the~~ sesterces ~~apiece~~ apiece to the soldiers on guard a.d. be 225 d. = 18 s. 9d.

Bis et vicies millies sestertium = 22,000 sestertium = 22,000 (100,000) sesterces = 2,200,000,000 sesterces = 2,200,000 sestertia = 2,200,000 ($£ 4\frac{3}{4}$) = £ 10,450,000, say 10 millions ~~and $\frac{1}{2}$~~

Sestertium = 1000 sestertii = $2\frac{1}{8}$ d. (1000) = £ 4 13s. 9d., say £ 4 14s., say £ 4 15s. = $£ 4\frac{3}{4}$

~~$\frac{1}{2}$~~ and a half

But take the sestertius for 2d, then 100 sesterces = 16s. 8d, and ~~the~~ sestertium or 1000 sesterces = £ 8 6s. 8d.

Bis et vicies millies sestertium = 22,000 sestertium = 22,000 (100,000) sestertii or sesterces = 2,200,000,000 sesterces = 2,200,000 sestertia = 2,200,000 (£ 8 6s. 8d.) = £ 17,600,000 + (13,200,00 s. = ~~6,600~~ 660,000 ~~s~~ £) + (17,600,000 d. = 1,465,000 s. = 73.250 £) = ~~22,873,250~~ £ 18,333,250

Temple of Apollo said to be west of Palatine, nearer Tiber. Tiberius' house on or near Palatine. Velabrum south at foot of Aventine. The milestone was at one end of the Forum Rom.

Stationem ~~etc~~, ~~has~~ ~~to~~ relief, on duty. Two cohorts of the praet. guards one on duty at the Palatine, the other at the camp and a ~~for~~ Tri-bune with each

$\underline{Cohort}$ tenth part of legion always; varied therefore with le-gion. But independent of legion, as with the praetorian guards, it is = battalion. The praetorian cohorts were 1000 strong each

Hick	1	2	3	4	
Hickson°	25	22	14	0	61
Bowden	25	15	22	0	62
MacWeeney	24	20	24	25	93
Maher	24	24	24	24	96
Kennedy	24	20	23	23	90
Lynch	13	17	19	0	39
MacKendry	0	0	0	10	10
Young	25	18	22	20	85

St. Cecily° — Praise God for her martyrdom
She told Valerian he cd. not see the angel till he was baptised.
Beati mundo corde, quoniam ipsi Deum videbunt, God and the things
of God.° The heart is what rises towards good, shrinks from evil, recog-
nising the good or the evil first by some eye of its own. We ought to
look to God first in everything, to seek first the kingdom of God and
his justice, his rightness, to be right with God and kin God to be
king or first principle, ἀρχήν in us. Pray for this more, in matters of
interest, of pleasure, and of of will. Ask St. Cecily's help

and the whole body 10,000 strong there were 10 of them, so
the whole body of Pretorians was 10,000 strong : Vitellius made
them 16,000 strong. They were raised in Italy, later from the home
provinces, last from the legionary l frontier provinces

Chapter + 61—Poeninis jugis : Pe Poenine or Pennine Alps° those
the highest, including Mt. Blanc and Monte Rosa, south of Geneva
and Switzerland and north of Savoy : the chief pass Mt. St. Be the
Gt. St. Bernard. Pennine possibly but not at all certainly a Celtic
word (Welsh penn , Irish ceann). No conn. prob. with Apennines, which
name is mostly taken from penn too, for who how comes the a there?
Cottian Alps between Dauphiny and Piedmont, lower. Highest pk.
Mont Genèvre

Trecenos sestertios = 600 d. = 50s. = 210 or tricenos =
60d. = 5s.

Hickson	1	2	3	4	20
	25	22	14	0	61
Bowden	25	15	22	0	62
MacWeeney	24	20	24	25	93
Maher	24	24	24	24	96
Kennedy	24	20	23	23	90
Lynch	13	17	19	0	39
MacKendry	0	0	0	10	10
Young	25	18	22	20	85

St. Cecily — Praise God for her martyrdom
She told Valerian he cd. not see the angel till he was baptised.
Beati mundo corde, quoniam ipsi Deum videbunt, God and the things
of God. The heart is what rises toward good, shrinks from evil, recog-
nising the good or the evil first (by some eye of its own). We ought to
look to God first in everything, to seek first the kingdom of God and
his justice, his rightness, to be right with God and ~~his~~ God to be
king or first principle, ἐν χϕν in us. Pray for this most, in matters of
interest, of pleasure, and of will. Ask St. Cecily's help

and ~~the whole body 10000 strong~~ there were 10 of them, so
the whole body of Praetorians was 10,000 strong. Vitellius made
them 16,000 strong. They were raised in Italy, later from the home
provinces, last from the ~~frequency~~ frontier provinces

Chapter 61 — Poeninus jugis : ~~the~~ Poenine or Pennine alps ~~these~~
the highest, including Mt. Blanc and Monte Rosa, south of Geneva
and Switzerland and north of Savoy ; the chief pass ~~not St.~~ Bes the
Gt. St. Bernard. Pennine possibly but not at all certainly a Celtic
word (welsh penn, Irish ceann). No conn. prob. with apennines, which
name is rashly taken from penn too, (or ~~how~~ how comes the a there?)

Cottian Alps between Dauphiny and Piedmont, lower. Highest pk.
Mont Genèvre

Trecenos sestertios = 600 d. = 50 s. = £2 10s, or trecenos =
60 d. = 5 s.

Earnest,° earthless, equal, attuneable, vaulty, voluminous, . . . stupen-
dous
Evening strains to be time's den, world's self, womb-of-all, home-of-
-all, hearse-of-all night.
Her fŏnd yellowy hornlight wound to the west, ~~and~~ her w̃ild willowy
hoarlight hung to the height
Waste ; her earliest stars, earlstars, stars principal, overbend us,
Firefeaturing heaven. And earth her being unbinds ; her dapple
is at an end—a-
Stray, aswarm, all throughther, in throngs ; self ín self steepèd
and stilled ; flush ; quite
Disremembering, dismembering all
⌠ and flush—fast ; quite
⌡   ⌠her being has unpenned ;
Firefeaturing heaven. For earth ⌊unpenned her being ; her
dapple's at an end — a-
Stray or aswarm, all throughther, in throng ; self ín self
steepèd and pashed — flush ; quite
Disremembering, dismembering all. My heart rounds me right
⌠Then : Evening is here one us, over us ; our night whelms,
⌡   whelms : when wìll ìt end us?

⌊That óur evening is over us, our night whelms, whelms : when
will it end us?

or
Only the crisp boughs beakèd ~~and~~ dragonish ⸗ damask the toolsmooth
beaked boughs, crispèd° and dragonish,
bleak light —, black
Ever so black on it. O this is our tale too !

⌠harbour
Evening strains to be time's ⌊hush, world's haven
dock, world's den
~~Evenin~~

doom-of-all, womb-of-all, hearse-of-all

Earnest, earthless, equal, attuneable, vaulty, voluminous, ... stupen
                              dous
Evening strains to be time's den, world's delf, womb-of-all, home-of
            -all, hearse-of-all night.
Her fond yellowy hornlight around to the crest, and her wild hollowy
                    hoarlight hung to the height
Waste; her earliest stars, earlstars, stars principal, overbend us,
Firefeaturing heaven. And earth her being unbinds - her dapple
                    is at an end - a-
stray, aswarm, all throughther, in throngs; self in self steep'd
                    and stilled; pluck; quite
Disremembering, dismembering all
                (and pluck - fast; quite

                                        her being has unpenned.
Firefeaturing heaven. For earth unpenned her being; her
                    dapple is at an end - a-
stray or aswarm, all throughther, in throng; self * in self
                    steep'd and packed - pluck; quite
Disremembering, dismembering all. My heart rounds me right
then: Evening is here over us, over us; our night whelms,
                    whelms: when will it end us?

          (that our evening is over us, our night whelms, whelms; when
                    will it end us?

Only the crisp boughs beaked and dragonish, damask the toolsmooth
          beaked boughs, crisped and dragonish,
                    bleak light, black,
ever so black on it. O this is our tale too!

                                Shadow
Evening strains to be time's hush, world's haven
                    dock, world's den
Somen

            doom-of-all, womb-of all, hearse-of all

ἄ - ρι - στος° εὐ - φρο - σύ - να πό - νων κε - κρι - μέ - νων
~~So do~~
Re° so fa s̅o̅ re   do ti do r̅e̅ mi ti la so

Μοι - σᾶν
ἰ - α - τρός, αἰ δὲ σο - φαὶ ~~Μοισαι~~   θύ - γα - τρες ἀ - οι - δαὶ
la mi so la so fa so   la   mi

~~θελ - ξαν νιν ἀ - πτό - με ναι~~

θέλ - ξαν νιν ἀ - πτό - με - ναι
re   la

My hĕart,° where have we been? | what have we seĕn, my mind?
What blow has Cradock dealt? What done? — A rebellious head

Struck off he has ; written | lãrge ~~o~~ ⌈~~on most~~⌉ , and on lovely limbs,
                                    ⌊~~upon lovely limbs~~⌋
In bloody letters lessons | of earnest, of revenge ;

Mŏnuments of ~~mighty~~ earnest, | rĕcords of ~~great~~ revenge
        my great   my
On one that went against me | whĕreas I had warned her —
Warned her! well she knows I warned her of this work.
What work? what harm is done ? There's no harm done, none yet;
                        we
Perhaps ~~I~~ struck no blow, Gwenvrewi lives perhaps ;
To makebelieve my mood was | — mock. O I might think so
But here ˵ is, hĕre is a workman after his day's task sweats.
~~Wipe it I am sure I did ; it seems~~
Wiped once
~~And wiped~~ I am sure it was — it seems, not well ; for still,
Still the scarlet swings and dances on the blade. ←————Be it so, be it!
Steel, I can scour thee ; curtain thee in thy dark scabbard ; these drops
Never, never, never in their blue banks again.
~~Cradock! O woeful word!~~   ~~What~~ Then whãt is it-
The   Caradoc   word!   ~~was done~~
O woeful word, ~~my heart~~ ; | woeful ^ + ~~What have we seen then,~~
~~What seen ?   — Her shining head, sheared from her shoulders, fall~~
    ~~did we see?   — Her head, sheared from her shoulders, fall~~
                        tresses
~~And lapped in shining hair roll to the bank's edge~~
We have seen ? — Her shining head, sheared down from her shoulders, fall
And lapped in its own loose locks roll to the bank's edge ; there
Down the beetliɴg banks, like water in waterfall ,
~~Stoop and~~   ran
It stooped and plashed and fell and ~~rolled~~ like water away,
And her eyes, and her eyes!
In all her body's beauty — and sunlight is but soot to it,
        bells are   to it ~~to it~~
Foam ~~is~~ not fresh ~~by it~~ to it , rainbows ᵇ by it not beaming—
                    ~~beside it~~
In all this beauty, I say, no place was like her eyes,
No piece like those eyes, kept most part much ~~k~~ cast down,
But being ~~lifted~~, ĭmmortal, | of ĭmmŏrtal ~~sweetness~~ brightness
        lĭfted
Several times I saw them, o'er and o'er they rolled
And still they strained towards heaven. Therefore the vengeances

ἄ-ει-στος εὐ-φρο-σύ-να πό-νων κε-κει-μέ-ναιϛ
so do
Re so fa so re do ti do re mi ti la so

ἰ-α-τρός, αἱ δὲ co-φαὶ ~~Νοι-σῶν~~ θύ-γα-τερς ἀ-οι-δαὶ
la mi so la so fa so la mi
~~Θέλ-ξαν νιν ἀ-πτό-με-ναι~~

Θέλ-ξαν νιν ἀ-πτό-με-ναι
re la

My heart, where have we been? / what have we seen, my mind?
What blow has Cradock dealt, what done? — a rebellious head
struck off he has; written large on lovely limbs,
in bloody letters lessons / of earnest, of revenge;
monuments of ~~might~~ great earnest, / records of ~~that~~ my revenge
on one that went against me / whereas I had warned her
Warned her! well she knows I warned her of this work.
What work? what harm is done? there's no harm done, none yet;
Perhaps I struck no blow, Guendricu lives perhaps
To make believe my mood — mock. I might think so
But here is, here is a workman after his day's task sweats.
~~I am sure blood I seem~~
wiped ~~and wiped~~ I am sure it was — it seems, not well; for still,
still the scarlet savings and dances on the blade. be it so, be it!
Steel, I can scour thee; curtain thee in thy dark scabbard; these drops
never, never, never in their blue banks again.
Cradock ~~I a resful work~~ ood! ~~what~~ they while thy ip
~~I a~~ ~~resful work and heart~~; a resful, ~~I what have we seen thy~~
~~what~~ Her shining head, sheared from her shoulders, fall
~~did we see?~~ ~~Her head sheared from her shoulders, fall~~
and lapped in shining ~~locks roll to the bank's edge~~
We have seen? — Her shining head, sheared from her shoulders, fall
and lapped in its own loose locks, roll to the bank's edge; there
Down the brutefing banks, like water in waterfall,
~~stoop and~~ and plashed and fell and ~~rolled~~ ran like water away,
crosses eyes, and her eyes!
In all her body's beauty — and sunlight is but soot to it,
Foam ~~bells are~~ not fresh ~~by it to it~~, rainbows by it not beaming —
~~beside it~~
In all this beauty, I say, no place was like her eyes,
No piece like those eyes, kept most part much cast down
Now being ~~lifted~~, immortal, ~~of~~ immortal ~~sweetness~~ brightness.
lifted
Several times I saw them, over and over they rolled
and still they strained towards heaven. Therefore the vengeance

Dec 20. — O Sapientia°

Desire this heavenly wisdom. Consider how the Sc[ripture] sets it above gold
and·all earthly goods, precious stones, by which you may understand gifts
of mind ~~as~~ for instance. Wish to see by its light

Consider what it is. Personally wisdom is ~~our~~ Christ^, as applied in
this antiphon ; also God the Holy Ghost as the spirit of wisdom ; also
the Bd. Virgin in that being which she had from the beginning, as ex-
pressed in the Book of Wisdom. Then also it is grace and charity

St. James says that God will give it to those who ask it and our Lord
says ~~that~~ your Father will give the good spirit to those who ask it

Attingens° a fine usque ad finem fortiter — Wish for the strength it
gives to reach through your life

Dec. 22 — St. Thomas°

Our Lord said to him before his Passion° | I am the way, the truth, and
the life : apply these words to the Resurrection , for if St. Thomas
had thought of them he wd. not have doubted or disbelieved

Dec. 24 — Christmas Eve —   married

Mary and Joseph were poor, strangers, travellers, ~~husband and
wife~~ that is to say | respectable, honest ; for this is a condition
in charity, to consider to whom you give and family life is the
greatest safeguard

The^y trials were hurry, discomfort, cold, inhospitality, dishonour

Their comfort was Xt's birth. Thank X God for your delivery
of today. Here think the Gloria in excelsis and bring yourself to
~~omit. Then cons~~ leave out of sight your own trials rejoicing over
Xt's birth. Wish a happy Xmas and all its blessings to all your
friends

Dec. 26 — St. Stephen°

St. Stephen's preparation for martyrdom — his labour, his
zeal, his fullness of the spirit of God, on which the Scp. dwells so
strongly

His love of his persecutors

Jan. 3 St. John, octave—Sic eum volo etc°

Consider the charity of these two to one another and what they
found ^, St. Peter that he shd. not betray our Lord, St. John that
he was to wait for God's coming.

Combining the two lives, active and contemplative, and here
consider Angelo Crover,° David Walsh etc

Jan. 5 — The three holy Kings°

We have seen his star in the east. They were watching for it.
Pray to be on the watch for God's providence, not determining where
or when but only sure that it will come. And apply this to all your
troubles and hopes, to England and Ireland, to ~~go~~ growth in virtue

Their offerings. Apply them thus : spiritual duties to Christ's
godhead ; , frankincense ; powers of mind to ~~his~~ the service of his
incarnation, gold ; mortification to his passion and death, myrrh

Jan. 6 — Continuing the above, pray, ~~f~~ acc[ording] to Fr. Foley's in-
structions° of tonight, for the spirit of love in all your doings. For°

Dec. 20 — O Sapientia

Desire this heavenly wisdom. Consider how the Scp. sets it above gold and all earthly goods, precious stones, by which you may understand gifts of mind and for instance. Wish to see by its light our Lord

Consider what it is. Personally wisdom is our Christ, as applied in this antiphon; also God the Holy Ghost is the spirit of wisdom; also the B.d. Virgin in that being which she had from the beginning, as expressed in the Book of Wisdom. Then also it is grace and charity.

St. James says that God will give it to those who ask it and our Lord says that your Father will give the good spirit to those who ask it

Attingens a fine usque ad finem fortiter — wish for the strength it gives to reach through your life

Dec. 22 — St. Thomas

Our Lord said to him before his Passion (I am the way, the truth and the life; apply these words to the Resurrection, for if St. Thomas had thought of them he wd. not have doubted or disbelieved

Dec. 24 — Christmas Eve —

Mary and Joseph were poor, strangers, travellers, married husband and wife that is to say (respectable, honest; for this is a condition in charity, to consider to whom you give and family life is the greatest safeguard

Their trials were hurry, discomfort, cold, inhospitality, dishonour

Their comfort was Xt's birth. Thank God for your delivery of today. Here think the Gloria in excelsis and bring yourself to leave out of sight your own trials, rejoicing over Xt's birth. Wish a happy Xmas and all its blessings to all your friends

Dec. 26 — St. Stephen

St. Stephen's preparation for martyrdom — his labour, his zeal, his fulness of the spirit of God, on which the Scp. dwells so strongly

His love of his persecutors

Jan. 3 St. John, octave — Sic eum volo etc.

Consider the charity of these two to one another and what they found out for each other, St. Peter that he shd. not betray our Lord, St. John that he was to wait for God's coming.

Concerning the two lives, active and contemplative, and here consider Cardinal Cyover, David Walsh etc

Jan. 5 — The three holy Kings

We have seen his star in the east. They were watching for it. Pray to be on the watch for God's providence, not determining where or when but only sure that it will come. And apply this to all your troubles and hopes, to England and Ireland, to growth in virtue

Their offerings, apply these thus: spiritual duties to Christ's godhead, frankincense; powers of mind to his the service of his incarnation, gold; mortification to his passion and death, myrrh

Jan. 6 — Continuing the above, pray, & act. to Fr. Foley's instructions of tonight, for the spirit of love in all your doings, for

Angelo,° ~~Harrington~~, ~~Fr. Bacon~~,° verses for Bridges,° ~~Statistics~~,° ~~Lu-
can~~, Mrs. ~~Delany~~°, Aunt Ann°, Fr. Rigby°, Fr. Cummins, ~~Milicent~~,°
verses for Fr. Bacon

---

indeed it seems a spirit of fear I live by. Consider the love shewn in
our Lord's appearances as a child and in the holy family
    Recommend to him with the holy kings all Gentiles
    Sunday in Oct[ave] of Epiphany° —
    Christ's three man[ifestatio]ns : at Bethlehem, at the baptism, at Cana
    (1) Consider to whom : ~~;~~ in (i) to the three Magi and by them to the Gentiles ; in (ii)
to St. ~~John's disciples and~~ Baptist, his disciples, and the Jews ; in (iii) to Christ's dis-
ciples. There were really ~~others~~ man[ifestatio]ns, as the ~~pr~~ Presentation and the Gloria
in Excelsis, the ~~finding in~~ questioning the Doctors in the Temple (this last is the Gospel
of the day)
    (2) Consider as what : in (i) as a child, helpless ; in (ii) as in the ^dis^guise of a
sinner, (in (iii) as in the disguise of common social life
    (3) By what means : in (i) of inanimate nature ~~;~~ in the star , ^ (ii) of the divine
Persons, in (iii) of his own incarnated power

‖ No. 8 ‖ —   Scholarship Examination°

(q. 1.) ✓✓✓✓~~✓~~ not very good . If each ✓ = 5 and v = 2 40 — 17

~~22 = 18 . Say 19~~ 23, say 24

                               Say 36
    No. 12 — ✓✓ . 40—7 = 33, besides marks of intelligence.

                    ✓
    No. 15 — ✓✓~~✓✓~~. 40—9 ~~11~~ = ~~29~~ 31 , but more intelligence than
the last. Say ~~34~~ 36

    No. 26 — ✓✓✓ . 40—9 = 31 . Style not good but as much int.
as the last. Give him 36

    No. 29 — ✓✓✓ . 40—14 = 26 . Int. little say I. 27

    No. 31 — ✓✓ , 40—7 = 33. Int. 3. 36

    No. 34 — ✓✓✓~~✓✓~~✓✓✓~~✓✓~~✓✓ . ~~39—40~~ 40—39 = 1 , poor fellow, and
no intelligence

    (Soph.) No. 8 — ✓✓✓ , call these 5. Intelligence say 2 . ~~40~~ 60—5 + 2 = 57
    (9. 1.) No. 12 — ✓~~✓~~✓✓ , say 11 . ~~40~~ 60—11 = ~~3~~ 49. Bad style, not much int.
                                ~~56 36~~ 57
    No. 15 — ✓✓~~✓~~ ~~40~~ 60—4 = ~~34~~ + 1 = ~~35~~ . Note : No. 8 the best yet
    No. 26 — ✓✓~~✓~~ . ~~40~~ 50—6 ~~4~~ = ~~34~~ 56 + 4 for knowledge (~~a~~ thorough study,
but no great judgment) = ~~38~~ ~~40~~ 60
                                51
    No. 29 — ✓✓✓~~✓~~ , say ~~19~~ . ~~40~~ 60—~~19~~ = ~~30~~, but give 4 for knowledge and int-
elligence = ~~34~~ 55
    No. 31 — ✓ and as much made up by knowledge. Therefore ~~40~~ 60

Angelo, Harrington, Fr. Bacon, verses for Bridges, Statistics, 1/4
cap., Mr. Delany, Aunt Ann, Fr. Rigby, Fr. Cummins, Millicent,
verses for Fr. Bacon

---

indeed it seems a spirit of fear I live by. Consider the love shewn in
our Lord's appearances as a child and in the Holy Family
Recommend to him with the holy kings all Gentiles
Sunday in Oct. of Epiphany —
Christ's three manifrs, at Bethlehem, at the Baptism, at Cana
(1) Consider to whom: in (i) to the three Magi and by them to the Gentiles; in (ii)
to St. John's disciples and Baptist, his disciples, and the Jews; in (iii) to Christ's dis-
ciples. There were really other manifrs, as the Presentation and the Gloria
in Excelsis, the finding or questioning the Doctors in the Temple (this last is the Gospel
of the day)
(2) Consider as what: in (i) as a child helpless; in (ii) as in the disguise of a
sinner, in (iii) as in the disguise of common social life
(3) By what means: in (i) of inanimate nature, in the star; (ii) of the divine
Persons, in (iii) of his own incarnated power

No. 8 — Scholarship Examination

(q.1.) ✓✓✓✓ not very good. If each ⌐ = 5 and ↲ = 2 40 - 17
= 18. Say 19 23, say 24   Say 36
no. 12 — ✓↲. 40 - 7 = 33, besides marks of intelligence.
no. 15 — ✓↲↲. 40 - 9 = 31, but more intelligence than
the last. Say 34 36
no. 26 — ↲↲↲. 40 - 9 = 31. Style not good but as much int.
as the last. Give him 36
no. 29 — ↲↲↲↲. 40 - 14 = 26. int. little say l. 27
no. 31 — ↲↲. 40 - 7 = 33, int. 3. 36
no. 34 — ↲↲↲↲↲↲↲↲↲↲↲↲↲. 39 = 40 40 - 39 = 1, poor fellow, and
no intelligence
(soph) no. 8 — ↲↲↲, call these 5. Intelligence say 2. 60 - 5 + 2 = 57
(q.1) no. 12 — ↲↲↲↲, say 11. 60 - 11 = 49. Bad style, not much int.
no. 15 — ↲↲↲ 60 - 4 = 56 + 1 = 57. Note: No. 8 the best yet
no. 26 — ↲↲↲. 60 - 4 = 56 + 4 for knowledge (through study,
but no great judgment) = 58 60
no. 29 — ↲↲↲, say 19. 60 - 19 = 41, but give 4 for knowledge and int-
elligence = 37 55
no. 31 — ↲ and as much made up by knowledge. Therefore 60

No. 34 — ✓✓✓✓ . 4̶0̶—20 = 2̶0̶ 40. Nothing to the good

Jan. 19 — S̶t̶. The devils° who tormented the demoniac b̶e̶g̶ ̶n̶o̶ pray not to
be tormented
 Remark the breaking of the bonds and how the swine broke loose and
drowned themselves. Remark the suicide. The man did not kill himself,
because the devils were not allowed to drive him to that. They are therefore
fettered themselves
 The Gerasenes asked him to g̶o̶ ̶a̶ depart, because they were possessed by fear ;
the cured demoniac asked to go t̶ with him. The̶y̶ swine t̶h̶r̶e̶w̶ ̶t̶h̶e̶m̶ ̶r̶a̶n̶
threw themselves into the sea, the Gerasenes threw away their salvation
by sending Christ back onto the sea. T̶h̶e̶ ̶d̶e̶v̶i̶l̶s̶
 The devils ask not to be sent out of the country (St. Mark, I think) ;
St. Luke says not sent into the abyss. It seems their request was granted.
I̶n̶ ̶w̶h̶a̶t̶ Where then did they continue to live, what did they possess?
Was it those who e̶a̶t̶ ̶o̶f̶ ate of the drowned swine's flesh?

 Tacitus° Histories bk. 1, chap. 8̶⧸3 —
 Illic° / là bas / real demonstrative ; ibi logical demonstrative, demonstrative
of context. So ille, is. Real dems. hic, ille, iste ; logical is, qui
 Crediderim / I could (not) h̶a̶ believe. You will not find t̶h̶a̶t̶ ̶I̶ ̶h̶a̶v̶e̶ ̶I̶ ̶s̶h̶a̶l̶l̶
that I have believed, I shall not be found to have believed. The subjunctive the mood
of assertion at a remove, of assertion delayed or qualified or reserved for want of some-
thing which being removed it becomes absolute, positive, unqualified, unreserved, cate-
gorical, indicative. The indic. the positive or categorical mood°   .
   eligendi
 Si ^ facultas detur° quas mentes imprecentur, quid optabunt? / If you suppose the
power given what must you say they pray for? then simply what will they pray for?
The English will and shall moods more than tenses. The subj. a future mood
 Vobis animus sit / Let y̶ the courage be yours, I want the courage to be yours°
 Ne° miles obsequatur / the soldiers not to obey
        the men to dare
 Non Germani audeant° / The very Germans are not b̶o̶l̶d̶ ̶e̶n̶o̶u̶g̶h̶ ̶t̶o̶ do such a thing
 Ulline Italiae a̶e̶ alumni d̶e̶ depoposcerit° ? Can i̶t̶ ̶b̶e̶ ̶t̶h̶a̶t̶ there c̶a̶n̶ be c̶h̶i̶l̶d̶r̶e̶n̶
sons of Italy that are (or will be) found to have demanded . . ?
 Sic fit ut hinc respublica constiterit° / So i̶t̶ is brought about (not quod / that but) how ⟩
the state is found to have ranged itself (on our side)
 Cujus splendore et gloria sordis et obscuritatem Vitellianarum partium prae-
stringimus / by the lightning stroke (stringere / rapid stroke, momentary tension) of
   cast
whose glory we p̶u̶t̶ ̶o̶u̶t̶ ̶o̶f̶ ̶s̶i̶g̶h̶t̶ into shade the dirt and dulness etc. Observe per-
stringere / to "touch up" , whip lightly,° w̶h̶i̶ below — V̶i̶t̶e̶l̶l̶i̶a̶n̶a̶r̶u̶m̶

No. 34 — LLL. $\frac{60}{40}$ - 20 = 40. nothing to the good

Jan. 19 — ✗ The devils who tormented the demoniac by no pray not to be tormented

Remark the breaking of the bonds and how the swine broke loose and drowned themselves, remark the suicide — the man did not kill himself, because the devils were not allowed to drive him to that. They are therefore fettered themselves

The Gerasenes ~~ay~~ him to go a depart, because they were possessed by fear; the cured demoniac ~~wished~~ to go forth with him. They ~~swine threw them can~~ threw themselves into the sea, the Gerasenes threw away their salvation by sending Christ back onto the sea ~~the devils~~

the devils ask not to be sent out of the country (St. Mark, I think), St Luke says not sent into the abyss. It seems their request was granted. ~~in which~~ where then did ~~they~~ continue to live, what did they possess? Was it those who ~~only~~ ate of the drowned swine's flesh?

Tacitus Histories bk. I chap. 8 ✗ 3 —

Hic / là tres preal demonstrative; hi logical demonstrative, demonstrative of context. Ho ille, is. Real dems, hic, ille, iste ; logical is, qui

Crediderim / I could (not) believe. You will not find, ~~that there I shall~~ that I have believed, I shall not be found to have believed. the subjunctive the mood of assertion at a remove, of assertion delayed or qualified or reserved for want of something which being removed it becomes absolute, positive, unqualified, unreserved, categorical, indicative. The indic. the positive or categorical mood

si ~~faculty~~ detur quas mentes imprecentur, quid optabant? / If you suppose the power given what must you say they pray for? then simply what will they pray for? The english will and shall moods more than tenses. the subj. a future mood

Velis animens sit / Sd the courage be yours, I want the courage to be yours

The rules obsequatur / the soldier not to obey

Non Germani auderent / the very Germans are not ~~bold enough to~~ do such a thing the ~~punto dare~~

ulline Italiae ~~at~~ alumni deposcerent / can ~~it be that~~ there ~~be children~~ sons of Italy that are ~~for~~ will supposed to have demanded ?

Sic fit ut hinc respublica constitit / to it is brought about (not quod/ that but) how the state is found to have ranged itself (on our side)

Cujus splendore et gloria sordes et obscuritatem Vitellianarum partium praestringens / by the lightning stroke (stringere/ rapid stroke, momentary tension) of whose glory we ~~find only light~~ into ~~shade~~ the dirt and dulness etc. observe perstringere / to "touch up", whip lightly, ~~alis~~ below — Vitellianarum

Bk. 2 cap. 1 —°

Berenice sister to Herod Agrippa I° (who killed St. James and imprisoned St. Peter), suspected of incest with her brother

Aerians, Aeria° seemingly Gk. versions of eastern words. Perhaps then it is Astarte,° Ἀφροδίτη Οὐρανία° . But the word may be a corruption, perversion of Asherah an eastern goddess. This word Asherah not the same as Astarte, Ashtaroth, Ishtar. It may be the corruption and confusion of both

Tamiram no role, prob. a false reading or variant of Thamy-
                         name
ras° and that the same as Thamyris, which ^ appears eastern and the same? as Thammuz . For I find that Adonis, that is Thammuz,° was called the son of Cinyras and his daughter Smyrna, incestuously begot. Now Thammuz or Adonis is the Spring or the Sun°

Look out Myrrha°

Adolere° to light the altar fire for sacrifice , like lighting candles for mass ; sign of ceremony begun. Hence ~~to~~ it means to ~~sacrifice, to~~
                        with
the sacrifice takes place ^, the service of the altar consists of / prayers and ~~bloodless~~ fire only , that is no ~~n~~ burnt offering, no bloods shed over it : incense these might be

Fibris rhetorical for viscera, vitals, ~~not entr~~, not entrails°
Explain the force of examining the vitals of the victim

Ratio in obscuro° — Prob. serpent worship, which is a most extra-
                        thing
ordinary and obscure ~~subject~~ and due in my opinion to a combination of causes, one of which I believe to be the wreathing of the sacrificial flame and smoke resembling a snake climbing to heaven The snake identified with the soul of the departed in the case of
                        a
a cremation, with the god sacrificed to in ~~an and~~ sacrifice. The Chinese say the deceased emperor mounts to heaven on a dragon.°

~~M~~ Nullis imbribus madescunt — It wd. be a struggle between fire and water

Secreto / secrecy. So secretum commissum, promissum / secrecy, not secret

Alliciendis etiam Muciani moribus / prob. just the man not only to pacify but even ~~to allu~~ win, to allure Mucianus°

Bk. 2 Cap. 1 —

Berenice sister to Herod Agrippa 1 (who killed St. James and imprisoned St. Peter), suspected of incest with her brother

Arrians, Asria seemingly gk. versions of eastern words. Perhaps then I is Astarte, Aphrodity Ouranea. But the word may be a corruption, perversion of asherah an eastern goddess. this word asherah, not the same as astarte, ashtaroth, Ishtar. it may be the corruption and confusion of both

Thamuras no note, prob. a false reading or variant of Thamyras and that the same as Thamyris, which appears name eastern and the same as Thammuz. For I find that Adonis, that is Thammuz, was called the son of Cinyras and his daughter Smyrna, incestuously begot. Now Thammuz or Adonis is the spring or the sun

Look out myrrha

Adolere to light the altar fire for sacrifice, like lighting candles for mass; sign of ceremony begun. Hence to it means to sacrifice, the sacrifice takes place the service of the altar consists of prayer and bloodless fire only that is no burnt offering, no blood shed over it: incense there might be

Filme rhetorical for viscera, vitals, not entia, not entrails Explain the force of examining the vitals of the victim

Ratio in obscuro — Prob. serpent worship, which is a most extraordinary and obscure thing and due in my opinion to a combination of causes, one of which I believe to be the wreathing of the sacrificial flame and smoke resembling a snake climbing to heaven the snake identified with the soul of the departed in the case of a cremation, with the god sacrificed to in sacrifice. the Chinese say the deceased emperor mounts to heaven on a dragon.

In nullis incluso inadescunt — It cd. be a struggle between fire and water

secreto / secrecy. So secretum commissum, promissum / secrecy, not secret

Allicienda etiam musicani mordres / prob. just the men not only to pacify but even to alluein, to allure / musicians

Monday Feb. 2° — Mr. Daly, ~~Mr~~ Malone, Lennox, Lynch, Young, Mac-
Weeney, Bowden, Murphy, Whittaker
Tuesday — Mr. Daly, Malone, Lennox, Lynch, Young, Bowden, Murphy,
Whittaker
Wednesday — The same + MacWeeney
Thursday — The same as yesterday
Friday —

Monday Feb. 9 — Mr. Bowden, Daly, Malone, Lennox, Lynch, Young, Mac-
Weeney, Murphy ⸗ , ~~Mr.~~ O'Brien, Whittaker
Tuesday — ~~MacWeeney away~~
Wednesday — ~~Malone away~~
Thursday — ~~at~~ The same
Friday—The same

Mithridates° was nominally at war
with Rome till his death in 63

                                                     Livius
        public   and M. ~~and L~~ Drusus
Great° ^ men of this period — two Gracchi ^; Marius, Cinna, and their opponent
                                               unsuccessful
Sulla ; first Triumvirs ; second Triumvirs — Cicero and his two ^ enemies Cati-
line and Clodius. Within this period then fall the two greatest names in Roman
statesmanship and literature, Caesar and Cicero

Monday Feb. 2 — Mr. Daly, ~~Mr~~ Malone, Lennox, Lynch, Young, Mac-Weeney, Bowden, Murphy, Whittaker

Tuesday — Mr. Daly, Malone, Lennox, Lynch, Young, Bowden, Murphy, Whittaker

Wednesday — the same + Mac Weeney

Thursday — the same as yesterday

Friday —

Monday Feb. 9 — Mr. Bowden, Daly, Malone, Lennox, Lynch, Young, Mac Weeney, Murphy, ~~Mr~~ O'Brien, Whittaker

Tuesday — ~~the same~~

Wednesday — ~~Malone only~~

Thursday — all the same

Friday — the same

Mithridates was nominally at war with Rome till his death in 63

Great men of this period — two Gracchi; Marius, Cinna, and their opponent Sulla; first triumvirs; second triumvirs; Cicero and his two enemies Catiline and Clodius. Within this period then fall the two greatest names in Roman statesmanship and literature, Caesar and Cicero

Notes° for <u>Roman Lit. and Antiquities</u> BC 133 —

Cicero

43 (death of Tib. Gracchus to death of ~~Julius Caesar~~)

Principal events of the period —

In first yr. <u>Numantia</u> taken ~~and~~ by Scipio the Younger ~~and in~~ and Spain
becomes Roman in the West, Attalus III leaves his <u>kin. of Pergamus</u> to Rome
in the East (province of Asia), at Rome agitation and <u>death of Tib. Gracchus.</u>
A slave war was going on in S~~e~~icily, ended in 99.

The popular movement led by the Gracchi goes on till 121, when <u>death of C.G.</u>
Same year <u>Narbovese Province</u> of Gaul established
Wars in Macedonia east, Jugurtha south, and the Cimbri and Teutones

~~Numidian~~ African

north. The ~~Numidian~~ war ~~with J.~~ came to an end by <u>Jugurtha's capture</u>

Marius'

106 ; the ~~Cimbrian~~ war in the north by ~~the~~ defeat of the ~~Cimbrians~~ Teu-
<u>tons</u> at Aquae Sextiae 102 <u>and Cimbrians</u> in the Raudine Plain next year

Popular party led by ~~Nim~~ Marius and Saturninus. The latter killed
in battle in the Forum 100. In that year J. Caesar born

Next year, <u>Slave War</u> in ~~Sei~~ Sicily brought to an end

The <u>Italian movement</u>, supported at Rome by M. Livius Drusus
trib. pl., who was murdered 91 . . The Social War followed and ended 88.

The <u>Mithridatic Wars</u> had meanwhile begun and went on till 65?°

Struggle of <u>Marius and Sulla</u>, popular and ~~a~~ aristocratic parties.
Marius died in his 7ᵗʰ consulship 86. ~~Sulla after defeating Mithrida~~
Cinna was killed 2 years later. Sulla, after defeating Mithradates, returns
to Italy. Proscriptions on both sides. Sulla dictator 82 to 79.

<u>War with Sertorius</u> in Spain, ~~and~~ <u>Pirates</u> on ~~see~~ sea, <u>slaves</u> in Italy
(besides Mithradates). Pompey receives extraordinary powers and be-

leading public

comes ~~chief~~ man at Rome

<u>Cicero's consulship</u> . <u>Catiline's conspiracy</u> 63
<u>First Triumvirate</u> of Caesar, Pompey, and Crassus 60
<u>Death of Crassus</u> at Carrhae 53. <u>Death of Clodius</u> next year
Caesar crosses the Rubicon 49
Battle of Pharsalus 48. Death of Pompey in Egypt. Caesar dictator
<u>Caesar murdered</u> ~~33~~ 44
<u>Second Triumvirate</u> of Octavian, Antony, and Lepidus. Murder of
Cicero ~~3~~ 43

---

age

The period then is the last ^ (century nearly) of the Republic. Abroad
during this period Rome became mistress of the Mediterranean world,

outside   of   countries on the

that is, ~~besides~~ Italy, ^ Gaul, Spain, Greece, and the ^ seaboard of the Adriat-
ic and part of Euxine seaboard, ~~there of~~ the Levant, Egypt, and the seaboard
of Africa. The Provincial administration was formed during this period.

~~At home during this time~~   races

In Italy there took place the struggle between the Italian ~~nationalities~~
and Rome. Rome was victorious, but most of what the Italians had strug-
gled for was yielded to them   Senate

At Rome this was the period of the struggle between the ~~people~~ and no-

Notes for <u>Roman Lit. and Antiquities</u> BC 133 — 24

43 (Death of Tib. Gracchus to death of ~~Julius Caesar~~ (Cicero))

Principal events of the period —

In first y. numantia taken ~~and~~ by scipio the ~~younger~~ ~~and~~ and spain becomes Roman in the West, Attalus III leaves his km. of Pergamus to Rome in the East (province of Asia), at Rome agitation and <u>death of Tib. Gracchus</u>. A slave war was going on in Sicily ended in 99.

The popular movement led by the Gracchi goes on till 121, then <u>Death of C.G.</u> same year <u>Narbonese Province of Gaul established</u>

Wars in macedonia east, Jugurtha south, and the Cimbri and teutones north. The ~~numidian~~ african war ~~with J.~~ came to an end by Jugurtha's capture 106 ; the ~~cimbrian~~ war in the north (y the (marius') defeat of the ~~cimbrians~~ Teutones at aquae sextiae 102 and Cimbrians in the Raudine Plain next year

Popular party led by ~~two~~ marius and Saturninus. the latter killed in battle in the Forum 100. In that year J. Caesar born

Next year, slave war in ~~sci~~ sicily brought to an end

The <u>Italian movement</u>, supported at Rome by m. Livius Drusus trib.pl., who was murdered 91, the Social War followed and ended 88.

the <u>mithridatic Wars</u> had meanwhile begun and went on till 65 ?

Struggle of <u>marius and Sulla</u>, popular and aristocratic parties. marius died in his 7th consulship, 86. ~~Sulla after defeating mithradates~~ Cinna was killed 2 years later. Sulla, after defeating mithradates, returns to Italy. Proscriptions on both sides. Sulla dictator 82 till 79

War with Sertorius in Spain, ~~and~~ Pirates on ~~the sea~~ sea, slaves in Italy (besides mithradates). Pompey receives extraordinary powers and be- comes ~~chief~~ leading public man at Rome

<u>Cicero's consulship</u> Catiline's conspiracy 63

<u>First Triumvirate</u> of Caesar, Pompey, and Crassus 60

Death of Crassus at Carrhae 53. <u>Death of Clodius</u> next year

Caesar crosses the Rubicon 49

Battle of Pharsalus 48. Death of Pompey in Egypt. Caesar dictator Caesar murdered 44

<u>Second Triumvirate</u> of Octavian, antony, and Lepidus. murder of Cicero B 43

The period then is the last (century nearly) of the Republic. Abroad during this period Rome became mistress of the mediterranean world, that is, ~~besides~~ italy of gaul, spain, Greece and ~~the~~ seaboard of the ~~adria~~ it and part of the euxine ~~seaboard~~, ~~those~~ of the Levant, Egypt, and the rest of africa. the provincial administration as passed during this period

In Italy there took place the struggle between the Italian ~~nationals~~ and slave. Rome was victorious, but most of what the Italians had strug- gled for was yielded to them

At Rome this was the period of the struggle between the ~~people~~ senate and

bles on the one hand and the popular party on the other which succeeded to the
struggles between the patricians and plebians. ~~It was like the other agrarian.~~
At last power passed into the hands of the army and its generals ; hence the
dictatorships, the triumvirates, and at last the principate agrarian

In ~~lite~~ social matters this period was the one in which the old order of
things having passed and the old virtues such as they were, passed with them.

                        gods were
The Roman ~~religion was~~ identified with the Greek, Eastern worships were in-
                                                              from
troduced, and morals ~~were~~ having less of a religious foundation ~~with~~ the decay
of belief, an attempt was made to rest them on Gk. philosophy , which now
gained ground. ~~as in the Roman empire~~ , as well as Gk. art and Gk. civilization in
general

In literature this was emphatically the age of the orators — from
the Gracchi to Cicero°

                                of Rome
In poetry it was the most original age ^ and led up to the brief Golden
                    at least   splendid   though
Age of Latin poetry. It produced ^ two poets of ~~brilliant~~ genius ~~but~~ imper-
fect execution, Lucretius° and Catullus.° These were besides L. Attius, Q. Lut-
atius Catulus, Laberius, Publilius Syrus, Volcatius Sedigitus, Furius Bibaculus, Cal-
vus, Cassius of Parma, Lucilius, Varro.° Caesar wrote verse . We may add Helvius Cinna
for Shakespeare's sake.° Caelius Rufus

History — Annalists, esp. Valerius of Antium ; historians of style ~~Salli~~
Sallust most eminent, Cornelius Nepos, Caesar. Also Atticus

General literature — Varro, Nigidius Figulus, Caesar, Auctor ad Herennium,
Valerius Cato what?

Philosophical — Cato the Younger, Cicero

                                        Lemonia
~~Jir~~ Jurists — Scaevola, C. Aquillius Gallus, Ser. Sulpicius ^ Rufus, C.
Trebatius Testa, Q. Aelius Tubero
Valerius Messala what ?
Tarpa
Letters

There was besides a P. Rutilius Rufus, ~~a~~ consular, a very up-
right man and banished for conscience sake ; ~~as an orator lea~~ a great
Stoic ; as an orator learned but dry

bles on the one hand and the popular party on the other which succeeded to the struggles between the patricians and plebeians. ~~It~~ ~~like the~~ ~~agrarian~~. At last power passed into the hands of the army and its generals; hence the dictatorships, the triumvirates, and at last the principate ~~established~~.

In ~~its~~ social matters this period was the one in which the old order of things having passed away, the old virtues such as they were, passed with them; the Roman ~~religion~~ identified with the greek, eastern worships were introduced, and morals ~~were~~ having less of a religious foundation ~~and~~ the decay of belief, an attempt was made to rest them on Gk. philosophy which now gained ground. ~~as in the Roman empire~~, as well as Gk. art and Gk. civilisation in general

In literature this was emphatically, the age of the orators — from the Gracchi to Cicero

In poetry it was the most original age of Rome, and led up to the brief golden age of latin poetry. It produced ~~two~~ two poets of ~~brilliant~~ splendid genius though imperfect execution, Lucretius and Catullus, there were besides L. Atheus Q. Lutatius Catulus, Laberius, Publilius Syrus, Volcatius Sedigitus, Furius Bibaculus, Calvus, Cassius of Parma, Lucilius, Varro. Caesar wrote verse, We may add Helvius Cinna for Shakespeare's sake. Coelius Rufus

History — annalists, esp. Valerius of Antium; historians of style ~~Sallu~~ sallust most eminent, Cornelius Nepos, Caesar. Also Atticus

General literature — Varro, Nigidius Figulus, Caesar, Auctor ad Herennium, Valerius Cato what?

Philosophical — Cato the younger, Cicero

Semonia

~~Jurists~~ — Scaevola, C. Aquillius Gallus, Ser. Sulpicius Rufus, C. Trebatius Testa, Q. Aelius Tubero

Valerius Messala what?

Tappa

letters

~~there was~~ besides a P. Rutilius Rufus, consular, a very upright man and banished for conscience sake; as an orator ~~had~~ a great type; as an orator learned but dry

M. Antonius Orator born 143, put to death by Marius and Cinna
87 and ~~set~~ his head set up on the Rostra, ~~orator~~ commander, orator,

er

and conservative statesman ; introduced as speak~~ing~~ in the De Oratore ;
grandfather of Mark Antony°

Wrote on Oratory (de Rat. Dicendi)

His

~~Published~~ speeches, ~~which~~ prosecutions and defences, were not published

not   down   reports   These

because ~~never~~ written^, by himself, but ~~notes~~ of them had been taken~~;~~ . ~~which~~
must have purported to be word for word for his diction was commented on.

not euphonious

It was unstudied and imperfect, though natural and manly ; but then his
delivery was admirable , and the impression his eloquence made was so great
that the soldiers sent to kill him cd. scarcely be got to do so

———

Cardinal MacCabe° died Feb. 11. News of Gordon's death° and tak-
ing of ~~Three dynamite explosions~~ Khartoom° about same time

The dynamite explosions° when ?

Winter in Ireland mild. Snow only in Feb.

———

Write to° ~~young Byrne, Fr. Rickaby,~~ ° Mr. Patmore°, Milicent°

———

Absent on Sat. Feb. 27 Mr MacWeeney, Mr Malone *Byrne*

———

Other orators of the ~~earlier~~ period are the three Curios, Carbo, Fimbria,

~~in politics on the conservative side,~~

~~G. S.~~ S. Scribonius Curio consul 76, a successful commander, ≙ became pont. max.,

Cicero

died 53, ~~a friend of Cicero and,~~ acc. to ~~him~~ , a good man, in politics on the
conservative side, ~~and~~ Cicero's friend, Caesar's bitter enemy. His Latin was pure,

for   even in Latin,

~~and~~ from some good home training, ^ he ~~was~~ had no culture, no reading, ^ and knew
scarcely any law. His father ~~had~~ was an orator before him, his son after him — both
bearing the same name, so that they made 3 generations of orators. The third, Antony's

nevertheless

infamous friend, whom ^ Cicero ~~never ceased to~~ loved, ~~was is cab~~ became a great ~~par~~ follow-

ed

er of Caesar ~~: he~~ and died ~~in~~ defeat^ in Africa 49. He is called a scoundrel of genius,
~~ingeniose~~ homo ingeniosissime nequam, or a man whose ~~r~~ rascality amounted to
genius.° He married Fulvia, afterwards Antony's wife. His debts were enormous

~~orators~~ orators

Much greater than Curio in Cicero's judgment were two ~~men~~ ^ who, he says, imi-
tated respectively Crassus and Antonius°—

Quintus   born 124   88   (not to be confounded with Lemonia)

~~Servius~~ Sulpicius Rufus ^ trib. pl. ^ carried on after Drusus' death the
work of constitutional reform and perished in Sulla's ~~pro return~~ first restor-
ation, when Marius escaped, the same year. He was the grandest and

rich

most tragic orator Cicero had ever heard ; his voice very ~~fine~~ ; his action

and animated   wordiness or excess

graceful and noble ; his delivery fluent^, but ~~all not~~ without ~~vehemence or exag-~~

His fault was that he cd.

geration. ~~However he cd. not descend and treat things be must always~~
not descend, his style was ~~he cd. not~~ was never ~~simple and~~ easy. It is plain
Roman oratory lost greatly by his early death . ~~at 36~~ He did not and said
he cd. not write , but forged speeches were fathered on him after his death

also

C. Aurelius Cotta, a contrast to the last, ^ a friend of Drusus and consul-
ar, ~~died~~ (75), died 2 years after strangely by the reopening of a very old
wound on the ~~very~~ eve of ~~a trumper~~ the triumph he had managed to get for a
trumpery affair in Gaul. He ~~was~~ had a philosophical training ; ~~was ingenious~~

M. Antonius Orator born 143, put to death by Marius and Cinna 87, and his head set up on the Rostra, commander, orator, and conservative statesman; introduced as speaking in the De oratore; grandfather of Mark Antony. Wrote on oratory (de Rate i Dicendi)

His speeches prosecutions and defences, were not published because not written by himself, but accounts of them had been taken, which must have purported to be word for word, for his diction was commented on. It was unstudied and imperfect, though natural and manly; but that his delivery was admirable, and the impression his eloquence made was so great that the soldiers sent to kill him cd. scarcely be got to do so

Cardinal MacCabe died Feb. 11. News of Gordon's death and taking of three dynamite explosions Khartoom about same time (the dynamite explosions when?)
Winter in Ireland mild. Snow only in Feb.

Write to young Byrne, T. Dickaby, Mr. Patmore, Millicent
Absent on Sat. Feb. 27 Mr. MacWeeney, Mr. Malone Byrne

Other orators of the earlier period are the three Curios, Cato, Fimbria,

S. S. Scribonius Curio consul 76, a successful commander, became pont. max. died 53, a friend of Cicero and, acc. to Cicero, a good man, in politics on the conservative side, and Cicero's friend, Caesar's bitter enemy. His Latin was pure, and from some good home training, for he had no culture, no reading, and knew scarcely any law. His father was an orator before him, his son after him — both bearing the same name, so that they made 3 generations of orators. The third, infamous friend, whom Cicero called to lord, became a great partner follower of Caesar and died a defeated in Africa 49. He is called a scoundrel of genius, homo ingeniosissime nequam, or a man whose rascality amounted to genius. He married Fulvia, afterwards Antony's wife. His debts were enormous, much greater than Curio in Cicero's judgment were two, who, he says, ranked respectively Crassus and Antonius —

Quintus Sulpicius Rufus born 124, trib. pl. 88, (not to be confounded with Servonia) carried on after Drusus' death the work of constitutional reform and perished in Sulla's first restoration, when Marius escaped, the same year. He was the grandest and most tragic orator Cicero had ever heard; his voice very rich, his action graceful and noble, his delivery fluent, but without exag- peration. this might be was descend and took things that he cd. always not descend, his style was never simple and easy. It is plain Roman oratory lost greatly by his early death. He did not and said he cd. not write, but forged speeches were fathered on him after his death

C. Aurelius Cotta, a contrast to the last, also a friend of Drusus and consul- ar (75), died 2 years after sharply by the reopening of a very old wound on the very eve of the triumph he had managed to get for a trumpery affair in Gaul. He had a philosophical training; ingenious and minute or detailed (subtile)

~~was~~ his treatment of his matter was ingenious ^ : his style had a graceful ease~~;~~ , it
was thoroughly sound and sensible ("nihil° erat in ejus oratione nisi sincerum,
nihil nisi siccum et sannum"). He had a brother Lucius, who used a
boorish style on purpose, thinking it effective

C. Flavius / Fimbria consul with Marius 104 , an able ~~but~~ but bitter
speaker, was famous ~~in his day as an~~ in his day but the fame of his orato-

~~w~~   away

ry soon waned ^. His son, an infamous and ~~violent~~ most violent man, spoke
in a way which was like raving

              an unscrupulous man,   partisan

C. Papirius Carbo, ~~of the consul 120,~~ ^ was first a ~~friend~~ of the Gracchi,
~~aft~~ and was suspected of the younger Scipio's murder ; afterwards he
changed sides and was universally despised. He was consul 120 and next
year being accused by the orator Crassus of what is not known, took can-
marides and died. He had little learning, but was, ~~a r~~ Cicero says, a re-

      forensic

ally great ^ orator, earnest and vigorous, yet graceful (dulcem) and witty, . ~~with~~

      ~~his pra~~

a his voice musical , and he ~~ear~~ practiced diligently. ~~There was another~~
~~a namesake of his surnamed Arvina~~ His son and namesake, but surnamed
                      an   orator

Arvina, was, Cicero says, a good man and ~~we ca~~ impressive ~~as a speaker~~

      died 87

T. Lutatius Catulus° ^ The ~~cons~~ soldier, ~~and stat,~~ ~~and~~ poet, ~~was als~~ and
historian, was also a fine orator. The ~~yon~~ younger Cato was also called e-
loquent and some of his speeches were politically important, but little is said of his
style.

The Asiatic, Rhodian, and Attic ~~styles~~ schools — In Asia Min-
or ~~the m~~, on the whole the most civilised part of the world at this time,

      ~~florid~~

had been developed a ᵔ school of oratory in which there was something
~~oriental~~ floridly and oriental. This school Hortensius represented at
Rome. At Rhodes, ~~the~~ after the fall of Corinth ~~of~~ the most ~~important~~
flourishing city of Greece, arose a ~~s~~ chaster school, ~~to~~ which Cicero was

      belong to

considered to ~~represent~~. But Cicero's younger contem[poraries] went back to the
golden age of Attic eloquence and esp. to the ~~purest~~ most lucid and pure
the most graceful of the Attic orators Lysias°

Lysias

Lysias

                                            John

such as we may perhaps recognise in its most beautiful form in St. ~~Gre~~
Chrysostom° and St. G[regory] Naz[ianzen].°

      besides Rome ~~and~~

though Cicero ~~himself~~ in fact ^ studied at ~~Rh~~ Athens, Rhodes, and in
Asia Minor all three

~~J.~~ C. Julius Caesar, ~~name~~ the Dictator's namesake but surnamed also
Strabo and Vopiscus, was of the aristocratic party ; he nearly brought on a
revolution by his efforts to win the consulship out of due course ; and was

                                  his

killed in Marius' prescriptions and Cinna's 87 . As an orator ~~he w~~
style was a novelty : it was ~~highly~~ graceful, easy, refined, and full of
humour, but without weight or force.

Pompey was a ~~dignifi~~ clear and dignified speaker. Antony was ~~to~~ unin-
telligible , ~~pompous~~ turgid, and would-be pathetic

was his treatment of his matter was ingenious; his style had a graceful ease; it
was thoroughly sound and sensible ("nihil erat in eius oratione nisi sincerum,
nihil nisi siccum et sanum"). He had a brother Lucius, who used a
crookish style on purpose, thinking it effective

C. Flavius Fimbria consul with Marius 104, an able but bitter
speaker, was famous in his day but the fame of his orato-
ry soon waned. His son, an infamous and most violent man, spoke
in a way which was like raving

C. Papirius Carbo, an unscrupulous man, was first a friend of the Gracchi,
and was suspected of the younger Scipio's murder; afterwards he
changed sides, and was universally despised. He was consul 120 and next
year, being accused by the orator Crassus of what is not known, took can-
tharides and died. He had little learning, but was, as Cicero says, a re-
ally great orator, earnest and vigorous, yet graceful (dulcem) and witty;
his voice musical and he practised diligently. His son and namesake, but surnamed
Arvina, was, Cicero says, a good man and an impressive orator as a speaker

2. Lutatius Catulus, the soldier, and poet, died 87
historian, was also a fine orator. The younger Cato was also called e-
loquent and some of his speeches were politically important, but little is said of his
style.

The Asiatic, Rhodian, and Attic schools — In Asia Mi-
or on the whole the most civilised part of the world at this time,
had been developed a school of oratory in which there was something
oriental florid and oriental. This school Hortensius represented at
Rome. At Rhodes, after the fall of Corinth the most important
flourishing city of Greece, arose a chaster school, which Cicero was
considered to belong to. But Cicero's younger contemps, went back to the
golden age of attic eloquence and esp. to the purest most lucid and for
the most graceful of the attic orators Lysias

Lysias

such as we may perhaps recognise in its most beautiful form in St. John
Chrysostom and St. G. Naz.

Though Cicero in fact studied at besides Rome and Athens, Rhodes, and in
Asia minor all three

C. Julius Caesar, the Dictator's namesake but surnamed also
Strabo and Vopiscus, was of the aristocratic party; he nearly brought on a
revolution by his efforts to win the consulship out of due course; and was
killed in the proscriptions and Cinna's 87. As an orator his
style was a novelty: it was graceful, easy, refined, and full of
humour, but without weight or force.

Pompey was a clear and dignified speaker. Antony was unin-
telligible, turgid, and would-be pathetic

A batch of orators better known for other things than their oratory are —

2   1

L. Appuleius Saturninus the demagogue and tribune killed 100, most eloquent
of revolutionists after the Gracchi
M. Livius Drusus tribune and reformer murdered 91

    St. Gregory the Great°—(1) His meeting with the boys in the market place
Angeli — natural endowments ; De Ira — state of sin ; Alleluia — em-
ployment in God's service. Consider under the first point the best you know of
England, under the second the worst, under the third the hopes of h̶ its conversion
and pray for that

    2. Hortensius born°

Explosions at House of Commons etc Jan. 24°
Khartoum fell Jan. 26°
Frost in March

The woman taken in adultery°
    The writing on the ground has something to do with the writing of the tables
of the law. Perhaps Xt meant to suggest that they must wait till he had drawn
up the law according to which he wished to decide, for they addressed him as a
new lawgiver
    Let him that is without sin etc — Pray to keep this spirit and as f̶o̶r̶ far
as possible rule in speaking of Mr. Gladstone° for instance

    March 16 — The feeding of the five thousand°   helpful
    St. Philip and St. Andrew : the one did, the other did not offer a ^ sug-
gestion . Every effort is good; God can make much of little when he will make
nothing out of nothing.
    March 17 St Patrick° — Recommend first to God the whole course
of his life, thanking God for the way he is glorified in him ; his exile and
sufferings, his piety and patience ; his selfsacrifice and zeal ; his miracles
and successes. Consider his hymn° : it breathes a̶ d̶e̶v̶o̶t̶i̶o̶n̶ an enthusiasm ,
which as far as feeling goes I feel but n̶o̶t̶ s̶o̶ a̶s̶ t̶o̶ a̶c̶t̶i̶o̶n̶ i̶t̶ my action
does not answer to this
    Ask for his help for Ireland in all its needs and for yourself in your
position A̶Y̶
    March 19 — St. Joseph°
    He was thought the father of Xt our Lord. Therefore there was nothing
in him visibly unworthy of what Xt visibly was. Consider how great then his
holiness and his humility, for the thought, the mistake made, was itself a
burden to him
    He is the patron of the hidden life ; of those, I shd. think, suffering in
mind and as I do. Therefore I will ask his help

---

rhet[oric]

    M. Calidius died 48, studied ^ under the emp. Aug's. master,
Apollodorus of Pergamus , from which it might seem he belonged to the Asi-
atic school, but this w̶a̶s̶ ̶s̶ does not agree with the accounts of him. Quint[ilian]
speaks of his subtilitas , fine finish or detail . Cicero admired his style greatly
            and choiceness ,   an̶d̶ enforced
and dwells on its originality ^ r̶e̶f̶i̶n̶e̶m̶e̶n̶t̶ , happy ^ use of figures, w̶i̶t̶h̶o̶u̶t̶ ̶p̶e̶r̶f̶e̶c̶t̶
and such a command of construction that the words seemed to fall into their places
like the pattern in mosaic. But h̶e̶ ̶w̶a̶s̶ his refinement made him calm even
to tameness, he used scarcely any gesture , never stamped his foot even ; so that Cicero

A batch of orators better known for other things than their oratory are — so
L. Appuleius Saturninus the demagogue and tribune killed 100, most eloquent
of revolutionists after the Gracchi

M. Livius Drusus tribune and reformer murdered 91

St. Gregory the Great — (1) His meeting with the boys in the market place
Angeli — natural endowments; Defra — state of sin; Alleluia — employment in God's service. Consider under the first point the best you know of England, under the second the worst, under the third the hopes of its conversion and pray for that

2. Hortensius born

Explosions at House of Commons etc Jan. 24
Khartoum fell Jan. 26
Frost in March

The woman taken in adultery
The writing on the ground has something to do with the writing of the tables of the law. Perhaps Xt meant to suggest that they must wait till he had drawn up the law according to which he wished to decide, for they addressed him as a new lawgiver
Let him that is without sin etc — Pray to keep to this spirit and as far as possible rule in speaking of Mr. Gladstone for instance

March 16 — The feeding the five thousand
St. Philip and St. Andrew: the one did, the other did not offer a helpful suggestion. Every effort is good; God can make much of little then he will make nothing out of nothing

March 17 St. Patrick — Recommend first to God the whole course of his life, thanking God for the way he is glorified in him; his exile and sufferings, his piety and patience; his selfsacrifice and zeal; his miracles and successes. Consider his hymn: it breathes a devotion an enthusiasm, which as far as feeling goes I feel but my action does not answer to this

Ask his help for Ireland in all its needs and for yourself in your position

March 19 — St. Joseph
He was thought the father of Xt our Lord. Therefore there was nothing in him visibly unworthy of what Xt visibly was. Consider how great then his holiness and his humility, for the thought, the mistake made, was itself a burden to him

He is the patron of the hidden life; of those, who think, suffering in mind and as I do, therefore I will ask his help

M. Calidius died 48, studied under the crop, Aug's master Apollodorus of Pergamus, from which it might seem he belonged to the Asiatic school, but this does not agree with the accounts of him. Quint. speaks of his subtilitas, fine finish in detail. Cicero admired his style greatly and dwells on its originality, happy use of figures, without result and such a command of construction that the words seem to fall into their places like the pattern in mosaic. But his refinement made him calm even to tameness, he used scarcely any gesture, never stamped his foot even; so that Cicero took advantage of it in court to argue he was not in earnest

The Annunciation° — Consider the persons — On earth the Bd. Virgin. She
was full of grace , that is / she had received and stored up in her every grace offered
and now overflowed in the Son of Christ. So the preparation for grace is grace cor-
responded with

The angel doing his office, his function . Everyone is admirable in his function
well performed , work well undertaken , and this also is matter of preparation

---

M. Caelius Rufus, born same day (May 28) and year (82) as Calvus the po-
et, and orator, friend ^and correspondent^ of Cicero , ~~also~~ of Catiline's ^friend^ and Clodius's , lover
of Clodius' sister Clodia Quadrantaria , espoused Caesar's side, then quarrelled
with him, ~~and~~ led a no-rent movement being himself deeply in debt and lastly ~~both~~
joined with Milo in ~~a raising an~~ a rising in S. Italy on ^the^ Pompeaan side in
which both were killed 48. As an orator he was remarkable for the passionate
force of his attack. Quintilian remarks on his indoles, individuality of style,
~~Cicero remarks on hi His diction~~ Cicero ^calls^ ~~says were way too broken or rugged hiulca~~ .
his oratory rich and grand and also full of wit . Later writers found a certain barbarism
M. Calidius , who died the same year, must have been a great contrast to Caelius
in the style
Asinius Pollio born 76, died AD. 4, served Caesar at home and in
the field and was a friend ~~of~~ ^to^ both Antony and Augustus. He withdrew
from political life ~~on~~ before ~~Art~~ Actium and practiced in the courts. He
is best known now as Virgil's and Horace's patron , but he was famous in
his day not only as a poet , historian, and critic, but most lastingly as an orat-
or. His style ^aimed at purity : it^ had something archaic about it, as though ~~it were earlier old~~ ^he belonged to an earlier^
~~era~~ ^era's^ ~~er~~ than Cicero ~~not younger~~ ; and later critics found ~~it~~ ^# it^ dry and wanting in
brilliancy , ~~but learn~~ though learned and very thorough in ^plan and^ execution (di-
ligentia). ^Of his sentences^ Quintilian says Cicero ends , Pollio stops. Sometimes however
he used a ~~m~~ more flowing style
M. Valerius Messala Corvinus born perhaps 64, studied at A-
thens with Horace and young Cicero, ~~was~~ first ~~with~~ Brutus and Cas-
sius, then ~~joined~~ ^joined^ Antony , lastly Augustus, whom he afterwards served
without loss of independence . Cicero implies that Messala was of his own
school of oratory ~~and highly~~ but owed more to study than genius. He was
admired by later critics ~~n~~ for the purity ^of his language^ ~~and aristocratic hi breeding~~
and a certain ~~noble breeding which~~ ^aristocratic air in^ his oratory ~~shewed~~ , which was choicer
though ~~not so~~ ^less^ powerful as Cicero's. He wrote poetry and grammatical works. ~~He~~
In his old age his mind gave way. He died AD. 9

<of Aquinum, St. Thomas's birthplace>°
~~(Decimo) J~~ <Decimus> Junius Juvenalis ^a^ rich freedman's son or fos-
ter son, it is not certain which , to middle age or thereabouts practiced
declamation rather for his own amusement than as a preparation for the
schools or the ~~court~~ courts. Then having

made him ~~pref~~ military prefect against the Scots>. This punishment was
chosen as ~~the most~~ best answering to ~~a trifling and a~~ ^the^ offence, which was
a trifle or a joke. Nevertheless the ~~victim~~ sufferer by it within a very
short time died of ~~wea~~ mortification and weariness. <Other accounts say

took advantage of it in court to argue he was not in earnest

The Annunciation — Consider the persons — On earth the Bsd. Virgin. She was full of grace, that is / she had received and stored up in her every grace offered and now overflowed in the Son of Christ. So the preparation for grace is grace corresponded with

The angel doing his office, his function. Everyone is admirable in his function well performed, work well undertaken, and this also is matter of preparation

M. Caelius, Rufus, born same day (may 28) and year (82) as Calvus the poet and orator, friend and correspondent of Cicero's, also of Catiline's and Clodius's, lover of Clodius' sister Clodia Quadrantaria, espoused Caesar's side, then quarrelled with him, and led a no-rent movement, being himself deeply in debt, and lastly both joined with Milo in a rising in S. Italy on Pompey's side in which both were killed 48. As an orator he was remarkable for the passionate force of his attack. Quintilian remarks on his indoles, individuality of style; Cicero remarks on his Cicero says he was too broken or up and down, his oratory rich and grand and also full of wit; later critics found a certain affectation

M. Calidius, who died the same year, must have been a great contrast to Caelius in the style

Asinius Pollio born 76 died A.D. 4, served Caesar at home and in the field and was a friend of both Antony and Augustus. He withdrew from political life after Actium and practised in the courts. He is best known now as Virgil's and Horace's patron, but he was famous in his day not only as a poet, historian, and critic, but most lastingly as an orator. His style had something archaic about it, a, though more archaic than Cicero's; and later critics found it dry and wanting in brilliancy, though learned and very thorough in execution (diligentia) Quintilian says cicero ends, Pollio stops. Sometimes however he used a more flowing style

M. Valerius Messala Corvinus born perhaps 64, then died at Athens with Horace and young Cicero, fought with Brutus and Cassius, then joined Antony, lastly Augustus, whom he afterwards served without loss of independence. Cicero implies that Messala was of his own school of oratory and owed more to study than genius. He was admired by later critics for the purity and for a certain aristocratic air which his oratory showed, which was chaste though not powerful as Cicero's. He wrote poetry and grammatical works. In his old age his mind gave way. He died A.D. 9

[Decimus] [Decimus] Junius Juvenalis [of Aquinum, St Thomas's birthplace] a rich freedman's son or fosterson, it is not certain which, to middle age or thereabouts practised declamation rather for his own amusement than as a preparation for the schools or the courts. Then having

made him military prefect against the Scots]. This punishment was chosen as the most best answering to a trifling offence, which was a trifle or a joke. Nevertheless the sufferer by it within a very short time died of mortification and weariness. [Other accounts say

~~The dates of~~

was

Dates for Juvenal°— Vespasian, ~~who d succeed~~, who died 79, was
succeeded by his son, Titus, ~~and Domitian who was~~ who died 81, and Do-
mitian, murdered 96. The Flavian House thus came to an end, having lasted
only 2 generations. Nerva, who succeeded, reigned only 2 years and was suc-

~~his adopted son~~   all but

ceded by ^ Trajan in 98 . Remark that ~~the 2ⁿᵈ century~~ his reign, ~~failing~~ 2
years, ~~serves to~~ begins ~~with~~ the 2nd century. He was succeeded in 117 by

his

Hadrian and he by ~~his adopted son~~ Antonius Pius in 138; he by ^ Aureli-

Marcus

us Antoninus, commonly called Marcus Aurelius° , in 161. ~~He~~ reigned to 180,
and these ~~four reigns~~ 5 reigns~~V~~ , making 84 years, V ~~are~~ are reckoned the
happiest of the Roman empire, the emperors being ~~acti~~ able, active, and

Each of

moderate men and their subjects contented and prosperous. ~~All~~ these emperors

his successor

adopted ~~as were~~ , unless perhaps Trajan Hadrian.

better

V between the tyrannies of Domitian and Commodus, bad sons of ~~good~~ fathers

~~The date of Juvenal's~~ Juvenal lived to be 80 or rather more. The
dates of his birth and therefore of his death are unknown. A late au-

This much is known :

thority, Friedländer,° fixes them as 67 and 147. ~~He began to write~~

he has   near the end

~~at or after middle life and there are~~ allusions to events ^ of Trajan's

and these were written when he was past middle life

~~and~~ reign and to Hadrian's succession^ . He was born at or came from
Aquinum, like St. Thomas ; from his height some thought him a Gaul.
He was a friend of Martial the poet's° — ~~The other~~ unless that is another
Juvenal. ~~The other facts known of him~~ There are several short lives
of him : the following one will serve.

a rich freedman's

< Decimus > Junius Juvenalis , ~~the~~ son or ~~else~~ foster son , ~~of~~ it is not

up

certain which , ^ to middle age practiced declamation, rather for his own

training

amusement than as a ~~preparation~~ for the schools or the courts. After

ing   having written a few   satire which was successful

this ~~he happened to write some~~ ^ lines of ~~not unsuccessful satire~~ on Paris
the pantomime <There were 2 of that name , ~~one Nero's, the other~~ ad-

the one   the other by

mired and put to death ^ by Nero, ~~and~~ Domitian ~~respectively~~ X> and upon

gave himself airs. on ~~one a soldier~~ the strength of   soldiering

a poet+ who ~~prided himself~~ ^ ~~on mac#~~ some trifling six months ~~source~~ or

began   to

so, he ^ carefully ^ ~~cultivated~~ that branch of composition. Yet it was long
before he had the courage to trust himself even to a small audience ;

     ~~when he did~~ though ~~when he did~~ in the end

X prob. it was the latter Paris   ~~in time~~ ^ he was listened ~~to with to~~

+ <Statius>   by such a crowd and with such

as

~~success that~~ encouragement ~~that~~

led him to   more

~~he~~ filled in his first attempts with ~~new~~ matter . ~~The~~ <He wrote : >

the great   To   the

What ~~princes~~ do not give a play actor shall give. ~~And do you give~~

or   the no-

~~a thought to the~~ Camerini ~~and~~ the Bareas, and all the halls of ~~noble~~
bility never you give a thought: that makes
~~men~~ It is Pelopea that makes prefects, Philomela ^ tribunes.

an actor

Now there was then ^ in high favour at court and many of his admi-
rers were promoted every day <according to one another account Trajan's,
to another Domitian's>. Juvenal therefore fell under the suspicion of meaning

by those lines

^ to stigmatise his own times : he was at once , though eighty years old, on

pretended honour of a   command

the ~~place of an honourable~~ military ~~service~~ , removed from Rome , and
sent < one account says at the end of Domitian's reign> to take the praet[or-]
ship of a cohort stationed in the furthest part of Egypt <or Tra###

The dates of

Dates for Juvenal — Vespasian ~~who~~ succeed, who died 79, was
succeeded by his son, Titus, ~~and~~ Domitian who was ~~who~~ died 81, and Do-
mitian, murdered 96. The Flavian house thus came to an end, having lasted
only 2 generations. Nerva, who succeeded, reigned only 2 years and was suc-
ceeded by ^ Trajan in 98. Remark that the ~~2nd~~ ~~century~~ his reign, ~~ed~~ all but
years, ~~seem to~~ begins ~~with~~ the 2nd century. He was succeeded in 117 by
Hadrian and he by ~~his~~ ~~adopted son~~ Antoninus Pius in 138; ** he by ^ Aureli-
us Antoninus, commonly called Marcus Aurelius, in 161. He reigned to 180,
and these ~~four~~ ~~reign~~ 5 reigns ** making 84 years, ~~the~~ are reckoned the
happiest of the Roman empire; the emperors being ~~able~~ able, active, and
moderate men, and their subjects contented and prosperous. ~~All these emperors~~
adopted ~~his~~ ~~successor~~, unless perhaps Trajan Hadrian, .

✓ between the tyrannies of Domitian and Commodus, bad sons of better ~~~~ fathers

The date of ~~Juvenal's~~ Juvenal lived to be 80 or rather more. The
dates of his birth and therefore of his death are unknown. A late au-
thority, Friedländer, fixes them as 67 and 147. He ~~began to work~~ this much is known
~~it~~ after middle life ~~and~~ ~~there are~~ allusions to events of Trajan's
~~and~~ reign and to Hadrian's succession. He was born at or came from
Aquinum, like St. Thomas; from his height some thought him a Gaul.
He was a friend of Martial the poet's ~~the other~~ unless that is another
Juvenal. ~~the~~ ~~chief facts known~~ of him there are several short lives
of him: the following one will serve. a rich freedman's

[Decimus] Junius Juvenalis; the son or else foster son, if it is not
certain which ** to middle age practised declamation, rather for his own
amusement than as a ~~preparation~~ for the schools or the courts. after
this ~~he~~ ~~happened~~ to write ~~~~ lines of ~~~~ ~~unsuccessful~~ satire on Paris
the pantomime [There were 2 of that name, one ~~~~, the other ad-
mired and put to death ~~by~~ Nero, Domitian ~~respectively~~] and upon
a poet who ~~~~ ~~himself~~ ~~on~~ ~~with~~ some trifling six-month soldier's or
so, he carefully cultivate that branch of composition. Yet it was long
before he had the courage to trust himself even to a small audience; ~~~~
~~in~~ ~~the~~ he was listened to ~~~~ ~~~~ by such a crowd and with such
~~~~ that encouragement that

✗ prob. it was the latter Paris

† [Statius]

led him to ~~he~~ filled in his first attempts with ~~new~~ matter. ~~the~~ [He wrote:]
What ~~~~ the great do not give a play actor shall give. ~~and do you~~ the
~~~~ ~~the~~ Camerini and the Bareas, and all the halls of noble-
~~~~ ~~~~ It is Pelopea that makes prefects, Philomela ~~that makes~~ tribunes.

Now there was then ^ an actor in high favour at court and many of his admi-
rers were promoted every day [according to one another account Trajan's,
to another Domitian's]. Juvenal therefore fell under the suspicion of meaning
~~to~~ stigmatize his own times: he was at once though eighty years old, on
the ~~~~ ~~~~ military ~~service~~ command removed from Rome, and
sent [one account says at the end of Domitian's reign] to take the prefec-
ship of a cohort stationed in the furthest part of Egypt [or the

From Fr. Hughes° July 24° £10. And I had, I think, 7s. besides.
Car 1s. — Porter 6d. — 2ⁿᵈ return Dublin to London £3 11s.
           ·
                           extortionate
— Welshman 3d. — # Tea 2s. 6d. (~~extravagan~~) — Porter 3d. — Cab
to Hampstead 3s. ⟋ July 24 and 25
    July 25 2nd to St. James's Park 1s.
    Later at church 6d.
    Railways 9d. or 11d.
    Exhibitions 1s. 6d.

————————

          The Pharisee
Luke xviii 9–14 . ~~Parable of th~~ and the Publican (Aug. 2 '85 Sydenham°)
    You know this Gospel well and must have listened to many discours-
es upon it ; yet when in the course of the year it comes round again we can-
      pass it by, we can
not ^ ~~with~~ but dwell upon these words of divine wisdom.

    Two men went to the Temple to pray. When they went home after their
                    made just
prayer one was justified, ~~the~~ that is was ~~become a just man~~, and the other
was not ; the one who was a great sinner, as we know from his own
words, had ~~become~~ become a just man and his sins were forgiven ; the other, whose
deeds, as we learn from himself, were good and just, went back worse than
          ~~by pride~~   The sin was   that of pride.
he came and sinned even in his prayers. ^ It is certain Xt our Lord in this
story gave to mankind a great warning.
                                       what
    I shall therefore examine the story more closely to shew ^ Xt our Lord's thought
is. And after that I shall advise myself and you against the sin of pride.

    Two men went up to the temple to pray — and ~~that~~ this one incident,
~~is all we hear.~~ which lasted perhaps but a few minutes, is all we hear.
~~There is then a suddenness about and in~~ In that short time all was done,
one man put in to the way of salvation ; the other, as wd. seem, of eter-
nal ruin. There is then a suddenness about the story and the sud-
denness seems rather to terrify than to comfort, as if the way of God were
full of incalculable ~~rev~~ hurricanes and reverses, in an instant build-
                         seem
ing up and in the same casting down, making it ^ seem better (which God for-
             a single
bid) to live recklessly and trust to ~~one~~ hearty act of sorrow than to toil
at prayers and mortifications which a breath of pride may in ~~one~~ one
            bring
fatal instant ~~throw to the ground for ever.~~ shatter and bring to nothing.
Look then somewhat nearer. <u>Two men went up to the Temple.</u> The Jews had
~~in every place~~ other places of worship than the Temple — synagogues. They
had them in every place, wherever Jews were and a running brook was —
for they needed that — was a synagogue and ~~even~~ in Jerusalem itself were
very many, hundreds. But the Temple was very different, ~~much~~ there was

From Fr. Hughes July 24 £10. and I had, I think, 7s. besides.

Car 1s. — Porter 6d. — In return Dublin to London £3 11s.
— Welshman 1d. — Tea 2s. 6d. (~~extravagant~~ extortionate) — Porter 3d. — Cab
to Hampstead 3s. * July 24 and 25
July 25 2nd to St. James's Park 1s.
Later at church 6d.
Railways 9d. or 11d.
Exhibition 1s. 6d.

Luke xviii 9 - 14. ~~Parable of the~~ the Pharisee and the Publican (aug. 2 '85 Sydenham)
You know this Gospel well and must have listened to many discourses upon it, yet when in the course of the year it comes round again we can not ~~pass it over but~~ but 'dwell upon these words of divine wisdom.

Two men went to the Temple to pray. When they went home after their prayer one was justified, ~~the~~ that is was ~~become a just was~~ made just, and the other was not; the one who was a great sinner, as we know from his own words, had ~~become~~ become a just man and his sins were forgiven, the other, whose deeds, as we learn from himself, were good and just, went back worse than he came and sinned even in his prayers. It is certain Xt our Lord in this story gave to mankind a great warning.

I shall therefore examine the story more closely to shew that Xt our Lord's thought is. and after that I shall advise myself and you against the sin of pride.

Two men went up to the Temple to pray — and ~~that~~ this one incident, ~~a all we hear~~ which lasted perhaps but a few minutes, is all we hear ~~here on then a suddenness about and In~~ that short time all was done one man put into the way of salvation, the other, as we seem, of eternal ruin. There is then a suddenness about the story and the suddenness seems rather to terrify than to comfort, as if the way of God were full of incalculable ~~not~~ hurricanes and reverses in an instant building up and in the same casting down, making it ~~run~~ better (which God forbid) to live recklessly and trust to a single hearty act of sorrow than to toil at prayers and mortifications which a breath of pride may in one one fatal instant ~~bring to the ground for ever~~ shatter and bring to nothing. Look then somewhat nearer. Two men went up to the Temple. The Jews had ~~in every place~~ other places of worship than the Temple — synagogues they had them in every place, wherever Jews were and a running brook was for they needed that — was a synagogue and even in Jerusalem itself were very many hundreds. But the Temple was very different, much there was

<u>Cornelius Tacitus</u>° (his forename is not certainly known) was born some-

it

where about 54 AD. , ~~where~~ is not known where ; in 78 he married the
daughter of Agricola the conqueror and also peacemaker of Britain ;

un Vespasian, continued under his sons Titus and

his political career, beg~~an~~ under ^ Domitian, when he rose to be praetor ;
under Nerva he became consul, being chosen to fill the place of the ~~geo~~

aged Verginius Rufus, who died suddenly in ~~his consulship~~ office, 97 ; ^
under Trajan in 100 he was chosen by the senate together with his

the younger   a great malefactor

friend ^ Pliny to prosecute ^ Marius Priscus for oppression of his province ; the
date of his death is unknown, but he lived at least to be 65. He was
famous in his own day, so that many persons unknown to him left him

chance acquaintance   him   games

legacies ; also we hear of a ~~provincial~~ saying to ~~Pliny~~ at the ~~theatre /~~
You are either Pliny or Tacitus, as if those were the most famous writers
of the ~~ag~~ ~~day~~ time. His works are the <u>Dialogue on Orators</u> (probably

certainly

and ~~certainly~~ the following ^ : the <u>Life of ~~Argi~~ Agricola</u>; the account of <u>Ger-
many</u> ; the <u>Histories</u> in 5 books incomplete ; the <u>Annals</u> in 16, also in-
complete. The Annals are a history of Rome from Augustus' death AD.

as we have them,   the one which

14 to Nero's 68 ; the Histories~~,~~ ^ are the history of one year only , ~~from~~

followed   but emperors

^ Nero's death ; ~~onwards and yet~~ of four ~~principates~~, Galba~~'s~~, Otho~~'s~~,
Vitellius~~'s~~, and Vespasian~~'s~~ begun ; ~~It is of course on a great scale~~ yet

they are

~~it is~~ said to have been written before the Annals. The work of course is

great   Tacitus

on a ~~minute~~ scale, which perhaps ~~he~~ did not mean to keep up throughout.
The Annals are the history of the Julian House from its founder Au-

was rather the   Caesarism or   itself

gustus' death (for Julius ~~its author and the~~ author of ^ all imperialism ^

than

~~was not exactly~~ ~~could scarcely be called~~ the founder of that dynasty). The

tell   how   the   passed ~~through several hands~~

Histories ~~is the story of the passing of~~ empire ^ from the Julian to the
Flavian Houses ~~, the hands~~ through what hands it so passed, and with

world,

what struggles. It was a struggle in which the four quarters of the Roman ^
that is the world of Mediterranean civilization , took part, like the four
winds in the prophet's vision contending over the sea ; ~~Clodiu~~ the south by

revolt ~~struggle~~

Clodius Macer, who however was crushed before the ^ could pass beyond the

of Africa

province ^; the west by Galba and then by Galba's murderer Otho, who

came from Germany to

came from Spain and Portugal; the North by Vitellius , who ^ defeat~~ed~~ Otho;

from Judea

the East by Vespasian , who ^ defeated Vitellius and left the empire to his sons.
The First Book tells of ~~Θ~~ Galba's fall, the Second of Otho's, the Third of

deals with   native

Vitellius's, the Fourth ^ ~~of~~ the great ^ revolt ~~of~~ on the Rhine and other mat-
ters, the Fifth ~~of the~~ begins the war with the Jews

the   for

^ He pronounced ~~Rufus's~~ funeral discourse , which on account of his fame ~~and~~ e-
loquence was thought ~~a great~~ to crown Rufus's good fortune ; also

<u>Tacitus' style</u>°

Cornelius Tacitus (his forename is not certainly known) was born at Rome
where about 54 AD, it is not known where; in 78 he married the
daughter of Agricola the conqueror and also peacemaker of Britain;
his political career, began under Vespasian, continued under his sons Titus and under Domitian, when he rose to be praetor;
under Nerva he became consul, being chosen to fill the place of the
aged Verginius Rufus, who died suddenly in the consulship office 97 in
under Trajan in 100 he was chosen by the senate together with his
friend Pliny to prosecute Marius Priscus for oppression of his province; the
date of his death is unknown, but he lived at least to be 65. He was
famous in his own day, so that many persons unknown to him left him
legacies; also we hear of a chance acquaintance saying to Pliny at the
you are either Pliny or Tacitus, as if these were the most famous writers
of the time. His works are the Dialogue on Orators & probably
and certainly the following: the Life of Agricola; the account of Ger-
many; the Histories in 5 books incomplete; the Annals in 16, also in-
complete. The Annals are a history of Rome from Augustus' death A.D.
14 to Nero's 68; the Histories are the history of one year only, from
Nero's death onwards and yet of four principates, Galba, Otho,
Vitellius, and Vespasian; it is of course on a great scale yet
it is said to have been written before the Annals. The work of course is
on a great scale, which perhaps Tacitus did not mean to keep up throughout.
The Annals are the history of the Julian house from its founder Au-
gustus' death (for Julius was neither the author of imperialism
than the founder of that dynasty). The
Histories tell the story of the passing of the empire from the Julian to the
Flavian House, through what hands it so passed, and with
what struggles. It was a struggle in which the four quarters of the Roman world,
that is the world of mediterranean civilisation, took part, like the four
winds in the prophet's vision contending over the sea; the south by
Clodius Macer, who however was crushed before the revolt's pass beyond the
province of Africa; the west by Galba and then by Galba's murderer Otho, who
came from Spain and Portugal; the North by Vitellius, who came from Germany & defeated Otho;
the East by Vespasian, who from Judaea defeated Vitellius and left the empire to his son.
The first Book tells of Galba's fall, the second of Otho's, the Third of
Vitellius's, the fourth deals with the great revolt on the Rhine and other mat-
ters; the Fifth begins the war with the Jews

¹ He pronounced the funeral discourse, which on account of his fame and
eloquence was thought to crown Rufus's good fortune; also

Tacitus' style

Eo i Histories° III ii 6. Eo ipso | the fact. Other uses of is iii. 1. ea statim contione qua

Procurator what — legatus legionis — legatus Caesaris°

Tanquam | on the ground or charge, not false charge°

Vim equitum : vis goes to make a termination like dom, ism etc. Perhaps enclitic — opum vim in hexameter°

Legions° — Flavian 7th Galliana ; 13th Gemina ; 7th Claudian (IX) ; 3rd (X and 8th (X.) (Also 1st Classicorum (ii 67. sent to Spain) ; 14th (ii 66. sent off to Britain etc)

11th legion (iii 50) ; 6000 Dalmatians (ib.); a legion (or something) from the Ravennese Fleet

8 Legions on Vitellius' side—5th (   ), 1st Italica (iii 14.) , 21st (ib.)

See iii 44. 1 adjutrix° (Othonian) sent sent to Spain) ; also in Spain 10th and 6th (Victrix)

2nd legion in Britain in Claudius' time

6th under Mucianus in D Moesia (iii 46.) Sexta Ferrata°

Lucan bk. 1° Analysis of speeches —
That of the Ariminensians 248 sqq. : Unhappy that we are here at Ariminum, exposed an outpost exposed to the first assault of Gauls,
                                                              planted
Carthaginians, and every enemy of Rome! Better have been ^ in the farthest East or coldest North than here°

Easy *Histories* III ii 6. *Eo ipso* / the fact, other uses of *is* . iii 1 . *ea statio continvitque gun*

Procurator what — legatus legionis — legatus Caesaris

Tanquam / on the ground or charge, not false charge

vin opulum : *ins* goes to make a termination like *don*, *ism* etc , Perhaps enclitic —
opuin vin in hexameter

Legions— Flavian 7th Galbiana ; 13th Gemina ; 7th Claudian (ix.) ;
3rd ⋈ and 8th (x.) (also 1st Classicorum (ii 67. sent to Spain) ; 14 th
(ii 66. sent off to Britain etc)

11 th legion (iii 50) , 6000 Dalmatians (ib.) ; a legion (or something) from the Flavian
ieee fleet

8 Legions on Vitellius' side — 5 th (   ), 1st Italica (iii 14.) , 21st
(ib.)

See iii 44. | adjutrix (Othonian) not sent to Spain) ; also in Spain
10 th and 6th (Victrix)

2nd legion in Britain in Claudius' time

6th under Mucianus in Moesia (iii 46) sixth Ferrata

Lucan bk. 1 Analysis of speeches —
that of the Ariminencians 248 sqq. : Unhappy that we are here
at Ariminum, exposed an outpost exposed to the first assault of Gaul,
Carthaginians, and every enemy of Rome ! Better have been planted in the
farthest East or coldest North than here

Curio's to Caesar 273 sqq. : As long, Caesar, as I cd. serve your cause

I can no more;

by ~~constitutional~~ peaceful means at Rome I did so: ~~against the senate ; but~~

that   *I am*

~~now~~ the constitution is overthrown and ~~am I now violently~~ driven into exile.

to repair   *from*

I ~~now~~ leave the lawless city gladly ~~and come~~ to you, ~~to~~ whom I look for the
restoration of my rights as citizen. Act at once: delay will do harm, not

taken ten   *warfare*

good. It is your own best interest. You have spent ^ years of ~~labour~~ in subdu-
ing Gaul ; ~~and~~ yet what is Gaul? Now a far grander prize is within yr.
reach, Rome and the Roman world. One or two ~~a~~ well directed blows and

else

Rome with all Rome owns is yours. You must do this: ~~otherwise~~ you

for   *An*

will lose all you have hitherto striven ~~war~~ . ^ Envious rivals will refuse you
your ~~tri~~ hard earned triumph, even an ovation : yr. very glory will be
your ruin. ˣHusband of your daughter though Pompey is, he hates you
and will never consent to share his sovereignty with you. To be plain,

get

~~you must be~~ rid of him and be master of the world ;°

   x Julia died however in 54. Crassus fell in 53°

to be our reward   ~~we beg and~~

   Caesar's to his troops : 299 sqq. : And is ~~not~~ this ^ ~~what our hard war~~

for all the   ~~we have borne in~~ *of our*

~~fare to get from our~~ hardships, ^ ~~of our~~ Gaulish wars? To be treated as

as ~~if it were~~ *though it were*

public enemies , ~~as~~ Hannibal himself with his Carthaginian host!

armaments

For that is what ~~ther~~ the ~~preparations~~ we hear of mean. And yet, fools,
they do not see ~~that~~ that they have to deal with ~~victors.~~ conquerors in

flush of   *must needs*   *me*   *my*

~~all~~ their ^ glory : they ~~wd. all pain~~ attack ~~us~~ in ~~our~~ hour of victory. Let
them come on; their leader ~~out of date , their~~ a veteran out of date ; their

soldiers

officers ~~civilians~~ babbling gownsmen ; their rank and file a ~~mob~~ hasty levy. And what of
their cause? It has no more right than it has might : Pompey, with his client mob, is to ~~be~~

For him

have everything ; I backed by my army nothing. ~~He has it,~~ it seems, ~~is to have~~ powers

first

~~prolonged~~ is to be prolonged till it it grows into a kingdom ; ~~first~~ he is ^ to

long   ~~is~~   *need*   *to begin with*

triumph ^ before the law allows and then ~~is he~~ ^ never ^ to lay down honours which ~~first~~
he had no right to wear <This refers to several breaches of law or precedent on

when only

Pompey's part, as his two triumphs, ~~as a merely~~ ^ a knight, but principally to his

legal

consulship hold before ~~his time~~ the ^ time and then ~~po~~ prolonged by the Gabinian
Billˣ> ; he for his purposes is to starve the people <this refers to Pompey's be-

on

ing made in 57, ~~at~~ Cicero's proposal, Prefect of the Cornmarket for 5 years> and to overawe

is to make   ~~on~~

the judges <~~a~~ at Milo's trial 52>; last of all he ^ ~~courts~~ war ~~with me~~ , a parricidal

on me

war, ^ . For he must have blood : ~~he~~ tiger ~~the cub~~ that he is, he learnt the taste of it in

from

his cubhood, ~~on~~ Sulla's prescriptions, and ~~in hi~~ still the craving ^ lasts. Yet even Sulla might
have taught him in his old age to withdraw to privacy. But no : he thinks of his triumphs

those triumphs   *more wea-*

over pirates, such as ~~they~~ were, and the old king of Pontus (who died indeed of poison ^

than   *Pompey*

ry of life ~~not~~ vanquished by ~~him~~), and he must crown them with a third, from Caesar.

forego

And why? Because I will not at his bidding lay down my arms and ~~lose~~ my triumph.
And if I do what of these, my comrades in arms? Are they to be cheated of their
well earned prize? My own rights I cd. waive, theirs I will not. They must have rest , they

else

must have a home and lands in town or ^ in country. What shall Pompey's beaten pir-

my conquering   ~~gallant~~

ates found colonies, and ^ ~~not my victorious~~ Romans none? Today they shall. ~~: if you say~~
~~no take~~ Make away with these victorious standards if you can, you who wd. deny me. No, we

had ~~shortly before~~   (50 and 49)

ˣ and to the intrigues by which Pompey ~~was at this time~~ lately ^ endeavoured to get Cae-
sar's power terminated and his army disbanded while he himself was to be prolonged in the pos-
session of both

Curio's to Caesar 273 sqq. : As long Caesar, as I cd. serve your cause
by constitutional peaceful means at Rome I did so; ~~against the~~ now ~~the~~
now the constitution is overthrown and ~~am I too~~ I am ~~violently~~ driven into exile.
I ~~will~~ leave the lawless city gladly ~~and~~ to ~~come~~ return to you. ~~To~~ From ~~you~~ I look for the
restoration of my rights as citizen. Act at once; delay will do harm, not
good. It is your own best interest. You have ~~taken~~ spent ten years of ~~labour~~ in subduing
Gaul; ~~but~~ and yet what is Gaul? Now a far grander prize is within yr.
reach, Rome and the Roman world. One or two ~~more~~ well directed blows and
Rome with all Rome owns is yours. You must do this; otherwise you
will lose all you have hitherto striven ~~for~~ an the. Envious rivals will refuse
your ~~too~~ hard earned triumph, even an ovation: yr. very glory will be
your ruin. Husband of your daughter though Pompey is, he hates you
and will never consent to share his sovereignty with you. To be plain,
~~you must be~~ get rid of him and be master of the world,
× Julia died however in 54, Crassus fell in 53

Caesar's to his troops: 299 sqq.: And is ~~not~~ this ~~that our hard won~~ to be our reward
~~fame to get from~~ for all the ~~friendship~~ ~~if we~~ Gaulish war? To be treated as
public enemies, ~~as if we were~~ Hannibal himself with his Carthaginian host!
for that is what ~~the~~ the ~~preparations~~ armaments we hear of mean. And yet forsooth
they do not see ~~that~~ that they have to deal with ~~victors~~ conquerors in
~~all~~ their ~~flush of~~ glory: they ~~must needs~~ ~~not~~ attack ~~us~~ in ~~our~~ my hour of victory. Let
them come on; their leader ~~out of date~~ there a veteran out of date; their
officers ~~could~~ babbling gownsmen, their rank and file a ~~mob~~ hasty levy. And what of
their cause? It has no more right than it has might: Pompey, with his client mob, is to have
everything; backed by my army nothing. ~~He backed~~ For if, it seems, ~~his~~ power
~~prolonged~~ is to be prolonged till I grows into a kingdom; ~~but he is~~ to lay down
triumph before the law allows and then ~~is to never~~ to lay down honours which
he had no right to wear [This refers to several breaches of law or precedent on
Pompey's part, as his two triumphs ~~necessary~~ Knight, but principally to his
consulship held before his time and then prolonged by the Galvinian
Bill]; he for his purposes is to starve the people [this refers to Pompey's be-
ing made in 57, × Cicero's proposal, Prefect of the Commissariat for 5 years] and to overawe
the judges [× at Milo's trial 52]; last of all he ~~to look~~ a parricidal
war. For he must have blood: ~~to typcrate~~ that he is, he learnt the taste of it in
his childhood, from Sulla's proscriptions, and still the craving lasts. Yet even Sulla might
have taught him in his old age to withdraw to privacy. But no: he thinks of his triumphs
over pirates such as ~~they were~~, and the old king of Pontus (who died indeed of poison,
of life that vanquished by ~~him~~) and he must crown them with a third, from Caesar.
And why? Because I will not at his bidding lay down my arms and ~~forgo~~ my triumph.
And if I do what of these, my comrades in arms? Are they to be cheated of their
well earned prize? My own rights I cd. wave this I will not. They must have rest they
must have a home and land in town or in country. What, shall Pompey's troops dis-
~~also~~ found colonies, and ~~they settle~~ Romans none? Today they shall. ~~if you say~~
~~to take~~ Make away with these victorious standards if you can, you who wd. deny me. No, the

× and to the intrigues by which Pompey ~~had shortly before~~ lately endeavoured to get Cae-
~~sar's power terminated and his army disbanded~~ while he himself was to be prolonged in the pos-
~~session of both~~

(50 and 49)

has grown and hardened on
~~have formed~~ our strength ^ ~~in~~ hard fought fields , now we will use it. Re-
    in justice   force take both our dues
fuse what we ask ~~of right~~ and we will by ^ ~~might ä take that~~ and more.
             neither
And heaven will help us too ; for the war on our side is ~~not~~ for power
     free   from
nor plunder : it is to ~~end~~ poor slavish Rome ~~of~~ her usurper.°

~~Caesar~~ Laelius the centurion's ~~to~~ on behalf of ~~the~~ Caesar's
                army
army 359 sqq. : If I am to speak the truth, Caesar, we yr. ~~soldiers~~
complain of nothing but your too great patience. Do you distrust
yr. soldiers that you thus endure to be curbed by gownsmen and se-
nators? Civil war! What is civil war? Lead ~~u~~ me where you
will, I follow : ~~th~~ I have followed you to the frozen North and
to the other world of Britain ; I follow you still. In enemy of yours
I recognize no countryman of mine. Nay kindred too, brother,
father , wife, child — though your orders were parricide towards
          I swear that
these , sacrilege towards the gods, ^ I must and would obey them.
No fear then that I shall not follow you to civil war : Rome itself
I am ready to storm , yet to wipe off from the ~~north,~~ earth°

have formed our strength on hardfought fields , now we will use it . Re-
fuse what we ask in [justice?] and we will [take both our ...] and more.
And heaven will help us too ; for the war on our side is not for power
nor plunder : it is to free poor slavish Rome of her usurper

Laelius the centurion's [speech] on behalf of Caesar's
army 359 399. : If I am to speak the truth, Caesar, we yr. [army]
complain of nothing but your too great patience. Do you distrust
yr. soldiers that you thus endure to be curbed by gownsmen and se-
nators ? Civil war ! what is civil war ? Lead me where you
will, I follow : I have followed you to the frozen North and
to the other world of Britain ; I follow you still . An enemy of yours
I recognise no countryman of mine . Nay kindred too, brother,
father, wife, child — though your orders were parricide 'towards'
these , sacrilege towards the gods [I swear apt] must and could obey them .
no fear then that I shall not follow you to civil war: Rome itself
I am ready to storm, yea to cope off from the [north] earth

Lucan bk. 1 392 sqq. : ~~ass~~ Caesar's forces etc°
Lemano 396 . | lake of Geneva . <u>Cavo</u> | embayed in mountains
<u>Vogesi</u> or <u>Vosegi</u> | Vosges mountains

<u>Lingonas</u> — <u>not</u> under the Vosges mountains, at the springs of the Marne°
Lyons
<u>Isarae</u> | Isère ~~falls~~ rises in Alps and falls into Rhone between (its meet-
ing with the ~~Dubis / Douls and the sea~~ Arar / Saône) and the sea
<u>Famae majoris in amnem</u> / Rhodanum, the Rhone
<u>Atax</u> / Aude
extended Italy so as to
<u>Varus</u> / Var. <u>Promoto</u>° # etc : Augustus ^ ~~included~~ Cisalpine Gaul and bounded
it by the Alps   sub
Quaque ^ etc. / ~~p~~Portus Herculeo <u>Monoeci</u> / Monaco

<u>Circius</u> / said to be WNW wind. If so it differs only a little from <u>Corus</u> /
NW wind. Is it the mistral?°

<u>Quaque jacet</u> / seemingly the ocean seaboard

<u>Aturi</u> / Adour
<u>Nemetis</u> / the Nemetes German race on the Rhine, but here it is
gn. of the Biscay coast. Nemes seems a river. <u>Nem</u> occurs in many Celtic
names . Possibly <u>nemet</u> may be the Irish and <u>Welsh</u> <u>nant</u> , valley
in Gascony and
<u>Tarbellicus</u> / the Tarbellian. These people ^ reached the Pyrenees.

<u>Santonus</u> / north of the Garonne. Hence Saintes and Saintonges
But
<u>Biturix</u> ~~g~~: round the Garonne. ~~Hence~~ Bourges, though from Bituriges,
belongs ~~Suessŏnes~~ to the B. Cubi a larger division of the race living ~~round~~
where
more inland and ~~midle~~ in the bay of the Loire, ~~round~~ it bends from a
N. to a W. course

~~Suessŏnes~~ / far north , on the Ase (Esa) and Marne (Matrona) .
Hence Soissons . Usually <u>Suessŏnes</u>°

<u>Leucus</u> / on the upper Moselle
on the upper Meuse.
<u>Remi</u> / between Suessones and Leuci ^ Hence <u>Reims</u>
<u>Gens.</u> . <u>Sequana</u> / on the Douls, next Switzerland
north of the Seine
<u>Belga</u> — all northern Gaul ^ called Belgica . Some say the Belgians
were German . Some have thought the Irish <u>Firbolgs</u> were <u>Belgae</u>°

<u>Arverni</u> ≠ at this, viz. Caesar's time they disputed ~~the sover~~ pre-

✱ Lucan bk. I 397 199. : Caesar's forces etc
Jemano 396. / Lake of Geneva. Caso / embayed in mountains
Vogeci or Vosege / Vosges mountains

Lingonas — not under the Vosges mountains, at the springs of the Marne
Isarae / Isère rises in Alps and falls into Rhone between its meet
                                    ly one
up with the ~~Dubis / Doula and the sea~~ Arar / Saône / and the sea
✱ Tanae majoris in amnem / Rhodanum, the Rhone
Atax / Aude
                              extended Italy so as to
Varus / Var. Pronota p etc : Augustus included Cisalpine Gaul and bounded
                  sub
it by the Alps Muague ? etc / Portus Herculis Monoeci / Monaco
            ^

Circius / said to be WNW wind. If so it differs only a little from Corus /
NW wind. Is it the mistral ?

Muague jacet / seemingly the ocean seaboard

Aturi / Adour
Nemetis / the Nemetes German race on the Rhine, but here it is
gn. of the Biscay coast. Nemos seems a river. Nem occurs in many Celtic
names. Possibly. nemet may be the irish and welsh naut, valley
                                            in Galway and
Tarbellicus / the Tarbellian. These people reached the Pyrenees
                                  ^

Santonus / north of the Garonne. Hence Saintes and Saintonges

Biturix ƒ : round the Garonne ~~Hence~~ But Bourges, though from Biturges,
belongs ~~Suessones~~ to the B. Cubi a larger division of the race living round
more inland and nside in the bay of the Loire, where it bends from a
N. to a W. course

Suessones / far north, on the Aisne (Isa) and Marne (Matrona).
Hence Soissons, usually Suessones

Leucus / on the upper Moselle
                          on upper Meuse.
Remi / between Suessones and Leuci, Hence Reims
                              ^
Sequ... Sequana / on the Doubs, next Switzerland
                  north of the Seine
✱Belga — all northern Gaul called Belgica, some say the Belgians
or German. some have thought the Irish Firbolgs were Belgae

Arverni ƒ at this, viz. Caesar's, time they disputed ~~the over pre~~

eminence in Gaul with the Aedui, with whom the Romans sided. Hence
Auvergne , on upper waters of Loire and bounded W. by Cévennes .
Under Vercingetorix they led the last gt. struggle of Gaul in 52°

    Ausi etc — ?

    Nervius — north of Remi, in Flanders. Bloody struggle with Caesar
in 54. Cottae / Aurunculeius Cotta killed by them that year°

    Vangiones / German tribe on both sides of Rhine, s. of S̶t̶. Moritz,
N. of Strasburg, abt. S̶p̶i̶r̶e̶s̶ Bormetomagus / Worms

    Sarmata

    Batavi

    Cinga

    Rhodanus . . Ararim — Arar , the river of incredible gentleness acc.
to Caesar's account

    Gebennas or Cebennas or Cevennas / Cévennes parallel to Rhone on
W.

    Pictones — S. of Loire on the Atlantic near the mouth°

    Turones° — on N. bank of the Loire above the Andegari

    Meduana — prob. Mayenne

    I̶f̶ ̶t̶h̶i̶s̶ ̶m̶e̶a̶n̶s̶ ̶t̶h̶e̶ ̶A̶n̶d̶e̶g̶a̶v̶i̶ ̶t̶h̶e̶y̶ ̶a̶r̶e̶ ̶o̶n̶ ̶t̶h̶e̶ ̶N̶.̶ ̶b̶a̶n̶k̶ ̶o̶f̶ ̶t̶h̶e̶ ̶l̶o̶w̶e̶r̶ ̶L̶o̶i̶r̶e̶ ̶.̶
        H̶e̶n̶c̶e̶ ̶A̶n̶g̶i̶e̶r̶s̶
ˣAndus — I̶ ̶f̶i̶n̶d̶ ̶a̶n̶ ̶A̶n̶d̶a̶c̶a̶m̶u̶l̶u̶m̶ ̶a̶m̶o̶n̶g̶ ̶t̶h̶e̶ ̶L̶e̶m̶o̶i̶r̶c̶e̶s̶ ̶i̶n̶ ̶A̶-̶
        t̶r̶i̶b̶u̶t̶a̶r̶y̶
q̶u̶i̶t̶a̶i̶n̶e̶ ̶o̶n̶ ̶a̶ ^ b̶r̶a̶n̶c̶h̶ ̶o̶f̶ ̶t̶h̶e̶ ̶L̶o̶i̶r̶e̶

    Genabos or Genalus or Genabum old o̶f̶ name of Aurelianorum
civitas / Orleans, which stands at the very northernmost point of
bow made by the Loire

    Dissolvitur seems = solvitur / is freed from and alis seems to mean
cavalry°

    Trevir —The Treveri whose capital Treverorum civitas | Treves is on the
Moselle

    Ligur —There he passes out of Gaul, for, i̶t̶ though the Ligurians once extend-
ed as far as the Rhone or indeed along the coast into Spain, they did not at
                                                still
this time. However Lucan may have thought or known there were ^ some Ligurians

    ˣAndus — no doubt same people as Caesar calls the Andes and that are
commonly called Andegavi, whose capital Andegavorum Civitas / Angers
stands where the Mayenne falls into the Loire. They are then on the north bank
of the L̶o̶i̶r̶e̶ lower Loire in Anjou

eminence in Gaul with the Aedui, with whom the Romans sided. Hence Auvergne, in upper waters of Loire and bounded W. by Cevennes, under Vercingetorix they led the last gt. struggle of Gaul in 52 _Auvi etc_ —

Nervii — north of Reme, in Flanders Bloody struggle with Caesar in 54. _Cotta_ / Aurunculeius Cotta killed by them that year

Vangiones / German tribe on both sides of Rhine, S. of the Nantz, N. of Strasburg, alt. ~~Civitas~~ Borbetomagus / Worms

Saxinata

Batavi

Cinga

Rhodanus .. Arasin — Arar the river of incredible gentleness acc. to Caesar's account

Gebennas or _Cebennas_ or _Cevennas_ / Cévennes parl. to Rhone on W.

Pictones — S. of Loire on the Atlantic near the mouth.

Turonas — on N. bank of the Loire above the Andegavi

Meduana — prob. Mayenne

x Andus — ~~If this means the Andegavi they are on the re. bank of the lower Loire~~ thence angers ~~Andacamulum among the Turones in a~~ ~~territory on a tributary of the Loire~~

Genabos or _Genalus_ or _Genalun_ old & name of Aurelianorum curtas / Orleans, which stands at the very northernmost point of bow made by the Loire

Dissolutus remis = solvitur / is freed from and alis seems to mean cavalry

Treviri — the Treveri whose capital treverorum curtas / Treves is on the Moselle

Ligur — Here he passes out of Gaul, for, though the Ligurians once extended as far as the Rhone or indeed along the coast into Spain, they did not at this time. However Lucan may have thought or known there were still some Ligurians

x Andus — no doubt same people as Caesar calls the Andes and that are commonly called Andegavi, whose capital Andegavorum curtas / angers stands where the Mayenne falls into the Loire. They are then on the north bank of the lower Loire in Anjou

in ~~Trans~~ Transalpine or Longhaired / Comata Gaul. It has been guessed that
this race entered Britain and gave ~~it~~ the name the Welsh still use for England as op-
posed to Wales and Scotland, Lloegr.°

    Teutates° — said to be Mercury, as ~~of~~ is also said of the ~~Teuton~~ German
                                           word
God Tuisco , Tiu = Ζεύς° ; from whose name Tuesday comes. The ~~name~~ enters
                               another king Teutoboduus
into many names, some perhaps German, others Celtic, as Teutones^, Silva Teu-
                                  matius
tobergi~~ch~~ensis Saltus (where Arminius defeated Varus) , Teuto~~boduus~~ king of
the Saluvii (Gauls)

                                       a
    Hesus°— represented with stags' horns, perhaps ^ solar deity

    Taranis — Welsh taran / thunder if I remember

    Caycos — ?? Perhaps the Chauci, a Graecised form.° They lived on the sea-
board between the Frisians and Denmark, but were not at this time threatening Gaul.
                            They became merged
afterwards in the Saxons

---

                                  the Duties
    Cicero de Officiis°—The Treatise de Officiis , on ~~Human~~
of Man was written in 44 ~~the~~ after Caesar's death and shortly be-
fore Cicero's own , in his retirement . It is the last or nearly so of Cicer-
o's philosophical works

                      in philosophy
    Cratippus ~~a~~ of Mitylene ^ a Peripatetic (that is Aristotelian, from A's.
practice of ~~delivering~~ giving his lectures pacing up and down in the Ly-
           great
ceum or ^ gymnasium sacred to Apollo Lyceius in the suburb~~s~~ east of
Athens) was a friend ~~of~~ and partizan of Pompey's, but at Cicero's in-
                  other great
stance, who did him ~~many~~ services, befriended by Caesar. Brutus after
Caesar's death attended his lectures. Young Cicero was very fond of him
and Cic. thought very highly of him°

    Cicero's principal authority Panaetius of Rhodes, the head of the Stoic
school of his time (the Stoics were so called from the Stoa Poecile, Painted
              of Citium
Colonnade , where Zeno° ^ their founder lectured) , a friend of the younger
Scipio's. His work on Duty, Περὶ τοῦ καθήκοντος , was ~~θ~~ finished by his
disciple Poseidonius of Apamea in Syria. Pos. ~~lectured~~ lived chiefly at
             he took part in politics. There
Rhodes, where ^ Cicero heard his lectures , and afterwards wanted him to
write the history of his consulship. He was a traveler and excelled in
physical science , which the Stoics somewhat neglected

    Ariston of Ceos a Peripatetic ~~ar~~ in 230 BC. became head of the
school and wrote.° But the Ariston Cic. means is he of Chios a Stoic
inclining to Cynicism, whom Cic. looked on as a ~~real~~ sceptic at bot-
tom, coupling him here and elsewhere with Pyrrhon. He flourished 260

in ~~three~~ Transalpine or longhaired / Comata Gaul. It has been guessed that this race entered Britain and gave it the name (the Welsh still use for England as opposed to Wales and Scotland, Sloegr

teutates — said to be Mercury, as of is also said of the ~~teuton~~ German god Tuisco, tiu — Zeus, (from whose name Tuesday comes), the name enters into many names, some perhaps German, others Celtic, as Teutones, another big Teutal etc., Teutoberg ensis saltus (where Arminius defeated Varus), Teutobodiacus king of the saluvii (Gauls)

Cernus represented with stag's horns, perhaps solar deity

Taranis — Welsh taran / thunder of I remember

Caycos — ∭ Perhaps the Chauci, a germanized form, they lived on the sea coast between the Frisians and Denmark, but were not at this time threatening Gaul. They became merged afterwards in the Saxons

Cicero de Officiis — the treatise de Officiis, on ~~Human~~ the Duties of man was written in 44 ~~the~~ after Caesar's death and shortly before Cicero's own, in his retirement. It is the last or nearly so of Cicero's philosophical works

Cratippus of Mitylene in philosophy a Peripatetic (that is Aristotelian, from his practice of delivering giving his lectures pacing up and down in the lyceum or gymnasium sacred to Apollo Lyceus in the suburbs east of Athens) was a friend of and partizan of Pompey's, but at Cicero's instance, who did him ~~many great~~ other great services, befriended I Caesar, Brutus after Caesar's death attended his lectures. Young Cicero was very fond of him and Cic. thought very highly of him

Cicero's principal authority Panaetius of Rhodes, the head of the Stoic school of his time (the Stoics were so called from the Stoa Poecile, painted colonnade, where Zeno their founder lectured), a friend of the younger Scipio's. His work on Duty, περὶ τοῦ καθήκοντος, was finished by his disciple Posidonius of Apamea in Syria. Pos. lectured lived chiefly at Rhodes, where Cicero heard his lectures, and afterwards wanted him to write the history of his consulship. He was a traveller and excelled in physical science, which the Stoics somewhat neglected

Ariston of Ceos a Peripatetic in 230 BC, became head of the school and wrote. But the Ariston Cic. means is he of Chios a Stoic inclining to cynicism, whom Cic. looked on as a ~~real~~ sceptic coupling him here and elsewhere with Pyrrhon. He flourished 260

terse and

Herillus of Carthage disciple of Zenon's the Stoic's, a ^ vigorous writer. He made
virtue equivalent to science, ἐπιστήμη°

Pyrrhon of Elis the founder of the Sceptics, whence skepticism in general
is sometimes called Pyrrhonism , was a contemp. of Alexander the Great's ⸴
and
~~who~~ honoured by him

Demetrius Phalereus (from Phalerum an old port of Athens, the deme he

great

belonged to) was the last of the ^ Attic orators.° He was, with the comic poet

pupil

Menander , a ~~disciple~~ of Theophrastus Aristotle's favourite pupil and
successor in the School. D. was a statesman too and a sort of dictator
at Athens in the Macedonian interest for 10 years , till at D. Poliorcetes'
approach he fled and lived long in Egypt at Ptolemy's court°

is   what we

Officium, duty , ^ that which we are to bound to in conduct , ^ must

for it is

do, not by a physical necessity, ~~but of free choice~~ for conduct is of free

by a ~~a necessary~~   alone

choice, but ^~~on a~~^ condition^, if we would ~~be~~ obey the sovereign lawgi-

by the enjoyment   of the reward   bestow

ver God, if we would be happy ~~with the happiness~~ ^ only he can ~~give or~~

or   God   God

^ not unhappy under the penalty only ~~he~~ can inflict. The necessity or must
is that of law , which the lawgiver is said to enforce, the force being the so-called sanction

Duty then is that which conscience or the moral sense recognizes as

Morality

the thing to be done. ~~Duty~~ ^ in gen. is the object of the moral sense and
this particular duty is the object of conscience. As the eye recognises
light, colour ; illumination ; the ear / sound ; the ~~intellect meaning~~ under-

a proper   own,

standing / meaning / so the conscience recognises ^ ~~an~~ object of its ~~bound,~~

some one

viz. law, an absolutely binding law, or rather ~~a~~ precept, a com-

the

mand, an imperative voice bidding and forbidding. Now ~~this voice~~
~~commands of this voice~~ this voice of command ⸴ is absolute , which is
the same as infinite , that is | under no conceivable circumstances to be
disobeyed or outweighing all possible motives and considerations to the

for a   poise

contrary ; ~~but the~~ weight which outweighs all possible counter ~~weight,~~

a

~~the~~ force which resists all possible countereffort, is infinite ; and there

which

is no infinite but God ; therefore the voice ~~of~~ commands conscience is

it is   so

the voice of God or ^ God as a lawgiver commanding, and ^ we have an

essence indeed   on us

immediate perception not of God's self and ~~natu essence~~ but of his ˣ action ^

the   and the will

or rather of ~~an~~ action ^ ~~on us~~ of some ~~power, as~~ being , some power which

for ourselves to be

we learn ~~to be God~~ from others or conclude ~~itself is~~ God Almighty

But the voice which conscience hears or, to speak less figuratively ,
the manifestation of will , the command and imperative which in matters
of conduct we are conscious of , is not arbitrary : ~~on~~ f its nature in-

being will,

deed, ^ it might be so, but in ordinary experience it is not ; it is al-

ˣ his will towards us, his

Herillus of Carthage disciple of Zeno's the Stoic's, *terse and* a vigorous writer. He made
virtue equivalent to science, sovereignty

Pyrrhon of Elis the founder of the sceptics, hence scepticism in general
is sometimes called Pyrrhonism, was a contemp. of Alexander the Great's,
and honoured by him

Demetrius Phalereus (from Phalerum an old port of Athens, the deme he
belonged to) was the last of the great Attic orators. He was, with the comic poet
Menander, a pupil of Theophrastus Aristotle's favourite pupil and
successor in the school. D. was a statesman too and a sort of dictator
at Athens in the Macedonian interest for 10 years, till at D. Poliorcetes'
approach he fled and lived long in Egypt at Ptolemy's court

Officium, duty is that which we are to bound to in conduct, what we must
do, not by physical necessity but of free choice for conduct is of free
choice, but by a necessary condition at once, if we would be obey the sovereign law-
ver God, if we would be happy with the happiness only God can give or
not unhappy under the penalty only God can inflict. the necessity or must
is that of law which the lawgiver is said to enforce, the force being the so-called sanction

Duty then is that which conscience or the moral sense recognises as
the thing to be done. Morality in gen. is the object of the moral sense and
this particular duty is the object of conscience. As the eye recognises
light, colour, illumination; the ear sound; the understanding/meaning/ is the conscience recognises as proper object of its ...
viz law, an absolutely binding law, or rather some one precept, a com-
mand an imperative voice bidding and forbidding. Now the ...
... this voice of command is absolute, which is
the same as infinite, that is under no conceivable circumstances to be
disobeyed or outweighing all possible motives and considerations to the
contrary.; the weight which outweighs all possible counter-weight,
the force which resists all possible countereffort is infinite; and there
is no infinite but God; therefore the voice which commands conscience is
the voice of God or of God as a lawgiver commanding, and we have an
immediate perception not of God's self and essence but of his action only
or rather of an action and the kind of some power being some power which
we learn to be God from others or conclude for ... is God Almighty

But the voice which conscience hears or, to speak less figuratively,
the manifestation of will, the command and imperative which in matters
of conduct we are conscious of, is not arbitrary: of its nature in-
deed it might be so, but in ordinary experience it is not; it is al-

x his will toward us, his

[*always*] directed towards, or directs us towards, the bringing about of one

[*th*]ing ^and^ the prevention of another~ . The thing it wd. bring about ~or~ bids
[*i*]s what we call Right or moral good, the thing it wd. prevent and

forbids is Wrong or moral evil . ~And t~These qualities of Right^ness^ and

Wrong^ness^ are present in all ,^ however various , ₓ ~which~ it bids and forbids

and constitute ^[duty and sin] respectively. ~We recognize them of them-~
~selves ^and~ for us , together with the command to do or forbear,
~we recognise their bindingness or unlawfulness, by the stress~
~put upon us by that voice of common , that law or conscience co~

which directs us to ~the doing of them~ or forbear~ing~ ^do^ , which bids or for-
bids us.

But what is the nature in general of that thing called Right
we are bidden to do ꝫ and of that thing Sin we are ^bidden^ ~not do?~ ^for^ ~not to~
the doing of?
In ordinary cases of experience, where, as said above, the inward
manifestation of will , is not arbitrary, ~the~ Right means that which
secures ~a~ the perfection of our nature ; Wrong means that which
is against our perfection , ~or~ ruins, and undoes it. Thus we feel that self-°

ₓ ~It that is~ duty is a right ^thing^ commanded, sin is a wrong ^thing^ forbidden ; so that ^That is to say^
there are in duty and sin two elements— ^ the ~ꜰ~ ^one^ command to do or for-
be~arear~; ~and~ ^the other^ the goodness, rightness / or evil, badness, wrongness / of the
thing bidden or forbidden. We recognise the ~g~ rightness or right, the good-
ness of good and on the other hand the wrongness of wrong, badness
of bad of themselves by an ordinary exercise ^of ~mind~ thought ~the mind~^ ~of reason~, just as we re-
[*c*]ognise that a line is straight or crooked, a ~loaded waggon balanced~ ^boat trimmed^ or
~t~lop~heavy~, a sheet of ~paper~ ^linen^ clean or spotted , either immediately or by ^sided^
applying some standard, rule, or principle ; but ^besides this^ duty ~as~ requires further
the notion of bindingness and law, ^ of ~sin~ unlawfulness, pro~bi~hibition, and
this we rec~gn~ognise in the stress put upon us by that voice of command which°

preservation is right and so a duty, self-destruction wrong and so a sin,
the sin of ~murder~ suicide , a case of murder. If there were not a power
outside of us forbidding, ~it might be unreasonable, wrong , that is~
~perverse or crooked to execute self slaughter~ if the Eternal, as Hamlet
says, had not fixed his canon gainst self slaughter,° it might be unreas-
onable , wrong in the sense of perverse or crooked, ~but it cd.~ to take
our own lives, but who cd. forbid it ? Only that same legislator, our-
[*se*]lves, who now , by as good a ~right~ ^title^ , ~abr annuls~ ^revokes^ his own ~law~ ^decree^
[##] ^ ~now~ we feel a higher ~power~ ^will^ than either ~ourselves~ ^as it is^ or any other ^ ^own^ whate- ^will^
[*v*]er forbidding the unreasonable ~act~ deed

Cicero strongly recognises and in other ~passages~ ^places^ (as
[*in*] a ~place~ passage from the last work <u>de Rep</u>. quoted by Lactantius
) beautifully expresses the derivation of duty from ~the un~ ^one eternal^ unchange-
[*a*]ble divine law binding all ; but in this treatise, either through haste or as tak-
[*en*] for granted, he leaves that fundamental point untouched
But on the other head, not <u>of the duty of doing</u> but of the duty to be done [####]

directed towards, or directs us towards, the bringing about of one
... the prevention of another, the thing it ... bring about ... ...
... we call Right or moral good, the thing it ... prevent ...
... is Wrong or moral evil. ... these qualities of Right and
Wrong, are present in all, however various, ... it ... and ...
and constitute duty and sin respectively. ... recognise them ...
... ... lawfulness or unlawfulness, by that stress
... ... by that voice, ... , that law or conscience ...
which directs us to ... doing of them or forbearing, which ... ...
bids us.

But what is the nature in general of that thing called Right
we are bidden to do? and of that thing Sin we are bidden not ...
in ordinary cases of experience, where, as said above, the inward
manifestation of evil, is not arbitrary, the Right means that which
secures ... the perfection of human nature; Wrong means that which
is against our perfection, ... ruins, and undoes it. Thus we feel that self-

× that is to say duty, is a right thing commanded, sin a wrong thing forbidden; so that
there are in duty and sin two elements—the command to do or for-
bear, and the goodness, rightness, or evil, badness, wrongness of the
thing bidden or forbidden. We recognise the rightness of right, the good-
ness of good and on the other hand the wrongness of wrong, badness
of bad of themselves by an ordinary exercise ... just as we re-
cognise that a line is straight or crooked, a ... balanced or
..., a sheet of ... clean or spotted, either immediately or by
applying some standard, rule, or principle; but duty ... requires further
the notion of bindingness and law, of unlawfulness, prohibition, and
this we recognise in the stress put upon us by that voice of command which

preservation is right and so a duty, self-destruction wrong and so a sin
the sin of murder suicide, a case of murder. If there were not a power
outside of us forbidding, ... that is
... ... to execute self-slaughter if the Eternal, as Hamlet
says, had not fixed his canon gainst self-slaughter, it might be unreas-
onable, wrong, in the sense of perverse or crooked, ... it ... to take
our own lives, but who could forbid it? Only that same legislator over our
lives, who now, by as good a title, revoked his own ...
... we feel a higher power than either ourselves or any other, that ...
forbidding the unreasonable ... deed

Cicero strongly recognises and in other places (as
a place passage from the lost work de Rep. quoted by Lactantius
) beautifully expresses the derivation of duty from the one eternal unchange-
able divine law binding all; but in this treatise, either through haste or as tak-
ing for granted, he leaves that fundamental point untouched
But on the other hand, not of the duty of doing but of the duty to be done ...

treats fully and first in chap. 4, where he identifies the <u>finis bon-</u>
<u>orum</u>, ultimate and sovereign good, with the <u>honestum</u>, τὸ κα-
λόν, the ~~morally beautif~~ noble or honourable or (most clearly) moral-
ly beautiful, and then divides this moral beauty into ~~four virtues,~~
the four cardinal virtues

He recognises a secondary moral good, the <u>utile</u>, and appears to
and that it is
think this is the <u>honestum</u> as applied to the conditions of life ^ not
~~an~~ absolutely good. This then will be the division he is making in
chapter 3 § 7

Good however is commonly divided into καλόν, χρήσιμον, and
ἡδύ°, honestum, utile, and dulce.° Of the last Cicero takes no notice,
seemingly because pleasure is not moral good. But this is illogical:
neither is beauty, which is τὸ καλόν simply, moral good ; nor con-
venience, usefulness, as of a key or ~~dictionary~~ bootjack or diction-
ary, moral good ; but the <u>morally</u> beautiful, the <u>morally</u> advant-
ageous, are moral good ; so then too ~~the~~ is moral pleasure, as
peace of conscience, and in fact happiness — for if pleasure be
our
extended to all time or beyond this life and to ~~the~~ highest, not our
lowest, faculties it will ~~be ha~~ not differ from happiness ; now
    and shd. be the
that happiness is ^ ~~a moral~~ object of moral action all allow

(perfectum)
At chap. 3 ~~ff~~ §8 he ~~seems to~~ divides duty into absolute ^ and
comparative ~~that is~~ (medium) , by which last he seems to mean
what is better ~~, but~~ done but not absolutely binding — a dist[inction] cor-
responding to the Xtian dist. of Precepts and Counsels. This dist.
only one thing
is Zeno's : Zeno seems to have recognised ~~nothing~~ as absolutely good

   Sulpicius
C. ~~Servilius ?~~ praetor BC. 169, served as legate to Paullus in Macedon-
ian war 167, consul 166 (Holden°)
α ἀστρολογία / <u>astronomy</u>, ἀστρονομία / the same.° The words afterwards distinguished

   Pompey the triumvir's
<u>Sex. Pompeius</u>,^ younger son, ~~of~~ was in the east with his mother when the battle
48
of Pharsalia was fought ^; joined his father in Egypt and there witnessed his murder,
went to Africa and Spain , where, when his brother Cneius was ~~de fell~~ was defeated
at Munda , and put to death, he fled to ~~a~~ the mountains 45 ; after Caesar's death
   esp. at sea,
he gathered power again, ^ was reconciled to the senate, and on the formation of the
second Triumvirate made himself master of Sicily and concluded a treaty in 39 with
   peace   some
the Triumvirs ; this ^ did not last and ~~Pomp. as a measure agst. the Triumvir~~ after ^ conside-
rable successes he was totally defeated ~~off~~ by Agrippa Augustus' lieutenant off Naulochus
   made
on the N. coast of Sicily 36 ; fled to the East, ~~tried to~~ raised war there, but was put
to death at Miletus 35 by Titius one of Antony's lieutenants. Cic[ero] speaks of him
as excelling in geometry , but in literature he was uneducated
§ 87 . 2. <u>Metellum</u> (2, Caecilium M. Macedonicum) — He was cons[ul]
143 , a very successful ~~p~~ statesman

<u>Theopompus</u> rhetorician and historian, contemp. of Alex. the great,° pupil of So-
crates

treats fully and first in chap. 4, where he identifies the finis bon-
orum, ultimate and sovereign good, with the honestum, τὸ κα-
λόν, the morally noble or honorable or (most clearly) moral-
ly beautiful, and then divides this moral beauty into four virtues,
the four cardinal virtues.

He recognises a secondary moral good, the utile, and appears to
think this is the honestum as applied to the conditions of life, and not, that is,
as absolutely good. This then will be the division he is making in
chapter 3 § [ ]

Good however is commonly divided into καλόν, χρήσιμον, and
ἡδύ, honestum, utile, and dulce. Of the last Cicero takes no notice,
seemingly because pleasure is not moral good. But this is illogical:
neither is beauty, which is τὸ καλόν simply, moral good; nor con-
venience, usefulness, as of a key or dictionary bootjack or diction-
ary, moral good; but the morally beautiful, the morally advant-
ageous, are moral good; so then too the moral pleasure, as
peace of conscience, and in fact happiness — for if pleasure be
extended to all time or beyond this life and to the highest, not our
lowest, faculties it will be not differ from happiness; now
that happiness is and also the object of moral action all allow

At chap. 3 § 8. he seems to divides duty into absolute (perfectum and)
comparative that is (medium), by which last he seems to mean
what is better not done but not absolutely binding — a dist. cor-
responding to the Xtian dist. of Precepts and Counsels. this dist.
is Zeno's: Zeno seems to have recognised nothing on this as absolutely good

C. Sulpicius Sominius [ ] praetor BC. 169, served as legate to Paullus in Macedon-
ian war 167, consul 166 (Holder)
ἀστρολογία (astronomy, ἀστεροσκοπία the same. the words afterwards distinguished)

Sex. Pompeius, younger son of Pompey the triumvir (a) in the east with his mother when the battle
of Pharsalia was fought, joined his father in Egypt and there witnessed his murder
went to Africa and spain, there, when his brother Cnaeus was de fell was defeated
at Munda and put to death, he fled to the mountains 45; after Caesar's death
he gathered power again, was reconciled to the senate, and on the formation of the
second triumvirate made himself master of Sicily and concluded a treaty in 39 with
the triumvirs; this did not last and Pompeius opposed the triumvirs after consider-
able successes he was totally defeated by Agrippa Augustus' lieutenant off Naulochus
on the n. coast of Sicily 36; fled to the east, tried to raise war there, but was put
to death at Miletus 35 by Titius one of Antony's lieutenants, Cic. speaks of him
as excelling in geometry, but in literature he was uneducated

§ 17. 2. Metellum (2. Caecilium M. Macedonicum) — He was consul
143; a very successful [ ] statesman

Theopompus rhetorician and historian, contemp. of Alex. the great, pupil of Iso-
crates

Antipater one of Philip's generals ; then regent of Macedonia ; father to Cassand[er]
himself afterwards king of Macedon. Cassander burst out laughing when he saw the pro-
estations at the court of Babylon and always hated the memory of Alexander

Antigonus° one of Alexander's generals , father to Demetrius Poliorcetes and one Phi-
lip, killed at battle of Ipsus 301

the ~~jurist~~ pontiff   honest
P. Rutilius legatus in Asia under Q. Mucius Scaevola ^ as proconsul, ~~incorrupt~~
man, condemned and banished on a scandalously unjust trial ~~op~~

father of the above, Quintus, a greater lawyer,
still, who was ~~Quintius~~ Cicero's
P. Mucius Scaevola, consul 133, great lawyer, ^ ~~father of a greater one Cicero's~~
teacher in law. ~~Q. Mucius~~ This latter is known as the Pontiff and was killed
in the Marian riots 82 at the Altar of Vesta.° 2: Mucius ~~Sa~~ Scaevola ~~als~~ known
as the Augur also taught Cicero law and died before the Pontiff his namesake

---

Martial° lib. 2 ep. 14° (Paley 72).
Remark on pettiness of Martial's mind. Cf. with Juvenal and Lucan
17. Per te : per governs te, but often the te depends on oro etc and per
anticipates its true object°

~~op~~

not") cf "but" whe[n]
Ep. 16° (73) — 2. "Si fuerit sanus" not as Paley says° "If he is not ill"; ~~but When~~ he
[is] not ill,
[ge]ts well what will the scarlet coverings do?"

Ep. 17° (74) — 3. "Argique letum", as if from Argi letum, a legend°; really argil-
in Ennius
latum . ep. ^ "Cere comminuit brum" and "Massili — portabant juvenes ad
[li]tora - tanas" (lagones), ~~imitated in~~ , others in Lucilius imitated by Auson-
[iu]s? ~~"Et Lucanis~~ "Villa Lucani — " max potieris — aca"

Ep. 24° (76) "Haerebo" / I am to, am expected : M. does not really promise nor mean ;
[that] wd. be pointless extravagance°
"Dat tibi" etc — strongest Latin antithesis without marker of antithesis°

79) ~~21~~ Ep. 30° "erat" — idiomatic use of indic[ative] imperf[ect] for a subjunctive°

Antipater one of Philip's generals, then regent of macedonia; father to Cassander himself afterwards king of macedon. Cassander burst out laughing when he saw the statue at the court of Babylon and always hated the memory of Alexander

Antigonus one of Alexander's generals, father to Demetrius Poliorcetes and one Phi...
p, killed at battle of Ipsus 301

P. Rutilius legatus in Asia under Q. Mucius Scaevola the ~~chief pontiff~~ as proconsul, ~~exconsul~~ ~~man~~, condemned and banished on a scandalously unjust trial 92

P. Mucius Scaevola, consul 133, great lawyer, father of the above, ~~Mucius~~ ~~greater lawyer~~. teacher in law. ~~a Mucius~~. This latter is known as the Pontiff and was killed in the Marian riots 82 at the Altar of Vesta. Q. Mucius ~~sc~~ Scaevola the ~~augur~~ also taught Cicero law and died before the Pontiff his namesake

__Martial__ lib. 2 ep. 14 (Paley 72).
Remark on pettiness of martial's mind. cp. with Juvenal and Lucan
17. Per te: per governs te, but often the te depends on ora etc and per anticipates its true object

✱

ep. 16 (73) — 2. "si fueris sanas" not as Paley says "if he is not ill"; but when he is well what will the scarlet coverings do?

ep. 17 (74) — 3. "Argique letum", as if from Argi letum, a legend; really argel letum. cp. "cete cominuit brem" and "massili- portabant juvenes ad tora -tanas" (Lagonas), others in Lucilius imitated by ~~Lucania~~ "Villa Lucani mox potieris -aca"

ep. 24 (76) "Haerebo"/ I am to, am expected: n, does not really praise nor mean, wd, be pointless extravagance
"Dat tibi" etc — strongest Latin antithesis without marks of antithesis

4) ep. 30 "Erat" — idiomatic use of indic. imperf. for a subjunctive

[   ]

———————————————————————————————
———————————————————————————————

[   ]

Revolts of Capito in ~~Africa~~ Germany and Clodius Macer in Africa, both crushed
                March 68   ~~March 68 AD.~~
~~Gaeo~~ Vindex revolts ^ in Gaul ^ and proclaims Galba emperor, but is cap[*tured*]
~~by Verginius Rufus and put to d~~ killed in a tumult at ~~Othe~~ Vesontio wh.
                                                    put down
[*fo*]llowed a conference with Verginius Rufus, who then ~~crushed~~ the revolt
    Galba advances from Spain against Nero under the name of legatus S.
P.Q.R.,° accompanied by Otho and the rhetorician Quintilian. Nero put
an end to his life June 9. Galba acknowledged emperor
    69 . Jan. 1 Galba consul
    Jan. 2 Vitellius proclaimed emperor by the armies of the Rhine at Cologne
    Galba and his adopted son Piso slain Jan. 15. Otho acknowledged emperor
            Otho engages the Vitellian troops   and
~~Vitellius and Otho engage~~ at Bedriacum ^ ~~Otho~~ being defeated puts an end to
his life April 16. Vitellius acknowledged emperor
    Vespasian proclaimed emperor at Alexandria July 1
    Vitellius slain Dec. 22. Vespasian acknowledged emperor, ~~died~~
    Vespasian died Jun. 23 79 and was succeeded by his son Titus. ,
    Who died Sept. 13 81 and was succeeded by his brother Domitian ,
    Who was slain Sept. 18 96 and succeeded by Nerva, who adopted Trajan
by whom he was succeeded on his death Jan. 25 98.
    Trajan died Aug. 8 117 and was succeeded by Hadrian , who claimed to
have been adopted by Trajan.
    There ~~als~~ followed the so-called Age of the Antonines , the happiest
period of the Roman empire , and then the decline°

Vindex revolt in Gaul and proclaims Galba emperor, but was killed in a tumult at Vesontio moved a conference with Verginius Rufus, who then crushed the revolt

Galba advanced from Spain against Nero under the name of legate of S.P.Q.R., accompanied by Otho and the rhetorician Quintilian. Nero put an end to his life June 9. Galba acknowledged emperor

69   Jan. 1 Galba consul

Jan. 2 Vitellius proclaimed emperor by the armies of the Rhine at Cologne
Galba and his adopted son Piso slain Jan. 15. Otho acknowledged emperor
Vitellius and Otho engage the Vitellian troops at Bedriacum, and being defeated put an end to his life April 16. Vitellius acknowledged emperor
Vespasian proclaimed emperor at Alexandria July 1
Vitellius slain Dec. 22. Vespasian acknowledged emperor

Vespasian died Jun. 23 79 and was succeeded by his son Titus,
who died Sept. 13 81 and was succeeded by his brother Domitian,
who was slain Sept. 18 96 and succeeded by Nerva, who adopted Trajan
by whom he was succeeded on his death Jan. 25 98.
Trajan died Aug. 8 117 and was succeeded by Hadrian, who claimed to have been adopted by Trajan.

There followed the so-called age of the Antonines, the happiest period of the Roman empire, and then the decline

EXPLANATORY AND TEXTUAL NOTES

Blank pages are excluded here.

Inside front cover

Gerard M. Hopkins: The signature, written in pencil, is an example of GMH's handwriting in the 1860s. Typically, he would put his name in a notebook when it was purchased, not when he began to use it. See also G.II (*CW* vi).

1ʳ

Matric. These lists of texts for the 1884–5 RUI examinations in Arts, Latin, and Greek (for the BA, Matriculation, First University pass and honours, Second University pass and honours; MA; and the Scholarship exam; see *RUIC* 1884, 31 ff.), also match the information provided in the *University College, Dublin. Prospectus* published in local newspapers.

References to Virgil, *Aeneid*, bk. 2 and 'Easy sentences into Latin' correspond to the fragments GMH cites while grading examinations (see below, fos. 10ʳ–16ᵛ). The texts cited are: Virgil, *Aeneid*; Caesar, *De Bello Gallico*; Sallust, *De Bello Catilinario*; Cicero, *Pro Milone*; Horace, *Epistles*; Cicero, *Philippics*; Virgil, *Georgics*; Horace, *Odes*; Cicero, *Pro Muraena* and *Pro Plancio*; Herodotus, *The Histories*; Homer, *Odyssey*; Sophocles, *Ajax* and *Philoctetes*; Plato, *Phaedo*; Sophocles, *Antigone* and *Oedipus Rex*; Thucydides, *History of the Peloponnesian War*; Aeschylus, *Agamemnon* and *Persae*; Sophocles, *Oedipus at Colonus*; Plato, *Gorgias*; Aristotle, *Rhetoric*; Demosthenes, *De False Legatione*; Aeschylus, *Agamemnon* and *Persae*; Aristophanes, *Nubes* and *Aves* {*The Clouds* and *The Birds*}; Pindar, *Nemean Odes*; Plato, *Republic*; Aristotle, *Politics*; Homer, *Iliad*; Euripides, *Bacchae*, *Ion*; Sophocles, *Trachinae*; Xenophon, *Hellenica*; Demosthenes, *In Leptinem*. Changes in texts, year to year, were announced in the Calendars.

Georgics bk. 1: GMH's extensive annotations for Virgil's poem are found in a volume now housed in the IJA (J11/19): *Corpus Poetarum Latinorum*, ed. William Sidney Walker (London: George Bell & Sons, 1878). See *CW* vi.

2ʳ

Aeschylus: GMH began studying the ancient Greek playwright's works at Highgate school; for his notes, see *CW* vi. The copy of Aeschylus' *Choephoroi* {*The Libation Bearers*} edited by A. Sidgwick (Oxford: Clarendon Press, 1884) that GMH used and annotated is now housed in the IJA (J11/21). The play was prescribed for the BA honours in 1885–6, 1886–7, and for the MA in 1885–6.

Pindar ÷: It is typographically impossible to indicate that GMH has cancelled a dash (or in other places, a short line); we are using the division sign (÷) to identify all such deletions.

Tauchnitz: Refers to the edition of Aristotle's *Politics* that GMH planned to use: *Aristotelis Politicorum libri VIII. et Oeconomica: Ad optimorum librorum fidem accurate edita* (Leipzig: Tauchnitz, 1831).

Scholarship: An example of GMH's practice of revisiting various pages and adding new material. See also Editorial Notes.

Rome: Details of Part III of the work prescribed for the Scholarships examinations continue on fo. 3ʳ, second item.

3ʳ

St. Peter's Confn.: Peter's celebrated confession of faith, as set forth in the synoptic gospels (Matthew 16: 13–20, Mark 8: 27–30, and Luke 9: 18–20), establishes his position as the foremost of the tweve apostles. While travelling with the disciples to the village of Caesarea Philippi (located in today's Golan Heights), Jesus asks, 'Who do men say that the Son of man is?' (Matthew 16: 13). The disciples propose various answers—John the Baptist, Elijah, Jeremiah—but Jesus meets them with a second question: 'But who do you say that I am?' (Matthew 16: 15). To this, Peter replies: 'You are the Christ, the Son of the living God.' Jesus then commissions Peter as the 'rock on which I will build my church' (16: 17–19). Within the Roman Catholic Church, this saying of Jesus forms the basis of the institution of the papacy. GMH's reminder to begin with 'Comp[osition of place'] is a standard part of Ignatian meditation in which one is to begin a meditation by using all the senses to enter into the scriptural scene. Similarly, 'fruit' is a reminder, in accordance with standard Ignatian prayer practice, to ask for the spiritual grace that he most truly desires. This is the first of some thirty instances in which GMH uses the *DN* to prepare 'points' for the following morning's meditative prayer—see the Introduction, above.

(b) Jan—Ins[truction]: Continuation of the requirements for the Scholarship examination. (*University College. Prospectus*; *RUIC* 1884, 63). 'Ins[truction] in Geography arising from above bks.' would have included the travels of Aeneas around the Mediterranean; details of Roman life as found in Horace, Sallust, and Cicero; and a military history of the Second Punic War, as treated in Livy's history of Rome, *Ab Urbe Condita*, books 21 to 23.

The Lance and Nails: In the gospel according to John, a Roman soldier uses his spear to pierce the side of Jesus, in order to confirm his death (19: 34), and doubting Thomas subsequently refers to the nail wounds and pierced side in Christ's risen body (20: 25). The Evangelist Luke, too, in his narrative of Jesus' resurrection, adverts to the nail wounds in Jesus' hands and feet (24: 39), and Jesus is traditionally represented as having been fixed to the cross in this manner. Metonyms for the ignominy and torture that Jesus underwent, the lance and the nails are, like the cross, celebrated by Christians as instruments of the salvation won by Christ through his passion, death, and resurrection. It would not have been lost on Hopkins that a commonly used seal of the Society of Jesus features a representation of the Holy Name under which are three nails, the whole surrounded by emanating rays representing the light of the resurrection. (Cf. *The Five Wounds*, below.)

The Transfiguration: Matthew (17: 1–13), Mark (9: 2–13), and Luke (9: 28–36) recount the transfiguration of Jesus, his assumption of heavenly glory as witnessed by Peter, James, and John. Bringing these apostles with him, Jesus ascends a mountain, usually said to be Mount Tabor (though Mount Hermon and, less probably, the Mount of Olives, have also been proposed), and 'is transfigured before them'. Radiant, he converses with Moses and Elijah, who appear at his side, while the voice of God, speaking from a cloud overhead, proclaims, 'This is my beloved Son, with whom I am well pleased; listen to him' (Matthew 17: 2–9).

Roehampton in the tertianship: GMH began his tertianship [from the Latin: *tertio*, meaning *third*], the 'third probation' before a Jesuit is admitted to take final vows, at Manresa House, Roehampton, in October 1881, professing his final vows in the Society of Jesus nine months later in August 1882. St Ignatius Loyola, in the *Constitutions of the Society of Jesus*, explains this final phase of Jesuit formation, 'after those who were sent to studies have achieved the diligent and careful formation of the intellect by learning, they will find it helpful during the period of last probation to apply themselves in the school of the heart, by exercising themselves in spiritual and corporal pursuits which can engender in them greater humility, abnegation . . . , and also greater knowledge and love of God our Lord' (no. 516). In this instance, GMH is recalling what he learned about Ignatian prayer during his tertianship and is reminding himself to apply this more affective method to his morning meditation.

The Five Wounds: Injuries sustained by Jesus during crucifixion, which became a focus of veneration from the Middle Ages. Of the canonical accounts of the Passion, only the gospel according to John directly testifies to the wounding of Jesus's side soon after his death, indicating that one of the Roman soldiers 'pierced his side with a spear, and at once there came out blood and water' (19: 34). Luke (24: 39) and John (20: 20, 27) refer to wounds in both the hands and feet, almost certainly from nails the soldiers would have used to affix him to the cross. Reverence of the Five Wounds reached its apex in the early modern cult of the Sacred Heart, as for instance in Richard Crashaw's poem, 'On the Wounds of Our Crucified Lord'. Devotion to the Sacred Heart of Jesus was traditionally characteristic of Ignatian spirituality.

4^{r}

The upper half of the leaf has been cut out.

crowned with thorns: Before crucifying Jesus, the Roman soldiers ridiculed his claim to being the 'King of the Jews' by dressing him in a scarlet robe, placing a crown of thorns on his head, and leading him in mock procession to the cross. See Matthew 27: 27–30, Mark 15: 17, and John 19: 2, 5.

tempted in the wilderness: Accounts of the temptation of Jesus are found in the synoptic gospels: Matthew (4: 1–11), Mark (1: 12–13) and Luke (4: 1–13). After Jesus' baptism in the River Jordan by John the Baptist, the spirit of God leads him into the wilderness, where he fasts for forty days and nights, then undergoes a series of temptations by Satan. First, Satan invites him to turn the stones before them into loaves of bread, thereby satisfying his hunger. He next urges Jesus to jump from the eminence of a temple, thereby proving his divinity, since angels of God will rescue him. Finally, he offers Jesus 'all the kingdoms of the world and the glory of them' (Matthew 4: 8), in exchange for Jesus' worship. That Jesus rejects these temptations even after a period of extreme self-denial is usually interpreted as reflecting his spiritual strength and his steadfast refusal to allow any temporal considerations to compromise his fidelity.

St Antony: St Antony of Egypt (251–356), considered the father of Christian monasticism, dedicated himself to asceticism at age 20. At 35, he retired to Pispir, a mountain on the Nile, where he lived inside an abandoned fort until 306. After emerging for five years to lead the disciples who had gathered around him, he took up residence in the desert between the Nile and the Red Sea, where he lived in semi-isolation. Primary source of information: the biography written by Athanasius (*c.*296–373) chronicles his spiritual combat and testifies to his great wisdom. Feast day: January 17.

St Cuthbert: St Cuthbert (*c.*634–87), probably born near Melrose in Northumbria, undertook an eremitic lifestyle on St Cuthbert's Island in 676; later that same year he retired to Inner Farne, in near-total solitude. In 685, he was appointed Bishop of Lindisfarne. Eleven years after his death, his body was found to be uncorrupted, leading to his widespread veneration in the Middle Ages. The Venerable Bede wrote a biography of Cuthbert (*c.*672), as did an anonymous monk of Lindisfarne. Feast day: March 20.

5^r

The upper third of the leaf has been removed. The first entry is written in ink; the remaining entries in pencil.

Our Lady's Sorrows: Commemoration of the 'seven sorrows' of Christ's mother, Mary, arose in the late Middle Ages. They consist of: (i) the prophecy of Simeon, the holy man, who appears at the temple during Jesus' consecration and foretells suffering for the child and mother (Luke 2: 34–5); (ii) the Holy Family's flight into Egypt to escape the massacre of first-born sons ordered by King Herod (Matthew 2: 13–15); (iii) searching for the child Jesus, later found among the elders in the temple courts, Jerusalem (Luke 2: 41–50); (iv) meeting Jesus on the road to Calvary (Luke 23: 27–31); (v) standing at the foot of the cross (John 19: 25–7); (vi) the deposition of Jesus' body from the cross (Luke 23: 53); and (vii) the burial of Jesus's body (Luke 23: 53). The feast of Mary's Seven Sorrows is celebrated on the third Sunday of September.

I set the Lord before me: Psalm 16: 8–9, 'I set the LORD always before me: because he is at my right hand, I shall not be moved. Therefore my heart is glad, and my glory rejoiceth: my flesh also shall dwell in safety.'

Rules of modesty: Set down by St Ignatius himself, the Rules of Modesty were to govern the Jesuit's conduct in all human interactions; they emphasized humility, gentleness, *gravitas*, religious decency, deportment, moderation, civility, and the preservation of one's chastity. GMH may have been thinking particularly of this last aspect of the Rules, which, among other counsels, emphasized the importance of 'custody of the eyes'. (See also fo. 6ʳ.)

Ways of life: GMH is recalling a passage in the *Spiritual Exercises*, an 'Introduction to the Consideration of Different States of Life' (no. 135), which adduces the young Jesus as moving from a simple state of obedience to the greater perfection of living the evangelical counsels in order to raise the question of 'how we ought to dispose ourselves in order to come to perfection in whatever state of life God our Lord would give us to choose'. This exercise is a prelude to meditations on the Two Standards and on the Three Classes of Men, which immediately follow; all three elements from the Second Week of the *Exercises* are designed to help the exercitant choose a manner of living that is spiritually best.

Corpus Christi: The Feast of Corpus Christi {the Body of Christ}, traditionally observed by the Catholic Church in the West on the Thursday following Trinity Sunday, dates to a Papal bull issued by Pope Urban IV in 1264; it commemorates Jesus' institution of the Eucharist (or Holy Communion) during the Last Supper and celebrates the the gift of Real Presence of Christ in the sacrament. Typically, immediately after Mass, there would be the public procession of the Blessed Sacrament accompanied by singing and acts of adoration, and, often, Benediction. The Feast of Corpus Christi in 1884 fell on 12 June.

Nobis datus: 'has been given to us'. GMH is citing *Pange lingua gloriosi* ('Sing, my tongue, the Saviour's glory'), attributed to Venantius Fortunatus (530–600) and St Thomas Aquinas. Composed for the feast of Corpus Christi and traditionally sung during Eucharistic processions, Adoration, and Benediction. One of the most famous texts in the Roman Catholic Breviary and missal, the opening lines are:

Pange, lingua, gloriosi	Sing, my tongue, the Saviour's glory,
Corporis mysterium,	of His flesh the mystery sing;
Sanguinisque pretiosi,	of the Blood, all price exceeding,
quem in mundi pretium	shed by our immortal King,
fructus ventris generosi	destined, for the world's redemption,
Rex effudit Gentium.	from a noble womb to spring.
Nobis datus, nobis natus	Of a pure and spotless Virgin
ex intacta Virgine[.]	born for us on earth below[.]

This translation is taken from *Lyra Catholica, containing all the Breviary and Missal Hymns* (London, 1849) by Edward Caswall (1814–78; *ODNB*), poet and translator, 'one of the most important hymnologists in the nineteenth-century English-speaking world' (de Flon, *Edward Caswell*, 1). Caswall, an Oxford graduate (BA, 1836), was ordained an Anglican priest in 1839. He and his wife Louisa converted to Catholicism; when she died in 1849, he joined Newman's Oratory of St Philip Neri in Birmingham and became a priest. Subsequently, he was a key financial donor and administrator, including during the months (September 1867–April 1868) when Hopkins was an instructor and resident at the Oratory.

Nobis natus ex intacta virgine: 'has been given to us from the untouched virgin'. From the *Pange lingua*.

6ʳ

The next three leaves have been removed; stubs remain.

Man was created to praise: The opening phrase of the 'First Principle and Foundation' of the *Spiritual Exercises* of St Ignatius Loyola: 'Man is created to praise, reverence, and serve God our Lord, and by this means to save his soul. The other things on the face of the earth are created for man to help him in attaining the end for which he is created. Hence, man is to make use of them in as far as they help him in the attainment of his end, and must rid himself of them in as far as they prove a hindrance to him. Therefore, we must make ourselves indifferent to all created things, as far as we are allowed free choice and not under any prohibition. Consequently, as far as we are concerned, we should not prefer health to sickness, riches to poverty, honor to dishonor, a long life to a short life. The same holds for all other things. Our one desire and choice should be what is more conducive to the end for which we are created' (no. 23). See also GMH's January 1889 retreat notes, Appendix I, 24ʳ.

Calix quem Pater: 'The chalice which my Father has given me, shall I not drink it?' (John 18: 11). GMH is probably citing from memory; the text of the Vulgate states: 'calicem quem dedit mihi Pater non bibam illum.' While *calix* is a grammatically acceptable change from the accusative *calicem*, GMH's *illud* is not quite right, since the pronoun *illud* is neuter, but here refers to the masculine *calix*. Yet, the sense is clear and grammatically GMH's shift is sustainable.

Facere nos indifferentes: 'Making ourselves indifferent.' From the 'Principle and Foundation' (no. 23), of the *Spiritual Exercises* of St Ignatius, an exhortation to become indifferent, or unattached, to created things in order to discern the divine will more readily and to use the creation most appropriately in service of the salvific purpose for which all was made by God (see above).

the part ex.: The Particular Examen, a practice of moral scrutiny repeated several times each day, is delineated in the First Week of the *Spiritual Exercises* in order to help one who wishes to grow in freedom 'to guard carefully against that particular sin or defect with regard to which he seeks to correct and improve himself' (no. 24; see also nos. 25–31).

Rules of modesty: see note at 5ʳ, above.

Foundation Exercise: The 'Principle and Foundation' of the *Spiritual Exercises*; see above.

Father D. M.: Denis Murphy, S.J. (1833–96), Hopkins's spiritual director during his first year in Dublin. Hopkins may have felt a particular connection with him, as Murphy too studied theology at St Beuno's (and was ordained there in 1862), and had shared interests in history, spirituality, and Irish language.

7^v

St Michael: The archangel Michael is mentioned by name four times in the Bible: twice in Daniel, where he is identified as the champion of Israel (10: 13 and 12: 1); once in the Catholic Epistle of St Jude, which refers to a legend of Michael fighting with Satan over the body of Moses (Jude 1: 9); and once in Revelation, where he is depicted as the leader of heaven's army in the battle against Satan (2: 7). St Michael is commonly celebrated as a warrior against Satan; rescuer of believers' souls at the time of their death; patron of the church; protector of God's chosen people; and the caller of souls to judgement. Michaelmas Day is traditionally celebrated on 29 September; 30 September marks the feast of St Jerome.

particular examen: See note at 6^r, above.

St Francis: Founder of the Franciscan Order, Francis of Assisi (1181/2–1226) was born to a wealthy Italian family. He served in the military as of age 20, but was felled by illness. Following his return to Assisi, he declared his intention to take up fasting, pilgrimages, and caring for the sick. Soon disinherited by his father, a cloth merchant, for his attempt to donate his father's draperies to the chapel of San Damiano, Francis in turn renounced all worldly possessions. Extreme asceticism, poverty, and devotion to the sick (especially lepers) distinguished the friars who joined Francis. Concern with doctrinal observance, papal fidelity, and worldly renunciation characterize *Regula Prima* (*c*.1210), the Rule that Francis penned for his order. The Penitents of Assisi, as they called themselves, were joined by two other orders: the Second Order of Poor Ladies, and the Third Order (for lay people who could not abandon their secular duties). In 1219, returning from a journey to the Holy Land, Francis drew up a modified Rule, *Regula Bullata* (1221), and resigned as the Order's leader. He received the stigmata (bleeding wounds to his hands, feet, and side, emblems of Christ's ordeal on the cross) in 1224 on Mount La Verna, an event commemorated by the Church on 17 September. Artistic representations often depict him preaching to birds; his belief in the unity of creation under God led him to refer to elements of the natural world as brothers and sisters. His devotion to St Michael appears in his Salutation to the Blessed Virgin Mary (see Francis, *Works of the Seraphic Father St. Francis of Assisi* (London: R. Washbourne, 1882), 168–9). Feast day: 4 October.

In the mid-1860s, GMH copied out an extract from St Bonaventure's *Life of St Francis*, ch. 9: 'Everything incited him to the love of God, he exulted in all the works of the Creator's hands and, by the beauty of His images, his spirit rose to their living origin and cause. He admired Supreme Beauty in all beautiful things, and by the traces impressed by God on all things he followed the Beloved. To him all creation was a stairway which led him up toward Him who is the goal of all desires. With an intensity of devotion unknown before him, he enjoyed the delights of the font of joy in every single creature, as in rivulets flowing from it. He perceived celestial harmonies in the concord of the virtues and activities which God had given the creatures and, like the Prophet David, he was sweetly reminded by them to praise the Lord.' *St Francis of Assisi: The Legends and Lauds*, trans. N. Wydenbruck, ed. Otto Karrer (London: Sheed and Ward, 1947), 164.

Bd. Peter Favre: Peter Faber (1506–46), one of the first companions of the nascent Society of Jesus, was born at Villaret, Savoy. He travelled to Paris in 1525 and shared quarters with Francis Xavier (1506–52) at the college of Saint-Barbe, where he also met and befriended Ignatius Loyola (1491–1556). In 1534, Faber was ordained a priest, and, along with Loyola, Xavier, and four others, pronounced private vows of poverty, chastity, and a pilgrimage to the Holy Land to convert infidels. When the pilgrimage proved unfeasible, they went to Rome instead, placing themselves at the disposal of the Pope to go wherever he judged they could produce the greatest apostolic benefit. Faber was subsequently sent to Germany to act as a Catholic envoy at the Diet of Worms (1540) and at the Diet of Regensburg (1541). He was also sent to assist at the Council of Trent in 1546, but died in transit, in Rome. He is chiefly remembered for his work in Germany, particularly his efforts to reform the Catholic clergy, and for founding Jesuit colleges there and in Spain. Beatified on 5 September 1872. The association of Faber with a devotion to angels comes from his custom of invoking the guardian angels of the parishes in which he travelled, especially in unwelcoming places. See Father Giuseppe Boero, *The Life of the Blessed Peter Favre* (London: Burns and Oates, 1873), 48–50. Feast day: variously given as 2, 8, and 11 August.

2 + 2: Markings on the stub of the leaf visible between fols. 7 and 8 suggest that it contained attendance lists.

8ʳ

Ode to Evening: by William Collins (1721–59; *ODNB*); first published in *Odes on Several Descriptive and Allegoric Subjects* (1746, dated 1747). See Appendix B for a published text. For GMH's musical setting of the Ode, see fo. 11ʳ.

With brede: anything woven, braided, or embroidered; poetically, it relates to the intermingling of colours, as in a rainbow.

9ʳ

Four leaves of the notebook were removed between fos. 8 and 9. The numeral '772', which appears at the top of the third stub, suggests that GMH was grading examinations (identifying candidates by their assigned number).

My heart: early draft of 'Caradoc's Soliloquy' from 'St Winefred's Well', a verse drama GMH worked on from 1879 to 1886 but never completed (see *PW* 438–41). Other segments include 'Leaden Echo' and three scenes from Acts I and II. In the mid-1870s, GMH composed a six-line English poem, 'On St. Winefred', and drafted several Latin stanzas, 'In S. Winefridam'. 'The characters in GMH's fragments are Winefred (or Gwenvrewi), her father Teryth, her mother Gwenlo, her uncle Beuno (referred to as 'Lord', the missionary saint), and her suitor (Prince) Carádoc (whose name is contracted to "Cradock")' (MacKenzie, *PW* 441). On New Year's Day 1885, GMH informed Bridges that 'I shall be proud to send you the fragments, unhappily no more, of my St. Winefred', but did not; the promise was renewed 1–2 April 1885 but only kept four months later. 'You will see that as the feeling rises the rhythm becomes freer and more sprung: I think I have written nothing stronger than some of those lines', he informed Bridges 1–2 April 1885; 'In the passage following Caradoc is to die impenitent, struck by the finger of God.'

Winefride (Gwenfrewi) was born to a noble family in north Wales in the seventh century. According to legend, when she rejected the advances of her suitor, Prince Caradoc, he pursued her and beheaded her in a rage; her uncle, St Beuno, restored her to life. She then became either an abbess at Holywell or a nun in a nearby valley. At the place where her head fell, a spring is said to have arisen; the site (Treffynnon/Holywell), which is within walking distance of St Beuno's College (where GMH studied theology), became a famous destination for pilgrimages well into the nineteenth century (and at present). In the late fifteenth and early sixteenth centuries a Gothic church was built on the site. See *The Life of St. Winefride*, ed. Canon John Dalton (London: C. Dolman, 1857); <www.saintwinefrideswell.com/contact.htm>.

My heart: the musical symbol that appears over 'heart' and 'seen' is the fermata or pause; these musical notes would be 'held' longer.

ɼ: GMH has cancelled a quaver rest (a pause that would last one-eighth of a measure).

10ʳ

Fo. 10ʳ to Fo. 16ᵛ. GMH is grading the 1884 Matriculation Examination; his notes correspond to the prescribed texts, Virgil's *Aeneid*, bk. 2, and Caesar's *De Bello Gallico*, bks. 1 and 2 (*RUIC* 1884: 31).

Then the Greeks: GMH is grading translations from the 'Helen Episode' of the *Aeneid*, bk. 2 (2. 567–88). Scholars generally reject the authenticity of the passage, which first appears in fourth-century manuscripts of the epic. See Charles Murgia, 'The Date of the Helen Episode', *Harvard Studies in Classical Philology*, 101 (2003), 405–26.

The Common Fury: A student has bungled *Aeneid* 2. 573 (*Troiae et patriae communis Erinys*), which refers to Helen as the 'Common ruin / Fury of Troy and her own homeland'. The Furies were avenging goddesses in Greek myth, born of Gaia and Chronos; depicted as women carrying torches and wrapped in snakes, they would punish sins perpetrated against family members. Originally known as the Erinyes; in the drama by Aeschylus (525–456 BCE), they are renamed the Eumenides, the change denoting a movement from purely visceral revenge to rationally determined punishment. Erinys is the singular form of Erinyes.

Most do not try: Students were told to scan two lines from the *Aeneid*. A similar question is found in the Summer 1885 Matriculation examination, featuring lines from *Aeneid* 3. Dactylic hexameter, the metre of classical epic, is perhaps the easiest ancient metre to identify: six feet of two long syllables each, the second of which may be resolved into two short syllables; the last syllable is an *anceps* (either short or long). Scanning the verse is not simply a metrical exercise; the lengths of vowels can affect translation, and thus the quantity of a syllable can change the meaning of a word (e.g. a *malum* is an evil, while a *mâlum* is an apple). Both Greek and Latin poetry are primarily scanned on the basis of vowel lengths as opposed to natural stress accent or *ichthus* (an issue relevant to GMH's treatment of Pindar's *Odes*, discussed below).

10ᵛ

Ariovistus in se consule: Probably taken from Julius Caesar, *De Bello Gallico* 1. 40. The student has failed to render the *oratio obliqua* into *oratio recta* (see note for fo. 11ʳ). The original Latin, which records a reported speech by Caesar himself, reads '*Ariovistum se consule . . . appetisse*'. In direct discourse (as pronounced by Caesar), it would read, 'In my own consulship Ariovistus sought' (the Latin should be, then, '*Ariovistus me consule . . . appetivit*'). Apparently the student changed the English from indirect to direct discourse successfully, but failed to translate that accurate rendering back into Latin, and composed nonsense instead. Ariovistus was the king of the Suebi, who invaded Gaul around 71 BCE and became a Roman ally, but was eventually defeated by Caesar in 58 BCE at Alsace.

11ʳ

as spoken: 'To render as spoken' refers to turning *oratio obliqua* into *oratio recta*, e.g., 'She said that she was sad' becomes 'She said, "I am sad"'. These students simply render the Latin more literally, aping the Latin word order.

   hours: The tedium of grading is interrupted by a snippet of musical composition; GMH is setting phrases from Collins's 'Ode to Evening'. See also Introduction; fo. 13ʳ; and the note for fo. 8ʳ.

11ᵛ

ecce trahebatur: *Aeneid* 2. 403–4, severely mistranslated. 'Lo! Priam's daughter, the maiden Cassandra, was being dragged with streaming hair from the temple and shrine of Minerva.' Virgil, *Aeneid I–VI*, trans. H. Rushton Fairclough (Cambridge, Mass.: Harvard University Press, 1999), 343.

   quotes Anthon: As the stub indicates, the subsequent folio, which probably contained additional grading work, has been cut away.

12ᵛ

"rupto turbine": *adversi rupto ceu quondam turbine venti / confligunt* {when a hurricane bursts forth, diverse winds clash}, *Aeneid* 2. 416.

   O wild west wind: The first line of Percy Bysshe Shelley's 'Ode to the West Wind' (1819; published 1820). GMH is composing using the sight-singing 'Tonic Sol-fa' method developed in the 1820s by Sarah Glover: *doh* = C; *ray* = D; *me* = E; *fa* = F; *sol* = G; *la* = A; *ti* = B; *doh* = C (see Introduction). Translated into a regular score by Bruce Douville, GMH's squib would look something like this (the time-values of the notes have been approximated):

O   wild west   wind,   thou breath of Au-tumn's being

13^r

Helen plainly: '"*Iamque adeo super unus eram, cum limina Vestae / servantem et tacitam secreta in sede latentem / Tyndarida aspicio; dant clara incendia lucem / erranti passimque oculos per cuncta ferenti. / illa sibi infestos eversa ob Pergama Teucros / et Danaum poenam et deserti coniugis iras / praemetuens, Troiae et patriae communis Erinys*"' {And now I alone was left, when I saw, sheltered in Vesta's shrine and silently hiding in the unfrequented fane, the daughter of Tyndareus; the bright fires give me light as I wander and cast my eyes, here and there, over the scene. She, fearing the Trojans' anger against her for the overthrow of Pergamum, the vengeance of the Greeks, and the wrath of the husband she abandoned—she, the undoing alike of her motherland and ours}, *Aeneid* 2. 567–73). Helen was the daughter of Leda (who, by some ancient accounts, was impregnated by Zeus in the form of a swan), wife of Tyndareus. Hence Helen was also known by the epithet *Tyndarida* (*Aeneid* 2. 569). Many of GMH's students failed to make the link between the epithets and the character of Helen. At the time of her abduction by Paris, a prince of Troy, Helen was married to Menelaus, king of Sparta.

For when thy folding star: GMH continues his work on Collins's 'Ode to Evening'. An approximation of the composition (again, the time-values of the notes were not indicated) would be:

For when thy fold-ing   star a-ri-sing shows   His

pa-ly circ-let, at his wan-ing_ lamp   That   slept in flow-ers the_

day   And_ ma-ny a   nymph who_   wreathes___ her_____

brows with sedge_   And_ sheds the fresh-en-ing dew and

wreathes her: As the digital image indicates, GMH would sometimes use diagonal lines to cancel material (in addition to the strikethroughs) or to indicate text that had been recopied elsewhere. See also fos. 15^r, 15^v, 17^r, 19^v, 20^v, 22^v, 24^v, 25^r, 25^v, 26^r, 26^v.

13^v

"dehevillished hair": A spelling error, probably in translating *Aeneid* 2. 401 ('streaming hair'; see fo. 11^v).

It is odd: On *oratio obliqua* and *oratio recta*, see 11^r above. Student 1458 confuses personal pronouns and adjectives in retranslating the *oratio recta* into Latin; *suis* {his own} would become *meis* {my own} in *oratio recta*.

14^r

"cum Cimbris": A reference to a passage taken from Caesar, *De Bello Gallico* 1. 40: '"Ariovistus," he said, "in my own consulship sought most eagerly the friendship of the Roman people. Why should anyone conclude that he intends recklessly to depart from his duty? For myself I am persuaded that, when my demands are made known, and the fairness of my terms understood, Ariovistus will not reject the goodwill of myself or of the Roman people. Even if, in a fit of rage and madness, he makes war, what, pray, have you to fear? Why do you despair of your own courage or of my competence? We have made trial of this foe in the time of our fathers, on the occasion when, in the defeat of the Cimbri and Teutoni by Gaius Marius, the army was deemed to have deserved no less praise than the commander himself."' Caesar, *The Gallic War*, trans. H. J. Edwards (Cambridge, Mass.: Harvard University Press, 1986), 61, 63. The Cimbrians were a proto-Germanic tribe who threatened Roman territory before their ultimate defeat *c*.101 BCE. See also fo. 10^v.

Rd. W. Dixon: For weeks in the autumn of 1884 GMH laboured over this biographical essay on his friend Richard Watson Dixon (1833–1900; poet and church historian; *ODNB*). See Biographical Register, and Appendix D.

Wm. Morris: London-born William Morris (1834–96; poet, writer, designer, and socialist visionary; *ODNB*) matriculated at Oxford, where he met Dixon (above) and Edward Burne-Jones (see fo. 16^r). Morris's focus soon shifted away from painting; he published his first volume of verse, *The Defence of Guinevere, and Other Poems* in 1858. In 1861 Morris co-founded Morris, Marshall, Faulkner & Co. (later Morris & Co.), a design firm that produced glass, textiles, wallpaper, and other decorative items. In later years Morris took up the cause of socialism, joining the Democratic Federation in 1883 and heading the Socialist League a year later. His Kelmscott Press, founded in 1890, was among the first in the private press movement.

late D. G. Rossetti: Dante Gabriel Rossetti (b. 1828; *ODNB*) died 9 April 1882. The poet and painter was a key figure in the original Pre-Raphaelite Brotherhood of the late 1840s and the subsequent Pre-Raphaelite movement (artists who opposed the constraints in form and subject matter imposed by the Royal Academy, and sought to reintroduce the vibrancy and intensity of pre-Renaissance painting). Rossetti produced innumerable paintings, sketches, and illustrations, along with stained-glass and furniture designs. His first volume of poetry appeared in 1870. See *CW* iii for GMH's initial interest in Rossetti's works, and the meeting with his sister, the poet Christina Rossetti

(1830–94; *ODNB*); and *CW* ii for GMH's letter to Dixon, 30 June–3 July 1886. For a discussion of the Rossetti paintings that GMH had seen in public and private collections, see Catherine Phillips, 'Gerard Manley Hopkins and Dante Gabriel Rossetti', *Ranam*, 36/1 (2003), 131–7.

Wellington: Arthur Wellesley, Duke of Wellington (1769–1851; *ODNB*), served as a general in the British Army, leading the forces that repelled French troops in the Peninsular War (1808–14). He later won fame by defeating Napoleon Bonaparte (1769–1821) at the Battle of Waterloo (1815), and was prime minister of England 1828–30.

Marlborough: John Churchill, first Duke of Marlborough (1650–1722; *ODNB*), enjoyed a very successful military career, and also served as a statesman. He campaigned on behalf of William of Orange in the Glorious Revolution of 1688; led the suppression of the Jacobite uprising in 1715; and won famous military victories against Louis XIV of France (1643–1715) at Blenheim (1704), Ramillies (1706), and Oudenaarde (1708). In honour of the Duke's victory at Blenheim, Queen Anne (1665–1714; *ODNB*) received parliament's approval to build Blenheim Palace on the grounds of the Duke's Woodstock estate (near Oxford), which she had given him following the battle. Begun in 1705, the vast and ornate structure was completed in 1725.

Franklin: Arctic explorer Sir John Franklin (1786–1847; *ODNB*) led three expeditions in search of the North-west Passage through the Arctic Ocean (1819–22; 1825–7; 1845). The first two resulted in a further mapping of the Canadian coastline of the Arctic; Franklin was knighted for his efforts. The last expedition never returned to England; subsequent search teams returned with news of the desperate demise of Franklin and his crew.

terza rima: Dante Alghieri (1265–1321) created the verse form *terza rima* for use in *The Divine Comedy* (*c.*1309–20). Tercets using the rhyme scheme aba bcb cdc, etc. are featured in iambic pentameter with one extra syllable (resulting in a hendecasyllabic, or eleven-syllable, line).

14^v

Two stubs indicate missing folios, the first of which included lines of Greek text.

no. 1761: Candidate 1761 translates *iubae*{crests} as 'plum' (misspelling 'plume'); *Nereus* (the sea god) is mistranslated as 'Nero'.

Tritronian woman: Candidate 1775 bungles *Tritonius*, an epithet for Neptune, to make it *Tritonia*, also misspelled ('the Tritonian woman').

next Ucalegon: A reference to *Aeneid* 2. 311–12, *proximus ardet / Ucalegon* {even now his neighbour Ucalegon blazes}. The student probably mistakes *proximus* ('next-door, neighbour') as 'next' in a temporal sense. The phrase is cited by the first-century CE grammarian Quintilian as an example of an inversion of a type of metonymy (*Institutio Oratoria* 8. 6. 25): the burning house next door is named by its owner (Ucalegon). Quintilian claims that 'only a poet' can devise and use such a trope.

15^r

Earnest: An early draft of 'Sibyl's Leaves', which GMH did not complete until 1886. The earliest extant draft, cut out of the *Dublin Notebook* and now housed in the Bodleian Library (MS Res. d.747 / MS. Eng. poet. c.48, fo. 51), features the first line and two variants of the second:

> Earnest, earthless, equal, attuneable, vaulty, voluminous, . . . stupendous
> Evening, dealing the dark down, time's drone, sullen hulk-of-all,
>   hearse-of-all night,
> Evening, dealing the drone-dark down, hollow hulk-of-all, home-of-all,
>   hearse-of-all night[.]

The Sibyl is mentioned in the opening stanza of '*Dies Irae*'{Day of Wrath}, a mid-thirteenth-century sequence on the Last Judgement sung during a Requiem Mass ('*Dies irae, dies illa / Solvet saeclum in favilla, / Teste David cum Sibylla*' {Day of wrath, day that will dissolve the world into burning coals, as David bore witness with the Sibyl}). See <www.franciscan-archive.org/de_celano/opera/diesirae.html>. GMH did not share the interest in mythological or 'pagan' figures that contemporary writers and artists such as Bridges, Alfred Lord Tennyson, Pater, and Burne-Jones enjoyed. As an undergraduate, GMH studied ancient Greek myth in George Grote's *A History of Greece*, 12 vols. (London: John Murray, 1846–56) (see *CW* iv); in the *DN* he reminds himself to read the 'Mythology' entry (by Andrew Lang) in the *Encyclopaedia Britannica* (see fo. 17^r).

15^v

~~*tragedy ic*~~: Before cancelling the the phrase, GMH mended 'tragedy' into 'tragic'.

16^r

to the stake: The scene underscores Mano's heroic stoicism prior to death (ll. 1440–5): 'Of Mano it was said that stone nor steel / No firmer countenance than he could show: / Nor he from silence did his lips unseal: / Save that to himself he smiled and muttered low, / "I feel the smell of nettles in warm shade". / This did I hear of him and nothing mo.' Dixon, *Mano: a Poetical History of the Time of the Close of the Tenth Century concerning the Adventures of a Norman Knight which Fell Part in Normandy Part in Italy*. In four books (London: George Routledge & Sons 1883), 188.

Burne Jones: Sir Edward Burne-Jones (1833–98, painter and designer; *ODNB*) also met William Morris at Oxford; he later studied painting with D. G. Rossetti. A major figure in the second wave of Pre-Raphaelitism, his style is distinguished by dream-like spaces, medieval and legendary themes, and the ethereal beauty of his female subjects. He also designed stained glass and tapestries for Morris and Co.

Keats: John Keats (1795–1821; *ODNB*), a central figure in the second generation of Romantic poets, was criticized for his early work in *Blackwood's Magazine*, which associated him with 'the Cockney School', a derisive term for a group of poets aligned with Leigh Hunt (1784–1859; *ODNB*) and maligned as working-class poetic pretenders. The richness of Keats's poetry, much of which is characterized by medievalism, won him recognition that intensified after his death. The synaesthesia of GMH's early verse is greatly indebted to Keats.

rhymes; and: The text continues on fo. 17ʳ, after nine rows of grading.

16ᵛ

his trident: Another mistake, from *Aeneid* 2. 418; the phrase '*silvae saevitque tridenti spumeus*' should be translated 'rages with his trident' (a reference to Nereus, the sea god who stirs up the waters during a storm).

17ʳ

Coleridge: Samuel Taylor Coleridge (1772–1834; *ODNB*), poet, critic, and philosopher of Romanticism. He and William Wordsworth (1770–1850; *ODNB*) became friends in 1797, and produced *Lyrical Ballads*, 1798. Now remembered for poems with exotic or otherworldly subject matter, such as 'The Rime of the Ancient Mariner' (1798) and 'Kubla Khan' (1816), Coleridge was a key figure in nineteenth-century English religious discourse. GMH's first school, in Highgate, was located near Coleridge's famous house; Thomas Carlyle had dubbed Coleridge 'the Sage of Highgate'. See also the 'Extracts' in *CW* iv.

To read: This short list of texts and sources articulates a variety of personal and pedagogical interests.

Plautus and Terence: Of Plautus (*c*.254–184 BCE) and Terence (*c*.195–159 BCE), two Roman comic authors, only Terence appears in the RUI examinations. The reference to Plautus and the phrasing ('to read a good deal of') suggests that GMH wanted to know these authors better, not for any classroom demands, but for personal interest.

Mr. Tyrrell: Robert Yelverton Tyrrell (1844–1914; *ODNB*), a brilliant classicist and professor of Latin and Greek at Trinity College, Dublin. GMH received at least one of Tyrrell's editions, a translation of Aristophanes' *Acharnians* (Dublin, 1883), as a gift; the book, now in the Irish Jesuit Archives (IJA J11/20), is inscribed on the flyleaf, 'Gerald Hopkins | from | R Y Tyrrell'. Tyrrell was one of the founders, in 1874, of the journal *Hermathena*, to which GMH considered making a submission. See J. A. Richmond, 'Classical Studies and Culture in Dublin in the 1880s', *Hopkins Quarterly* (Special Issue: *Hopkins and Dublin: The Man and the City*), 14/1–4 (Apr. 1987–Jan. 1988), 151.

Wordsworth's: John Wordsworth's *Fragments and Specimens of Early Latin* (Oxford: Clarendon Press, 1874), a volume that includes both a grammar and pronunciation guide to early Latin as well as collected fragments from early authors. Wordsworth does not include Plautus and Terence in his volume, since adequate editions for them already existed. Lucan occurs later in the *DN* as classroom material; see below.

Has Madvig: the esteemed nineteenth-century Danish critic and editor Johan Nicolai Madvig (1804–86) edited Livy in 1861–6. See also the Second University Examination in Arts (Pass), September 1884, and First University Examination from Autumn 1885: familiarity with Madvig's edition of Livy is presumed in the exam itself (RUI Examinations 19 [41]). GMH may have used Madvig, *A Latin Grammar*, trans. George Woods (Oxford: Clarendon Press, 1856).

Ency. Brit.: GMH first began consulting the *Encyclopaedia Britannica* as an undergraduate. Given the paucity of books available at UC, using the *Britannica*'s extensive articles for lesson preparations and personal musical instruction was a wise choice.

Athenaeums at Royal Irish Academy: Since his youth, and like many Victorians, GMH had been an avid reader of periodicals, ranging from family-focused journals such as *Once a Week* to literary, cultural, and political serials including *Fraser's Magazine*, *Cornhill*, and the *Westminster Review* (see Introduction to *CW* iii). In December 1884, he was trying to locate reviews of Bridges's new volume, *Prometheus the Firegiver*, in the *Academy* and the *Athenaeum* (see postcard dated 17 Dec. 1884, *CW* ii). The Royal Irish Academy (RIA) was located on Dawson Street, just a few blocks north of St Stephen's Green (the RIA moved from the 'Navigation House', now 114 Grafton Street, to no. 19 Dawson in 1851, where it remains to this day). Of the periodicals GMH often consulted, the RIA library's holdings included the *Academy*, the *Athenaeum* (every year but 1842, and July–December 1857), the London *Times*, *Irish Monthly*, and *Freeman's Journal*.

Pharsalia: Marcus Annaeus Lucanus (39–65 CE), the Roman poet, considered one of the outstanding figures of the 'Silver Latin' period, is discussed in Tacitus's *Annals* and is the subject of an ode by Statius. A grandson of Seneca the Elder, Lucan was tutored by his uncle, Seneca the Younger. Initially he found favour and success under Nero, but in 65 CE he joined the conspiracy of Gaius Calpurnius Piso against Nero. When his treason was discovered, he was forced to commit suicide. His epic poem *Pharsalia* (identified as *De bello civili* in the manuscripts) narrates the civil war between Julius Caesar and Pompey. For GMH's annotations of *De bello civili* {The Civil War}, which he made in *M. ANNAEI LUCANI | PHARSALIAE | LIBER PRIMUS* (1884; now housed in Gonzaga University), see *CW* vi, and Fredric Schlatter, S.J., 'Poetic Fragments, Comments on Lucan', 33–4. GMH's notes on Lucan begin on fo. 28ᵛ.

lectures: Robert Prescott Stewart (1825–94; *ODNB*), born in Dublin, received musical training at the school of Christ's Church, Dublin, where he became church organist in 1844. Two years later, he was named conductor of the Dublin University Choral Society; D.Mus., 1851. In 1861 he became professor of music at Dublin University; in 1872, he was knighted and made professor of theory at the Royal Irish Academy of Music. Stewart also conducted the Dublin Philharmonic and the Belfast Harmonic Society, and served as vice-president of the Royal Academy of Music and the Royal College of Organists. As a composer, Stewart was both prolific and acclaimed, winning numerous awards and prizes for his compositions, and commissions for public events. His public lectures on music were widely popular, and included topics such as eighteenth-century Irish musicians, Bach's fugues, and lyric drama. See Lisa Parker, 'For the Purpose of Public Music Education: The Lectures of Robert Prescott Stewart

(1825–1894)', in Michael Murphy and Jan Smaczny (eds.), *Irish Musical Studies 9: Music in Nineteenth-Century Ireland* (Dublin: Four Courts Press, 2007).

Dr. Gunn's book: There are two likely possibilities: William Gunn (1750–1841; *ODNB*), Church of England clergyman and antiquarian, author of *Inquiry into the Origin and Influence of Gothic Architecture* (1819) and *Cartonensia, or, An Historical and Critical Account of the Tapestries in the Palace of the Vatican; Copied from the Designs of Raphael, etc.* (1831); and John Gunn (*c.*1765–*c.*1824; *ODNB*), a Scottish writer on music whose books included *The Theory and Practice of Fingering for the Violoncello* (1793), *Forty Scotch Airs, Arranged as Trios for Flute, Violin, and Violoncello* (1793), and *Essay . . . on the Application of the Principles of Harmony, Thorough Bass, and Modulation to the Violoncello, Explaining how to Harmonize a Bass Line on the Cello* (1801).

Gibbon: Edward Gibbon (1737–94; *ODNB*), author, military officer, parliamentarian; author of *The History of the Decline and Fall of the Roman Empire* (6 vols., 1776–88).

17ᵛ

ἐκ σέθεν {from you}: Notes on scanning Pindar's *Isthmian Odes* 3/4; see Appendix E. Although *Odes* 3 and 4 are distinct poems in the manuscript tradition, they are the only metrically identical poems in the poet's surviving corpus and therefore originally constituted a single piece. GMH treats the two parts as one, following the consensus of his time.

18ʳ

like Abraham's and Lot's: Abraham, the Old Testament patriarch formerly known as Abram, is considered a founder of Judaism, Christianity, and Islam. GMH refers to Genesis 13: Abram leaves Egypt and, in the company of his nephew Lot, travels to Bethel. Unable to sustain their flocks on one tract of land, the two part ways, Lot taking the fair pastures of the Jordan Valley near Sodom, and Abram taking the land of Canaan.

adjoining pastures: In addition to the metrical analysis, GMH offers a brief discussion of the closing lines—'And, being related to the Labdacids on their mother's side, they followed a path of wealth with the toil of their four-horse teams. But the whirling days of a man's lifetime change many things. Only the children of the gods are unwounded'—offering a translation that is slightly more bleak than the Greek suggests ('dangerous road of wealth'). GMH is correct that the reference to wealth refers back to the first lines of the ode.

ὤπασεν {and in the games of Adrastos at Sikyon}: This rejected note dealing with Pindar's *Isthmian Ode* 3/4, 'For Melissos of Thebes, Winner, Pancration', indicates GMH's thorough grasp of Greek linguistics. The marks, including gamma (γ) in parentheses, signal a digamma in the original spelling of *Isthmiois*. The digamma was a consonant in archaic Greek that had disappeared by Pindar's day, but whose presence could be detected in the metrical lengthening of vowels in poetry. GMH, almost in passing, recognizes that the word *Isthmios* originally began with a digamma, which would render long the final *alpha* in the preceding word, *ephanās*.

shews another thing: This discussion of varieties of vowel lengths in Pindar reflects nineteenth-century methods of scanning the verse.

this is common: An astute observation concerning Pindaric shifts in imagery.

Re: GMH indicates changes, but not for the pitch of the starting note; the *sol-fa* notations could become:

Images: From *Ode* 3/4, words evoking the abundance of nature: θάλλειν {to bloom, flourish}; βάσσαισιν {woody glens}; στεφάνους {crown-like victory wreaths}; νάπᾳ {woody glen}; θάλλοντες {flourishing}; φοινικέοισιν ἄνθησεν ῥόδοις {has blossomed with crimson roses}; φύλλ' ἀοιδῶν {leaves of songs}.

*: *dal segno*, a musical notation meaning 'repeat from the sign' (?). *Πλαγίαις*: From *Ode* 3/4, words evoking change, succession, and diversity: πλαγίαις φρένεσσιν {with crooked minds}; διέστειχον {they followed the path; GMH: 'they made their way down the dangerous road'}; κυλινδομέναις ἀμέραις {with the whirling days}; εὐμαχανίαν {inventive skill}; διέρχονται {travel towards}; ἄλλοτε δ'ἄλλος {at different times}; ποικίλων μηνῶν {of the changing months}; γέφυραν ποντιάδα {at the sea bridge}; καμπύλον δίφρον {curved chariot}; τέχνα καταμάρψαισα {the skill overtakes}; ἔρνει Τελεσιάδα {offspring of Telesiadas}.

18ᵛ

spreading: The phrase κατὰ ῥάβδον {according to the minstrel's wand} interested GMH in Homer as well; see Anderson, 'The Dublin Notes on Homer', 75–6.

or three: A textual difficulty in Pindar. Following Heyne's emendation (Gottingen, 1773), most editors suggest emending the reading θηρῶν ('of the wild [beasts]') by changing it to the singular θήραν. GMH's objection reflects the general scholarly consensus. Mommsen's 1866 edition offers two alternative readings, which GMH rejects.

Year 68: These notes on Tacitus' *Histories* include various historical details, probably intended for the classroom; the more amusing digressions may have been meant to engage students' imaginations. Tacitus' *Histories* treats the so-called Year of Four Emperors (69 CE), after the death of Nero and the end of the Julio-Claudian line of Roman rule, which began with Julius Caesar. Rome was governed by a rapid succession of emperors in a period marked by military violence and political intrigue: Galba, Otho, Vitellius, and finally Vespasian, who founded the Flavian dynasty. These notes often function as little more than repetitions of Tacitus' original, with the insertion of certain dates; Nero's death, for instance, occurred in June 68 CE.

Nymphidius Sabinus: The praetorian prefect (commander of the emperor's bodyguards).

Sicilies: GMH notes that the plural *Galliae* refers to the 'Gallic provinces', or the provinces that made up the territory of Gaul, in the same way one would refer to the kingdom of 'Russias' and the 'two Sicilies' (or one might speak of 'the Netherlands'), a point that could be missed by students.

Tanquam: *Tanquam*, 'as though', is often inserted in a passage to signal the author's doubts about a reported event. GMH seems to be referring to *Historiae* 1. 8: '*quem non remitti atque etiam reum esse tamquam suum crimen accipiebant*' {The fact that he was not sent back, but was actually brought to trial, the soldiers regarded as an accusation against themselves}. The adverb *tamquam* modifies *suum crimen*, presenting the charge brought against Verginius as though it were an accusation against the soldiers themselves.

Tacitus: Tacitus the historian was also consul; he delivered the panegyric for Verginius, his predecessor, in 97 CE. GMH was using William Henry Simcox's edition of *The History of Tacitus*, which uses the text of Drelli, *Cornelii Taciti Historiae*, Books III, IV, V (London, 1876); the book, now housed in the IJA (J11/18), features GMH's textual glosses and conjectures (see *CW* vi). See fo. 28ʳ for additional work on Tacitus.

correct this: The problem, although unclear, could refer to a point of textual criticism.

Consularis: Explaining the workings of the Roman army. Only a general of consular rank, that is, a former consul (or, later in the empire, a senator raised to the dignity to govern one of the provinces) was considered a *consularis*.

Dum: GMH notes that *dum* {while, until} can be used with the subjunctive mood in temporal clauses, yet the only appearance of *dum* in that passage occurs at 1. 9, where it is used with the indicative (and not subjunctive) *cunctantur*. *Antequam iuberentur* {before they received orders to take action}, from 1. 7, does provide an example of the subjunctive in a temporal clause.

Provinces: A brief discussion of *provincia*, the 'province', which for the Romans designated the sphere in which a magistrate had influence (not primarily a geographic area). GMH includes a digression on the title of the governor, who could be called a *praeses* {president}. Wondering why they were not 'Provincials', GMH develops a lengthy explanation. He is correct about the etymology of *provincia*; it remains obscure.

19ʳ

Inchoavere: Perhaps noted because of special problems the form could create for beginners. Initially, it appears to be an infinitive, but it is an alternative derived from the less correct form of the verb *incoho* in the perfect: 'They began'.

Ultimum, supremum: Highlighting the literary effects of juxtaposing *ultimum* and *supremum*, which can be synonyms meaning last or 'ultimate'; GMH is playing on the fact that the last year (chronologically) in the life of Galba was almost the 'end', the last year ever, for Rome.

I shd. think: A reference to Tacitus, *Histories* 1. 18, when Emperor Galba adopted the inexperienced aristocrat Piso as his son, thereby establishing his succession for the throne (both Galba and Piso were soon murdered by military opponents). In this section, GMH finds a possible reference to the military form of adoption (since Galba says that he is adopting according to the example of Augustus and in the *mos militaris* {the military manner}).

Dein generum: Perhaps *Dein generum Agrippam* {his son-in-law Agrippa} may have given GMH trouble because he needed to decipher the relationship between Augustus and Augustus' favourite general, Agrippa, who married the emperor's daughter Octavia and thereby became his son-in-law, or *gener*.

the flattered: GMH explains the difficult aphorism *pessimum veri adfectus venenum sua cuique utilitas* {that worst poison to genuine affection, namely, each one's benefit} as explained by *sine adfectu peragitur* {a thing accomplished without feeling} from *Histories* 1. 15. Galba, who is addressing Piso, observes that mutual utility, expressed especially as flattery, can infect genuine affection with manipulation. This virus spreads from the flatterer, the subordinate, to the flattered, the superior, and 'poisons' (as GMH notes, stretching the metaphor) their relationship.

19ᵛ

Sestertius: A lengthy analysis of Roman currency, a topic that could easily confuse students reading Tacitus' *Histories*; GMH tries to disentangle the relationships among the various types of Roman coins and to find English equivalents for the denominations. A *sestertius*, from *semis-tertius* {a two-and-a-half}, and often translated 'sesterce', was originally worth two and a half *asses* (singular *as*) and one fourth of a *denarius* (literally, a 'tenner'—a name maintained even when the denarius came to be worth 16 *asses*). Philologically-minded GMH suggests the term *sestertium* {1000 sestertii} came originally from a confusion of the literal designation *mille sestertiorum* {1000 of sesterces}. This original form gradually disappeared when later Romans took the *sestertiorum* to be a genitive plural form of *sestertium*, whose plural would then be *sestertia*. (GMH performs a similar, much briefer exercise in the margins of his copy of Cicero's *De Officiis*, pp. 82–3; see *CW* vi.)

Temple of Apollo: Located on Rome's Palatine Hill, near the Circus Maximus, the Temple of Apollo Palatinus was dedicated by Octavian Augustus to his patron god in 28 BCE, to give thanks for victories over Sextus Pompeius and Marc Antony and Cleopatra. The emperor's private house was connected to the temple sanctuary. According to ancient sources, the temple was graced with ivory doors and included many works of sculpture; the surrounding portico featured black marble statues of the fifty Danaids (daughters of Danaus, ordered by their father to kill their husbands). The archaeological remains were excavated in the 1960s. See Olivier Hekster and John Rich, 'Octavian and the Thunderbolt: The Temple of Apollo Palatinus and Roman Traditions of Temple Building', *Classical Quarterly*, 56 (2006), 149–68.

on duty: Tacitus, *Histories* 1. 28: *Stationem in castris agebat Iulius Martialis tribunus* {Julius Martialis the tribune was the officer of the day in the camp}.

20ʳ

Hickson: GMH records and then tallies the results of quizzes or recitation exercises. The students can only be tentatively identified, partly due to spelling mistakes in the surnames and lack of initials. *Hickson*: perhaps H. A. Hinkson, First University Class in 1884, who received 2nd class honours in the Autumn 1884 RUI examinations. *Bowden*: unknown. *MacWeeney*: two are listed: Edmund J. M'Weeney, candidate for BA Class, who won a scholarship in Modern Languages and placed first in the RUI examinations in Autumn 1884; and Henry C. M'Weeney, in the First University Class, who received 2nd class honours in Latin in Autumn 1884. *Maher*: either Thomas Maher, Second University class, who passed his RUI exams; or Martin Maher, in the First University Class, who also passed his RUI exams. *Kennedy*: perhaps J. J. O'Kennedy, who passed the Secondary University exams. *Lynch*: Patrick Lynch, First University Class. *MacKendry*: James M'Kendry, Second University Class. *Young*: Edmund Young, First University Class.

St. Cecily: Cecilia, patron saint of music; feast day, 22 November. Martyred, either during Marcus Aurelius' reign, between 176–80 CE, or *c.*230, under Emperor Alexander Severus. Henry Purcell (1659–95; *ODNB*), the composer so admired by GMH, set three odes to Cecilia to music in 1683; John Dryden (1631–1700; *ODNB*) published 'A Song for Saint Cecillia's Day, 1687', with music by Giovanni Baptista Draghi (1640–1708), in 1687; his ode 'Alexander's Feast; Or The Power of Musique. An Ode, In Honour of St. Cecilia's Day' appeared in 1697. George Frederic Handel (1685–1759) set 'Alexander's Feast' to music in 1736, and in 1739 he paired the piece with music written to accompany Dryden's 'A Song for Saint Cecillia's Day'.

things of God: 'Blessed are the pure in heart, since they will see God' (Matthew 5: 8).

Pennine Alps: Philological digression on the Pennines (*Poeninis iugis*: 'the Pennine range'). According to the 'Pennines' entry in *The Cambridge Dictionary of English Place-Names*, (ed.) Victor Watts (2004), 'The genuine *Alpes Penninae* do indeed derive from Celtic *penno* – "a mountain summit"'; the *Oxford Dictionary of World Place-Names*, (ed.) John Everett-Heath (Oxford 2005), relates the *ap-* in Apennines to the Latin *apex* ('peak'). A reference to the etymology of the name 'Pennines' occurs in the Summer 1885 First University Examination ('Examination Papers' 15/23); in book 21 of *Ab Urbe Condita* Livy mentions some who attribute the name to the 'Punic' crossing in Hannibal's invasion of Italy.

20ᵛ

Earnest: Another draft of 'Sibyl's Leaves'. See also fo. 15ʳ.

crisped: GMH has cancelled the stress on the second syllable, 'ed'.

21ʳ

ἄριστος: The opening three lines of Pindar's *Nemean Ode* 4 (For Timasarchos of Aegina: Boys' Wrestling, *c*.?473 BCE), prescribed for the RUI MA exam, 1884–6. (See also Appendix E.) GMH includes his musical notation, in tonic *sol-fa*, which does not correspond to any scientific theories of the poet's lyrical qualities.

ἄριστος εὐφροσύνα πόνων κεκριμένων
ἰατρός· αἱ δὲ σοφαὶ
Μοισᾶν θύγατρες ἀοιδαὶ θέλξαν νιν ἁπτόμεναι.

{The best healer for toils judged successful / is joyous revelry, but songs too, those wise / daughters of the Muses, soothe them with their touch.} Pindar, *Nemean Odes, Isthmian Odes, Fragments*, trans. William H. Race (Cambridge, Mass.: Harvard University Press, 1997), 35.

Re: GMH's melody, as conjectured by Bruce Douville:

My heart: Another draft of 'Caradoc's Soliloquy'. See fo. 9ʳ.

21ᵛ

O Sapientia {O Wisdom}: The Advent 'O Antiphon' for 17 December: '*O Sapientia, quæ ex ore Altissimi prodiisti, attingens a fine usque ad finem fortiter, suaviterque disponens omnia: veni ad docendum nos viam prudentiae*' {O Wisdom, that came out of the mouth of the Most High, reaching from end to end mightily, and sweetly disposing all things: come to teach us the way of prudence}. During Advent, the seven days preceding Christmas Eve are marked by a series of prayers addressed to Christ under various titles, with each 'O Antiphon' following sequentially on a particular date.

Attingens: GMH focuses on the fullness and extent, the 'reaching', of the Word Incarnate as the wisdom of God. He dates the entry to 20 December, for which the antiphon is 'O Clavis David' {O Key of David}, but recalls the earlier antiphon from the 17th, which begins the antiphonal cycle.

St. Thomas: St Thomas (1st century CE) is named as one of Jesus' twelve disciples in each of the gospels. In St. John's gospel, he declares himself ready to die with Jesus (11: 6); expresses uncertainty about the path that Jesus is going to take to his Father's house (14: 5); and doubts Jesus' resurrection until he is able to verify the identity of the risen Christ by touching his wounds, afterward becoming the first to declare Jesus' divinity (20: 24–8).

before his Passion: John 14: 5–6, Thomas said to Christ, 'Lord, we don't know where you are going, so how can we know the way?' Jesus replied, 'I am the way and the truth and the life. No one comes to the Father except through me.' This exchange takes place at the Last Supper.

St. Stephen: All that is known of St Stephen (d. *c*.35) comes from Acts 6–7, in which he is identified as among the first deacons, as a miracle worker, and as the first Christian martyr. Filled with the Holy Spirit, Stephen testified to Christ's divinity and denounced Israel for resisting the message of Jesus and the prophets before him, and was stoned to death without trial, asking forgiveness as he died for those responsible.

Sic eum volo etc {So I wish that he . . . }: (John 21: 22). Jesus responds to Peter's question about John, the beloved disciple, saying, 'If I wish that he remain until I come, what is that to you?' GMH is preparing his notes for meditating on the story of Christ's resurrection appearance to seven of his disciples on the shore of Lake Tiberias (John 21: 1–23).

Angelo Crover: unidentified; cf. David Walsh.

three holy Kings: The Magi, or three Wise Men from the East, who journey to Bethlehem to do homage to the infant Jesus, as recounted in Matthew 2: 1–12. GMH is preparing for his morning meditation on the feast of the Epiphany (6 January).

Fr. Foley's instructions: Fr Foley, conducting a preached retreat for GMH and others, was giving 'points' for the retreatants' individual meditation.

For: the entry continues on fo. 22ʳ, second item.

22ʳ

~~*Angelo*~~: A miscellaneous list of names and commissions; as was his practice in his diaries, GMH cancelled a memorandum as he completed the task. *Angelo* and *Harrington* are unidentified.

Fr. Bacon: Francis Edward Bacon, S.J. (1839–1922); see Biographical Register.

Bridges: Robert Bridges (1844–1930; *ODNB*), poet; see Biographical Register.

Statistics: For his father's book *Cardinal Numbers, with an Introductory Chapter on Numbers Generally* (London: Sampson Low, Marston, Searle & Rivington, 1887), GMH provided the sections on Welsh calculation methods and 'spectral numbers' (the 'mental visibility of numbers'), and mathematical observations woven throughout the text. As White observes, 'it is difficult to say with certainty where Manley's contributions ended and Gerard's began' (*Hopkins, A Literary Biography*, 6). When the book was reviewed in the *Saturday Review* (22 September 1888), GMH's contribution regarding 'the mental visibility of numbers' was treated dismissively.

Mrs Delany: unidentified (perhaps the mother of Fr William Delany, S.J., but his biographer does not record the date of her death).

Aunt Ann: Ann Hopkins (1815–87), Manley's sister; see Biographical Register. GMH's paternal grandmother ('Grandmamma') was Ann Manley Hopkins (1785–1875).

Fr. Rigby: Most probably Fr John Rigby, S.J. (1809–89), in retirement at the Stonyhurst Jesuit community, where GMH had been (August 1882–February 1884) before coming to Dublin, but also possibly another English Province Jesuit, Fr Thomas Rigby, S.J. (1842–1912), then doing parish work in Liverpool. There is no surviving correspondence between GMH and either of these men; neither is mentioned in GMH's diaries.

Fr. Cummins: Most likely Fr John Ildephonsus Cummins, OSB (1850–1938), an Ampleforth Benedictine assigned during 1885–7 to the parish of St Peter's, Seel Street, Liverpool. He later served as Prior of of Belmont Abbey (1901–5). For GMH's connections with Belmont, see *CW* iii.

Milicent: GMH's younger sister, Milicent (1849–1946), an Anglican nun. See also fo. 25ʳ, and Biographical Register. GMH once explained to Baillie that Milicent 'is given to Puseyism: she is what is called an out-sister of the Margaret Street Home [All Saints' Home, Margaret Street, London]. . . . Consequently she will be directed by some Ritualist, which are the worst hands she could fall into: these men are imperious, uncommissioned, without common sense, and without knowledge of moral theology' (6 Jan. 1877; *CW* i. 257).

Octave of Epiphany: The eight days following the feast of the Epiphany (6 January), or 'manifestation' of the newborn Christ to the visiting Magi, which symbolizes that Jesus is not only the Jewish Messiah, the 'one who was to come', but also the light to all nations, the saviour of the world. The feast of Christ's baptism is celebrated on the Sunday immediately following the Epiphany; as recounted in the gospels, it is another manifestation of Jesus' true identity and mission. Similarly, his first public miracle during the wedding feast at Cana, which inaugurates his public ministry in the Gospel of John, is itself a kind of epiphany, or revelation—and is also associated with the Epiphany, particularly in the writings of Clement of Alexandria.

Scholarship Examination: For the list of texts required, see fo. 2ʳ.

22ᵛ

The devils: GMH is preparing notes to pray about Jesus' exorcism of the Gerasene demoniac, recounted in all three synoptic gospels (Matthew 8: 28–34; Mark 5: 1–20; and Luke 6: 26–39), who is possessed by so many devils that the narratives of Mark and Luke identify them collectively as 'Legion'.

Tacitus: The following notes focus on Tacitus' use of the subjunctive in *Histories* 1. 83–4 (words and phrases cited by GMH appear in **bold**):

'*[83] An et **illic** nocte intempesta rapientur arma? Unus alterve perditus ac temulentus (neque enim pluris consternatione proxima insanisse **crediderim**) centurionis ac tribuni sanguine manus imbuet, imperatoris sui tentorium inrumpet? [84] "Vos quidem istud pro me: sed in discursu ac tenebris et rerum omnium confusione patefieri occasio etiam adversus me potest. **Si Vitellio et satellitibus eius eligendi facultas detur**, quem nobis animum, quas mentis **imprecentur, quid** aliud quam seditionem et discordiam **optabunt**? Ne miles centurioni, ne centurio tribuno obsequatur, ut confusi pedites equitesque in exitium ruamus. Parendo potius, commilitones, quam imperia ducum sciscitando res* *militares continentur, et fortissimus in ipso discrimine exercitus est qui ante discrimen quietissimus. Vobis arma et **animus sit**: mihi consilium et virtutis vestrae regimen relinquite. Paucorum culpa fuit, duorum poena erit: ceteri abolete memoriam foedissimae noctis. Nec illas adversus senatum voces ullus usquam exercitus audiat. Caput imperii et decora omnium provinciarum ad poenam vocare **non hercule illi**, quos cum maxime Vitellius in nos ciet, **Germani audeant. Ulline Italiae alumni** et Romana vere iuventus ad sanguinem et caedem **depoposcerit** ordinem, **cuius splendore et gloria sordis et obscuritatem Vitellianarum partium praestringimus?** Nationes aliquas occupavit Vitellius, imaginem quandam exercitus habet, senatus nobiscum est: **sic fit ut hinc res publica**, inde hostes rei publicae constiterint.'*

{Suppose in the field you have to take your arms in the dead of night, shall one or two worthless and drunken men—for I cannot believe that the recent madness was due to the panic of more than that—stain their hands in the blood of a centurion or tribune? Shall they burst into the tent of their general? [84] "You, it is true, did that for me. But in time of riot, in the darkness and general confusion, an opportunity may also be given for an attack on me. Suppose Vitellius and his satellites should have an opportunity to choose the spirit and sentiment with which they would pray you to be inspired, what will they prefer to mutiny and strife? Will they not wish that soldier should not obey centurion or centurion tribune, so that we may all, foot and horse, in utter confusion rush to ruin? It is rather by obedience, fellow-soldiers, than by questioning the commands of the leaders, that success in war is obtained, and that is the bravest army in time of crisis which has been most orderly before the crisis. Yours be the arms and the spirit; leave to me the plan of campaign and the direction of your valour. Few were at fault; two shall pay the penalty: do all the rest of you blot out the memory of that awful night. And I pray that no army may ever hear such cries against the senate. That is the head of the empire and the glory of all the provinces; good heavens, not even those Germans whom Vitellius at this moment is stirring up against us would dare to call it to punishment. Shall any child of Italy, any true Roman youth, demand the blood and murder of that order through whose splendid glory we outshine the meanness and base birth of the partisans of Vitellius? Vitellius has won over some peoples; he has a certain shadow of an army, but the senate is with us. And so it is that on our side stands the state, on theirs the enemies of the state."}

Tacitus, *The Histories. Books I–III*, trans. Clifford Moore
(Cambridge, Mass.: Harvard University Press, 1980), 142, 144, 143, 145.

Illic: Discussing the demonstrative pronoun *illic* {there, at that place}, GMH seems to distinguish 'real' demonstratives, pronouns that point out a location or event, from demonstratives of context, which simply hold the place of a noun (thus, the Latin *is* would simply refer to a third person, masculine agent).

categorical mood: The use of this subjunctive instead of the indicative for the verb *credo* {I believe} suggests that there is some hypothetical remove that distinguishes the act of not believing from the present reality, i.e. 'Were you to offer evidence, I still would not believe.'

detur: Again, the subjunctive is used. GMH claims that the subjunctive in the protasis of the conditional ('If the power of election be given') implies that the future indicative in the apodosis ('they will pray') takes on a subjunctive mood ('they would pray'). Tacitus uses a future indicative, as one would do in English.

be yours: GMH takes *sit* as a jussive subjunctive, resembling a third-person command.

Ne miles: GMH takes *ne* as introducing a clause dependent, indirectly, on *optabunt* {would they wish?}.

audeant: GMH takes the subjunctive verb *audeant* to suggest an implied conditional ('if X were to occur, the Germans would not dare').

depoposcerit: The form is ambiguous: it can be a future perfect indicative or perfect subjunctive; GMH offers both readings in his note. GMH is fond of including the modifying phrases 'is found'/'will be found' in his translation.

constiterit: GMH is explaining the use of the subjunctive in *constiterit* after the conjunction *ut* (which can mean 'that' or 'how').

whip lightly: Working out difficult translations from *Histories* 1. 84. GMH also alludes to a textual variant, *perstringimus* for *praestringimus*.

23ʳ

Cap. 1: Focusing on various points of Roman religion and mythology, as found in Tacitus's *Histories* 2. 1.

Herod Agrippa I: Originally named Marcus Julius Agrippa, Herod Agrippa I (10 BCE–44 CE) was the grandson of Herod the Great, and son of Aristobulus IV and Berenice. He is the king named Herod in the New Testament's Acts of Christ's apostles. One of GMH's attempts to connect the classical text to Christian history.

Aeria: GMH tries to relate the name of the Cyprian temple at Aeria (*Histories* 2. 3) to the names for eastern goddesses, but the connections are doubtful.

Astarte: The Greek name for Ashtart, the Canaanite 'Queen of Heaven', and goddess of fertility, sexuality, and war. Associated with the sea, moon, and stars, Astarte (or Ashtaroth) is often depicted with the horns of a bull. Ishtar, the Assyrian-Babylonian goddess of sexuality and war, is identified with Astarte, as is the Greek goddess of love, Aphrodite.

Ἀφροδίτη Οὐρανία: Aphrodite Ourania. In Plato's *Symposium* (180 E), Pausanias explains that there are two goddesses of beauty and love: the elder is the 'heavenly' Aphrodite Urania, daughter of Ouranos, who inspires male–male erotic desire; and the younger, Aphrodite Pandemos ('of all the people' or 'common'), who inspires heterosexual desire.

Thamyras: Legendary Thracian musician and poet Thamyris (or Thamyras) asserted that he would best the Muses in a musical contest; the Muses responded by blinding him and depriving him of his musical abilities.

that is Thammuz: The ancient Greek god of sexuality, Adonis, born from the union of Kinyras and his daughter Myrrha, was beloved by Aphrodite and Persephone. When Adonis was killed by a wild boar, Aphrodite turned his blood into the anemone flower; consequently Adonis is associated with rituals of death and rebirth. The Mesopotamian story of Thammuz is thought to arise from the same tradition.

the Sun: From *Histories* 2. 3; GMH tries to relate the figure mentioned by Tacitus, Tamiras the Cilician, to the mythical character of Adonis, by way of etymological links to the character Thamyras, a mythical bard mentioned in the *Iliad* ii. 594 ff., and

Thammuz, a Sumerian figure often linked to Adonis. The conjectures are not supported by classical scholarship.

Myrrha: In Ovid's tale of Adonis's birth, Myrrha, daughter of Kinyras and Cenchreis, lusts after her father; appalled, she attempts to hang herself. Her nursemaid intervenes, then helps to devise the plan whereby Kinyras is intoxicated and then seduced in the dark. When Kinyras discovers his lover's identity, he attempts to kill his daughter. Myrrha flees; after nine months of wandering and praying to the gods for forgiveness, she is transformed into a tree, and the child Adonis is delivered. The baby is nursed by the Naiads and bathed in myrrh, his mother's tears (*Metamorphoses* 10. 298–518). In other versions, Myrrha is named Smyrna and her father Theias.

Adolere: GMH relates the verb *adolere* {to burn ritually} to the bloodless sacrifices of fire and prayer of the altar, which he finds parallel to Catholic worship.

not entrails: GMH would disagree with the Loeb translator, Moore, who renders *fibris* as 'entrails' rather than as 'vitals'. As Schlatter notes, GMH comments on *fibra* in his notes on Lucan ('Comments on Lucan' [2000] 44–5); see also *CW* vi.

Ratio in obscuro: Bk 2. 3: '*sed ratio in obscuro*' {the reason for this is obscure}.

dragon: GMH planned to explain the Roman ritual of divination overseen by the *haruspices*, in which the entrails (in this case, of kid goats) are examined for portents. By preferring the translation 'vitals', GMH emphasizes that the insides of the animal would be expected to reveal secret meanings precisely because they preserved the vital force of the living animal's spirit. GMH assumed Tacitus' record of Roman religion offers profounder insights into common Roman attitudes than most modern commentators would allow.

Mucianus: A reference to Titus, who presented himself to Vespasian as the perfect man to pacify and even seduce Mucianus, Vespasian's rival in the Middle East.

23ᵛ

Monday Feb. 2: A series of attendance lists for UC classes. The names of students not included on fo. 20ʳ: *Daly*: unidentified; *Malone*: James Malone; *Lennox*: unidentified; *Murphy*: either Denis Murphy or P. J. Murphy, First University Class, who received a pass in the Autumn 1884 RUI examinations; *Whittaker*: J. J. Whitaker, First University Class, who also received a pass in the Autumn 1884 examinations; *O'Brien*: either Edward T. O'Brien, who received 2nd class honours in the Third Year RUI Examinations in Autumn 1884, or more likely D. Edward O'Brien, who received a pass for the First University Examination; *Malone*: James Malone, a member of the Second University Class in Autumn 1884; *Byrne*: John Byrne, First University Class. In June 1947, Bischoff interviewed Fr Whitaker, S.J., who recalled GMH as being 'very small, quiet, soft-spoken. GMH used to come into class laden down with books, usually a huge Latin dictionary balancing precariously on top of the pile. . . . On one occasion . . . GMH devoted an hour to lecturing on the various uses and meanings of "*atque*" {and, as well as}, only to come in the next day and devote another whole hour to adding remarks . . . omitted on the previous day' (BRC 41a:8).

2 February, 'Candlemas', commemorates the purification of the Mary, according to Mosaic law, forty days after the birth of Christ. Before the Mass, candles were blessed and then featured in a procession.

Mithridates: GMH's gloss for the lines on fo. 24ʳ beginning, 'The <u>Mithridatic Wars</u>'. Persian king Mithridates (120–63 BCE) fought against Rome for decades, losing more than once before he was finally defeated by Pompey in 68 BCE. He died after ordering a bodyguard to run him through with a sword.

Great: GMH's gloss for the lines on fo. 24ʳ beginning 'The period then is the last age (century nearly) of the Republic'.

24ʳ

Notes: The first draft of his lecture outlines. GMH substantially revised and expanded this work twice in the other major Dublin-era notebook, G.II (now housed in Campion Hall, Oxford; see *CW* vi for a transcription). In G.II, the first set of corrected notes is headed 'Notes for <u>Roman Literature and Antiquities</u> | BC. 133–43 (from death of Tib. Gracchus to that of Cicero)'; the second, 'Notes on the Course of Roman Antiquities for Second Arts ~~Examination~~ 1888'.

till 65?: The date is not firmly established, but GMH's guess is credible.

24ᵛ

Gracchi to Cicero: A list of famous authors in various genres. Most literature from the period does not survive; scholars rely on the judgements and summaries made by later grammarians to reconstruct the literature from 133 to 43 BCE. Assessments of the orators reflect the judgements drawn originally from Quintilian and other grammarians, which were received as authorities in the history of classical education. Students were often expected to imitate the vocabulary and style of a particular author; GMH's notes provide some idea of the distinctions among stylists.

Lucretius: Little is known about Titus Lucretius Carus (*c*.99–*c*.55 BCE), poet and author of *De rerum natura* {On the Nature of Things}. Consisting of six books in hexameter verse, the work, a treatise on Epicurean philosophy, is designed to demonstrate the materiality and mortality of the human soul, the atomistic nature of the universe, and the error of believing in providence.

Catullus: Gaius Valerius Catullus (*c*.84–*c*.54 BCE) is known for his infusion of Hellenistic tendencies into Roman poetry. Love poems to the woman he called Lesbia are his most famous works.

L. Attius . . . Varro: A list of famous orators.

Shakespeare's sake: GMH is discussing Gaius Helvius Cinna, a poet during the late Roman Republic (1st century BCE), author of *Smyrna*, and friend of Catullus. In *Julius Caesar*, Shakespeare follows Plutarch's *Life of Brutus* in suggesting that Cinna the poet, not Lucius Cornelius Cinna, is threatened with death by a mob accusing him of being a conspirator against Caesar. When he responds that he is not Cinna the conspirator, but Cinna the poet, the crowd demands he be punished for 'his bad verses' (III. iii. 26–31).

25^r

Mark Antony: The Roman statesman Marcus Antonius (*c*.83–30 BCE) won fame by accompanying Julius Caesar (100–44 BCE) on his campaign to Gaul (54–50 BCE), where Antony was made quaestor in 51 BCE. He then served as Caesar's tribune. Following Caesar's death, Antony's charisma rendered him the presumed successor. Octavian (63 BCE–14 CE; see note above, fo. 19^r) and Marcus Junius Brutus (*c*.85–42 BCE), however, banded together to challenge Antony, and he was thrust back to Transalpine Gaul before he called for peace. Together, the three men formed the Second Triumvirate of Rome, with Antony awarded rule of Asia. In 40 BCE Antony married Octavia, the sister of Octavian, despite his ongoing relationship with Cleopatra, queen of Egypt, with whom he had three children. In 32 BCE the Roman Senate stripped Antony of his authority; Octavian's forces defeated those of Antony and Cleopatra at the decisive Battle of Actium in 31 BCE. The following year Octavian invaded Egypt, and Antony took his own life. Featured in Shakespeare's plays *Julius Caesar* and *Antony and Cleopatra*, his name appears as 'Marcus Antonius' among the *dramatis personae* for *Julius Caesar* in Knight's *Pictorial Edition of the Works of Shakspere* (p. 226), which GMH consulted as an Oxford student, but the text of the play uses the spelling 'Mark Antony'. Both the *dramatis personae* (p. 278) and the text of *Antony and Cleopatra* in the Knight edition use the spelling 'Mark Antony'.

Cardinal MacCabe: Edward McCabe (1816–85), born in Dublin, was ordained a Catholic priest at St Patrick's College, Maynooth, in 1839; made canon in 1855; and the following year, vicar-general of his archdiocese. He became bishop of Gadara in 1877. Given the failing health of Cardinal Cullen (1803–78), McCabe was named his auxiliary, and consecrated archbishop in 1879, after Cullen's death. Three years later he was made cardinal. As a member of the RUI Senate, he spoke publicly about the disadvantages faced by Roman Catholics in Ireland's university education system (see 'The Roman Catholic Clergy in Ireland', *The Times* [*London*], 29530 (1 Apr. 1879), 11). Otherwise, McCabe was conservative in his politics; he opposed the Land League and the campaign for Home Rule, and was consequently unpopular with the nationalist Dublin populace. He died 11 February 1885 and was buried at Glasnevin Cemetery. His papers are housed in the Archdiocese of Dublin: <www.dublindiocese.ie>.

Gordon's death: Charles George Gordon (1833–85; *ONDB*) fought in the Crimean War (1853–6) and the second Opium War (1856–60), and conducted mapping expeditions of the Russian and Ottoman frontiers. Governor of Equatoria, 1873–6; in 1877–9 and 1884–5, governor-general of Sudan, where he worked against the slave trade. In 1884 he was sent to Khartoum in response to the Madhist rebellion. Gordon evacuated 2,600 people from the city before it was blockaded; he was killed 26 January 1885. Public outcry was enormous, leading to the resignation of Prime Minister William Gladstone (see note to fo. 25^v, below); subsequently England renewed its efforts to consolidate power and wealth in Egypt and the Sudan.

Khartoom: On 21 August 1881, Muslim mystic Mohammed Ahmad, the Mahdi, declared a jihad (holy war) on the Sudan's Egyptian ruler and supporters. On 22 November 1883, London and Cairo received news of the Mahdi's victory over the army commanded by Al-ed-Deel Pacha and British General Hicks (the battle took place 3–4 November); a significant shift in British policy resulted. On 18 January 1884 the government enlisted General Gordon to superintend the evacuation of Egyptian garrisons. Gordon's expedition escalated the situation, provoking rumours of an impending English conquest of the region and an Arab slaughter; some hitherto friendly tribes fomented against Gordon. On 12 March 1884 a large force of tribesmen appeared on the right bank of the Blue Nile within sight of Khartoum, capital of Sudan, and cut the telegraph line; Gordon decided to defend the capital. Two days later he sent out a force of one thousand Egyptian and Sudanese soldiers but the two commanding officers decamped to join the Mahdi. On 26 May, the fall of Berber to the Mahdi ended all hope that Gordon could evacuate Khartoum without British assistance. On 12 August, the British government sanctioned a relief expedition to the Sudan. The Mahdi and his forces arrived at Khartoum on 21 October. When they captured the steamer *Abbas*, its cargo included papers detailing Khartoum's food stores and garrison population. On 13 November, they surrounded Khartoum and cut off supplies; starvation ensued. On 26 January 1885, the Mahdi made a final assault and entered Khartoum. The exact circumstances of Gordon's death were a mystery, but a small group of Ansar attacked and killed Gordon and a group of soldiers heading to a church. Khartoum fell to the Mahdi that day. The British relief expedition arrived 28 January 1885.

dynamite explosions: Known as the 'Dynamite Outrages' to Londoners, thirteen explosions occurred in public places such as railway stations between March 1883 and February 1885. GMH is referring to 'Dynamite Saturday': at about 2.00 p.m. on 24 January 1885, explosions occurred at the Tower of London, in the Crypt leading from Westminster Hall, and in the chamber of the House of Commons. No lives were lost, but many injuries were reported. The attacks were carried out by a militant wing of Irish nationalists and their Irish-American associates. As GMH informed his mother, news of the attacks was 'cried in the streets' of Dublin that same day (24 Jan. 1885).

Write to: another list of letters to be sent, with the names cancelled after the task was completed.

young Byrne: perhaps John Byrne, one of his UC students.

Fr. Rickaby: Joseph Rickaby, S.J. (1845–1932) distinguished himself at Stonyhurst (novitiate) and St Mary's Hall, Stonyhurst (Philosophy), and obtained his MA from the University of London. He taught at Stonyhurst before going to St Beuno's in 1874 to begin his theology studies (GMH arrived at St Beuno's in August 1874). From 1879 to 1896, he taught ethics and natural law, and was the Prefect of Studies at St Mary's Hall. His publications include *Moral Philosophy, Ethics, and the Natural Law* (1889); *Waters that Go Softly* (1906); *Index to the Works of Cardinal Newman* (1914); an English translation of the *Spiritual Exercises of St. Ignatius* (1915); a translation of Alphonsus

Rodriguez's *The Practice of Perfection and Religious Virtues* (1929); and fifty-eight articles in *The Month*.

Mr. Patmore: Coventry Patmore (1823–96; *ODNB*), poet; see Biographical Register.

Milicent: GMH's sister; see fo. 22ʳ and Biographical Register.

genius: From Velleius Paterculus (*c*.19 BCE–*c*.31 CE), *Historiae Romanae*, 1. 48, a basic reference work.

Antonius: Standard information from reference works.

25ᵛ

nihil: Cicero, *Brutus*, 202: '*Nihil erat in eius oratione nisi sincerum, nihil nisi siccum atque sanum*' {In his language everything was genuine, everything sane and healthy}.

Catulus: Appears in the First University Examination for Autumn 1885 ('Examination Papers' 19/41).

Lysias: Son of a wealthy Athenian craftsman, Lysias (459/8–*c*.380 BCE) travelled to Thurii in the south of Italy, where he probably studied rhetoric. He returned to Athens in 412 BCE; nine years later, he was arrested by the Thirty Tyrants, a Spartan-sponsored Athenian oligarchy, on the pretext of dissidence. Lysias escaped to Megara; when he returned to Athens later that year, he was impoverished. He took up speech-writing as a means of survival, writing primarily for court appearances, but also public occasions such as the Olympic festival in 388 BCE. Famous for his clarity and persuasiveness; his style is associated with the natural, unembellished 'Attic' school of oration, as distinct from the more ornate or 'Asiatic' style.

St. John Chrysostom: St John Chrysostom (347–407 CE), born in Antioch, became a religious hermit around 373; for more than a decade he lived according to a severely ascetic regimen. He returned to Antioch in 381; was ordained a priest in 386; and worked as a bishop's assistant before being made Archbishop of Constantinople in 398. Outspoken critic of the city's moral corruption and its empress, Eudoxia (d. 404). Chrysostom was deposed in 403 after collusion on the part of the Patriarch of Constantinople, Theophilus (d. 412). After a brief return he was exiled to Pontus, where he died. (In ancient Greek texts, the Black Sea was the *Pontus Euxeinos*, or Hospitable Sea; Pontus—named as such in Xenophon's *Anabasis*—referred to the southern coast of the Black Sea, now north-eastern Turkey. People in the region were among the first to convert to Christianity; see 1 Peter. It became a Roman province in 62 CE, and then part of the Byzantine empire.) St John is remembered in the Western Church as one of the Four Greek Doctors; in the Eastern Church, as one of the Three Holy Hierarchs and Universal Teachers. The epithet 'Chrysostom', meaning 'golden-mouthed' in Greek, honours his eloquence in preaching. For GMH's translation of Chrysostom's sermon on Eutropius, see *CW* v.

St. G[regory] Naz[ianzen]: St Gregory of Nazianzus (329/30–389/90 CE), son of the bishop of Nazianzus, studied in Athens before leaving in 359 to become a monk at Pontus in the company of his friend St Basil (*c*.330–79). When, after two years, he returned to Athens, he was ordained a priest; in 372 he became Bishop of Sasima. After the death of Emperor Valens (d. 378), Gregory worked to revive the beleaguered Christian Church in Constantinople, and preached in favour of the Nicene faith (as opposed to the Arianism of Valens). In 381 he was made Bishop of Constantinople, but soon resigned. Gregory is one of the Four Eastern Doctors.

26ʳ

St. Gregory the Great: Gregory (*c.*540–604), born in Rome to an aristocratic family, was urban prefect from 572–3, and papal representative in Constantinople, 579–86, before becoming pope in 590. He negotiated peace accords with the hostile Lombards in 592–3, and appointed governors to Italian cities, thereby asserting the temporal authority of the church. He delegated St Augustine of Canterbury (d. *c.*605) to convert England to Christianity in 596. According to legend, the decision was motivated by a scene Gregory happened upon in a Roman marketplace, where he witnessed the sale of English boys as slaves. When told that the beautiful young men were Angli (Angles), he punningly suggested they had the faces of *Angeli* (angels). He later requested that Anglian slave boys be purchased, baptized, and entered into monasteries (see Henry Chadwick, *The Church in Ancient Society: From Galilee to Gregory the Great* (Oxford: Oxford University Press, 2001), 671–2). Feast day: 12 March. See also GMH's 'Mortal Beauty', which he sent to Dixon dated 'Aug. 23 1885'. Following a traditional method of Ignatian prayer, GMH gives himself three points to reflect upon during his morning contemplation; see the Introduction, ' "Consider your own misery" '.

Hortensius born: Continuing the list of famous Roman orators; Quintus Hortensius Hortalus (114–49 BCE) was, after Cicero, the most famous speaker in the late Republic.

Jan. 24: See note on *dynamite explosions* above, fo. 25ʳ.

Jan. 26: see note on siege of Khartoum above, fo. 25ʳ.

taken in adultery: A story uniquely found in the gospel of John (8: 1–11), in which Jesus, when the Pharisees ask for his judgement on a woman caught *in flagrante delicto*, enigmatically bends down to the ground and writes in the dirt with his finger before rendering his famous pronouncement that the man who is without sin should cast the first stone at her. Reflecting upon Christ's teaching about self-righteousness, GMH applies it to himself.

Mr. Gladstone: William Ewart Gladstone (1809–98; *ODNB*), born in Liverpool to a wealthy merchant family, educated at Eton and Christ Church, Oxford. First elected to the House of Commons as a Tory representative in 1832; he was vice-president and later president of the Board of Trade from 1841 to 1845, under the government of Sir Robert Peel (1788–1850), and Chancellor of the Exchequer four times between 1852 and 1882. Gladstone adopted increasingly radical positions on topics such as extending the franchise and the disestablishment of the Anglican Church in Ireland. In 1868, elected as prime minister in the Liberal Party, a position from which he retired in 1874 after calling and losing a general election. He returned as prime minister in 1880, his party passing the Irish Land Act of 1881 and the Reform Act of 1884. He stepped down in 1885, stymied in attempts to broker a system of local government for Ireland. He was elected again the next year, but left office after calling and losing a general election following the defeat of his Home Rule Bill; during his final tenure as prime minister, 1892 to 1894, the second Home Rule Bill failed. In addition to his political career, Gladstone published widely on topics such as classical studies, literature, and politics (see Frank Turner, *The Greek Heritage in Victorian Britain* (New Haven: Yale University Press, 1981), esp. chs. 4, 5).

The question of Irish independence dogged Gladstone throughout his career. GMH objected to his concessions to Irish nationalists. In a letter to Baillie, GMH agrees that Gladstone 'ought to be beheaded on Tower Hill', then adds, 'As I am accustomed to speak too strongly of him I will not further commit myself in writing' (24 Apr. 1885); three years later, GMH describes Gladstone as being 'without foresight, insight, or resolution' (1 May 1888). See also Norman White, *Hopkins: A Literary Biography*, 364, 431.

feeding of the five thousand: Also known as the miracle of the five loaves and two fish, this story, told in all four gospels (Matthew 14: 13–21; Mark 6: 31–4; Luke 9: 10–17; John 6: 5–15), tells of Jesus feeding a multitude by blessing and distributing a ration fit for a few. GMH's notes indicate that he was reading the account in the gospel of John.

St. Patrick: Born in the late fourth century to a British family; his father was a church deacon. According to the *Confessions*, which Patrick almost certainly did not write, he was kidnapped by Irish raiders as a youth and kept in slavery for six years in Ireland, tending flocks. He escaped back to England, and was ordained a priest, but accepted a commission to bring Christianity to the Irish. Arriving in Ireland *c*.435, he established an episcopal see in Armagh and set up a system of sees organized by geographical location. It is difficult to separate the historical man from the Patrick of legend. His reputation for miracles and humility helped to win over Druidic followers. He is the patron saint of Ireland. Feast day: 17 March.

his hymn: GMH particularly admired 'St Patrick's Breastplate', which historians have traced back to the early eighth century. Tradition ascribes the text to St Patrick, but linguistic evidence refutes this claim. Translated from the Irish, the hymn begins: 'I bind to myself today / The strong virtue of the Invocation of the Trinity: / I believe the Trinity in the Unity / The Creator of the Universe.' The full text is available at: <www.newadvent.org/cathen/11554a.htm>. Writing to Bridges on 13 Oct. 1886, GMH asks, 'Did I ever send you St. Patrick's "Breastplate" or prayer? I do now at all events. Read it and say if it is not one of the most remarkable compositions of man.'

St. Joseph: Joseph was the husband of Mary, the mother of Jesus. Matthew 1: 18–25 tells the story of Joseph's intention, on learning that his betrothed spouse was pregnant with a child not his own, to divorce her quietly, but a revelation in a dream led him instead to marry her. He then became a stalwart protector of both mother and child. Feast day: 19 March.

26ᵛ

The Annunciation: The Gospel of Luke (1: 26–38) recounts that the angel Gabriel announced to Mary that God had chosen her to be the mother of Jesus. Mary, although confused and afraid, agreed to serve God and his salvific design. The feast is celebrated on 25 March, nine months before Christmas Day; following his usual practice, GMH most probably made these notes on the evening of Monday, 24 March 1885 in preparation for his prayer the following morning.

St. Thomas's birthplace: Thomas Aquinas (*c*.1225–74) was born to a noble family near Aquinum (now Aquino), in south-eastern Italy. After studying at the Monte Cassino monastery and the University of Naples, he joined the Dominican friars in 1244, against his family's wishes. A famous scholar by 1269, he was summoned to Paris to be a consultant for King Louis IX (1214–70). He returned to Naples in 1272; two years later, he died on his way to the Council of Lyons, to which he had been called by Pope Gregory X (1210–76). He was canonized in 1323, and declared a Doctor of the Church in 1567. Known as the pre-eminent medieval scholastic; his prolific writings include translations of Aristotle; theological treatises; and biblical commentaries. His central texts are the *Summa contra Gentiles* {Against the Errors of the Infidels}, which argues that revealed truth cannot be judged on the basis of scientific truth; 1261–4), and *Summa Theologiae* {Summation of Theology}, a manual for theology students; *c*.1266–74).

27ʳ

This folio was loose before the MS was repaired; undoubtedly one or more subsequent folios are missing.

Dates for Juvenal: Introductions to the lives and writings of Juvenal and Tacitus, two of the great 'Silver Latin' authors. Along with Horace, Juvenal (Decimus Iunius Iuvenalis, *c*.60–70 to early 2nd century CE) was the pre-eminent Roman satirist. He wrote five books of verse in hexameters (16 satires) attacking the *mores* of his contemporary society. Virtually nothing of his life is known that does not rely on the very doubtful information he provides in his own verse. On Tacitus (*c*.56–118 CE), who was the major historian of the Roman Empire, see the notes that follow.

Marcus Aurelius: Marcus Aurelius Antoninus Augustus (121–80 CE) was adopted by the Emperor Antoninus Pius (86/7–161) in 138; his political career was also furthered by the mentorship of the Emperor Hadrian (76–138; emperor, 117–38). He ruled with Lucius Verus as co-emperor from 161 until Lucius' death in 169, and then as emperor until 180. As a young man, Marcus Aurelius was tutored by Herodes Atticus and Fronto. He studied the works of Epictetus and was personally acquainted with Apollonius of Chalcedon, an eminent Stoic philosopher; the influence of both informs Aurelius' famous *Meditations* (written in Greek, 170–80), first published in 1558. In the nineteenth century, those who wrote admiringly about the *Meditations* included Johann Wolfgang von Goethe, John Stuart Mill, and Matthew Arnold. Walter Pater, Hopkins's former tutor, critiqued Aurelius's stoicism in the historical novel *Marius the Epicurean* (1885).

Friedländer: Ludwig Friedländer (1824–1909), who edited Juvenal's five books of *Satires* and an important volume on Roman culture, *Darstellungen aus der Sittengeschichte Roms in der Zeit von Augustus bis zum Ausgang der Antonine* (Leipzig, 1862–4).

Martial the poet's: Marcus Valerius Martialis (*c*.40–103 CE), Latin satirist and epigrammatist, was born in Bilbilis, Spain but spent most of his adult life in Rome, where Seneca and Lucan assisted him. 'His concise, pointed, often obscene epigrams are quintessentially urban writing. Their abrasive edge, discontinuities, paradoxes and juxtapositions' are deployed to attack 'social and moral hypocrisy, insiders and outsiders'. A. J. Boyle, 'Our Page Tastes of Man', *Times Literary Supplement* (5 October 2007), 9. See also fo. 33^r.

27^v

Fr. Hughes: John J. Hughes, S.J. (1843–1912), Vice-President of UC and Dean of Residence. A Dublin native, he entered the Society of Jesus in October 1860.

July 24: GMH's vacation in England began at his parents' home in Hampstead (they were poised to move to Haslemere, in Surrey), and included their summer residence in the village of Eastbourne, South Downs; a trip to Sydenham, to see the ailing William Addis (see Addis's letter 10 July 1885); and a visit with Patmore and his family in Hastings, on the east Sussex coast. 'I have been in England', GMH informed Bridges 1–8 Sept. 1885; he had not visited the Bridges family because Monica was pregnant (she subsequently miscarried): 'I was with my people first at Hampstead, then at Midhurst in Sussex in a lovely ~~laud lan~~ landscape: they are there yet. And from there I went to Hastings to Mr. Patmore's for a few days. I managed to see several old friends and to make new ones, amongst which Mr. W. H. Cummings the tenor singer and composer, who wrote the Life of Purcell: he shewed me some of his Purcell treasures and others and is going to send me several things. I liked him very much but the time of my being with him was cut short.' Regarding the Patmore visit, GMH informed his mother, 20 Aug. 1885: 'We went to see Battle, Winchilsea [*sic*], Rye, and so on.' None of his extant letters mentions the exhibitions that he saw. Admission to the Royal Academy, in that era, was 1 shilling; catalogues could be purchased for an additional 6*s*. GMH returned to Ireland on 19 August. See also the letter to Patmore, 21 Aug. 1885.

Sydenham: See *CW* v for the text of the sermon, a revised version of one he had written and delivered previously.

28^r

Tacitus: A page on the life of Tacitus, very similar to the treatment of Juvenal, above.

Tacitus' style: GMH has left room for additional commentary. The IJA has one unruled sheet, 28 × 22.5 cm, folded to create four pages (the booklet format GMH favoured), featuring notes on 'Tacitus's Style' (J11/15; see *CW* vi). The notes treat chapters from the *Histories* not otherwise mentioned in the *DN*; yet, GMH's example of the second characteristic, 'varietas, variety or studied irregularity', from *Histories* 1. 1, and his example of the third, '^color^ poeticus, poetical colouring', from *Histories* 1. 2, are both passages treated in the Notebook. These passages from the *Histories*, required by the curriculum, provided easy classroom references to explain Tacitus' prosody. In some instances GMH may exaggerate to make a pedagogical point; *opimum*, from *Histories* 1. 2, is not uncommon in Latin prose, and thus not quite a 'tropical and poetical word'.

28ᵛ

Histories: *Histories* 3. 2 includes a use of the pronoun *is* ('this', masculine; 'he'); GMH finds other examples later in the book. *Eo ipso* {the fact itself} probably refers to the phrase in 3. 2, '*Quin potius eo ipso*' {Rather let us take advantage of the fact that . . . }; '*ea statim contione qua*' {this harange . . . which} comes from 3. 3; the feminine form *ea* anticipates the relative pronoun *qua*. GMH points out the different uses of the pronoun, both for emphasis and for demonstration.

   legatus Caesaris: *Procurator* probably comes from *Histories* 3. 4; GMH wants to relate the office to the *legatus legionis* {the ambassador of the legion} and *legatus Caesaris* {the ambassador of Caesar}, apparently referring to phrases in *Histories* 1. 7. The *procurator* 'signified an agent or, in legal proceedings, representative, and under the Principate came to be the distinctive term for the employees of the emperor in civil administration' (*OCD* 1251); in the provinces, the *procurator* was governed by the *legatus*. GMH could be refreshing his memory of Roman bureaucracy for use in the classroom.

   false charge: Probably *Histories* 3. 4, where the adverb is used to mean 'as' instead of 'as though', which would imply that the charge made (that Flavianus remembered his former friendship with Vitellius, which he did) was false.

   in hexameter: 'The strength of the knights', *Histories* 3. 5; the declension of the noun *vis* is unusual. The reference to *opum vim* in hexameter may be to the oracle given to Croesus when he consulted Delphi about invading Persia, as quoted by Cicero (*De divinatione* 1. 115): '*Croesus Halyn penetrans magnum, pervertet opum vim*' {Croesus, crossing the great Halys, will overcome the strength of an empire}; GMH may be interested in the use of *vis*, which works as an 'enclitic', added after another word (here, *opus*) almost as a particle (hence the comparison with the English suffixes 'dom' and 'ism').

   Legions: Mapping out the legions involved in the Roman imperial wars after 68 CE.

   adjutrix: 'Helper', *Histories* 3. 44, a reference to the legion sent to Spain to support Otho.

   Sexta Ferrata: 'Sixth iron [clad]', *Histories* 3. 44; a legion of the Roman army, active in the province of Palestine; the reference is unclear.

   Lucan bk. 1: The RUI Calendar for 1886 lists Lucan, *Pharsalia*, bk. 1, as a subject of examination in the Second University Examination in Arts, honours (administered 20 June to 10 July 1886). This section is more a liberal paraphrase than a literary analysis of the text. GMH simplifies Lucan's text to convey the Latin's rhetorical effect. Lucan's epic is most famous for its speeches; even the narrative is described as rhetorical. These students, preparing for an advanced examination, would be more competent Latinists than those whose examinations GMH graded earlier in the *DN*, but Lucan's liberties could well confuse even skilled translators.

North than here: A nine-line lament (not really a speech, since it is silent) is compressed into a few sentences. The Ariminensians were exposed also to the Senones, the Cimbrians, and the Germans, not only to the Gauls and the Carthaginians. GMH tends to ignore Lucan's famous *sententiae*, aphorisms that capture a variety of sentiments in a compressed phrase. Thus, he does not really translate *quotiens Romam Fortuna lacessit, / hac iter est bellis* {whenever Fortune strikes Rome, here is the site of the battles}.

29^r

master of the world: Again, GMH gives a paraphrase, ignoring the more 'Lucanian' *sententiae*. He avoids a literal translation of *tua nos faciet victoria cives* {Your victory will make citizens of us}, which captures the irony of sentiment in a single verse (Caesar, whose victory, in fact, brings tyranny to Rome's citizens, will give Curio's party citizenship).

fell in 53: the fact that Pompey was Caesar's son-in-law is not mentioned by most commentators. The title was not accurate when the speech was delivered in 49 BCE, since Caesar's daughter Julia died in 54 BCE, yet one could continue to refer to Pompey as a *gener* even after his wife's death.

29^v

her usurper: GMH translates this long speech (ll. 299–351), but unlike the previous two, makes explanatory additions. He renders l. 317, *ille semel raptos numquam dimittet honores* {That man [i.e. Pompey] will never give up honours that have once been robbed} as 'then never need to lay down honours which to begin with he had no right to wear'. GMH's loose rendering does not include details of these violations of the law. Haskins's edition (Cambridge, 1875) clarifies (19): Pompey had triumphed over Hiarbas in 81 BC, at the age of 24; the legal age was 30.

earth: GMH paraphrases significantly, ignoring most of the details and inserting exclamations ('Civil War!') that would not appear in a literal rendering. He captures the force and the contradictions present in Laelius' speech, in which he rejects all norms of fraternal piety in the service of Caesar, his general.

30^r

forces etc: The geographical details of Lucan's *Pharsalia* 1. 392–465, a passage treating the areas from which Caesar gathered his military forces; GMH is also reviewing the layout of the Roman republic at the time. The occasional etymological speculations are idiosyncratic, but some of GMH's difficulties with particular locations are shared by Haskins in his edition (the location of the river *Nemetis* (1. 419), for example, remains obscure). GMH includes the geographical references on ll. 436–40, although that passage was regarded as spurious as early as Haskins. As Schlatter notes in his commentary, some of this vocabulary would be familiar to GMH from teaching Caesar's *De Bello Gallico*, bks. 1 and 2. See also *A Dictionary of Greek and Roman Geography*, ed. William Smith (London: John Murray, 1876).

Marne: Lucan may be right and GMH mistaken, as the Lingones evidently migrated to Cisalpine Gaul (northern Italy), near the Po River, a movement which may have brought them through or closer to the south.

Promoto: *Promoto*, literally 'extended'; the Italian territory was extended to the river Var by Augustus.

mistral: J. D. Duff, in the Loeb translation, takes the distinction not to refer to a north-west wind in general—which would make the Circius more or less identical to the Corus—but rather to refer to a local wind particular to Monaco. The Mistral blows from northern Spain to northern Italy, through the Rhône valley in France, into the Mediterranean. An early nineteenth-century nature handbook indicates the Mistral as another name for the wind pattern that Aulus Gellius (b. between 125 and 128 CE) calls Circius in *Noctes Atticae* (Lib. II, cap. 22). See Edward Polehampton, *The Gallery of Nature and Art; Or a Tour through Creation and Science*, iv (London: R. Wilks, 1815), 234. 'Corus' is a Latin term for any north-westerly wind.

Suessŏnes: GMH notes that Lucan makes the 'o' in this word metrically long, although it is normally short.

Belgae: In Irish myth, the Fir Bolg (Fir Bholg, Firbolg) was one of the races that inhabited the island prior to the arrival of the Tuatha Dé Danann. The origin of their name is the subject of dispute: many commentators consider them the 'men of Builg' or 'men of bags', or possibly 'men with spears', from *bolg* meaning spear or by comparison with the modern Irish word *bolg* meaning 'belly' (and originally meaning 'bag'). Alternatively they may be related to the Belgae tribe, whose name meant the 'shining ones' (from Proto-Celtic *belo*, meaning 'bright').

30ᵛ

Gaul in 52: GMH is referring to Lucan's gloss on the Arverni tribe: 'who falsely claim descent from Troy and brotherhood with Rome'. In Caesar's time they were in dispute with the Aedui (both tribes lived in the centre of modern France) and claimed Trojan ancestry and therefore fraternity with the Romans of Latium. The Aedui eventually joined the Gaulish coalition against Rome. Vercingetorix was their last ruler and Rome's last great foe in Gaul. The reference to 52 refers to the battle of Alessia between Caesar's and Vercingetorix's forces, a classic moment in the history of siege warfare.

that year: A Belgic people occupying parts of Hainault and Flanders were defeated by Caesar after a fierce struggle in 57 BCE.

near the mouth: The next few entries (from *Pictones* to *Genabos*) are from ll. 436–40. Haskins notes: 'These verses wanting alike in taste and Latinity are not found in the old MSS.' GMH follows most standard editions at the time.

Turones: *Turonas*, l. 437; most editions now read *Turones*.

cavalry: The verb *dissolvitur*, although containing the prefix *dis-*, is virtually equivalent to *solvitur*, 'to set loose, free'.

31ʳ

Lloegr: Lucan refers to them as *tonse*, with their hair cut, as opposed to *comata*, long-haired, as the Ligurians had been previously.

Teutates: A god of the Celts; equated by the Romans (along with Esus and Taranis) with Mars, Mercury, and Jupiter. The name inspires a philological digression.

Ζεύς: Zeus, son of Cronus and Rhea, the most powerful of all the ancient Greek gods (Roman equivalent, Jupiter).

Hesus: The Gaulish god Hesus (more commonly, Esus) is associated with Mercury and Mars; some scholars postulate he is a god of war. His followers were said to engage in human sacrifice and ritual wounding. Depictions link him with the sacred bull, as well as cranes and egrets. With Esus and Teutates, Taranis was one of the three central gods of Gaul and Britain mentioned by Lucan (39–65). Represented by the wheel and by lightning, he is the spirit of thunder.

Graecised form: GMH is correct about the derivation.

Cicero de Officiis {The Duties of Man}: Another unfinished Classics project, preparing a commentary or lecture on Cicero's famous treatise. Previously edited and published by Norman MacKenzie, 'The Imperative Voice—An Unpublished Lecture by Hopkins', *Hopkins Quarterly*, 2 (1975–6), 101–16, and 'An Unpublished Hopkins Manuscript', *Hopkins Research Bulletin*, 7 (1976), 3–7; and Schlatter, S.J., 'Gerard Manley Hopkins: Poetic Fragments'. Schlatter's introduction (51–3) is helpful for dating the essay. While working in Dublin, GHM used and annotated an Oxford Pocket Classics edition of Cicero (M. Tullius Cicero, *De Officiis, De Senectute, et De Amicitia* (Parker and Co., 1882); now BRC 9:14). The prefatory notes on Cicero's 'authorities' and mentors are indebted to *A Dictionary of Greek and Roman Biography and Mythology*, ed. Smith.

highly of him: For additional background, see Holden's commentary (Leipzig: Teubner, 1866), especially 140 (note for l. 12).

Zeno: Zeno of Citium (*c*.335–*c*.263 BCE) arrived in Athens from Citium (Cyprus) around 313 BCE, and studied under philosophers of various schools before teaching in the Painted Colonnade (*Stoa Poikile*), from which Stoicism takes its name. Known as the school's founder, Zeno crystallized Stoicism into the three foundational principles of logic, physics, and ethics. As a Stoic, he was associated with ethical and epistemological absolutism, and the belief in adapting oneself to live in conformity with universal reason. His lost text, *Republic*, envisions a utopian community, and stresses the importance of universal laws and institutions. See GMH's notes in *CW* iv. 321–2.

and wrote: Holden has 'Ariston of Chius (B. C. 260)' (145 (note for 1.16)), which corresponds to GMH's correction of himself.

31ᵛ

ἐπιστήμη {episteme}: Scientific knowledge, or a system of understanding.

Attic orators: Cicero mentions Demetrius of Phalerum (*De Officiis* 1. 3) as a Greek model of both subtle, 'philosophical' oratory and forensic skill.

Ptolemy's court: GMH's language follows Holden's note on Demetrius (142 (note for 1.10)).

32ʳ

that self-: The sentence ('preservation is right . . . ') and paragraph conclude below, after the addendum marked by 'X'.

command which: This added gloss continues below, beginning 'Cicero strongly recognises . . . '

self slaughter: Hamlet enjoins: 'O, that this too too solid flesh would melt, / Thaw, and resolve itself into a dew! / Or that the Everlasting had not fix'd / His canon 'gainst self-slaughter!' *Hamlet* I. ii. 129–32 in *The Pictorial Edition of the Works of Shakespere*, ed. Charles Knight, vi (London: C. Knight and Co., 1843).

32ᵛ

ἡδύ: καλόν {beautiful, good}, χρήσιμον {useful}, and ἡδύ {pleasurable}.

dulce: 'Good', 'Useful/Practical', 'Pleasing'. *Honestum*—Cicero's translation of καλόν (*kalon*, 'good') might be closer to 'honourable' in English. See Schlatter, S.J., 'Commentary on Lucan and Cicero' (2000), 78, and GMH's own note recorded in his edition of *De Officiis*, *CW* vi.

Holden: The edition, with introduction and commentary, by H. A. Holden, 1866.

the same: *Astrologia* {the reasons of the stars} and *astronomia* {the laws of the stars} were originally deemed interchangeable. The modern distinction between astrology and astronomy appears around the end of the fourteenth century.

Alex. the great: Alexander of Macedon (356–323 BCE), born in Pella to King Philip II (382–336 BCE) and Queen Olympias (*c*.375–316 BCE); studied under Aristotle in his youth. Following his father's murder, he undertook Philip's planned war against the Persian Empire: after quashing a nascent insurrection in Thebes in 335 BCE, he crossed the Hellespont and entered Asia. In the battle at Issus in 333 BCE, his army defeated Darius III (*c*.380–330 BCE), king of Persia; two years later, the Macedonians effected a decisive victory over the Persians at Arbela. From 330 to 327 BCE Alexander's forces moved across the Persian Empire; in 327 BCE he entered India, where he fought his last major battle in 326 BCE. Although his empire collapsed shortly after his death, his efforts generated an unprecedented and lasting mingling of Hellenistic and Asian culture.

33ʳ

Antigonus: The first two names seem to be additions from the Greek BA course on History and Literature from 430 to 322, which would include the life and times of Alexander the Great and, hence, Antipater, and Antigonus.

Altar of Vesta: The temple of Vesta, ancient Roman goddess of the hearth, was located in the Forum. Its inner sanctum housed sacred objects such as the Palladium, the legendary wooden image of Athena. On the shrine's altar was kept the sacred hearthfire, signifying the state's link to the private home. The fire, kept burning day and night, was ritually relit on 1 March. Tending the fire always were the Vestal Virgins, Rome's sole female priesthood, comprised of six women chosen from high-ranking families. The virgins, supervised by the *pontifex maximus*, were charged with preparing salt cakes for public offerings. Failure to maintain one's chastity was punishable by live entombment. In a letter to his brother Lionel of 1 March 1889 GMH outlines plans for an article on the *Argei*, the Vestal Virgins' 'Bridge-ceremony' whereby, standing on the Pons Sublicius, they would throw images of men, fashioned in rushes, into the Tiber river.

Martial: Comments on Martial, using Paley's expurgated edition (*Grammar School Classics*; *Epigrammata Selecta* (London: Whitaker & Co., 1875)), which would have included only Martial's less objectionable material. Martial's 'pettiness of mind', in comparison with Juvenal and Lucan, rankles GMH; Martial's epigrams treat mundane, and sometimes vulgar, topics (Lucan and Juvenal, while cynical and satirical, generally employ a loftier style and treat more elevated themes). GMH would have found support in Paley's comments: 'However brilliant the wit, however valuable the details of domestic Roman life and of Roman topography, and however admirable the poetry and the latinity of Martial, there is this valid ground of objection to the use of his epigrams in schools, that not less than a fourth part of them is exceedingly gross, and quite unfit for general reading. The same, indeed, may justly be said of Catullus, Juvenal, Aristophanes, and some others' (*Grammar School Classics*, p. iv). Paley adopted the text of F. G. Schneidewin (Leipzig: Teubner, 1853):

Ep. 14: Martial, Book II, Epigram 14

Nil intemptatum Selius, nil linquit inausum,
    cenandum quotiens iam videt esse domi.
currit ad Europen et te, Pauline, tuosque
    laudat Achilleos, sed sine fine, pedes.
si nihil Europe fecit, tunc Saepta petuntur,
    si quid Phillyrides praestet et Aesonides.
hic quoque deceptus Memphitica templa frequentat,
    assidet et cathedris, maesta iuvenca, tuis.
inde petit centum pendentia tecta columnis,
    illinc Pompei dona nemusque duplex.
nec Fortunati spernit nec balnea Fausti
    nec Grylli tenebras Aeoliamque Lupi:

> *nam thermis iterum ternis iterumque lauatur.*
> *omnia cum fecit, sed renuente deo,*
> *lotus ad Europes tepidae buxeta recurrit,*
> *si quis ibi serum carpat amicus iter.*
> ***per te** perque tuam, vector lascive, puellam,*
> *ad cenam Selium tu, **rogo**, taure, voca.*

{Selius leaves nothing untried, nothing unventured, whenever he sees that he has to dine at home. He runs to Europa [a portico in the Campus Martius featuring paintings of the rape of Europa] and praises you, Paulinus, and your feet fast as Achilles'—interminably. If Europa does nothing, he heads for the Enclosure [the Saepta Julia, in the Campus Martius, begun by Caesar and completed by Agrippa] to see whether the son of Phillyra and the son of Aeson will furnish anything. Disappointed here too, he goes and hangs around the goddess of Memphis' [Isis], temple and seats himself beside your chairs, sorrowful heifer. Thence he seeks the roof supported by a hundred columns [the Hecatostylon, close to the Portico and the Theatre of Pompey], and from there the gift of Pompey and the double wood. Nor does he scorn the baths of Fortunatus nor those of Faustus nor yet the gloom of Gryllus and Lupus' Aeolian cavern. As for the three hot baths, he uses them again and again. When he has tried everything but the god refuses, he runs after his ablutions back to the box shrubbery of sunwarmed Europa, in case a friend may be taking his way there late. Wanton mount, I beg you in your own name and your girl's, o bull, *you* invite Selius to dinner [i.e. and give him grass to eat, or nothing].}

true object: GMH is noting a poetic ambiguity in Martial's use of *per te* with the verb for begging (here *rogo*, but GMH uses a synonym, *oro*); *rogo* (or oro) *per* can simply mean 'I beg for', which can also be expressed without the preposition *per*. In Epigram 14, Martial's use of *per te* {by, on your authority} thus hints that the poet is begging *for* the listener himself:

Ep. 16: Martial, Book II, Epigram 16

> *Zoilus aegrotat: faciunt hanc stragula febrem.*
> *si fuerit sanus, coccina quid facient?*
> *quid torus a Nilo, quid Sidone tinctus olenti ?*
> *ostendit stultas quid nisi morbus opes?*
> *quid tibi cum medicis? dimitte Machaonas omnis.*
> *vis fieri sanus? stragula sume mea.*

{Zoilus is ill. His bedclothes make this fever. If he gets well, what will be the use of his scarlet coverlets or an underblanket from Nile or one dyed in smelly Sidonian purple? What but sickness shows off such silly wealth? What do you want with doctors? Dismiss all the Machaons. Do you want to get well? Take *my* bedclothes.}

as Paley says: Paley comments, '"if he is *not* ill, what is the fine scarlet-dyed bed covering to do," viz. in order to be seen and admired', taking the verb *fuerit* (a future perfect) to have a merely conditional meaning. GMH corrects Paley's note, insisting that one should maintain a future perfect meaning, 'If / when he will be healthy'.

Ep. 17: Martial, Book II, Epigram 17

Tonstrix Suburae faucibus sedet primis,
cruenta pendent qua flagella tortorum
Argique Letum multus obsidet sutor.
sed ista tonstrix, Ammiane, non tondet,
non tondet, inquam. quid igitur facit? radit.

{A female barber sits right at the entrance of Subura, where the bloody scourges of the torturers hang and many a cobbler throngs Argiletum. But that female barber, Ammianus, does not clip, she doesn't clip, I say. What does she do then? She shaves [i.e. she fleeces her clients].}

a legend: Martial's use of *tmesis*, the separation of a word into two parts, with another word or phrase placed between the parts, is analysed. GMH points out that *argique letum* really is the tmesis of the word *argiletum*[*que*] (where the *que* is an 'enclitic particle' meaning 'and'). This leads him to recall some of the wilder examples of tmesis in Latin poetry, including two cases long attributed to Ennius: *Cere comminuit brum*, from *Cerebrum comminuit*, and *Massili—portabant ad* [*li*]*tora—tanas* for *portabunt* [*juvenes*] *ad litora Massilitanas*. GMH seems to be citing from memory, but may have referred to Wordsworth (*Fragments and Specimens of Early Latin*, 585; see fo. 17ʳ), who cites the passages on 585, 'some barbarous licences (unpoetical is too good a name for them)'. Attribution to Ennius is doubtful, especially for the second phrase. GMH also includes a citation from the Roman satirist Lucilius, which is preserved in the Christian Latin poet Ausonius: '*villa Lucani—mox potieris—aca* [*o?*]' {soon wilt thou gain the Lucani—villa—acus}for *Villa Lucaniaca mox potieris* (Ausonius, *Epistula* 16. 36; *PL* 19: 918D), which does not appear in Wordsworth. These examples were notorious in Roman literature, especially offensive to the tastes of later Latin grammarians, and were considered doggerel. It seems that GMH had memorized these passages (they do not appear in Paley's notes), since, while writing about Martial, these examples would not have been ready to hand. Perhaps he gave them special attention on account of his own interest in the poetic technique. Stephanie West links GMH's use of tmesis to his reading of Virgil ('Classical Notes on Gerard Manley Hopkins', *International Journal of the Classical Tradition*, 13/1 (2006), 21–32 at 27). She refers to Ennius only as an exaggeration of the technique. But GMH's note suggests he saw the lines attributed to Ennius as something of an exemplar for the technique.

Ep. 24: Martial, Book II, Epigram 24

Si det iniqua tibi tristem fortuna reatum,
squalidus haerebo pallidiorque reo:
si iubeat patria damnatum excedere terra,
per freta, per scopulos exulis ibo comes.

> *dat tibi divitias: ecquid sunt ista duorum?*
> *das partem? 'multum est.' Candide, das aliquid ?*
> *mecum eris ergo miser: quod si deus ore sereno*
> *annuerit, felix, Candide, solus eris.*

{If unkind Fortune should put you in the sad situation of a man on trial, I shall stand by you in mourning, paler than the accused. If she have you found guilty and order you to leave your native land, I shall bear the exile company through seas and cliffs. She gives you riches. Are they for us both? Do you give me half a share? 'That's a lot.' Candidus, do you give me anything? Very well, in trouble you will be with me, but if the god nods with face serene, in prosperity, Candidus, you will be alone.}

extravagance: Interested in teaching points, GMH notes that the future tense in *haerebo* 'I will cling/stand by' should emphasize the sense of future obligation ('I am to go to the doctor' or 'Shall we take his advice?'); this interpretation departs from Paley, who takes the future to imply a promise.

antithesis: GMH follows Paley's note: Fortune has *not* given the addressee, Candidus, suffering—as the previous lines described—but rather fortune has given him riches.

Ep. 30: Martial, Book II, Epigram 30

> *Mutua viginti sestertia forte rogabam,*
> *quae vel donanti non grave munus erat.*
> *quippe rogabatur fidusque vetusque sodalis*
> *et cuius laxas arca flagellat opes.*
> *is mihi 'dives eris, si causas egeris' inquit.*
> *quod peto da, Gai: non peto consilium.*

{I happened to ask for a loan of twenty thousand sesterces, no burdensome present even as a gift. He of whom I asked it was [i.e. had been] a faithful old friend, whose coffer whips up his ample wealth. Says he to me: 'You'll be a rich man if you plead cases.' Give me what I ask, Gaius; I'm not asking advice.}

subjunctive: GMH responds to a standard pedagogical need in teaching elementary Latin: explain the unexpected absence or presence of the subjunctive. One expects to find *esset* in this relative clause ('contrary to fact'). Paley offers no note.

33ᵛ

legatus S.P.Q.R.: *Senatus Populus Que Romanus* {ambassador of the Senate and the People of Rome}.

the decline: A brief overview of the period discussed in Tacitus, which concludes with a reference to the succession of Flavian emperors, ending with Hadrian (d. 138), after whom was founded the Antonine dynasty, the rule of the so-called *Pax Romana*, when the Empire reached its greatest expanse and the peak of its bureaucratic efficiency. GMH may have Edward Gibbon's work in mind (*The History of the Decline and Fall of the Roman Empire*, i (1776); ii–iii (1781); iv–vi (1788) as he notes the decline.

APPENDIX A

Documents Related to Hopkins's Academic Appointments

1. Letter from George Porter, the English assistant to the Jesuits' Superior General,[1] to William Delany, S.J., President of University College (BRC 41b: 12).

San Girolamo
5th Nov. 1882

Dear Rev. Father,

P. C. [*Pax Christi*, the peace of Christ]

Many thanks of your letters of the 28th October and its predecessor.

I think F. Purbrick might be induced to let you have Hopkins or Walford: I do not think he would part with Rickaby or Lucas. Walford is a first class teacher; Hopkins is clever, well trained, teaches well but has never succeeded well: his mind runs into eccentric ways . . .

2. Letters from Edward J. Purbrick, S.J. (English Provincial) to William Delany, S.J. (IJA J456 / 51 (2)).

111 Mount Street,
London, W.

Nov. 10, 1882

My Dear Fr Delany,

P.X. [*Pax Christi*]

I am delighted to hear that all difficulty with the Bishops has passed away.

The remaining difficulties are formidable enough, except that the want of men surprises me. Would that I could help in so great & important a work, but our good men, such as you name, are just the cream of the Province, & absolutely not to be spared. Fr Perry & the Observatory are inseparable—I do not know one to replace him for years to come. Fr Hunter is a treasure absolutely indispensable. Mr Walford is not yet ordained & is at last in proximate preparation for ordination. Fr J. Moore has no health—We cannot use him for Mathematics, or full work of any kind. Fr Rickaby fills three important offices, & I could not replace him.

Fr Sicour fills up the gap caused by Fr Moore's bad health.

---

[1] Although Pieter Jan Beckx, S.J. (1795–1887) had been Superior General since 1853, a general congregation of the Society in 1883 had elected Anton Anderledy, S.J. (1819–92) as Coadjutor with right of succession.

Fr Hopkins is very clever & a good scholar. But I should do you no kindness in sending you a man so eccentric. I am trying him this year in coaching B.A.s. at Stonyhurst, but with fear & trembling—This <u>inter nos</u> [between us].

My perpetual struggle is with paucity of men for the teaching posts, & I could not in conscience weaken the Province by sending any one of that kind to work elsewhere.

I am too sure of the welcome any of them would receive with you to have any hesitation except on the score of our dearth of men.

Ever R. Y^r
servus in X° [your servant in Christ]

E. J. Purbrick, S.J.

3. Letter from Edward J. Purbrick, S.J. to William Delany, S.J. (IJA J11 / 456 (3))

111 Mount Street,
London, W.

Nov. 29, 1883

My Dear Fr Delany,
                    P.X. [Pax Christi]
As far as I am concerned I have no objection to your writing Fr Gerard Hopkins to stand as a Candidate for a Fellowship. He is the only man <u>possible</u>. You know him. I have the highest opinion of his scholarship & abilities—I fancy also that University work would be more in his line than anything else.

Sometimes what we in community deem oddities are the very qualities which outside are appreciated as original & valuable.

If you can coax R. Fr Provincial to give me a Father in exchange for Honduras, I shall be so much the better pleased & duly grateful.

I have not said anything to Fr Hopkins because I thought an invitation direct from you with my sanction more complimentary & appetising to him.
    Ever Rd yr
    servus in X°
    E. J. Purbrick

4. Letter from William Delany, S.J. to Lord Thomas O'Hagan (1812–85), Lord Chancellor of Ireland) (BRC 36:13)

University College
85 & 86 Stephen's Green
Dublin
February 13 1884

My dear Lord

I am very sorry indeed to learn that your strength is coming back so slowly and that sleeplessness has come to make the weary days of illness so much more wearisome. It was such a pleasure to us a week or so ago to hear that you were nearly all right again, and I looked forward to seeing you amongst us again at an early date; I hope and pray that with God's blessing these cheering accounts may still be realised and speedily.

Your Lordship's absence was much felt on all sides at the late Crisis: had you been there, it is certain that no crisis of the kind could possibly have occurred. At least I have that conviction.

Such as it was, it came like a thunderstorm on a fine summer's day without a moment's notice.

The two Fellowships for Catholics in Natural Philosophy and Classics were advertised early in the Autumn. It was found in October that there was absolutely no qualified Catholic Candidate for Natural Philosophy except England or Queen's College Cork. The Catholic Senators objected on principle to appointing a Queen's College Professor to one of the Catholic Fellowships, and one of them came to me to beg of me to find a suitable candidate and accordingly I put forward a Mr Curtis who had had a most distinguished career in T.C.D. [Trinity College, Dublin] and of whom Casey & Williamson had a very high opinion. From the first it was plain that he was the most eligible Candidate, but as there was some informality about the dates of giving notice, the whole Election was postponed to the January meeting.

In December therefore I sought and obtained from Fr Purbrick consent to bring over as a candidate in Classics Fr Gerard Hopkins, a convert who had had a most brilliant career at Oxford.

I sent his testimonials & those of Mr Curtis to the leading Catholic Senators. I waited on the Cardinal and not finding him I wrote a letter respectfully asking his support for Hopkins and Curtis on the two grounds that their appointment would most directly attain the end of the whole Fellowships scheme which was to help to build up a teaching College here, and that they would most help because a. They would give all their time and energies to University College whilst extern Fellows give only 8 hours a week b. they would contribute to the unity of purpose and harmony of action which are vital elements of success for a College & c. They would devote their salaries to the payment of the supplemental Professors who will always be a necessity for the efficient working of a University College.

The second ground on which I asked support was that I believed them to be unmistakeably the most highly qualified amongst the candidates, and therefore deserving the appointment even independently of any other consideration. I wrote also to Dr. Woodlock in the same sense. The latter replied in a friendly tone, but saying that he should consult the Cardinal [McCabe]. The Cardinal himself did not reply.

Early in January I brought Mr Curtis to present him to his Eminence who received us graciously. In the conversation that took place, I mentioned Fr Hopkins' name, and the Cardinal said that he did not like to have any more Englishmen, but on my explaining the special distinction of Fr Hopkins and the benefit it would be to us vis à vis of Trinity College to have a man of Fr Hopkins' literary powers and original scholarship, his Eminence seemed quite satisfied. He gave no hint whatever of preferring any other Candidate.

So things stood until Monday Jan 28. On that day Dr. Walsh lunched here and told me that he had been speaking to the Cardinal about the Fellowships that the Cardinal had again mentioned his objection to the Englishman, that he Dr. Walsh had shown him that there was abundant reason to overlook that objection—and that he looked on it as quite settled that the Cardinal would propose Fr Hopkins and Mr Curtis.

That same day, however, Dr Walsh at the Standing Committee brought forward a request from French College [Blackrock] to be "approved" by the Senate, and moved that it be put on the agenda paper for the meeting of the Senate on Wednesday. This was strongly opposed at the Committee by Lord Emly, Dr Kavanagh and others.

1. Because it would be recognising an Intermediate School as a University College—things that should be perfectly distinct.
2. Because French College once admitted, Carlow, St Malachy's, Tullabeg, Rumpel and other places should be recognised, and 3ᵈ there would be thus frittered away the whole boon of the paid teaching Fellows, and all hopes would be put an end to of building up a great central College of which there seemed now, at last, some likelihood.

The discussion ended in Dr Walsh not finding even a Seconder.

The next day, Tuesday, Jan 29, there met the Committee of Bishops who had to deal with Education, and to whom therefore it fell to make the arrangements with the Jesuits when coming here.

As I explained before to Your Lordship it happened unfortunately for us that their Committee had on it a more determined opponent of ours, Dr. Moran of Ossory. The other Bishops were Dr Woodlock and Dr Gilloolly, not unfriendly to us, but much influenced by the Cardinal and Dr Moran, and Dr Butter of Limerick our staunch and strong friend, but who was unfortunately absent from ill health.

There were present therefore the Cardinal, Drs Moran, Gilloolly and Woodlock. At the request of the latter who acts as Secretary I prepared for the meeting a memorandum dealing with some matters of business of which I sent Your Lordship a copy. This memorandum introduced under the head of Financial Condition the question of the Fellowships. I beg Your Lordship to read it here and the Financial Statement that accompanied it.

———

On that Tuesday eve of the election Lord Emly called on the Cardinal before the Bishops' meeting. His Eminence then promised him that he would propose Fr Hopkins and Mr Curtis, Lord Emly would second them and the Election would be a matter of course.

This news Lord Emly brought me at six o'clock. I telegraphed to Fr Hopkins, and sent word to some leading Senators who took a deep interest in this College and our attempt to work it up that all was right –

At nine o'clock that same evening the Provincial came to tell me that he had just had a visit from Dr Woodlock who came to tell him that the Cardinal would propose Fr Reffé of Blackrock instead of Fr Hopkins but that his Eminence would see him (Fr Browne) next morning, if he had any thing to urge on the other side.

The Provincial replied that he feared he had no new arguments to offer his Eminence, and would hardly feel it to be respectful to ask him to change his mind at the last moment. Thus they parted and the Provincial came in hot haste to me.

I was much taken aback: I did not see that we could do anything to avoid a division. Fr Hopkins was at Stonyhurst, it was past 9. P.M. Telegraphic offices closed. He had just had a message that all was right. So had the Senators. How get a withdrawal physically, even if withdrawal were advisable? and even if Fr Hopkins were withdrawn, there still remained as Candidates two more eligible laymen, Quinn & Starkie. F. Reffé is personally most disliked by all the Queen's College men. Starkie had personal recommendations to many of them and was fresh from Cambridge with the highest honours. What chance was there of Reffé having a walk over brought forward in such a manner without a single word to one of the Catholic Senators, who on the contrary had all been led to believe that the Cardinal was going to propose Fr Hopkins?

There was no choice for it but to let the matter be settled by the Senate. However next morning before the Meeting the Catholic Senators gathered round the Cardinal and asked him not to propose a candidate who would be surely rejected.

His Eminence persevered however and proposed as his candidates Fr Reffé and Mr Curtis. In proposing them he said that, left to himself personally, he would not have taken the course he was about to take, but that he thought he was the mouthpiece of the Bishops and in that capacity he put forward Fr Reffé leaving the matter to the judgment of the Senate.

The nomination was supported by Dr Woodlock. Lord Emly proposed as an amendment to substitute Fr Hopkins' name for Fr Reffé's and pointed out that <u>on principle</u> it was most desirable to concentrate the Fellowships in University College for which they were originally created, that the appointment of Fr Reffé would indirectly recognise French College, a point on which they had been practically unanimous in their rejection of it and <u>on personal grounds</u> they had the highest evidence of Fr Hopkins' qualifications whilst they had absolutely none of Fr Reffé's fitness for a Classical Fellowship.

Cllr. Redington seconded the amendment and said that Fr Hopkins was a contemporary of his at Oxford, and was one of the most brilliant perhaps even the most brilliant and original men in the University at that time. Dr Ball followed on the lines of Lord Emly, clearly and strongly advocating the doing all the Senate could to build up a central place here. Dr. Walsh supported the Cardinal, but (as he told me afterwards) having no evidence to put forward for Fr Reffé's fitness, he confined himself to speaking of the success of the French College.

Dr Kavanagh took him up in a very clear speech—Chief Justice Morris, Dr Cruise and others followed in the same strain and ultimately it proved there were for Fr Reffé and the Cardinal in a Senate of 26 merely 3, the Cardinal Dr Woodlock and Dr Walsh.

This no doubt was an amazing result: and no one was more amazed than I was when I heard it. I deplored and deplore the division and the very foolish advice that placed the Cardinal in so very painful a position at the Senate when he had been all powerful, and might have easily remained so.

But as a Protestant Senator remarked the Bishops of Ireland have put the Jesuits in charge of University College and already it gives great hope of success.—there is vacant in that College under Jesuit management a Fellowship in Classics for which the head of the College puts forward a University man of the most brilliant qualifications. Cardinal McCabe himself accepted him and promised to propose him, and at the eleventh hour some one or two Bishops get at him and induce him to propose for a University Professorship of Classics, a foreigner about whose Classics we know nothing whatever and whose chief recommendation is that he has worked up a <u>rival</u> College. The Catholic Senators would have befooled themselves to have accepted such a nomination and forward with such a total want of courtesy towards them.

———

On Thursday, the day after the election those who saw the Cardinal reported that he seemed very good humoured over the defeat but on Friday other influences had worked and he sent in his resignation, against Dr Woodlock's advice, and without a word to Dr Walsh, who would have done all he could to dissuade him, had [he] been consulted.

There was great anxiety of course in official quarters to avert this trouble, for it would, no doubt, have disturbed for a while the successful working of the new University and at last when other appeals had failed Lord Spencer tried a personal appeal and succeeded in inducing his Em[inence] to hold on.

Whilst the resignation was still under consideration, Dr Gilloolly wrote a very singular letter to the Provincial [Fr Browne], calling on him to withdraw Fr Hopkins even now that he had been elected. The Provincial in reply showed that such withdrawal would only make the affair a hopeless muddle. The Senate would resent it as a dictation, and Fr Reffé's chances would be made hopeless by proposing him under such circumstances.—Dr Gilloolly on reflection seems to have thought better of his proposal.

Here are (at, I fear great length) all the facts of the case as far as I know them. I daresay the effect will be to make the relations of the Cardinal with this place a little strained for some time. This I regret very much, and whatever can be done to smooth things down I shall be only too happy to get a chance of doing.

Meantime we must only work on and try to make the College a success. So far thank God success has come beyond my more sanguine hopes. From Nov 12, when we opened, to this date,—that is in barely 3 months and not the best months of the year,—there have enrolled their names on the Book, 121 Students of whom nearly 80 are matriculated students of the University. In Clonliffe students do not come this year, and therefore form no part of this number. There are amongst them however 29 Jesuit Scholastics reading for Degrees some of them young men of high promise and 5 Marist Scholastics but the remaining 87 are lay students.

This I am sure Your Lordship will regard as good progress and promising anyway for the future.

There is already a capital tone growing up. Students eager contented and hard working and Professors working with great zeal and in perfect harmony.

Finance forms my chief difficulty, as will be seen from the figures given. If this could be met by Fellowships or otherwise I think the College may win for itself even within the next five years, a brilliant position.

I keep hoping that God who has guided things so far, will help us still to do His work. When things get smoother I daresay we shall obtain the leaves for spiritual work which it is rather surprising should be withheld from us now, dealing as we are with a class which needs help far more than any other in the community—those poor young men that are scattered about a city like Dublin, many of them fresh from innocent country homes and totally unfitted by their very innocence for the struggle of a student's life amidst such temptations.

———

Of the immediate future the pressing question for us is that of the Modern Language Fellowships. I am putting forward Fr. O'Carroll for one. I believe him to be in every way most brilliantly qualified. I know from Jesuits of the various countries speaking of their own languages that he speaks and knows thoroughly German, French, Italian, Spanish, Dutch, Illyrian, and Polish. He knows Irish also as few scholars know it in Ireland. Besides the foregoing languages I have myself heard him speak with natives Modern Greek and Swedish, and he is familiar with Danish, Bohemian, and Russian. He is a most accurate and widely read Classical scholar and outside all this is cyclopedic in his knowledge of all imaginable things.

In other circumstances I think his election would have been certain, as the Cardinal had very great respect for his parents and would probably have taken him up as his own Candidate. As things are now, I am doubtful.

There is also vacant a Natural Science Fellowship (beside Dr Sigerson[2]): but we have no qualified candidate.

I fear I must have long since tried your attention & patience: please put it down to my desire to put before you in the simplest & fullest way any knowledge that I had that might help you to form a judgment on these events.

Please give my kindest respects to Lady O'Hagan. She has had my most sincere sympathy in all her anxious solicitude on your account & wishing you both every blessing

Believe me my dear Lord
        Ever most sincerely yours
            William Delany

[2] Dr George Sigerson (1836–1925), a physician, was president of the National Literary Society from 1893–1925.

APPENDIX B
William Collins, 'Ode to Evening'

GMH, who began setting Collins's ode to music in 1884, while living at Stonyhurst, writes out the poem in full on fos. 8ʳ and 8ᵛ of his Dublin notebook. The ode, composed in 1746, features unrhymed stanzas and a distinctive metre. Roger Lonsdale suggests that Collins was influenced by Milton's unrhymed translation of Horace's 'Pyrrha' ode (and Milton's 'Comus'); by Joseph Warton's 'Ode to Evening'; and by Thomas Warton's 'Pleasures of Melancholy'.[1]

If aught of oaten stop or pastoral song
May hope, chaste Eve, to soothe thy modest ear,
    Like thy own solemn springs,
    Thy springs and dying gales,
O nymph reserved, while now the bright-haired sun
Sits in yon western tent, whose cloudy skirts,
    With brede ethereal wove,
    O'erhang his wavy bed;
Now air is hushed, save where the weak-eyed bat
With short shrill shriek flits by on leathern wing,
    Or where the beetle winds
    His small but sullen horn,
As oft he rises midst the twilight path,
Against the pilgrim borne in heedless hum:
    Now teach me, maid composed,
    To breathe some softened strain,
Whose numbers stealing through thy darkening vale
May not unseemly with its stillness suit;
    As musing slow, I hail
    Thy genial loved return!
For when thy folding star arising shows
His paly circlet, at his warning lamp
    The fragrant Hours, and elves
    Who slept in flowers the day,
And many a nymph who wreathes her brows with sedge,
And sheds the freshening dew, and, lovelier still,
    The Pensive Pleasures sweet,
    Prepare thy shadowy car.

[1] *The Poems of Thomas Gray, William Collins, and Oliver Goldsmith*, (ed.) Roger Lonsdale (Harlow: Longmans, 1969), 461–7.

Then lead, calm vot'ress, where some sheety lake
Cheers the lone heath, or some time-hallowed pile,
     Or upland fallows grey,
     Reflect its last cool gleam.
But when chill blustering winds or driving rain
Forbid my willing feet, be mine the hut
     That from the mountain's side
     Views wilds and swelling floods,
And hamlets brown, and dim-covered spires,
And hears their simple bell, and marks o'er all
     Thy dewy fingers draw
     The gradual dusky veil.
While Spring shall pour his showers, as oft he wont,
And bathe thy breathing tresses, meekest Eve!
     While Summer loves to sport
     Beneath thy lingering light;
While sallow Autumn fills thy lap with leaves,
Or Winter, yelling through the troublous air,
     Affrights thy shrinking train,
     And rudely rends thy robes;
So long, sure-found beneath the sylvan shed,
Shall Fancy, Friendship, Science, rose-lipped Health,
     Thy gentlest influence own,
     And hymn thy favourite name!

Lonsdale follows the text of the poem published in the second edition of Robert Dodsley's *Collection* (1748). In several nineteenth-century editions of the ode, however, the second line states: 'May hope, O pensive Eve, to soothe thine Ear', which is how Hopkins remembers it. See *The Poems of William Collins*, (ed.) Christopher Stone (London: Frowde, 1907), 51–2.

APPENDIX C

Gerard Manley Hopkins, 'Spelt from Sibyl's Leaves'

From *Poetical Works*, 190–1.

Earnest, earthless, equal, attuneable, | vaulty, voluminous, . . .
      stupendous

Evening strains to be time's vást, | womb-of-all, home-of-all,
      hearse-of-all night.

Her fond yellow hornlight wound to the west, | her wild hollow
      hoarlight hung to the height

Waste; her earliest stars, earlstars, | stárs principal, overbend us,

Fire-féaturing héaven. For éarth | her béing has unbóund; her dápple
      is at énd, as-

Tray or aswarm, all throughther, in throngs; | self ín self stéepèd and
      páshed—qúite

Disremembering, dismémbering | áll now. Heart, you round me right

With: Óur évening is óver us; óur night | whélms, whélms, ánd will
      énd us.

Only the beakleaved boughs dragonish | damask the tool-smooth
      bleak light; black,

Ever so black on it. Óur tale, O óur oracle! | Lét life, wáned, ah lét life
      wind

Off hér once skéined stained véined variety | upon, áll on twó spools;
      párt, pen, páck

Now her áll in twó flocks, twó folds—bláck, white; | ríght, wrong;
      réckon but, réck but, mind

But thése two; wáre of a wórld where bút these | twó tell, éach off
      the óther; of a ráck

Where, selfwrung, selfstrung, sheathe- and shelterless, | thóughts
      agaínst thoughts ín groans grínd.

APPENDIX D

Gerard Manley Hopkins, 'Richard Watson Dixon'

This is the text of GMH's biographical notice as it appears in Thomas Arnold (ed.), *A Manual of English Literature, Historical and Critical*, 5th edn., rev. (London: Longmans, Green, and Co., 1885), 470–1.

Richard Watson Dixon, now vicar of Warkworth and hon. canon of Carlisle, was born at Islington, near London, in 1833, and educated at King Edward's School, Birmingham, and Pembroke College, Oxford. At Oxford he became the friend and colleague of William Morris, Burne-Jones, and others of the mediaevalist school, to which, as a poet, he belongs. The chance reading of his earlier poems also won for him the friendship of D. G. Rossetti.

He is engaged on a history of the Church of England on a great scale; of this three volumes have appeared. In verse he has published—in 1859, *Christ's Company, and Other Poems*; in 1863, *Historical Odes* (on Marlborough, Wellington, Sir John Franklin, &c.); in 1883, *Mano* (his greatest work, a romance-epic in *terza rima*: Mano is a Norman knight put to death A.D. 1000, and the story, darkly and affectingly tragical, turns upon the date); in 1884, *Odes and Eclogues*.

In his poems we find a deep thoughtfulness and earnestness, and a mind touched by the pathos of human life, of which *Mano* is, in a strange but a typical case, the likeness; noble but never highflown, sad without noise or straining—everything as it most reaches and comes home to man's heart. In particular he is a master of horror (see Mano's words about the nettles on his way to the stake) and pathos; of pathos so much that here it would be hard to name his rival. We also find the very rare gift of pure imagination, such as Coleridge had (see the song 'Fallen Rain,' and the one on the sky wooing the river). But he is likest and owes most to Keats, and his description and imagery are realised with a truth and splendour not less than Keats' own (see the scene of the nine lovers in *Love's Consolation*; the images of the quicksilver and of the heart fastened round with hair, *ibidem*). This richness of image, matched with the deep feeling which flushes his work throughout, gives rise to effects we look for rather from music than from verse. And there is, as in music, a sequence, seeming necessary and yet unforeseen, of feeling, acting often with magical strokes (see, *e.g.*, in *Love's Consolation*, 'Ah, God! Thy lightnings should have wakened me three days before they did'; in *Mano*, 'She would have answered underneath the boughs').

He is faulty by a certain vagueness of form, some unpleasing rhymes, and most by an obscurity—partly of thought, partly of expression—suggesting a deeper meaning behind the text without leaving the reader any decisive clue to find it. This fault injures the general effect of *Mano*. He employs sometimes the archaic style now common, but with such a mastery and dramatic point as justify a practice otherwise vicious.

Arnold's footnote: 'Notice by Rev. G. Hopkins.'

APPENDIX E
Hopkins's Notes on Pindar

As the Introduction explains, GMH's attempts to scan and understand Pindar's complex metrical arrangements in the *Nemean Odes* and *Isthmian Odes* inspired his theory of the 'Dorian Measure'—what he believed to be a prototypical rhythm of classical verse. Folios 17ᵛ, 18ʳ, and the first four lines of 18ᵛ show GMH trying to determine the pattern of long, short, rising, and falling syllables that Pindar—notorious among classical authors for the variety of his lyric metres—uses in *Isthmian Ode* 3. (*Odes* 3 and 4, although distinct texts in the manuscript tradition, are the only metrically identical poems in the poet's surviving corpus and are therefore often considered as a single piece—using 'Doric' or 'verse' scansion.)

Isthmian Ode 3

ΜΕΛΙΣΣΩΙ ΘΗΒΑΙΩΙ ΙΠΠΟΙΣ

εἴ τις ἀνδρῶν εὐτυχήσαις
    ἢ σὺν εὐδόξοις ἀέθλοις
ἢ σθένει πλούτου κατέχει φρασὶν αἰανῆ κόρον,
ἄξιος εὐλογίαις ἀστῶν μεμίχθαι.
Ζεῦ, μεγάλαι δ᾽ ἀρεταὶ θνατοῖς ἕπονται
ἐκ σέθεν· ζώει δὲ μάσσων
    ὄλβος ὀπιζομένων, πλαγίαις δὲ φρένεσσιν
οὐχ ὁμῶς πάντα χρόνον θάλλων ὁμιλεῖ.

εὐκλέων δ᾽ ἔργων ἄποινα
    χρὴ μὲν ὑμνῆσαι τὸν ἐσλόν,
χρὴ δὲ κωμάζοντ᾽ ἀγαναῖς χαρίτεσσιν βαστάσαι.
ἔστι δὲ καὶ διδύμων ἀέθλων Μελίσσῳ
μοῖρα πρὸς εὐφροσύναν τρέψαι γλυκεῖαν
ἦτορ, ἐν βάσσαισιν Ἰσθμοῦ
    δεξαμένῳ στεφάνους, τὰ δὲ κοίλᾳ λέοντος
ἐν βαθυστέρνου νάπᾳ κάρυξε Θήβαν
ἱπποδρομίᾳ κρατέων. ἀνδρῶν δ᾽ ἀρετὰν
σύμφυτον οὐ κατελέγχει.
ἴστε μὰν Κλεωνύμου
δόξαν παλαιὰν ἅρμασιν:
καὶ ματρόθε Λαβδακίδαισιν σύννομοι
πλούτου διέστειχον τετραοριᾶν πόνοις.
αἰὼν δὲ κυλινδομέναις ἀμέραις ἄλλ᾽ ἄλλοτ᾽ ἐξ
ἄλλαξεν. ἄτρωτοί γε μὰν παῖδες θεῶν.

For Melissos of Thebes, Winner, Chariot Race

If a man is successful,
      either in glorious games
or with mighty wealth, and keeps down nagging excess in his mind,
he deserves to be included in his townsmen's praises.
Zeus, great achievements come to mortals
from you, and men's happiness has a longer life
      when they are reverent, but does not flourish
as well for all time when it dwells with shifty minds.

In recompense for glorious deeds
      one must hymn the good man
and must exalt him, as he revels, with gentle poems of praise.
Melissos has the good fortune of twin prizes
to turn his heart to sweet
festivity, for he won crowns in the Isthmian
      glens, and then in the hollow valley
of the deep-chested lion he had Thebe proclaimed
by winning the chariot race. He brings no disgrace
upon the prowess inherited from his kinsmen.
Surely you know the ancient fame
of Kleonymos with chariots,
and on his mother's side as relatives of the Labdakidai
they devoted their wealth to the toils of four-horse chariots.
As the days roll by, one's life changes now this way
now that, but the sons of the gods remain unwounded.

(English translation from *The Odes of Pindar including the
Principal Fragments*, trans. Sir John Sandys (Cambridge,
Mass.: Harvard University Press, 1937), 157, 159.)

Pindar (*c*.518–*c*.446 BCE), a lyric poet from Boeotia, composed each of his odes according to a unique and complex metrical scheme, far more complex than the rather repetitious dactylic hexameters of the Homeric poems or the iambs of tragic dialogues. Analysis of these patterns has always been subject to debate; a determination of GMH's place in the history of these controversies would require a great deal of labour by scholars more expert than those who have so far examined the materials. Further connections with Greek music would require a study of their own. For summaries of nineteenth-century knowledge of ancient Greek music, see W. Chapell's entry in Sir John Stainer and W. A. Barrett (eds.), *Dictionary of Musical Forms* (London: Novello, Ewer, and Co., 1888), and the *Grove Dictionary of Music* (1906).

GMH apparently followed the text in *Pindari Carmina cum deperditorum fragmentis selectis*, (ed.) W. Christ (Leipzig: Teubner, 1869); for his notes, he may have had access to Pindar's *Nemean and Isthmian Odes*, (ed.) H. M. Fennell (Cambridge: Cambridge University Press, 1883). GMH's references to line numbers in Pindar refer to the old system of line divisions, now superseded according to new metrical analysis (both are offered in all modern editions).

A full analysis of even just the transcription of Pindar is beyond the scope of this volume, and the details of GMH's subsequent melange of vocabulary study and analysis of the poem certainly deserves a separate article. As a brief example of what such analysis might include, we are grateful to Ross G. Arthur for the following speculations about GMH's primary working procedures on the first line cited on 17ᵛ:

The first line of the excerpt reveals details of his involvement with the materials of the poem. Christ prints it this way:

$$\text{ἐκ σέθεν·}\quad \text{ζώει δὲ μάσσων ὄλβος ὀπιζομένων, πλα-}$$
$$\text{γίαις}\quad \text{δὲ φρένεσσιν}$$

and provides the following scansion:

$$\ddot{\smile}\ \smile\ —\ —\ —\ \smile\ —\ —\ \acute{\smile}\ \smile\smile\ —\ \smile\smile\ —\ \smile\smile\ \lrcorner\ \acute{—}\ \smile\ —\ \asymp$$

It would today be scanned thus:

$$\bar{\breve{\text{ἐκ}}}\ \bar{\text{σέ}}\bar{\text{θεν}}·\ |\ \bar{\text{ζώ}}\ |\ \bar{\text{ει}}\ \text{δὲ}\ \breve{\text{μάσσ}}\ |\ \bar{\text{ων}}\ |\ \bar{\text{ὄλβ}}\breve{\text{ος}}\ \bar{\text{ὀπι}}\bar{\text{ζο}}\breve{\text{μέ}}\breve{\text{νων}},\ \pi\lambda\bar{\text{αγ}}\breve{\text{ίαις}}\ |\ \text{δὲ}\ \bar{\text{φρέ}}\bar{\text{νεσσ}}\ |\ \breve{\text{ιν}}$$

GMH starts by writing just the letters of the Greek:

$$\text{'εκ σέθεν · ζώει δε μάσσον}$$

Here, as elsewhere, accents and breathings often appear to the left of the vowel; this suggests that GMH writes the accent first and the vowel second. Such a procedure is unusual, and perhaps reveals a writer more obsessive about accentuation than most Hellenists, although it must be confessed that some of his acute accents come close to being vertical. He leaves a space before the raised dot (and later, the comma), as if he regards punctuation more as a break between clauses than the mark of the end of a clause. At this early point, he realizes that he has mistakenly written a short omicron instead of a long omega in μάσσον, so he crosses it out, separately cancelling the accent. Then he continues:

$$\text{'εκ σέθεν · ζώει δε} \cancel{\mu\acute{\alpha}\sigma\sigma\sigma\nu}\ \text{μάσσων ὄλβος ὀπιζομένων , πλαγίαις}$$
$$\overline{\overline{}}\ \text{δὲ}\quad \text{φρένεσσιν .}$$

The brace before δὲ indicates that the last two words are a continuation of the previous words, not a new poetic line. The macron over δὲ marks it as being metrically long. It is the only syllable in the verse which might be problematic, since the combination of the following consonants would not lengthen the preceding vowel according to the rules of later verse. GMH is therefore drawing attention to a particularly Doric feature of the most basic aspects of scansion.

Then he proceeds to divide the verse into metrical feet with short vertical lines:

ἐκ σέθεν · ζώει δὲ ~~πασσον~~ μάσσων | ὄλβος ὀπιζομένων , πλαγίαις

δὲ   φρένεσσιν .

He begins to add arrows, long and short, above particular vowels—

ἐκ σέθεν · ζώει δὲ ~~πασσον~~ μάσσων | ὄλβος ὀπιζομένων , πλαγίαις

δὲ   φρένεσσιν .

—but he stops after the sixth arrow. Discovering that something is wrong, he crosses out the entire verse:

~~ἐκ σέθεν · ζώει δὲ πασσον μάσσων | ὄλβος ὀπιζομένων , πλαγίαις~~

~~δὲ   φρένεσσιν .~~

He starts again, but with some differences. Divisions are now inserted into the metrical feet as he goes along, as can be seen by the extra space surrounding the ones that occur mid-word. (He may well have written in the arrows at the same time.) He makes the same mistake with μάσσον/μάσσων but this time just crosses out the ον rather than the whole word. He marks the metrical break in πλαγίαις with a double bar. Elsewhere, this is the sign for a caesura or for the end of a period; what it means to GMH one can only speculate. In this iteration he does not bother to mark the length of δὲ, nor does he indicate the wrap-around; the comma after ὀπιζομένων is forgotten.

ἐκ σέθεν · ζώ | ει δὲ μάσσ~~ον~~ων | ῎ολβος ὀπι | ζομένων πλαγί ‖ αις

δὲ φρένεσσιν ‖

Again, however, he decides something is wrong. He cancels the last three letters of πλαγίαις, adds a hyphen to show the break in the word, and then writes those last three letters on the next line, prefacing them with two musical crotchet rests; I am unable to account for the declaration that the letters before and after the equals sign are equivalent, or for the stumbling over δὲ.

ἐκ σέθεν · ζώ | ει δὲ μάσσ~~ον~~ων | ῎ολβος ὀπι | ζομένων πλαγί ‖ αις –

𝄽 𝄽 αις | δὲ φρένεσσιν ‖ (= -αις δὲ δὲ φρένεσσιν

At the risk of being repetitious, this is complex and interesting material, and it is to be hoped that it receives the attention it deserves from a range of competent scholars.

APPENDIX F
RUI Matriculation Examination, September 1884

Reprinted in 'Examination Papers, 1884–85', Royal University of Ireland, *The Calendar for the Year 1885* (Dublin: Royal University, 1885), 58–9.

MATRICULATION EXAMINATION.

Autumn, 1884

PASS.

LATIN

FIRST PAPER — October 1 — 9.30 to 12.30.

Examiner, REV. PROFESSOR HOPKINS, B.A.

Virgil, Aeneid, Bk. ii.; Caesar, De Bello Gallico, Bks. i., ii.

1. Translate:

Heu nihil invitis fas quemquam fidere divis!

. . . .

Spumeus atque imo Nereus ciet aequora fundo.

Aen. ii. 402–419.[1]

---

[1]
Heu nihil invitis fas quemquam fidere divis!
Ecce trahebatur passis Priameia virgo
Crinibus a templo Cassandra adytisque Minervae,
Ad caelum tendens ardentia lumina frustra,—
Lumina, nam teneras arcebant vincula palmas.
Non tulit hanc speciem furiata mente Coroebus,
Et sese medium iniecit periturus in agmen.
Consequimur cuncti et densis incurrimus armis.
Hic primum ex alto delubri culmine telis
Nostrorum obruimur, oriturque miserrima caedes
Armorum facie et Graiarum errore iubarum.
Tum Danai gemitu atque ereptae virginis ira
Undique collecti invadunt, acerrimus Aiax,
Et gemini Atridae, Dolopumque exercitus omnis;
Adversi rupto ceu quondam turbine venti
Confligunt, Zephyrusque Notusque et laetus Eois
Eurus equis; stridunt silvae, saevitque tridenti
Spumeus atque imo Nereus ciet aequora fundo.
<http://meta.montclair.edu/latintexts/vergil/aeneid_georgics/aeneid2.html>.

2. Give the 1ˢᵗ person singular present and perfect indicative active, and the nominative singular masculine past participle passive of the verbs from which come — (a) *passis*, (b) *arcebant*, (c) *obruimur*, (d) *ciet*; and mark the quantity of the vowels.

3. Scan the line *armorum*, etc., and the following.

4. Translate:—

  (a) Hic Dolopum manus, hic savus tendebat Achilles.[2]
  (b) Sanguine quarendi reditus animaque litandum Argolica.[3]
  (c) .   .   .   . proximus ardet Ucalegon.[4]
  (d) Who is meant by—

       .   .   .   Trojae et patriae communis Erinys?[5]

5. Translate:—

  Haec cum animadvertisset, convocato consilio, ... quos tamen aliquid usus ac disciplina, quam a nobis accepissent, sublevarent.[6] — *De Bello Gallico*, i. 40

6. Give Caesar's words *as spoken* from *Ariovistum* down to *repudiaturum*.

ADDITIONAL MATERIAL:

Two samples of GMH's handwriting are featured in the Tracts on English Handwriting that Robert Bridges wrote or commissioned for the Society for the Preservation of English (SPE).[7] Tract XXII, written by Roger Fry and E. A. Lowe (Oxford: Clarendon Press, 1926), includes a GMH fragment (source unspecified) headed 'Matriculation: Pass'. The notes were written on a single sheet, ruled with faint blue lines.

[2] *Aeneid*, ii. 29.
[3] *Aeneid*, ii. 108.
[4] *Aeneid*, ii. 311–12.
[5] *Aeneid*, ii. 573.
[6] Haec cum animadvertisset, convocato consilio omniumque ordinum ad id consilium adhibitis centurionibus, vehementer eos incusavit: primum, quod aut quam in partem aut quo consilio ducerentur sibi quaerendum aut cogitandum putarent. Ariovistum se consule cupidissime populi Romani amicitiam adpetisse; cur hunc tam temere quisquam ab officio discessurum iudicaret? Sibi quidem persuaderi cognitis suis poslulatis atque aequitate condicionum perspecta eum neque suam neque populi Romani gratiam epudiaturum. Quod si furore atque amentia impulsum bellum intulisset, quid tandem vererentur? Aut cur de sua virtute aut de ipsius diligentia desperarent? Factum eius hostis periculum patrum nostrorum emoria Cimbris et Teutonis a C. Mario pulsis [cum non minorem laudem exercitus quam ipse imperator meritus videbatur]; factum etiam nuper in Italia servili tumultu, quos tamen aliquid usus ac disciplina, quam a nobis accepissent, sublevarint. (Web version from <www.ibiblio.org/caesar/>.)
[7] In Tract XXVIII, edited by Bridges, Plate 33 features lines from a GMH letter to Dixon, 1886. See *CW* ii.

Matriculation: Pass

Latin Sentences

(1) Caecilius, when he understood that ambassadors were going to be sent, fearing greatly that they would ask more than the enemy was likely to (future in rus) grant, managed (efficere) himself to be ~~of the number~~ made one of them.

(2) Some payment (stipendium) there must be; which, if they receive (future) three shillings (denarius: use distributive numerals) apiece, will, in my judgment, be enough.

(3) But you say that you sent messengers? What messengers? (surely not) those who, that son-in-law (gener[8]) of yours found drunk in the forum at midday (meredie)?

---

[8] See the observation regarding, 'Dein generum Agrippam : meaning?', fo. 19ʳ.

APPENDIX G

Documents from the Campion Hall Archive

The Hopkins Collection at Campion Hall, Oxford includes several fragments related to the *Dublin Notebook* and GMH's academic activities. These incidental papers include examination drafts, undated comments on students' RUI examination papers, and syllabus changes.

1. Examination paper for the Royal University. Although signed and 'approved' by his colleagues James Stewart and John F. Davies, GMH notes on fo. 1ʳ that the exam was 'Drawn up by mistake' (CH M.VII.1). In fact, the examination was set by another RUI colleague, Prof. MacMaster.

| M.VII.1ʳ |

Royal University

First Examination in Arts:

Pass

Livy book XXII

1. Translate <6 cap. xxxix 9d 6 — 10.> Ominis ~~causa~~ ^etiam^ . . . ego gessi.
2. In the above ^a^ put the words ~~"~~priusquam to insanit into the past;
   ~~(b) Derive extempla;~~
   (b) Turn "Atqui si hic . . . cladibus erit," leaving out "belli hoc genus, hostem ~~him~~ hunc", into ~~i~~Indirect ~~Utte~~ Utterance, both after dicit and after dixit understood, and for shortness do it in one sentence only, bracing or bracketing the words ~~in~~ which differ in the two cases;
   (~~d~~c) ~~Parse~~ ^Explain the construction of^ hoc genus; and
   (e) Excesserim
3. Where were ^(a)^ Faesulae, ^(b)^ Cercina, ^(c)^ Geronium, (d) the Paeligni, (e) the Insubriân Gauls?
4. ^Translate and, where needed,^ Explain (a): "Sortes sua sorte attenuatas unamque ~~it~~ excidisse ita scriptam' etc. ; < ~~(b)~~ i 11.>;
   (b) "Qui faciet quando volet quaque lege volet facito; quo modo faxit probe factum esto . . . Si quis clepsit ne populo scelus est neve cui cleptum erit"
   ((c) "Debellarique

| M.VII.1ᵛ |

(c) "Debellarique ni cessatum foret ~~potuisse~~ potaisse" <XLI 3.> ;

(d) "Si quibus argentum in praesentia deesset dandam ex aerario pecuniam mutuam praedibusque ac praediis cavendum populo" <LX 4.>;

(e) "In singulos equites . . quadrigatos nummos quinos vicenos et pediti denos . . . dederunt" <LIV 2.>.

5. Translate the following unprescribed passage, ~~<Livy iii book iii chap. XLVI>~~: ~~"Carretato ^Lictores . . . pateretur"~~ ~~Li Lictores . . . pateretus",~~ <Suetonius ~~?~~ Octavius 90>:

Circa relligiones talem accepimus: tonitrua et fulgura paulo infirmius expavescebat, at semper et ubique pellem vituli marini circumferret pro remedio atque ad omnem majoris <tempestatis suspicionem in abditum et concamaratum> locum se reciperet, consternatus olim per nocturnum iter transcursu fulguris, ut praediximus. Somnia neque sua reque aliena de se neglegebat. Philippensi acie, quamvis statuisset non egredi tabernaculo propter valetudinem, egressus est tamen amici somnio monitus, cessitque res prospere, quando captis, <castris> lectica ejus, quasi ibi cubans remansisset, concursu hostium confossa atque lacerata est.

Approved

James Stewart

John F Davies

2. Syllabus changes for 1886–7 and notes as to which editions to consult. (CH M.VII.2)

| M.VII.2ʳ |

Changes for 1886 ^and^ 1887	
For	*Read*

1 Univ. Pass
   Herod[otus] V
Hon.
   Hom[er] Il[iad] 9, 17, 18
	Herod[otus] VI
	
	Hom[er] Il[iad] 17—20

2 Univ. Hon[ours] *Phaedo Plato*	*Ar[istotle] Poetics* *Plato Ion*
B.A. Hon. *Plato Gorgias*	*Aristoph[anes] Nubes*
M.A. *Aristoph[anes] Aves* *Plato Rep[ublic] 1–3.*	*Aristoph[anes] Equites* *Plato Rep[ublic] 8–10.*
Schol. *Demosth[enes] in Sept.*	*Plutarch Life of Themi-stocles by Holden*[1]

[1] The bottom of the piece of paper is missing.

| M.VII.2ᵛ |

(Macmillan)	
Acting ed[ition] of the Clouds by Green in the Catena Class.[2] *A better in Clarendon Press by Merny "for Schools"* *Frogs expurgated by Mitchell* <u>*Acharnians*</u> *and* <u>*Knights*</u> *in the Catena* <u>*Poetics*</u> *(Sutsemihl late; Ritter:* ∉ *Latin notes, very good* *indeed; Turning very good in–* *deed)*	

3(a) and (b). Notes on students' translation exercises (compare with *DN*, fos.10ʳ–11ᵛ). In September 1885, GMH and Professor James MacMaster ('Mr: MacM', below) set and graded together the Latin paper for the First University Examination and the Matriculation exam.

| M.VII.3aʳ |

"N.B. I cannot even call to mind suitable words for composition or arrange them aright" He translates <u>money</u> / <u>munnian</u> (420)

"What Charybdis so glutinous" (420)

"So many drinking saloons are patronized by the most wicked men" (430)

Shew Mr: MacM[3] no. 432 for effects of cram and 433

"Quo me teste convinces? An chirographo? in quo habes scientiam quaestuosam" / "With what experiment would you convince me? O surgeon. I seek a knowledge of the science in which you have been engaged. This means that the speaker wishes to learn surgery but before doing so ~~a~~ he wishes to see an operation"

---

[2] Refers to the series: Arthur Holmes, MA, and Charles Bigg, MA, *Catena Classicorum* (Cambridge, 1868). The title of the collection of school texts means the 'Chain', i.e. series of classical texts; the volume with Aristophanes, *Clouds*, is edited by William Charles Green, MA.

[3] His RUI colleague James McMaster, McGee College.

Remark how they harp on <u>foil</u> — a sword of lath covered with foil; "can I foil so good a combatant so quickly?" ⸔ " . . . be so easily foiled"

No. 445 raving throughout

| M.VII.3aᵛ | "Such drunkness"

⸗ "Apothecae totae nequissimis hominibus condonabantur / "Every cartaker was abandoned to the most worthless of men" (459)

| M.VII.3bʳ |

Quae Charybdis? What "charyb."?

Being so good a gladiator have you become a rustic all at once? (and he alleges reasons for this rendering)

⸗ Male parta male dilabuntur / Evil loves evil (what can he mean?)

"The passage Cui Bono Fuerit refers to a passage in one of Cicero's epics which was satirized by Antony"

No. 233 writes like me

No. 275 is an original and very promising

"As good as the caller is so the sooner his voice becomes rude"

The people rose a cheer

Although a good gladiator yet rood on that account

| M.VII.3bᵛ |

Was so good a gladiator so vulgar with his food?

Ingurge

Gladiators were those who carried the lash in front of the magistrates emblematic of punishment

So good a gladiator yet red so suddenly!

So good a gladiator so quickly (become) rough!

<u>Taetra⁴ bellua</u> / fourheaded beast

So good a gladiator though certainly rude

Another thing / <u>aliud rem</u>

Instead of / <u>in lieu</u> (given as Latin)

A good rough gladiator though hasty

Antony had permission granted him by the Senate to forge ad libitum up to the Ides of March, after which it was forbidden by law to do so

Apothecae totae nequissimis hominibus condonabantur / every apotheosis was pardoned by these most abandoned men

---

⁴ The five lines beginning 'Taetra' and ending 'hasty' are written in a purple ink similar to that found in the *DN*.

APPENDIX H
Cicero, *On Duty*

The essay *On Duty* was written by Marcus Tullius Cicero in 44 BCE. Composed in the form of a letter to his son Marcus, then studying in Athens at the school of Cratippus, the treatise combines ethical and political insights. After a preamble, and summaries of key figures in Cicero's personal or intellectual life, GMH launches into a commentary; there is also an extended gloss comparing duty and sin. See *CW* vi for an edited version of the text and a fuller explication. GMH's annotated copy of Cicero, *De Officiis, De Senectute, et De Amicitia* (Oxford: Henry Parker and Sons, 1882) is now housed at Gonzaga University (BRC 9:14).

Cicero, *Treatise on the Duties of Man*

Cicero de Officiis—The Treatise de Officiis, on the Duties of Man was written in 44 after Caesar's death and shortly before Cicero's own, in his retirement. It is the last or nearly so of Cicero's philosophical works[.]

Cratippus of Mitylene[,] in philosophy a Peripatetic (that is Aristotelian, from A[ristotle]'s practice of giving his lectures pacing up and down in the Lyceum or great gymnasium sacred to Apollo Lyceius in the suburb east of Athens) was a friend and partizan of Pompey's, but at Cicero's instance, who did him other great services, befriended by Caesar. Brutus after Caesar's death attended his lectures. Young Cicero was very fond of him and Cic[ero] thought very highly of him[.]

Cicero's principal authority Panaetius of Rhodes, the head of the Stoic school of his time (the Stoics were so called from the Stoa Poecìle, Painted Colonnade, where Zeno of Citium their founder lectured), a friend of the younger Scipio's. His work on Duty, Περὶ τοῦ καθήκοντος {On Duty}, was finished by his disciple Poseidonias of Apamea in Syria. Pos[eidonias] lived chiefly at Rhodes, where he took part in politics. There Cicero heard his lectures, and afterwards wanted him to write the history of his consulship. He was a traveler and excelled in physical science, which the Stoics somewhat neglected[.]

Ariston of Ceos[,] a Peripatetic[,] in 230 BC. became head of the school and wrote. But the Ariston Cic[ero] means is he of Chios a Stoic inclining to Cynicism, whom Cic[ero] looked on as a sceptic at bottom, coupling him here and elsewhere with Pyrrhon. He flourished 260[.]

Herillus of Carthage[,] disciple of Zenon the Stoic's, a terse and vigorous writer. He made virtue equivalent to science, ἐπιστήμη {knowledge}[.]

Pyrrhon of Elis the founder of the Sceptics, whence skepticism in general is sometimes called Pyrrhonism, was a contemp[orary] of Alexander the Great's and honoured by him[.]

Demetrius Phalereus (from Phalerum an old port of Athens, the deme he belonged to) was the last of the great Attic orators. He was, with the comic poet Menander, a pupil of Theophrastus Aristotle's favourite pupil and successor in the School. D[emetrius Phalereus] was a statesman too and a sort of dictator at Athens in the Macedonian interest for 10 years, till at D[emetrius] Poliorcetes' approach he fled and lived long in Egypt at Ptolemy's court[.]

[* * *]

Officium, duty, is that which we are to [sic] bound to in conduct, what we must do, not by a physical necessity, for conduct is of free choice, but by a conditional one, if we would obey the sovereign lawgiver God, if we would be happy by the enjoyment of the reward only God can bestow or not unhappy under the penalty only God can inflict. The necessity or must is that of law, which the lawgiver is said to enforce, the force being the so-called sanction[.]

Duty then is that which conscience or the moral sense recognises as the thing to be done. Morality in gen[eral] is the object of the moral sense and this particular duty is the object of conscience. As the eye recognises light, colour; illumination; the ear / sound; the understanding / meaning / so the conscience recognises a proper object of its own, viz. law, an absolutely binding law, or rather some one precept, a command, an imperative voice bidding and forbidding. Now this voice of command is absolute, which is the same as infinite, that is | under no conceivable circumstances to be disobeyed or outweighing all possible motives and considerations to the contrary; for a weight which outweighs all possible counterpoise, a force which resists all possible countereffort, is infinite; and there is no infinite but God; therefore the voice which commands conscience is the voice of God or it is God as a lawgiver commanding, and so we have an immediate perception not of God's self and essence indeed but of his will towards us, his action on us or rather of the action and the will of some being, some power which we learn from others or conclude for ourselves to be God Almighty[.]

But the voice which conscience hears or, to speak less figuratively, the manifestation of will, the command and imperative which in matters of conduct we are conscious of, is not arbitrary: of its nature indeed, being Will, it might be so, but in ordinary experience it is not ; it is al[so] directed towards, or directs us towards, the bringing about of one [th]ing and the prevention of another. The thing it wd. bring about and bids [i]s what we call Right or moral good, the thing it wd. prevent and forbids is Wrong or moral evil . These qualities of Rightness and Wrongness are present in all that, however various, it bids and forbids and constitute for us, together with the command to do or forbear, respectively duty and sin,[x] which directs us to do or forbear, which bids or forbids us.

But what is the nature in general of that thing called Right we are bidden to do and of that thing Sin we are forbidden the doing of? In ordinary cases of experience, where, as said above, the inward manifestation of will, is not arbitrary, Right means that which secures the perfection of our human nature; Wrong means that which is against our perfection, ruins, and undoes it. Thus we feel that selfpreservation is right and so a duty, self-destruction wrong and so a sin, the sin of suicide, a case of murder. If there were not a power outside of us forbidding, if the Eternal, as Hamlet says, had not fixed his canon gainst self slaughter, it might be unreasonable, wrong in the sense of perverse or crooked, to take our own lives, but who cd.. forbid it ? Only that same legislator, our[*se*]lves, who now, by as good a title, revokes his own decree. [*But*] as it is we feel a higher will than either our own or any other will whate[*v*]er forbidding the unreasonable deed[.]

But on the other head, not of the duty of doing but of the duty to be done [*he*] treats fully and first in chap. 4, where he identifies the finis bonorum, ultimate and sovereign good, with the honestum, τὸ καλόν, the noble or honourable or (most clearly) morally beautiful, and then divides this moral beauty into the four cardinal virtues[.]

He recognises a secondary moral good, the utile, and appears to think this is the honestum as applied to the conditions of life and not that it is absolutely good. This then will be the division he is making in chapter 3 §7

Good however is commonly divided into καλόν, χρήσιμον, and ἡδύ, honestum, utile, and dulce. Of the last Cicero takes no notice, seemingly because pleasure is not moral good. But this is illogical: neither is beauty, which is τό καλόν simply, moral good; nor convenience, usefulness, as of a key or dictionary bootjack or dictionary, moral good; but the morally beautiful, the morally advantageous, are moral good; so then too is moral pleasure, as peace of conscience, and in fact happiness — for if pleasure be extended to all time or beyond this life and to our highest, not our lowest, faculties it will not differ from happiness; now that happiness is and shd. be the moral object of moral action all allow[.]

At chap. 3 §8 he seems to divide duty into absolute (perfectum) and comparative (medium), by which last he seems to mean what is better done but not absolutely binding — a dist[inction] corresponding to the Xtian dist[inction] of Precepts and Counsels. This dist[inction] is Zeno's: Zeno seems to have recognised only one thing as absolutely good[.]

[*GMH's note*]

ˣ That is to say duty is a right thing commanded, sin is a wrong thing forbidden; so that there are in duty and sin two elements—one the command to do or forbear; the other the goodness, rightness / or evil, badness, wrongness / of the thing bidden or forbidden. We recognise the rightness or right, the goodness of good and on the other hand the wrongness of wrong, badness of bad of themselves by an ordinary exercise of thought, just as we re[*c*]ognise that a line is straight or crooked, a boat trimmed or lopsided, a sheet of linen clean or spotted, either immediately or by applying some standard, rule, or principle; but besides this duty requires further the notion of bindingness and law, sin of unlawfulness, prohibition, and this we recognise in the stress put upon us by that voice of command which Cicero strongly recognises and in other places (as a passage from the lost work de Rep. quoted by Lactantius) beautifully expresses the derivation of duty from one eternal unchange[*a*]ble divine law binding all ; but in this treatise, either through haste or as tak[*en*] for granted, he leaves that fundamental point untouched[.]

APPENDIX I

Hopkins's Retreat Notes, 1889

In January 1889, GMH began his annual retreat, this time at St Stanislaus's College, Tullabeg (near Tullamore), which had recently become the novitiate of the Irish Province. The manuscript of GMH's retreat notes, now housed in the Bodleian Library, Oxford,[1] consists of eight sheets, with text on rectos and versos. The first and third sheets are written on stationery bearing the imprint: 'LOYOLA HOUSE, | DROMORE, | CO. DOWN'.

| *Bod* a.8, 24ʳ | Jan. 1 1888[2] St. Stanislaus' Collgege, Tullabeg.

Principium seu Fundamentum: "Homo creatus est ut laudet" etc—All moral good, beg in all man's being good, lies in two things—in being right, or ^being^ in the right, and in doing right; in being on the side of right side, on the side of good, and then ^on that side^ of doing good. Neither of these will do by itself. Doing good but on the wrong side, promoting a bad cause, is rather doing wrong. Doing good but ^not^ in no good cause is no merit: of whom or what does the doer deserve well? Not at any rate of God. Nor plainly is it enough to be on the right side and not promote it.

But men are variously constituted to make much of one of these things and neglect the other. The Irish think it enough to be Catholics or on the right side and that it is no matter what they say and do on ^to advance^ it; practically so, but what they think is that all they and their leaders do to advance the right side is and must be right. The English think, as Pope says for them, he can't be wrong whose life is in the right.[3] Marcus Aurelius seems in his Meditations to be leading the purest ^and most unselfish^ life of virtue; he thinks, though, with hesitation, that ^Reason governs the universe and that^ by this life he ranks himself on the side of that Reason which governs the universe; and indeed, if this was all he had the means of doing, it was enough; but he does not know of any particular standard the rallying to which is the appointed signal of taking God the sovereign Reason's, God the Word's made flesh's, side; and yet that standard was then raised in the world ^and the Word and sovereign Reason was then made flesh^ and he persecuted it. And in any case his principles are principles of despair and , besides, ^again^ philosophy is not religion

| *Bod* a.8, 24ᵛ | But how is it with me? I was a Christian from birth; or baptism, ^later I was^ converted to the Catholic faith, and am enlisted 20 years in the Society of

---

[1] Bodleian MS Eng, Misc, a.8, fos. 24–31.

[2] GMH's misprint for '1889'.

[3] Alexander Pope, *Essay on Man* (Epistle III, Part VI, ll. 305–6): 'For modes of faith let graceless zealots fight; / His can't be wrong whose life is in the right.'

Jesus. I am now 44. I do not waver in my allegiance, I never have ^since my conversion to the Church^. The question is how I advance the side I serve on. This may be ~~by~~ inwardly or outwardly. Outwardly I often think I am employed to do what is of little or no use. Something else which I ~~might~~ ^can^ conceive myself doing might indeed be ^more^ useful~~ler~~, but still it is an advantage for there to be a ~~Catholic~~ course of higher studies for Catholics in Ireland and that that shd. be partly in Jesuit hands; and my ^work and my^ salary keep~~s~~ that up. Meantime the Catholic Church in Ireland and ~~our~~ the Irish Province in it and our College in that are ~~half~~ ^greatly^ given over to ~~an immoral~~ ^a partly unlawful^ cause, promoted by partly ~~immoral~~ unlawful means, and against my will ~~my wearin~~ pains, laborious and distasteful, like prisoners made to serve the enemies' gunners, go to ~~serve~~ ^help on^ this cause. I do not feel then that outwardly I do much good, much that I care to do or can much wish to prosper; and this is a mournful life to lead. ~~Yet it seems to me that I ca~~ In thought I can of course divide the good from the evil and live for the one, not the other: this justifies me, but it does not alter the facts. Yet it seems to me that I could lead this life well enough if I had bodily energy and cheerful spirits. However these God will not give me. The other part, the more important, remains, my inward service.

I was continuing this ~~reflexion~~ ^train of thought^ this evening when I began to enter on that course of loathing and hopelessness which I have so often felt before, which made me fear madness and led me to give up the practice of meditation except, as now, in retreat, and here it is again. I could therefore do no~~w~~ more than repeat <u>Justus es, Domine, et rectum, judicium tuum</u> and the like, and then being tired I nodded and woke with a start. What is my wretched life? Five wasted years almost have passed | *Bod* a.8, 25^r^ | in Ireland. I am ashamed of the little I have done, of my waste of time, ~~and yet~~ ^although^ my helplessness ~~is su~~ and weakness is such that I could scarcely do otherwise. And yet the Wise Man warns us against excusing ourselves in that fashion. I cannot then be excused: but what is my life with ~~am~~ aim, ~~and~~ without a spur, without help? All my undertakings miscarry: I am like a straining eunuch. I wish then for death: yet if I died now I shd. die imperfect, no master of myself, and that is the worst failure of all. O my God, look down on me

| *Bod* a.8, 25^r^ | Jan. 2—This morning I made the med. on the Three Sins, with nothing to enter but loathing of my life and a barren submission to God's will. The body cannot rest when it is in pain nor the mind be at peace as long as something bitter distills in it and it aches. This may be at any time and is at many: how then can it be pretended there is ^for those who feel this^ anything worth calling happiness in this world? There is a happiness, hope, the anticipation of happiness hereafter: it is better than happiness, but it is not happiness now. It is as if one were dazzled by a spark or star in the dark, seeing it but not seeing by it: we want a light ~~spea~~ ^shed^ on our way and a happiness spread over our life

Afternoon: on the same—more loathing and only this thought, that, I can do my spiritual and other duties better with God's help. In particular I think it may be well to resolve to make the examen every day at 1.15 and then say vespers and compline if not said before. I will consider what next

| *Bod* a.8, 25ʳ | Jan. 3—Repetition of 1st and 2nd exercise—Helpless loathing: Then I went out and I said the Te Deum and yet I thought what was needed was not praise of God but amendment of life

| *Bod* a.8, 25ʳ | . . . Jan. 5—Rep. of meds. on Incarnation and Nativity—All that happens in Christendom and so in the whole world is affected, ~~by the Incarnation,~~ markedly on a great scale, and like any other historical event, ~~and~~ ^and^ in fact more than any other ~~by the Incarnation~~ ^event, by the Incarnation^; at any rate by Christ's life and death, whom we by faith hold to be God made man. Our lives are affected by the events of Roman history, by Caesar's victory and murder for instance. Yet one might perhaps maintain that at this distance of time individuals wd. not find a difference in their lives, except in what was set down in | *Bod* a.8, 25ᵛ | books of history and works of art, if Pompey instead of Caesar had founded the empire or Caesar had lived 20 years longer. But our lives and in particular those of religious, as mine, are in their whole direction, not ~~in~~ only ~~outward but~~ ^inwardly^ but mostly visibly and outwardly, shaped by Christ's. Without that even outwardly the world wd. be so different that we cannot even guess it. And my life is determined by the Incarnation down to most of the details of the day. Now ~~and~~ this being so that I cannot even stop it, why shd. I not make the cause that determines my life ^both^ as a whole and in much detail determine it in greater detail still and to the greater efficiency of what I in any case shd. do and to my greater happiness in doing it? It is for this that St Ignatius speaks of the angel <u>discharging his mission</u>; it being qn. of action on leading up to, as now my action leads from, the Incarnation. The Incarnation was for my salvation and that of the world: this work goes on in a great system and machinery which even drags me on with the collar round my neck ~~even if~~ ^though^ I wd. and do neglect my duty in it. But I say to myself that I am ~~now~~ ^only^ too willing to do God's work and help on the knowledge of the Incarnation. But this is not really true: I am not willing enough for the piece of work assigned me, the only ~~one~~ ^work^ I ~~can have~~ ^am given^ to do though I could do others if they were given. This is my work at Stephen's Green. And I thought how the Royal University was to me ~~a descripti~~ what Augustus's enrolment was to St. Joseph: <u>exiit sermo a Caesare Augusto etc</u>; so resolution of the Senate of the R.U. came to me, inconvenient and painful, but the journey to Bethlehem was inconvenient and painful; and then I am bound in justice, and paid. I hope to bear this in mind

| *Bod* a.8, 26ʳ | Jan. 6 Epiphany—Yesterday I had ever so much light about the ~~Wise Men and~~ the mystery of this feast and the historical interp[retatio]n of the Gospel and ~~had~~ last night on the Baptism and today on that and the calling of Nathanael and so on, more than I can easily put down. However I had better have at least some notes

The Wise Men were Magians, either Zoroastrians or at least of a religion or sect of philosophy ^(Sabaeism)^ in which astrology played a part. And astrology is astronomy, ordinary science, with an extraordinary science ^added^. This is called after them <u>magic</u> and there is therefore acc. to the Scp. a good or "white" magic, ~~though it~~ lawful in itself though positively or from its dangers, it may be, unlawful. ^That is^ there is ~~then in fact~~ above all ~~ha~~ natural science a ~~no~~ science which bridges over the ~~gap~~ ^gulf^ between human and superhuman knowledge, that is, enters a world of spirits, not departed souls but angels. And therefore natural bodies like the stars may exercise not only a natural, ~~but als~~ as by their light and weight, but also a preternatural influence on man. That they cannot determine his fate is plain from many reasons, among which I now see that those which convinced St. Austin ^and St. Gregory^—are good. For ~~the~~ ^a^ horoscope is the momentary cast or determination of the whole heaven, to which acc. to the ancients, and we may say in truth, the earth is like a point: in this enormous, infinite, disproportion only one thing is to be ~~as~~ considered, the aspect of the ~~point~~ ^place^ of birth, that is the relation between that and the heavenly sphere; this alone decides the horoscope, for all differences ^here below,^ <u>within</u> the same aspect, so long as they make no difference in the horoscope itself; can count for nothing, any more than differences of position ~~in the~~ between two men ^or houses^ make any ^sensible^ difference in the parallelism of their shadows in the sun. ~~But~~ So then two men born within a few seconds ^or minutes^ of one another, too few to change the horoscope, and in the same street, must have the same fate; which is not the case. But that the stars might ~~conceivably~~ not determine ~~but~~ a fate but influence ^a man's^ constitution and with it his history is not inconceivable. ~~However~~ From their great distance this is either small or at least difficult to observe: astro- | *Bod* a.8, 26ᵛ | nomy succeeds with difficulty in measuring for instance the heat ~~of~~ ^shed by^ Sirius upon the earth; his activism may be more considerable: these are natural influences; it wd. seem the Magians professed ~~and succeeded in discerning~~ to observe preternatural, that is angelic, influences, and did so

The star ~~no~~ was nothing to ordinary observers, perhaps not visible at all to them. For ~~even~~ ^as^ in modern science most of the phenomena are known to astronomers, ^to^ the specialists, only; the public wd. scarcely ~~know~~ ^remark^ if a star of the first magnitude were withdrawn from Orion; so still more ~~of~~ with a secret art. So the Magi behave: nothing of <u>the star which</u> ~~ap~~ <u>appeared</u> or <u>has appeared</u>; it is <u>we have seen</u>; they speak of their art, their observation, magisterially. So that the star may even have been an altogether preternatural appearance, only visible after the practice of their art, some sort of evocation, had been gone through, not necessarily ~~then~~ always then; as in fact it disappeared

If they were Persian Magians they may of course have come from Bactria and the ~~bound~~ borders of India, more reasonable to suppose the East bears its scriptural meaning of Arabia east of the Holy Land. They were then of the Sabean, the very ancient religion of ~~Arab the en~~ those parts, in them seemingly not idolatrous. <u>The king of the Jews</u> more natural to people of that country; also that they shd. be chiefs or kings than if they had been ~~kings~~ Persians

Date of coming uncertain. For the mystery one wd. suppose <u>after</u> the Circumcision, by which Xt. so to say, qualified as king <u>of the Jews</u>. Twelve days = 6 + 6 = Creation and Redemption, also a sort of mystical year, meaning the fulness of time. As a round number a chosen for the feast one wd. rather have expected 14, octave of New Year's day | *Bod* a.8, 27ʳ | or 10. It must have been before the Purification, as then prob. the Holy Family wd. leave Bethlehem.

<u>Where is he</u> etc—They know when, they ask where. Jerusalem troubled; their coming unwelcome, they knew more than the Jews, came to teach them. The Jews looked for the homage of the Gentiles: when it came it brought an unexpected circumstance with it, as God's works always do; the Gentiles, the teachers, more honoured than themselves—though only in one partic.

The Scribes called together secretly as far as poss., and the information ^at least^ given secretly to the Wise Men. They get away by night, it may be by their own wish, to lose no time; but also by Herod's, that ~~it may~~ their going may be, unlike their coming, without noise. (Presumably night, for they see the star.) He sent them to Bethlehem, that is sent a guide ~~with them,~~ ^to shew the road^, courtesy so requiring. Writers ask why did he not send some one to report where they went. There wd. be a difficulty: it must be secretly, and from them. He wd. not commit himself by any known messenger: he wd. then seem to be recognising the Pretender. In the urgency he might not find a secret follower, and he thought there was no need.

Then prob. they do not enter Bethlehem. The stable was outside. The Bethlehemites saw little of them, did not know where they went. They wd. encamp near the spot and the dream was that very night; they set out before morning and Herod altogether lost sight of them

Herod had meant to say on their return, that they were mistaken, this cd. not be the expected king etc, and afterwards to treat the matter as a conspiracy. No doubt he still more treated it so when he found himself 'mocked'. He ~~does~~ prob. | *Bod* a.8, 27ᵛ | does not act at once, but waits some ^weeks or^ months for a pretext, for the conspiracy to shew itself. But the Bethlehemites had no plot and little knowledge on the subject. There was the story of the shepherds, but, so to say, nothing had followed it. After the Purification ~~fa~~ the Holy Family had prob. ~~gone~~ ^disappeared^. Herod of course availed himself of the registration and found St. Joseph's name and place of abode and so marked out Xt for death; but not as a likely, rather as an unlikely, case. For by enquiring of Nazareth it wd. have appeared that the birth of Joseph's child at Bethlehem must have been a chance (and no doubt they had stayed ~~ti~~ at home till the last date possible), so that there cd. not well have been a plot. When Herod acted at last he must have pretended a conspiracy, required a confession, and getting none made this proof of general guilt, and so justified a general slaughter. The ~~num~~ number of children killed cannot have been great, <u>a bimatu et infra</u>, that is prob. from the beginning of the second year, one full year ~~and a little more~~ ^from birth^. The Magians had been clear about the star shewing ^the fact of^ the Christ's <u>being</u> ^now^ born, and ^born^ within a year: they did not know or they did not tell Herod it meant he was born at the hour of the star's appearance. Some of the children born within the year may have left Bethlehem: Herod wd. ascertain this and have them killed where found, but no doubt most were still at Bethlehem, and it wd. be a point with him to strike suddenly and once only, to give no alarm; he must then have meant the Nazareth murder to take place on the same day as the Bethlehem one. It was then the night before this day prob. that St. Joseph was warned and fled. When Herod heard this, he must have | *Bod* a.8, 28ʳ | been torture then at last have suspected this was the most dangerous of his rivals and have been tortured by the thought till he died. He must have thought his agents had betrayed him too

Why to Egypt, not Syria? Perhaps it is nearer or no farther; since Herod's kingdom included Abylina in Syria. Secondly it was less suspicious to go Jerusalemwards, than northwards, and less easy to track. Thirdly extradition from the Syrian princes was easier than from Egypt, which was most strictly ^jealously^ watched by Rome. And if Herod had heard ^heard^ anything of the way the Holy Family went this wd. ^must^ have surprised and balled him yet more

Remark that Herod died long before the claimant pretender he wanted to destroy ed was of age to do anything and so indeed did his son Archelaus, in whose more especial interest he might be thought to have acted. And at his own death his kin[gdom] was broken up, and at his son Archelaus' death its best part was forfeited altogether, and all this not by a Jewish pretender but by the Romans. Then his son Antipas who did live to see Christ proclaimed king of the Jews and had him sent to him and put in his power, with even the leave and the wish for him to use it ^Holy power^, and he neglected just put it aside, as wholly needless. And then Christ died by the s Roman sentence, the same sentence that had divided Herod's kin[gdom]. And when these crimes ^agst. Xt^ were all over, as if then it nothing mattered, Herod Agrippa came to inherit nearly most of Herod the Great's kingdom. And then in that ^Antipas too finding himself assured in his^ position and free from hi rivals he affected a more than messiasship, a godhead himself and with applause; and for it miserably died. So wholly futile was all this wicked worldliness

Defuncti sunt enim, whereas in the first dream it had been said Futurum est enim ut Herodes. St. Jerome therefore concludes the Scribes too had sought Xt's death. And therefore we cannot be sure it was at once on Herod's death that St. as at a signal that the St. Joseph was called from Egypt, esp. as it had been till I shall tell thee, not till Herod dies.

The Baptism etc—St. John baptised by immersion. (1) For his baptism did not differ ^in form^ from Christ's seemingly except in the words used; now early Xtian baptism was by immersion. (2) This is the most natural form of the symbol of ^for^ a baptism of penance, where defilement, dirt, covering the whole man stands for utter guilt. (3) Though he | *Bod* a.8, 28ᵛ | addressed all Israel he preached only in and the valley of the Jordan (and through all of that Luke iii 3.) and places where there was plenty of water (viz. Aenon near Salem: John iii 23., quia aquae multae in eo erant): but much water wd. not be needed but for that; any fountain wd. do. (4) In saying he was not fit to unfasten or to carry Xt's shoes he implies / so far from being fit to baptise him, I am not even to undress him for baptism. (5) Xt was in fact so baptised (see Matt. and Mark) and he was baptised like others

The ᵇ penitents then went down into the water, but this was their own act and for the symbol this was far from enough. John was the Baptist and must baptise them. For this prob. he used affusion, throwing water on them, and for this some shell or scoop, ~~and this he~~ as he is represented. And he seems to allude to this in contrasting himself with Xt: ego quidem aqua baptizo . . . cuius ventilabrum in manu eius Luke iii 16, 17. ~~Then ba—~~he baptises with ~~wind~~ ^breath^ and fire, as wheat is winnowed in the wind and sun, and uses no shell like this which only washes ~~only~~ once but a ~~fen~~ fan that thoroughly and for ever parts the wheat from the chaff. For the fan is a sort of scoop, a shallow basket with a low back, sides sloping down from the back ~~to the front~~ forwards, and no rim in front, like our ~~fire~~ dustpans, it is said. The grain is either scooped into this or thrown in by another, then tossed out against the wind, and this vehement action St. John compares to his own repeated "dousing" or affusion. The ~~contrasts also~~ separation it makes is very visible too: the grain lies heaped on one side, the chaff blows away the other, between them the winnower stands; after that nothing is more combustible than the chaff, and yet the fire he calls unquenchable. It will do its work at once and yet last, as this river runs for ever, but has to do its work over again. Everything about himself is weak and ineffective, he and his instruments; everything about Xt strong. He dwelt with enthusiasm on this thought, representing Xt as a ~~gigantic~~ heroic figure, of ~~heroic~~ ^gigantic^ ~~st~~ size, strength, and equipment; to whom he was a pigmy child. To his hearers too this point of view was not ~~offens~~ unwelcome: the Jews, St. Paul says, ~~love~~ signa petunt (~~Rom.~~ 1 Cor. i 22.), signs of power; the Gk. has δυνάμεις. They wanted a strong Messias and that he shd. use his strength against their enemies: moreover the multitude are not offended by terrorstriking thoughts of religion. But then Xt was not what they expected from this; for prophecy must be interpreted by a spiritual light and if it does | *Bod* **a.8, 29ʳ** | not enlighten it misleads. Partly for this St. John himself changed his style and when he pointed Xt out said Ecce Agnus Dei. But now he uses terms of force and, though he was well understood to speak of moral greatness and dignity, yet, in ~~as~~ terms, physical ~~power~~ ^force^. I take yr. garments and your footgear from you when you go down into the water; all sorts of men come to me and I know the difference between a light sandal and the soldier's heavy caliga: I tell you my fingers have not the force to wring open this man's laces, ~~st~~ though I stoop and bend my body to the task; ^if he washed himself^ my arms have not the strength to ~~bear~~ ^lift^ his ~~buskins.~~ ^boots.^ He uses this imagery because he was the forerunner and smoothed the way; not, he wd. have said, for his sake, for it is nothing to him where he treads, but for yours, hard hearts, which like ~~stones~~ ^sandstone^ ~~he~~ ^his tread^ may grind to powder; brood of adders, whose heads they may crush in blood. He wd. be well shod as a traveller, soldier, on the march, or ~~farmer~~ labourer in the forest (securis ad radicem arboris posita est)

There may be added the contrast between baptising one by one and tossing the whole basketfull of grain, each grain a man, at one throw empty

The struggle between Xt and St. John, two innocent lambs, over Xt's baptism was like the momentary encounter of two rams: then St. John recognising himself the weaker withdraws. Yet it was which shd. humble himself: Xt being stronger humbled himself more

Which does the Scp. mean saw the heavens open ^etc^ after the Baptism, Xt or St. John? St. John certainly saw this (John i 33, 34.), but St. Matt.'s and Mark's words imply or almost imply it was Xt. It was then both; the form of words is remarkable and is no doubt a case of the Threefold Tradition. They said he saw and the evangelists supplied a sense: the Tradn. probably meant St. John

The baptism was at Bethania beyond Jordan seemingly John i 28. and so the temptation wd. be in the desert beyond Jordan; but is that the tradn.? However neither of these points is clear. St. John speaks of 3 certain days—28. Haec in Bethania facta sunt . . 29. Altera die | *Bod* a.8, 29ᵛ | vidit Joannes Jesum venientem ad se . . 35. Altera ~~antems qui / esse~~ die iterum stabat Joannes . . ~~43. In crastin~~—but do these mean the next day or on another day,² St. John singling certain notable days? And does 29. ~~mean Nathanael under the fig tree⁴~~ mean ~~the~~ Xt's baptism?, ~~mean~~ which is in silence supposed at 32.? or was this on Xt's return from the temptation? If so he lodged near where John was and made some disciples, waited for them to be handed over to him

36. Respiciens Jesum ambulantem, that is / passing; not coming to him as at 29. He ~~told~~ meant them to follow the Lamb quocumque ierit. Two of his disciples take this hint: conversus autem Iesus et videns eos sequentes se dicit eis, 38., this, though literally true, is rather the idiom, for saying Jesus in his turn, on his side, as, seeing, they were following etc

43. In crastinum must be meant literally, but ~~ter~~ et die tertia ~~iii~~ ii 1. may perhaps mean on a third day, that is / later than the two just mentioned. This inexactness marks that nothing depends on the difference; see also 43. voluit exire in Galileam et invenit Philippum may be Xt or Andrew: both wd. be true, for both went to the wedding at Cana no doubt and both wanted Philip, but rather Andrew is meant, since it ~~seems~~ ^is^ less becoming for the writer to seem to know Xt's thoughts and we are never without reason to suppose anything revealed to the sacred historians. Andrew then knew that ^Philip would^ gladly come if ~~called and therefore~~ Xt chose to call and it proved that he did, and the Gospel does not even give his answer meaning he was only too glad, as his enthusiastic words in 45. shew. He was sort of chamberlain to Xt afterwards (as ~~Nathanael under~~ vi 5, xii 21.)

Nathanael under the figtree—The ~~presum~~ ^chances^ were that Philip was wrong and the presumption was agst. Nazareth in particular, but Philip wisely said come and see and Nathanael went. And this is why he is called an Israelite without guile: an Israelite,

---

⁴ In whole or in part, the phrase 'Nathanael under the figtree' appears three times on fo. 29ᵛ, in preparation for a new meditation topic. Yet GMH extends the discussion of Christ and his disciples twice—hence the cancellations—before finally changing topics.

that is looking for the ~~hope and~~ redemption of Israel (Luke ii 38.), and without guile, that is / not refusing it when offered, nor dissembling nor like Herod ~~persecuting~~ trying to extinguish it or, as the whole nation, choosing a Barabbas instead; nor pressing his objection like the Pharisees to the point | *Bod* a.8, 30ʳ | [5] not of searching but of telling someone else to search and that then he cd. not find

(John i) 48. Priusquam te Philippus vocaret / before he answered a call or had a call to answer, cum esses sub ficu, that is / in ^his^ ease and his privacy, when his will was less good and he ~~did not think~~ ^never thought^ of God through anyone concerning himself about him. ~~The~~ To be under one's own figtree is to be at one's ease and the figleaf stands for concealment—here privacy, a luxurious concealment: the leaves shut out the sun and shine themselves and without stirring one can pull the figs. Vidi te / I ~~set my heart~~ ^had my eye^ on thee: it does not imply miraculous knowledge, but it implies more knowledge than was supposed by Nathanael. He is touched and gives his allegiance. We must also suppose something that Philip or a bystander cd. not know of that came home to him, either something that really took place under a figtree or that it was a great insight into what he secretly recognised as the ~~fact of~~ fault of his life, selfish ease, idleness, and so on, and that Xt nevertheless chose this idler especially for his kingdom. 50. Quia dixi tibi: vidi te sub ficu credis: ɇ cf. this with what is said to Thomas; but this is praise. Majus his videbis, and then this will not be private or singular, therefore now he speaks in the plural including Philip and all his disciples—videbitis coelum apertum: instead of living at earth on ~~a~~ ^the^ little spot of earth that a fig^tree^ ~~shelters you shall see heaven a~~ hides from heaven and heaven from it, you shall see ~~hea~~ bare heaven open; and instead of idleness in men activity in angels; and instead of men selfishly helping each himself angels ~~all~~ ministering to a man. ~~He~~ ^Xt^ is the man, but they who help to minister to the king are to share the kingdom. There is of course an allusion to Jacob's ~~ladder~~, Israel's, ladder Gen. xxviii: Jacob had then been sleeping under the bare sky, so far from luxury was he then, and stones were his pillow. There is further an allusion to the angels which had just been ministering to Xt after his fast: this is meant by the Evangelist but was not known to Xt's hearers. And lastly the first fulfilment of the promise was at the marriage of Cana, when crediderunt in eum discipuli eius ii 11. We may perhaps conclude that in working ~~Xt's~~ miracles Xt used the ministry of angels, but the words might be | *Bod* a.8, 30ᵛ | taken more figuratively. The servers at the wedding being ~~engaged~~ ^concerned^ in a miracle might be called God's angels

Remark also that Nathanael ~~no~~ ceases to live under a figtree, ~~an~~ the Jewish church, and ^comes to^ ~~lives~~ in ~~a vine,~~ and be part of a vine, Xt and the church of Xt

ii 1, 2. Et erat Mater Jesu ibi; that is / already or at least as a matter of course, as a friend of the family. Vocatus est autem et Jesus et discipuli eius ad nuptias—a pointed distinction made: she was there ~~w~~ he was asked; she was there before, ~~the wedding~~ he

---

[5] Fos. 30ʳ and 30ᵛ are written on sheets of stationery printed: 'St. Stanislaus' College, | Tullamore'.

was asked to the wedding. It is true, he must, it wd. seem, have been a friend of the family too, but now he was a public character and had disciples and if ^he^ were asked they must; at least it was so done in her honour. But this overburdened the house: it was not provided for so many and Mary knew this. She did not notice it then first at the time, for it wd. seem ^that^ from her modesty, ~~that she~~ in spite of her charity, she wd. not have been attending to such a thing till others saw it and so the hosts wd. have been put to pain. But now she knows how they stand throughout and warns Xt in time

4. <u>Nondum venit hora mea</u> / my moment; because he knew and was ready to act, but did not need so soon. That is / he tells her there was no need to speak. She knew he did not need reminding, but she did not know he might not need requesting. This was a point insoluble to her, ^of itself^ not admitting of certainty; and she must act: she took the side of charity and exposed herself to rebuke. Her words to the servers are a great light to us on her knowledge of Xt's power and will. Further it appears she said to herself he wd. send for wine and it wd. appear, perhaps ^send them^ out of doors to ~~be~~ ^have it^ delivered, ^to them^ say, by angel hands. But Xt makes the ~~gu~~ supply seem to come from the hosts, and further the guests see, from the great <u>hydriae</u>, that they are amply supplied. This conceals the miracle more at the moment and increases it afterwards.

~~It was~~ The miracle was in fact forestalled ~~g~~. It was too soon; for when drawn the wine was not served to the guests, but the master of ceremonies is consulted about | *Bod* a.8, 31^r^ | ^it^ and he also remonstrates with the bridegroom before anything more is done. Further it took long filling the great watervessels: the guests then cannot have been waiting and the <u>architriculinus</u> notices nothing in this respect: rather they have had plenty, there has been no stint, but there has been an unwise order in the serving

BIOGRAPHICAL REGISTER OF PERSONS FREQUENTLY CITED

An asterisk (*) denotes a separate entry.

BACON, S.J., FRANCIS EDWARD JOSEPH (1839–1922). Raised in London by Protestant parents, Bacon received 'a commercial education' before turning his talents to teaching. The latter, coupled with a desire to see the world, took him to Georgetown, British Guiana for four years at the end of the 1850s. Bacon was 'quietly preparing' for the Anglican ministry when he made the decision, in 1866, to convert to Roman Catholicism.[1] After a year in a Lisbon seminary, he entered the Society's novitiate at Roehamptom on 9 October 1867. From 1868 to 1875 (the novitiate through to Bacon's ordination; GMH was ordained in 1877), Bacon and GMH crossed paths or co-resided throughout the English Province: Roehampton, Stonyhurst, and St Beuno's. They were also members of a holiday party in Scotland 'on the Argyleshire coast of the Frith of Clyde' in 1871 (see *CW* iii). From his ordination until his death, Bacon lived and served at St Aloysius's College in Glasgow, Scotland; he had a particular gift for working with young people. Bacon, who wrote verses as a young man and copied poems GMH shared with him (by Manley *Hopkins and Digby Dolben) into his commonplace book, was one of the few Jesuits who both recognized and responded to GMH's eclectic brilliance, and appreciated his poetry. When Fr Keating's articles on GMH appeared in *The Month* in 1909, Bacon wrote to Keating: 'What a pity his verse was not appreciated before by S.J.'s . . . I regret that he received so little recognition from [the Society] during his life, I mean in regard to his poetic endowments. I venerated him as a saintly man, and especially in his great humility, and cheerful submission to the Will of God under much depreciation and many disappointments.'[2] For more on Bacon, see Lesley Higgins, 'Uncommon Lives: Fr. Hopkins and Fr. Bacon', *Hopkins Quarterly*, 21/3–4 (Summer–Fall 1994), 77–96.

BAILLIE, ALEXANDER WILLIAM MOWBRAY (1843–1921). Educated at the Edinburgh Academy, Baillie won an exhibition to Balliol in 1862; Greats, 1866. He joined the Inner Temple in 1866; called to the Bar, 1871. Due to ill health, he travelled to Egypt beginning in 1874 and pursued his interests in archaeology and languages. When GMH died, Baillie wrote to Kate *Hopkins: 'It is impossible to say how much I owe to him. He is one figure which fills my whole memory of my Oxford life. There is hardly a reminiscence with which he is not associated. All my intellectual growth, and a

---

[1] Obituary notice, *Letters and Notices*, 38 (1923), 250.
[2] Quoted in House and Storey, *Journals and Papers*, 411–12 n. 208.

very large proportion of the happiness of those Oxford days, I owed to his companionship. It has been a subject of unceasing regret to me that circumstances have made me see so little of him since. His rare visits gave me the keenest pleasure, and were eagerly looked forward to. Apart from my own nearest relatives, I never had so strong an affection for any one' (17 June 1889). For the letters exchanged with GMH, see *CW* i and ii.

BRIDGES, ROBERT (1844–1930; *ODNB*). Bridges, a physician and poet (British poet laureate, 1913–30), was one of GMH's closest friends and correspondents (see *CW* i and ii); they met while studying at Oxford in the 1860s. On 3 September 1884, Bridges married (Mary) Monica Waterhouse (1863–1949), daughter of the architect Alfred Waterhouse; they had three children. Among Bridges's most highly regarded volumes: *The Growth of Love* (1876) and *Testament of Youth* (1929). He was a founding member of the Society of Pure English, for which he wrote or edited several tracts (1919 to 1930). Bridges carefully preserved copies of GMH's poems (autographs and transcriptions) in albums now housed in the Bodleian Library, Oxford. For the first edition of GMH's poems, he provided a critical introduction and explanatory notes. Bridges also edited poems, and provided instructive memoirs, for *Dixon (*Poems by the Late Rev. Dr. Richard Watson Dixon*, 1909) and his distant cousin, Digby Dolben (*The Poems of Digby Mackworth Dolben*, 1911; see *CW* iii). GMH's letters to Bridges during the Dublin years are especially informative; the poem 'To R. B.' was written in April 1889.

CASSIDY, MARY. 'Who is Miss Cassidy?' GMH explained to Bridges, 29 April 1889: 'She is an elderly lady who by often asking me down to Monasterevan and by the change and holiday her kind hospitality provides is become one of the props and struts of my existence' (Monasterevan, Co. Kildare, is a village on the river Barrow some 20 km (39 miles) from Dublin). Fr Delany had introduced GMH to Mary, known as Miss Cassidy, and Eleanor, widow of Daniel O'Connell Wheble, then in their late fifties or early sixties, who were the sisters of the current owner of the distillery, James Cassidy (the village's chief employer). The family were Catholic but loyal to the British government and served as magistrates, insisting on adherence to British law. GMH's duties at Monasterevan were to say Mass for the family and to assist at Sts Peter and Paul, the local Catholic church opened in 1847. See White, *Hopkins in Ireland*, 114–19. A pastel painting of Mary Cassidy's niece and nephew, the Wheble children, was displayed in her home. GMH first saw it during his Christmas 1886 visit; it inspired his elegiac poem 'On the Portrait of Two Beautiful Young People'. An initial draft was sent to *Bridges in winter 1887, but GMH continued to work on it until summer 1888.

CURTIS, S.J., ROBERT (1852–93). Curtis, 'the first Catholic entrant' to Trinity College 'after Gladstone had abolished religious tests',[3] was a gifted mathematician. He

---

[3] White, *Gerard Manley Hopkins*, 374.

entered the Society of Jesus in May 1875, but, due to his epilepsy, was not able to be a candidate for ordination. A member of the UC faculty as of 1883, in mathematics and science, he was named RUI Fellow in Natural Science in January 1884. By November 1884, GMH described Curtis to his mother as 'my comfort beyond what I can say and a kind of godsend I never expected to have. His father Mr. Stephen Curtis Q.C. and mother live in town and I often see them and shd. more if I had time to go there' (26 Nov. 1884). Known for his sense of humour, he was keen on walking and swimming. GMH and Curtis hiked throughout northern Wales in July 1886; in August 1888, they travelled in western Scotland (see letter to Bridges, 18–19 Aug. 1888). See Martin, *Gerard Manley Hopkins*, 377–9; and Feeney, 'Hopkins's Closest Friend in Ireland: Robert Curtis, S.J.' in *Hopkins and Dublin: The Man and the City*, (ed.) Richard F. Giles, special issue of *Hopkins Quarterly*, 14/1–2 (Apr. 1987–Jan. 1988), 211–38.

DELANY, S.J., WILLIAM (1835–1924; *ODNB*). Delany, who joined the Society of Jesus in 1856, studied theology in the Gregorian University, Rome, 1865 to 1866, when he was ordained a priest. In 1868, he became prefect and administrator of St Stanislaus' College, Tullabeg, and established himself as a devoted educationist. In October 1883, he was named president of UC; his plans for the new RUI were supported by William Monsell, Lord *Emly. Overall, his goal was to establish a Catholic rival to Trinity College, Dublin; recruiting GMH was part of that plan. For his summary of the Irish university 'question', see *Irish University Education: A Plea for Fair Play* (1904). A determined leader, Delany was praised by GMH as someone who 'wholly lives for the success of the place. He is as generous, cheering, and open hearted a man as I ever lived with' (letter to Kate *Hopkins, 26 Nov. 1884). Delany was Provincial of the Irish Jesuits 1909–12.

DIXON, RICHARD WATSON (1833–1900; *ODNB*). Born in London, Dixon matriculated at Oxford in 1852. Together with William Morris and Edward Burne-Jones, Dixon founded *The Oxford and Cambridge Magazine* (1856), based on the short-lived Pre-Raphaelite journal *The Germ* (1848). The three men studied painting with Dante Gabriel Rossetti, but Dixon soon left the group and took Anglican orders. Assistant master at Highgate School, Middlesex, in 1861–2; GMH was among his students. Six years later, Dixon became a minor canon in Carlisle. In addition to his religious duties, he published poetry and a magisterial six-volume *History of the Church of England* (1878–1902). He and GMH began corresponding in 1878 (see *CW* i and ii), encouraging each other's creative efforts and sympathizing about the burdens of work. Although Dixon's verse received little recognition, it found favour with poets such as Algernon Charles Swinburne (1837–1909; *ODNB*). See Appendix D above for the published version of GMH's biographical sketch, which he informed *Bridges was finished 11–12 November 1884. GMH had transcribed various poems by Dixon in the 1860s; Bodleian MS Eng. Poet. e.91 includes 'St Paul' and 'St John' from *Christ's Company* and 'Love's Consolation'. In a much later hand, GMH transcribed five more poems, and noted: 'The three songs <u>Fallen Rain</u>, <u>Sky that rollest ever</u>, and <u>Does the South Wind</u> I know by heart and can write down at any time.' For his discussion of Dixon's *Mano* with Dixon and Coventry Patmore, see *CW* ii. GMH's possessions at the time of his death included Dixon's *Odes and Eclogues* (1884), *Lyrical Poems* (1887), and *The Story of Eudocia & Her Brothers* (1888). See also Florence Boos, 'Christian Pre-Raphaelitism: G. M. Hopkins' Debt to Richard Watson Dixon', *Victorian Poetry*, 16/4 (Winter 1978), 314–22.

EMLY, WILLIAM MONSELL, first Baron Emly (1812–94; *ODNB*). Born in Limerick, Ireland, the politician was educated at Winchester College (1826–30) and Oriel College, Oxford (he left before taking his degree). He represented Limerick in the British parliament from 1847 to 1874 as a member of the Liberal party. Converted to Roman Catholicism in 1850, and became a close friend of John Henry *Newman. In the early 1870s, Emly was involved in Gladstone's first plan to establish a national university in Ireland; in January 1874 he was created a peer, Baron Emly. Although an advocate of agricultural reform, he opposed the Land League movement, and Home Rule. He was appointed to the RUI Senate in 1884, and became vice-chancellor in 1885.

THE HOPKINS FAMILY. GMH was raised in an affluent, accomplished, middle-class Church of England family. His parents, **Kate Smith** (1821–1920) and **Manley Hopkins** (1818–97), were married in 1843; Gerard was their first child. His siblings: **Cyril** (1846–1932); **Arthur**, a well-known artist and illustrator (1847–1930); **Milicent** (1849–1946), who became an Anglican nun; **Lionel** (1854–1952), a Chinese scholar; **Kate** (1856–1933); **Grace** (1857–1945), a musician who encouraged her brother's interests; and **Everard** (1860–1928), an illustrator. **Felix**, a fourth brother, died in infancy in 1852. **Ann Hopkins** (1815–87), Manley's sister, was a visual artist and pianist who encouraged her nephew's creative talents and intellectual pursuits (including an interest in archaeology). For many years she lived with her brother's family. Kate Hopkins fostered her children's educational and artistic interests. Manley Hopkins, an insurance broker who eventually owned his own firm specializing in maritime insurance products, was the author of *A Handbook of Average* (1857; a guide to 'adjusting' expenses and financial losses when a ship was damaged or wrecked) and *A Manual of Marine Insurance* (1867). He also dabbled in poetry and belles-lettres. For Manley's study of *Cardinal Numbers with an Introductory Chapter on Numbers Generally* (London, 1887), GMH provided the sections on Welsh calculation methods and 'spectral numbers' (the 'mental visibility of numbers'), and mathematical observations woven throughout the text. As biographer Norman White observes, 'it is difficult to say with certainly where Manley's contributions ended and Gerard's began'.[4]

---

[4] Norman White, *Hopkins: A Literary Biography* (Oxford: Oxford University Press, 2002), 6.

KLEIN, LOUIS LEOPOLD MARTIAL BAYNARD DE BEAUMONT (1849–1934). Klein's life was eclectic enough for two people: raised in France, he served as a cavalry officer during the Franco-Prussian War of 1870–1; studied medicine in France and England; and entered the Society of Jesus in 1878 (family lore suggested a conversion from Judaism, but this was not the case). He studied theology at St Beuno's in the 1880s, and was ordained a priest in 1884 (at the theologate of exiled French Jesuits established at St David's College, North Wales). In December 1884, he was appointed Professor of Biology at UC and Fellow of Natural Science at RUI. Critical of the Irish nationalist movement, Klein was convinced that he should advise the Vatican on the matter, but his Jesuit superiors refused permission to do so. In June 1887, he disobeyed orders not to attend a garden party in honour of Queen Victoria (he hoped to address her son, Prince Edward, the guest of honour) and was subsequently disciplined. His letter of resignation from the RUI, dated 20 August 1887, was accepted on 26 October 1887 (BRC 41b:11 (3)). Edward Purbrick, S.J., the English Provincial, recalled Klein in mid-October; Klein left the Society a month later and was formally dismissed on 4 November. Subsequently he became a Unitarian minister, embraced the Positivist teachings of Auguste Comte, and in 1897 married Kathleen O'Hagan (1876–1974), the daughter of a distinguished Anglo-Irish family (Lord O'Hagan, a staunch Catholic who became Chancellor of Ireland in 1868, died in February 1885; his widow left the Church in 1895). Klein was a Fellow of the Linneaean Society and of Regents Park Zoo. In 1913, he changed his German-sounding surname to de Beaumont, his mother's maiden name. For GMH's observations of a lecture by Klein, see the comments on Lucan in *CW* vi; and Schlatter, 'Gerard Manley Hopkins: Poetic Fragments', 41–2. See also Schlatter, 'Martial Klein, Hopkins's Dublin Colleague', 80; and Richard Cohen, 'Beaumont, Charles-Louis Leopold Alfred de (1902–72)', *ODNB*.

NEWMAN, JOHN HENRY, (1801–90; *ODNB*). One of the most compelling figures in Victorian religious and cultural life, Newman was a brilliant writer and apologist. Educated at Trinity College, Oxford. While a Fellow of Oriel College in the 1830s, he contributed to *Tracts for the Times* and the controversial 'Tractarian' or reform movement within the Church of England. In 1845, he converted to Roman Catholicism, a decision that was as polarizing as it was famous. A decade later, he was in Ireland, as rector of the new Catholic university (1854–8; see *The Idea of a University Defined and Illustrated*, 1873). In 1879, he was created a cardinal. From Newman's prolific canon, the texts most important to GMH were *Tract XC* (1841), *Loss and Gain* (1848, a novel in which an Oxford undergraduate 'goes over' to Rome), the autobiographical *Apologia pro Vita Sua* (1864), and *The Grammar of Assent* (1870). At four key junctures in his life, GMH tried to emulate Newman. GMH first wrote to Newman, explaining that he was 'anxious to become a Catholic', on 28 August 1866; they met at the Birmingham Oratory on 21 October and GMH was received into the Church of Rome (Newman also advised GMH how to conduct himself, at Oxford and with his family, once converted). The second experience was professional: after completing his studies at Oxford, GMH served as a schoolmaster at Newman's Oratory of St Philip Neri (in Edgbaston, a Birmingham suburb) from September 1867 to April 1868. A decade later, when Fr Hopkins, S.J. returned to Oxford as assistant pastor at the Jesuit-run St Aloysius's, many hoped he too would 'fire up' the 'towery city' for Rome—but that did not happen. Soon after arriving in Dublin, in February 1884, GMH wrote to Newman to inform him of his new position and to lament that current circumstances at St Stephen's Green were antithetical to their 'idea of a university' (see *CW* ii).

PATMORE, COVENTRY (1823–96; *ODNB*). Patmore, whose father Peter (1786–1855) was a literary journalist, was educated at home; he published his first volume of *Poems* in 1844. Two years later, when his father's investments failed, he went to work in the printed book department of the British Museum (he retired in 1865), and became a well-regarded essayist. His early verse was admired by members of the Pre-Raphaelite Brotherhood ('The Woodman's Daughter' inspired John Everett Millais's painting) and he contributed to the PRB journal, *The Germ*. His first marriage, to Emily Andrews, from 1847 until her death in 1862, resulted in six children and the archetypal Victorian hymn to marriage and conventional femininity, *The Angel in the House* (1854–63). In 1864, he travelled to Rome, met, and subsequently married his second wife, Marianne Byles, a Roman Catholic; he then converted. *The Unknown Eros*, a series of odes, was published in 1877. His second wife died in 1880. Patmore was especially close to two children, both of whom published poetry: his daughter Emily (Sister Mary Christina, of the Society of the Holy Child Jesus), considered a mystic, who died in July 1882; and his son Henry, who died in February 1883. Patmore married again, in 1881, to Harriet Robson, the children's governess. In later years, he published essays on cultural and religious subjects in the *St James's Gazette*; many were collected in *Principle in Art* (1889; 1890) and *Religio poetae* (1893; 1898). Patmore and GMH met at Stonyhurst College in late July 1883, when Patmore was a guest at 'Great Academy' or speech day; they began corresponding (see *CW* ii). For GMH's sketch of Patmore, dated 1 August 1883, see *LPM* 355 and *CW* vi.

RUSSELL, S.J., MATTHEW (1834–1912; *ODNB*). In Dublin and Irish cultural circles, Russell was, in Katharine *Tynan's words, the 'reconciler': 'Everywhere he touched, he dispelled a prejudice. No Protestant who had ever known Fr. Russell could go on believing evil of Catholics and Catholicism.'[5] Raised near Newry, Co. Down and Killowen, Russell, whose parents were strict Catholics, was educated at home, Castleknock College, and St Patrick's College, Maynooth. His uncle, Charles William Russell, 'who became president of St Patrick's College in 1857, had been instrumental in converting John Henry *Newman to Catholicism, and helped Cardinal Wiseman to edit the *Dublin Review*. . . . Russell's three surviving sisters all became nuns in the order of Mercy, while his brother, Charles Arthur Russell (1832–1900), a barrister, rose to be

[5] Tynan, 'Dearest of Friends', 552.

lord chief justice of England in 1894'.[6] Russell, who joined the Jesuits in 1857, was ordained a priest in 1864. For nine years, he carried out teaching and Society work in Limerick; in 1873, he was transferred to Dublin. Later that year, he established the *Irish Monthly*, which he edited until his death. 'He was a minor poet himself, and he admired the poetry of Bridges', Martin states.[7] Through the pages of the *Irish Monthly*, he encouraged the intellectual and creative efforts of 'the Catholic upper middle classes'[8] and diplomatically promoted the Irish literary revival (publishing, among others, W. B. Yeats, Oscar Wilde, Katharine Tynan, Rose Kavanagh).[9] (In 1954, the *Irish Monthly* suspended publication and merged with *Studies*.) GMH's Latin rendering of two songs by Shakespeare appeared in the periodical in 1886 and 1887.[10] 'From 1877 to 1886 Russell served as a priest at St Francis Xavier's Church in Gardner Street, Dublin, and from 1886 to 1903 taught' at UC, where he took charge of the residential students.[11] In 1903, he returned to St Francis Xavier. In October 1886, 'Father Matt' walked Hopkins across St Stephen's Green to the studio of John Butler Yeats, in order to meet the agnostic painter; his son, the fledgling poet William Butler Yeats; and his current sitter, Katharine Tynan.

TYNAN, KATHARINE (1859–1931; *ODNB*). A prolific writer of verse and prose, Katharine Tynan Hinkson (she married Henry Albert Hinkson, a classicist and legal author, in 1893) was a vital part of the emergence of a middle- and upper-class Catholic cultural scene in Dublin in the later nineteenth century (greatly energized by Matthew Russell, S.J.) and was also connected with Irish 'renaissance' figures such as W. B. Yeats, 'A. E.' (George Russell), John O'Leary, and Douglas Hyde. *The Wind in the Trees* (1898) is considered her best volume of lyric poetry. For the letters exchanged between GMH and Tynan, see *CW* ii. For Tynan's recollections of GMH, 'small and child-looking, yet like a child-sage, nervous too and very sensitive, with a small ivory-pale face', see her *Memories* (London: Eveleigh Nash & Grayson, 1924), and *The Middle Years* (Boston: Houghton Mifflin, 1917).

---

[6] John Kelly, 'Russell, Matthew (1834–1912)', *ODNB*. For Russell's biography of his sisters, see *The Three Sisters of Lord Russell of Killowen and their Convent Life* (1912).

[7] Martin, *Gerard Manley Hopkins*, 403.

[8] O'Keefe, 'A Man for Others', 62.

[9] Ibid. 62–70.

[10] *Irish Monthly*, 14 (1886), 628 and 15 (1887), 92.

[11] Kelly, 'Russell, Matthew'. See also [McKenna], 'Father Gerard Hopkins, S.J., and his Poetry'. The article is signed 'The Editor'; previous commentators misattributed it to Russell, but he died in 1912, after which McKenna assumed the editor's responsibilities.

BIBLIOGRAPHY

Addis, William E., and Arnold, Thomas, *A Catholic Dictionary, containing Some Account of the Doctrine, Discipline, Rites, Ceremonies, Councils, and Religious Orders of the Catholic Church* (London: Kegan Paul, 1884).

Aeschylus, *Choephoroi*, (ed.) A. Sidgwick (Oxford: Clarendon Press, 1884).

Allaby, Michael (ed.), *A Dictionary of Earth Sciences* (Oxford: Oxford University Press, 2008). Oxford Reference Online.

Anderson, Warren, 'Hopkins's Dublin Notes on Homer', *Hopkins Quarterly*, 14/1–4 (Apr. 1987–Jan. 1988), 179–91.

Anon., *Ireland and the English Catholics, By One of Them* (London: John Sinkins, 1887).

Anon., 'Irish Jesuits since 1800', *Irish Monthly* (Jan. 1890), 1–16.

Archbold, W. A. J., 'McCabe, Edward (1816–1885)', rev. David C. Sheehy, *ODNB*.

Aristotle, *Aristotelis Politicorum libri VIII. et Oeconomica: Ad optimorum librorum fidem accurate edita* (Leipzig: Tauchnitz, 1831).

Arnold, Matthew, 'The Nadir of Liberalism', *Nineteenth Century*, 19 (May 1886), 645–63.

Arnold, Thomas, *Letters of Thomas Arnold the Younger 1850–1900*, (ed.) James Bertram (Auckland: Auckland University Press, 1980).

Baldick, Chris, *The Oxford Dictionary of Literary Terms* (Oxford: Oxford University Press, 2008). Oxford Reference Online.

Baxter, Lucy, *The Life of William Barnes: Poet and Philologist* (New York: Macmillan and Co., 1887).

Becker, Joseph, *The Re-Formed Jesuits* (Ft. Collins, CO: Ignatius Press, 1997).

Bennet, Douglas, *The Encyclopaedia of Dublin* (Dublin: Gill & Macmillan Ltd., 2005).

Bergonzi, Bernard, *Gerard Manley Hopkins* (New York: Macmillan, 1977).

Bew, Paul, 'Parnell, Charles Stewart (1846–1891)', *ODNB*.

Biagini, Eugenio F., *British Democracy and Irish Nationalism 1876–1906* (Cambridge: Cambridge University Press, 2007).

Boero, Giuseppe, *The Life of the Blessed Peter Favre* (London: Burns and Oates, 1873).

Bonaventure, St, *St Francis of Assisi: The Legends and Lauds*, trans. N. Wydenbruck, (ed.) Otto Karrer (London: Sheed and Ward, 1947).

Boos, Florence, 'Christian Pre-Raphaelitism: G. M. Hopkins' Debt to Richard Watson Dixon', *Victorian Poetry*, 16/4 (Winter 1978), 314–22.

Bosanquet, R. H. M., 'Music. Part II: — Scientific Basis', *Encyclopaedia Britannica*, 1889 edn. (Chicago: R. S. Peale Reprints, 1992), xii. 102–6.

Bowker, John (ed.), *The Concise Oxford Dictionary of World Religions* (Oxford: Oxford University Press, 2000). Oxford Reference Online.

Boylan, Henry, *A Dictionary of Irish Biography* (Dublin: Gill and Macmillan, 2000).

Boyle, A. J., 'Our Page Tastes of Man', *Times Literary Supplement* (5 Oct. 2007), 9.

Bradley, J. L., *A Ruskin Chronology* (New York: St. Martin's Press, 1997).

Brady, Joseph, and Simms, Anngret, 'Dublin at the Turn of the Century', in Joseph Brady and Anngret Simms (eds.), *Dublin through Space and Time* (Dublin: Four Courts Press, 2001), 221–81.

—— 'Dublin in the Nineteenth Century: An Introduction', in Brady and Simms (eds.), *Dublin through Space and Time*, 159–65.

'Breastplate of St Patrick', in E. A. Livingstone (ed.), *The Concise Oxford Dictionary of the Christian Church* (Oxford: Oxford University Press, 2006).

Buisseret, David (ed.), *The Oxford Companion to World Exploration* (Oxford: Oxford University Press, 2007).

Caesar, Julius, *The Gallic War*, trans. H. J. Edwards (Cambridge, Mass.: Harvard University Press, 1986).

The Cambridge Dictionary of English Place-Names, (ed.) Victor Watts (Cambridge: Cambridge University Press, 2004).

Cannon, John (ed.), *A Dictionary of British History* (Oxford: Oxford University Press, 2001). Oxford Reference Online.

Casey, Christine (ed.), *The Buildings of Ireland: Dublin* (New Haven: Yale University Press, 2005).

Caswall, Edward, *Lyra Catholica: Containing All the Breviary and Missal Hymns with Others from Various Sources* (London: James Burns, 1849).

The Catholic Encyclopedia: An International Work of Reference on the Constitution, Doctrine, Discipline, and History of the Catholic Church, 15 vols. (New York: Appleton, 1907–12). Electronic version: <www.newadvent.org>.

Chadwick, Henry, *The Church in Ancient Society: From Galilee to Gregory the Great* (Oxford: Oxford University Press, 2001).

Chapell, W., 'Greek Music', in Sir John Stainer and W. A. Barrett (eds.), *Dictionary of Musical Terms* (London: Novello, Ewer and Co., 1888).

Chilvers, Ian (ed.), *The Oxford Dictionary of Art and Artists* (Oxford: Oxford University Press, 2009). Oxford Reference Online.

Clark, Anne, *Lewis Carroll: A Biography* (New York: Schocken Books, 1979).

Cohen, Richard, 'Beaumont, Charles-Louis Leopold Alfred de (1902–1972)', *ODNB*.

Colin, Thomas, *Historical Dictionary of Ireland* (Lanham, Md.: Scarecrow Press, 1997).

Connolly, S. J. (ed.), *The Oxford Companion to Irish History* (Oxford: Oxford University Press, 2007). Oxford Reference Online.

Corcoran, S.J., Timothy, *The Clongowes Record, 1814 to 1932: With Introductory Chapters on Irish Jesuit Educators, 1564 to 1813* (Dublin: Browne and Nolan, 1932).

Corpus Poetarum Latinorum, (ed.) William Sidney Walker (London: George Bell & Sons, 1878).

Costello, Peter, *Clongowes Wood: A History of Clongowes Wood College, 1814–1989* (Dublin: Gill and Macmillan, 1989.

——*James Joyce: The Years of Growth 1882–1915* (London: Kyle Cathie Limited, 1992).

Coulston, J. C., and Dodge, Hazel, *Ancient Rome: The Archaeology of the Eternal City* (Oxford: Oxford University School of Archaeology, 2000).

Cox, Michael (ed.), *The Oxford Chronology of English Literature*, 2 vols. (Oxford: Oxford University Press, 2000).

Cronin, Mike, *A History of Ireland* (Basingstoke: Palgrave, 2001).

Cunningham, Bernadette, and Fitzpatrick, Siobhán (eds.), *Treasures of the Royal Irish Academy Library* (Dublin: Royal Irish Academy, 2009).

Curtis, Edmund, *A History of Ireland: From Earliest Times to 1922* (London: Routledge, 2002).

Daly, Mary, 'Dublin in the 1880s', *Hopkins Quarterly*, 14/1–4 (Apr. 1987–Jan. 1988), 96–103.

——*Dublin, the Deposed Capital: A Social and Economic History 1860–1914* (Cork: Cork University Press, 1984).

de Flon, Nancy Marie, *Edward Caswall: Newman's Brother and Friend* (Leominster: Gracewing, 2005).

Delaney, John J., and Tobin, James Edward, *The Dictionary of Catholic Biography* (New York: Doubleday, 1961).

DeLaura, David, 'Such Good Friends: Four Letters of Gerard Manley Hopkins to Katharine Tynan', *Studies* (Winter 1974), 389–96.

A Dictionary of Greek and Roman Geography, (ed.) William Smith, 3 vols. (London: John Murray, 1876).

Dixon, Richard Watson, *Mano: A Poetical History of the Time of the Close of the Tenth Century concerning the Adventures of a Norman Knight which Fell Part in Normandy Part in Italy. In Four Books* (London: George Routledge & Sons, 1883).

—— *Poems by the Late Rev. Dr. Richard Watson Dixon: A Selection with a Portrait & a Memoir by Robert Bridges* (London, Smith, Elder & Co, 1909).

Drabble, Margaret (ed.), *The Oxford Companion to English Literature* (Oxford: Oxford University Press, 2000). Oxford Reference Online.

—— and Stringer, Jenny (eds.), *The Concise Oxford Companion to English Literature* (Oxford: Oxford University Press, 2007). Oxford Reference Online.

Dryden, John, *The Works of John Dryden*, iv, (eds.) A. B. Chambers, William Frost, and Vinton A. Dearing (Berkeley: University of California Press, 1974).

Dunlop, Storm, *A Dictionary of Weather* (Oxford: Oxford University Press, 2008). Oxford Reference Online.

'Dynamite Outrages: Attempts on the House of Commons, Westminster Hall, and the Tower of London', *The Times* [London], 31353 (26 Jan. 1885), 10.

Encyclopædia Britannica, 2009. *Encyclopædia Britannica Online*.

Fathers of the Society of Jesus (eds.), *A Page of Irish History: Story of University College, Dublin 1883–1909* (Dublin: The Talbot Press, 1930).

Farmer, David Hugh, *The Oxford Dictionary of Saints* (Oxford: Oxford University Press, 2003). Oxford Reference Online.

Feeney, S.J., Joseph, 'Hopkins and the MacCabe Family: Three Children who Knew Gerard Manley Hopkins', *Studies*, 90 (2001), 299–307.

—— 'Hopkins's Closest Friend in Ireland: Robert Curtis, S.J.', *Hopkins and Dublin: The Man and the City*, (ed.) Richard F. Giles, special issue of *Hopkins Quarterly*, 14/1–2 (Apr. 1987–Jan. 1988), 211–38.

Francis, St, *Works of the Seraphic Father St. Francis of Assisi* (London: R. Washbourne, 1882).

St Francis of Assisi: The Legends and Lauds, trans. N. Wydenbruck, ed. Otto Karrer (London: Sheed and Ward, 1947).

Fredeman, William E., and Nadel, Ira (eds.), *Dictionary of Literary Biography*, xxxv: *Victorian Poets after 1850* (Detroit: Gale Research, 1985).

Geraghty, Tony, *The Irish War: The Hidden Conflict between the IRA and British Intelligence* (Baltimore: Johns Hopkins University Press, 2000).

Gibbon, Monk, *The Masterpiece and the Man—Yeats as I Knew Him* (London: Hart-Davis, 1959).

Grinstein, Alexander, *Wilkie Collins: Man of Mystery and Imagination* (Madison, Conn.: International Universities Press, 2003).

Grote, George, *A History of Greece*, 12 vols. (London: John Murray, 1846–56).

Grove Music Online. Oxford Music Online, <www.oxfordmusiconline.com/public/book/omo_gmo>.

Guide to Royal University of Ireland. Matriculation. Tildesley's Royal University of Ireland series (Edinburgh: S. J. Tildesley & Co., 1889).

Gunn, Ian, Hart, Clive, and Beck, Harald, *James Joyce's Dublin: A Topographical Guide to the Dublin of* Ulysses (London: Thames and Hudson, Ltd., 2004).

Hahn, Daniel, and Robins, Nicholas (eds.), *The Oxford Guide to Literary Britain and Ireland* (Oxford: Oxford University Press, 2009). Oxford Reference Online.

Hallowell, Gerald (ed.), *The Oxford Companion to Canadian History* (Oxford: Oxford University Press, 2004). Oxford Reference Online.

Hekster, Olivier, and Rich, John, 'Octavian and the Thunderbolt: The Temple of Apollo Palatinus and Roman Traditions of Temple Building', *Classical Quarterly*, 56 (2006), 149–68.

Higgins, Lesley, 'Uncommon Lives: Fr. Hopkins and Fr. Bacon', *Hopkins Quarterly*, 21/3–4 (Summer–Fall 1994), 77–96.

Hilton, Tim, *John Ruskin: The Later Years* (New Haven: Yale University Press, 2000).

Holmes, Richard (ed.), *The Oxford Companion to Military History* (Oxford: Oxford University Press, 2001). Oxford Reference Online.

Honan, Park, *Matthew Arnold: A Life* (New York: Mc-Graw Hill, 1981).

Hopkins, Gerard Manley, *Journals and Papers*, (eds.) Humphry House and Graham Storey (Oxford: Oxford University Press, 1959).

Hopkins, Manley, *Cardinal Numbers with an Introductory Chapter on Numbers Generally* (London: Sampson Low, Marston, Searle & Rivington, 1887).

Hornblower, Simon, and Spawforth, Antony (eds.), *The Oxford Companion to Classical Civilization* (Oxford: Oxford University Press, 1998). Oxford Reference Online.

————— *Who's Who in the Classical World* (Oxford: Oxford University Press, 2000). Oxford Reference Online.

House, Humphry, *The Youth of Gerard Manley Hopkins, 1844–1868*, (ed.) Lesley Higgins, *Hopkins Quarterly*, 37/1–4 (2010), 1–218.

Howatson, M. C. (ed.), *The Oxford Companion to Classical Literature* (Oxford: Oxford University Press, 1989).

—— and Chilvers, Ian (eds.), *The Concise Oxford Companion to Classical Literature* (Oxford: Oxford University Press, 1996). Oxford Reference Online.

Hyde, Derek, *New Found Voices: Women in Nineteenth-Century English Music*, 3rd edn. (Aldershot: Ashgate, 1998).

Igoe, Vivien, *James Joyce's Dublin Houses* (London: Mandarin Paperbacks, 1990).

Isaacs, Alan (ed.), *A Dictionary of World History* (Oxford: Oxford University Press, 2000). Oxford Reference Online.

Keaveney, Raymond, 'A Brief History', *National Gallery of Ireland: Essential Guide* (London: Scala Publishers, 2002), 1–10.

Keenan, Desmond J., *The Catholic Church in Nineteenth-Century Ireland* (Dublin: Gill & Macmillan, 1983).

Kelly, John, 'Russell, Matthew (1834–1912)', *ODNB*.

Kerr, D. A., and Sheehy, David C., 'Walsh, William Joseph (1841–1921)', rev. *ODNB*.

Knowles, Elizabeth (ed.), *A Dictionary of Phrase and Fable* (Oxford: Oxford University Press, 2006). Oxford Reference Online.

Kot, Halvden, *Life of Ibsen*, trans. and ed. Einar Haugen and A. E. Santaniello (New York: Benjamin Blom, 1971).

Kupperman, Joel J., *The Oxford Companion to Philosophy* (Oxford: Oxford University Press, 2005). Oxford Reference Online.

Lahey, S.J., G. F., *Gerard Manley Hopkins* (London: Oxford University Press, 1930).

Lang, Andrew, 'Myth', *Encyclopaedia Britannica*, 1889 edn. (Chicago: R. S. Peale Reprints, 1992), xii. 135–58.

Leeming, David (ed.), *The Oxford Companion to World Mythology* (Oxford: Oxford University Press, 2004). Oxford Reference Online.

Legge, R. H., rev. Nilanjana Banerji, 'Prescott, Sir Robert Stewart', *ODNB*.

The Life of St. Winefride, ed. John Dalton (London: C. Dolman, 1857).

Livingstone, E. A. (ed.), *The Concise Oxford Dictionary of the Christian Church* (Oxford: Oxford University Press, 2006). Oxford Reference Online.

Loyola, S.J., Ignatius, *Constitutions of the Society of Jesus*, trans., intro. and commentary by George E. Ganss (St. Louis: Institute of Jesuit Sources, 1970).

—— *The Spiritual Exercises of St. Ignatius: Based on Studies in the Language of the Autograph*, trans. Louis J. Puhl (Chicago: Loyola Press, 1968).

Lyons, Francis Stewart, '"Parnellism and Crime". 1887–90', *Transactions of the Royal Historical Society*, 5th ser. 24 (1974), 123–40.

Lydon, James, *The Making of Ireland: From Ancient Times to the Present* (London and New York: Routledge, 1998).

McCartney, Donal (ed.), *Parnell: The Politics of Power* (Dublin: Wolfhound Press, 1991).

—— *UCD, a National Idea: The History of University College, Dublin* (Dublin: Gill & Macmillan, 1999).

McConkey, Kennet, *A Free Spirit: Irish Art 1860–1960* (London: Antique Collectors' Club, 1990).

McConville, Seán, *Irish Political Prisoners, 1848–1922: Theatres of War* (London: Routledge, 2003).

McDermott, John, 'Hopkins in Liverpool', in McDermott (ed.), *Hopkins' Lancashire: Sesquicentennial Essays* (Wigan: North West Catholic History Society, 1994), 19–25.

Macfarren, Sir George, 'Music. — Part I. History', *Encyclopaedia Britannica*, 1889 edn. (Chicago: R. S. Peale Reprints, 1892), xii. 77–102.

McGrath, Joseph, 'Recollections of Tullabeg', *The Clongowian*, 1/1 (Christmas 1895), 19–22.

McGuire, John, *Music and Victorian Philanthropy: The Tonic Sol-fa Movement* (Cambridge: Cambridge University Press, 2009).

[McKenna, S.J., Lambert], 'Father Gerard Hopkins, S.J., and his Poetry', *Irish Monthly*, 47/554 (1919), 441–8.

MacKenzie, Norman, 'Hopkins, Yeats, and Dublin in the Eighties', in Joseph Romsley (ed.), *Myth and Reality in Irish Literature* (Waterloo, Ont.: Wilfred Laurier University Press, 1977), 77–97.

—— 'The Imperative Voice—An Unpublished Lecture by Hopkins', *Hopkins Quarterly*, 2 (1975–6), 101–16.

—— 'The Making of . . . "Spelt from Sibyl's Leaves"', in *Festschrift for E. R. Seary* (St. John's, Newfoundland: Memorial University, 1975), 151–69.

—— 'Spelt from Sibyl's Leaves', *Malahat Review* (Apr. 1973), 218–28.

—— 'An Unpublished Hopkins Manuscript', *Hopkins Research Bulletin*, 7 (1976), 3–7.

McKillop, James, *A Dictionary of Celtic Mythology* (Oxford: Oxford University Press, 1998). Oxford Reference Online.

MacLaren, Andrew, *Dublin: The Shaping of a Capital* (London: Belhaven Press, 1993).

Macran, H. S., 'Greek Music', in J. A. Fuller Maitland (ed.), *Grove's Dictionary of Music and Musicians* (London: Macmillan & Co., Ltd., 1906).

Madvig, Johan Nicolai, *A Latin Grammar*, trans. George Woods (Oxford: Clarendon Press, 1856).

Mariani, Paul, *Gerard Manley Hopkins: A Life* (New York: Viking, 2008).

Marsh, Jan, *Christina Rossetti: A Writer's Life* (New York: Viking, 1994).

Martial, *Epigrammaton libri*, (ed.) F. G. Schneidewin (Leipzig: Teubner, 1853).

—— *Grammar School Classics*; *Epigrammata Selecta*, (eds.) F. A. Paley and W. H. Stone (London: Whitaker & Co., 1875).

Martin, Robert Bernard, *Gerard Manley Hopkins: A Very Private Life* (New York: G. P. Putnam's Sons, 1991).

Metzger, Bruce M., and Coogan, Michael D. (eds.), *The Oxford Companion to the Bible* (Oxford: Oxford University Press, 1993). Oxford Reference Online.

—— —— *The Oxford Guide to People and Places of the Bible* (Oxford: Oxford University Press, 2001). Oxford Reference Online.

Moody, T. W., '*The Times* versus Parnell and Co., 1887–90', *Historical Studies*, 6 (1968), 147–82.

Morrissey, Thomas J., 'Delany, William (1835–1924)', *ODNB*.

—— *Thomas A. Finlay, S.J., 1848–1940: Educationalist, Editor, Social Reformer* (Dublin: Four Courts Press, 2004).

—— *Towards a National University: William Delany S.J. (1835–1924): An Era of Initiative in Irish Education* (Dublin: Wolfhound Press, 1983).

—— *William J. Walsh, Archbishop of Dublin, 1841–1921: No Uncertain Voice* (Dublin: Four Courts Press, 2000).

Morwood, James (ed.), *The Pocket Oxford Latin Dictionary* (Oxford: Oxford University Press, 1994). Oxford Reference Online.

Muller, Jill, *Gerard Manley Hopkins and Victorian Catholicism: A Heart in Hiding* (New York and London: Routledge, 2003).

Murgia, Charles, 'The Date of the Helen Episode', *Harvard Studies in Classical Philology*, 101 (2003), 405–26.

Murphy, J. J., 'Typhoid Fever', *Freemans Journal and Daily Commercial Advertiser*, 23 Nov. 1889. Gale Group: <www.galegroup.com>, accessed 14 July 2009.

'Music', in Thomas Stewart Traill (ed.), *Encyclopaedia Britannica, or, Dictionary of Arts, Sciences, and General Literature*, 8th edn., vol. xv of xxi (Edinburgh: Neill, 1853–60), 700–42.

'Mythology', ibid. 759–68.

Nelson, Brian, (ed.), *The Cambridge Companion to Zola* (Cambridge: Cambridge University Press, 2007).

'Notices', *Musical Standard*, 2/397 (9 Mar. 1872), 113.

O'Flynn, Gráinne, 'Hopkins's Teaching', *Hopkins Quarterly*, 14/1–4 (Apr. 1987–Jan. 1988), 163–78.

O'Keefe, Declan, 'A Man for Others and a Beacon in the Twilight: Matthew Russell, S.J. and the *Irish Monthly*', *Studies*, 99/394 (Summer 2010), 62–70.

O'Raifeartaigh, T. O. (ed.), *The Royal Irish Academy: A Bicentennial History, 1785–1985* (Dublin: Royal Irish Academy, 1985).

Oxford Dictionary of World Place-Names, (ed.) John Everett-Heath (Oxford: Oxford University Press, 2005).

The Oxford English Dictionary, 2nd edn. 1989. *OED* Online.

Parker, Lisa, 'For the Purpose of Public Music Education: The Lectures of Robert Prescott Stewart (1825–1894)', in Michael Murphy and Jan Smaczny (eds.), *Irish Musical Studies 9: Music in Nineteenth-Century Ireland* (Dublin: Four Courts Press, 2007).

Parnell, John Howard, *Charles Stewart Parnell: A Memoir* (New York: H. Holt and Company, 1914).

Parnell, Katharine, *Charles Stewart Parnell: His Love Story and Political Life* (London: Cassell and Company, 1914).

Parry, C. H. H., 'Fermata', in J. A. Fuller Maitland (ed.), *Grove's Dictionary of Music and Musicians* (London: Macmillan & Co., Ltd., 1906).

Pater, Walter, *Three Major Texts*, (ed.) William E. Buckler (New York: New York University Press, 1986).

Phillips, Catherine, 'Gerard Manley Hopkins and Dante Gabriel Rossetti', *Ranam*, 36/1 (2003), 131–7.

Pindar, *Nemean Odes, Isthmian Odes, Fragments*, trans. William H. Race (Cambridge, Mass.: Harvard University Press, 1997).

Polehampton, Edward, *The Gallery of Nature and Art; Or a Tour through Creation and Science*, iv (London: R. Wilks, 1815).

Porter, J. R., 'Louis Pasteur Sesquicentennial (1822–1972)', *Science*, NS 178/4067 (22 Dec. 1972), 1249–54.

Preston, Margaret H., *Charitable Words: Women, Philanthropy, and the Language of Charity in Nineteenth-Century Dublin* (Westport, Conn.: Praeger Publishers, 2004).

Rainbow, Bernarr, 'Glover, Sarah Anna (1786–1867)', *ODNB*.

—— *The Land without Music* (London: Novello, 1967).

Richmond, J. A., 'Classical Studies and Culture in Dublin in the 1880s', *Hopkins Quarterly* (Special Issue: *Hopkins and Dublin: The Man and the City*), 14/1–4 (Apr. 1987–Jan. 1988), 145–62.

Roberts, John (ed.), *Oxford Dictionary of the Classical World* (Oxford: Oxford University Press, 2007). Oxford Reference Online.

Roche, John, 'Typhoid Fever', *Freeman's Journal and Daily Commercial Advertiser*, 13 Nov. 1889. Gale Group: <www.galegroup.com>, accessed 14 July 2009.

The Roman Breviary: Reformed by Order of the Holy Ecumenical Council of Trent, ii, trans. John Patrick Crichton-Stuart Bute (London: William Blackwood and Sons, 1879).

'The Roman Catholic Clergy in Ireland', *The Times* [*London*], 29530 (1 Apr. 1879), 11.

'Sacred Musicians of the XIXth Century', *Frank Leslie's Sunday Magazine*, 16/2 (Aug. 1884), 142–5.

Salmon, Nicholas, *The William Morris Chronology* (Bristol: Thoemmes Press, 1996).

Sambrook, James, *A Poet Hidden: The Life of Richard Watson Dixon* (London: Athlone Press,1962).

Schlatter, S.J., Fredric W., 'Gerard Manley Hopkins: Poetic Fragments, Comments on Lucan and Cicero, Essay on Duty', *Hopkins Quarterly*, 27/3–4 (Summer–Fall 2000), 1–106.

—— 'Hopkins and Baillie', *Studies in Philology*, 103 (2006), 522–44.

—— 'Martial Klein, Hopkins's Dublin Colleague', *Hopkins Quarterly*, 29/3–4 (Summer–Fall 2002), 69–105.

Shakespeare, William, *The Pictorial Edition of the Works of Shakespere*, (ed.) Charles Knight, vi (London: C. Knight and Co., 1843).

—— *The Tragedy of Antony and Cleopatra*, in *The Pictorial Edition of the Works of Shakespere*, (ed.) Charles Knight, vii (London: C. Knight and Co., 1843), 275–338.

—— *The Tragedy of Hamlet, Prince of Denmark*, in *The Pictorial Edition of the Works of Shakespere*, (ed.) Charles Knight, vi (London: C. Knight and Co., 1843), 85–176.

—— *The Tragedy of Hamlet, Prince of Denmark*, in *The Riverside Shakespeare*, (ed.) G. Blakemore Evans (Boston: Houghton Mifflin, 1997), 1183–1245.

—— *The Tragedy of Julius Caesar*, in *The Pictorial Edition of the Works of Shakespere*, (ed.) Charles Knight, vii (London: C. Knight and Co., 1843), 215–74.

—— *The Tragedy of Julius Caesar*, in *The Riverside Shakespeare*, (ed.) G. Blakemore Evans (Boston: Houghton Mifflin, 1997), 1146–81.

Shelley, Percy Bysshe, 'Ode to the West Wind', in Percy Bysshe Shelley, *The Major Works*, (eds.) Zachary Leader and Michael O'Neill (Oxford: Oxford University Press, 2003), 412–14.

—— 'Ode to the West Wind', in *The Complete Poetical Works of Percy Bysshe Shelley*, (ed.) William Michael Rossetti, iii (London: Reeves and Turner, 1878), 48–50.

Smith, Andrew, 'Gerard Manley Hopkins as Classicist', *Irish University Review*, 20/2 (Autumn 1990), 299–317.

Sobolev, Dennis, 'Hopkins's Portraits of the Artist: Between the Biographical and the Ideological', *Connotations: A Journal for Critical Debate*, 10/2–3 (2000–1), 304–27.

Societas Jesu, *Catalogus Provinciae Hiberniae* (Dublin: Browne and Nolan, 1885).

Somerville-Large, Peter, *Dublin: The Fair City* (London: Sinclain-Stevenson, 1996).

Squire, W. B., 'Curwen, John (1816–1880)', rev. Peter Ward Jones, *ODNB*.

Stanford, Sir Charles Villiers, *Pages from an Unwritten Diary* (London: Edward Arnold, 1914).

Stanford, Donald (ed.), *Dictionary of Literary Biography*, xix: *British Poets, 1880–1914* (Detroit: Gale Research, 1983). Literature Resource Center.

Stevens, Robin, *The Curwen Method* (Melbourne, Victoria, Australia: Deakin University, 2008), <http://www.deakin.edu.au/arts-ed/education/music-ed/curwen-method/index.php>, accessed 30 July 2008.

Swift, Jonathan, *The Essential Writings of Jonathan Swift*, (eds.) Claude Rawson and Ian Higgins (New York: Norton, 2010).

Tacitus, *The Histories, Books I–III*, (ed.) Clifford H. Moore (Cambridge, Mass.: Harvard University Press, 1980).

Tamark, M., *Cecil Rhodes and the Cape Afrikaners: The Imperial Colossus and the Colonial Parish Pump* (London: Frank Cass, 1996).

Tanselle, G. Thomas, 'Reproductions and Scholarship', *Studies in Bibliography*, 42 (1989), 25–54.

Taylor, Patrick (ed.), *The Oxford Companion to the Garden* (Oxford: Oxford University Press, 2006).

Thomas, Donald, *Robert Browning: A Life within Life* (New York: Viking Press, 1982).

Thornton, R. K. R., 'Dublin and Hopkins in the 1880s', *Hopkins Quarterly*, 14/1–4 (Apr. 1987–Jan. 1988), 105–11.

Tierney, Michael (ed.), *Struggle with Fortune: A Miscellany for the Centenary of the Catholic University of Ireland, 1854–1954* (Dublin: Brone and Nollan, 1954).

Turner, Frank, *The Greek Heritage in Victorian Britain* (New Haven: Yale University Press, 1981).

Tylenda, Joseph N., *Saints and Feasts of the Liturgical Year* (Washington, DC: Georgetown University Press, 2003).

Tynan, Katharine, 'Dearest of Friends', *Irish Monthly*, 45 (1912), 551–4.

—— *Memories* (London: Eveleigh Nash & Grayson, 1924).

—— *The Middle Years* (Boston: Houghton Mifflin, 1917).

University College, Dublin. Prospectus (Dublin: Browne and Nolan, 1884).

Virgil, *Aeneid I–VI*, trans. H. Rushton Fairclough (Cambridge, Mass.: Harvard University Press, 1999).

Weliver, Phyllis, *The Musical Crowd in English Fiction, 1840–1910: Class, Culture, and Nation* (Basingstoke: Palgrave, 2006).

West, Stephanie R., 'Classical Notes on Gerard Manley Hopkins', *International Journal of the Classical Tradition*, 13/1 (2006), 21–32.

White, Harry, *The Keeper's Recital: Music and Cultural History in Ireland, 1770–1970* (Notre Dame, Ind.: University of Notre Dame Press, 1998).

White, Norman, 'G. M. Hopkins's Contributions to the English Dialect Dictionary', *English Studies*, 68/4 (1987), 325–35.

—— 'Gerard Manley Hopkins and the Irish Row', *Hopkins Quarterly*, 9 (1982), 91–107.

—— *Hopkins: A Literary Biography* (Oxford: Oxford University Press, 2002).

—— *Hopkins in Ireland* (Dublin: University College Dublin Press, 2002).

Wile, Frederick William, *Emile Berliner: Maker of the Microphone* (Indianapolis, Ind.: Bobbs-Merrill Company, 1926).

Williams, Adrian, *Portrait of Liszt: By Himself and his Contemporaries* (Oxford: Clarendon Press, 1990).

Williams, Basil, *Cecil Rhodes* (London: Constable and Co., 1938).

Wordsworth, John, *Fragments and Specimens of Early Latin* (Oxford: Clarendon Press, 1874).

Woudhuysen, Henry, '"Work of permanent utility": Editors and Texts, Authorities and Originals', in Lukas Erne and Margaret Jane Kidnie (eds.), *Textual Performances: The Modern Reproduction of Shakespeare's Drama* (Cambridge: Cambridge University Press, 2004), 37–48.

Yeats, William Butler, *Letters to Katharine Tynan*, (ed.) Roger McHugh (Dublin: Clonmore and Reynolds, 1953).

INDEX

Bold numbers denote references to illustrations. Dates of birth and death are provided for all those listed in the *Oxford Dictionary of National Biography* or cognate volumes.

For my wonderful
family and friends,
for being my wind.
— L.Y.

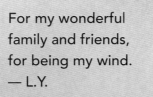

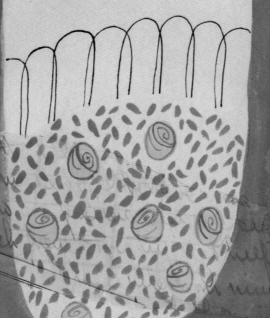

Lindsey Yankey

Bluebird

SIMPLY READ BOOKS

Early one spring morning, a little bluebird woke up in her nest
eager to *fly*. She was about to take off, when she stopped.
Something was different. Something was missing —
her friend the wind! Not a leaf in her tree was stirring.

"I've never flown without the *wind*," she thought.
"I'd better find my friend right away!"
So she jumped down into the park
to do just that.

She landed by a group of *dandelions* to see if the *wind* was there, blowing their seeds away, making wishes.

But the dandelions were still, and each had all its *seeds*.

She found a *kite* resting on a bench.

The *wind* loved to help kites perform acrobatics high in the sky.

But this kite just lay there looking lonely.

Confused but curious,
she hurried over to
the *willow* tree at the end of the park.

Just the day before, the *wind* had been
tickling the grass with the willow branches.
But now her friend was nowhere
to be found.

"Maybe the wind is taking the day off to enjoy the *city*," she thought.

So the little bluebird left the park to
search for the *wind* there.

In the city, at a café, people were drinking tea and reading

newspapers

She hoped the *wind* would be eagerly flipping pages along with them.

But it wasn't.

Only people were turning the pages.

She found a man selling *scarves* near the square.

There was no sign of the *wind* trying on the pretty fabrics.

Not even the fringes fluttered in a breeze.

Maybe the *wind* was hiding somewhere higher. Sometimes she had seen it dancing with brightly colored balloons, dipping and spinning them high in the sky.

But this *balloon* wasn't being carried away by the wind.

It was being carried away by a girl.

Surely she would find the wind
down an alleyway helping
dry the clothes on the *lines*.

But the *wind* wasn't there either.

The clothes hung straight down.

Determined to find her missing friend,
the little bluebird visited the *flagpole*
to see if the *wind* was proudly
waving the flag
in the air.

But today the *flag* drooped instead of waved.

She searched
for the *wind* at the pond where
it liked to race the *boats*
across the water.

But the boats all *floated* motionless,
out of reach.

And then it occurred to her.
Why had she not thought of it before?

There was one place where the wind always
went — if she couldn't find it there, then
she wouldn't be able to find it anywhere.

Finally, she reached the wind's favorite window.

The *wind* loved to make music with Grandma Brooks' wind chimes.

But even here,
she couldn't hear a *whisper*
of her friend.

The little bluebird stopped to rest. She was
getting tired of searching and didn't
understand why she couldn't find the *wind*.

How could she ever *fly*
without her
friend's help?

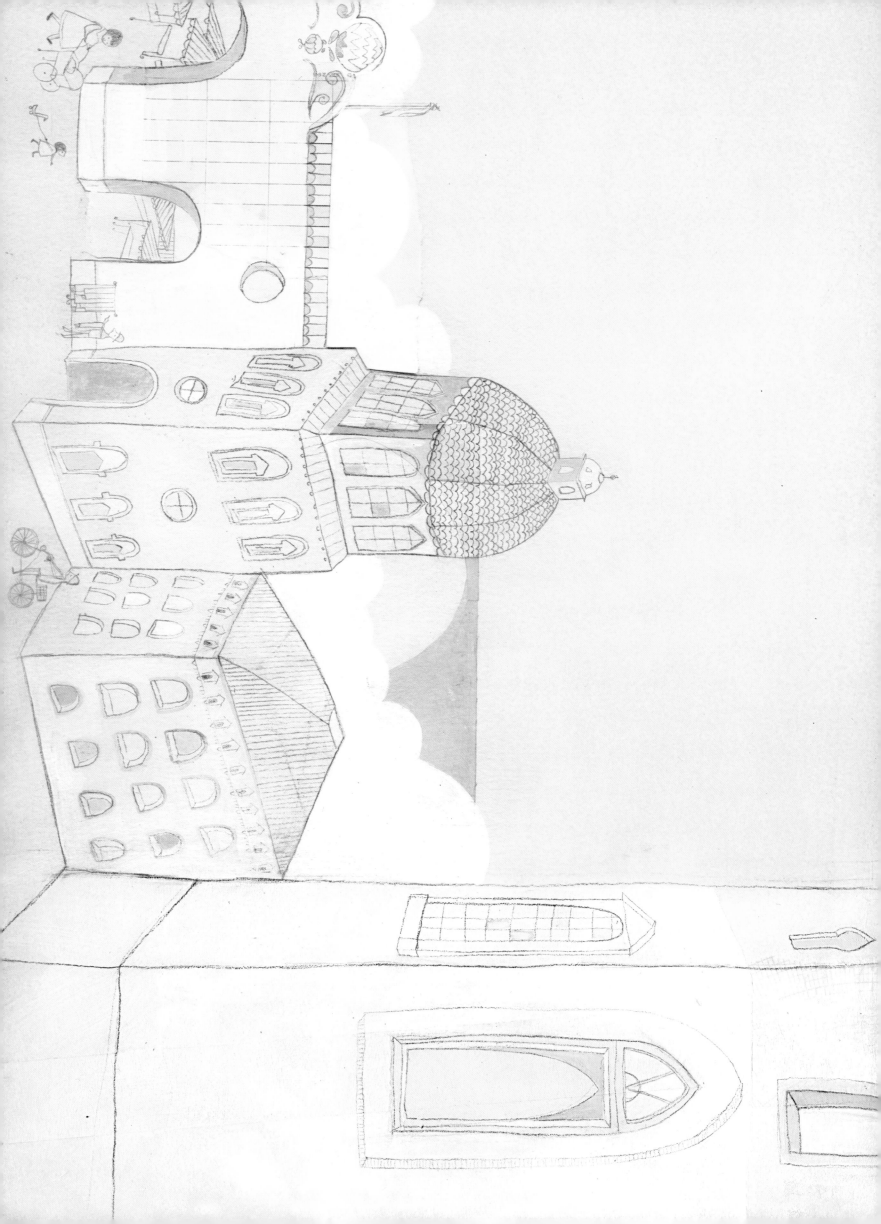

She sighed and looked around.

Suddenly, she realized what she had done. She had flown to the top of the *tallest building* all on her own!

Very excited and quite pleased with herself, she held her head high and spread her wings. Just as she was about to take off, she felt something.

It was the *wind*, blowing down from the clouds, high above the city. It must have been resting there, watching her fly.

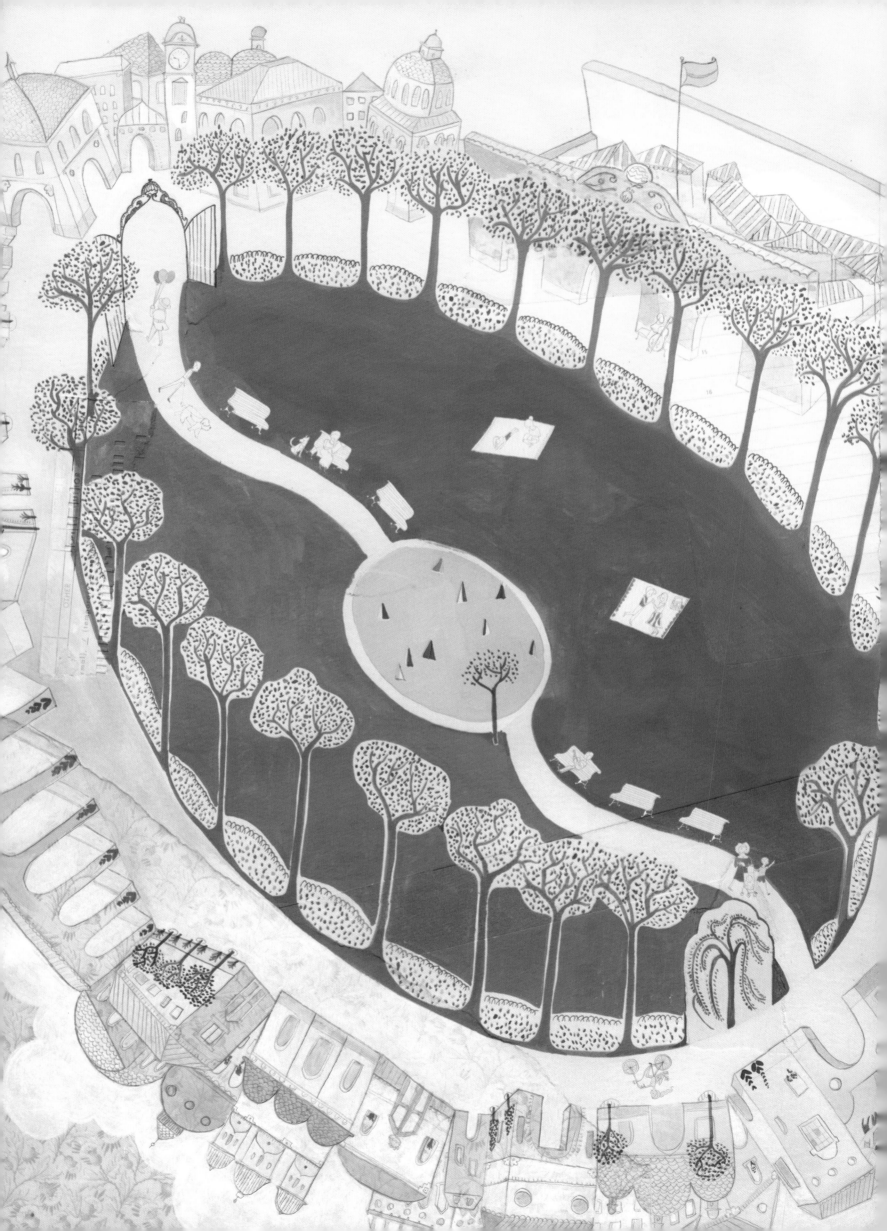

The bluebird's feathers rustled softly
as she soared off
with her *Friend.*

Published in 2014 by Simply Read Books
www.simplyreadbooks.com

Library and Archives Canada Cataloguing in Publication
Yankey, Lindsey
         Bluebird / written and illustrated by Lindsey Yankey.
ISBN 978-1-927018-33-0
I.   Title.
 PZ7.Y2Bl 2013   j813'.6   C2013-901262-1

We gratefully acknowledge for their financial support of our publishing program the Canada Council for the Arts, the BC Arts Council, and the Government of Canada through the Canada Book Fund (CBF).

Manufactured in Malaysia.

Book design by Robin Mitchell Cranfield for hundreds & thousands

10 9 8 7 6 5 4 3 2 1